Stranger Danger

Stranger Danger

*Family Values, Childhood, and the
American Carceral State*

Paul M. Renfro

OXFORD
UNIVERSITY PRESS

OXFORD
UNIVERSITY PRESS

Oxford University Press is a department of the University of Oxford. It furthers
the University's objective of excellence in research, scholarship, and education
by publishing worldwide. Oxford is a registered trade mark of Oxford University
Press in the UK and certain other countries.

Published in the United States of America by Oxford University Press
198 Madison Avenue, New York, NY 10016, United States of America.

Library of Congress Cataloging-in-Publication Data
Names: Renfro, Paul M., author.
Title: Stranger danger : family values, childhood, and the American carceral state /
Paul M. Renfro.
Description: New York : Oxford University Press, [2020] |
Includes bibliographical references and index.
Identifiers: LCCN 2019034331 (print) | LCCN 2019034332 (ebook) |
ISBN 9780190913984 (hardback) | ISBN 9780190914004 (epub) |
ISBN 9780190914011 (online) | ISBN 9780190913991 (updf)
Subjects: LCSH: Kidnapping—United States—History. |
Kidnapping—Press coverage—United States. |
Missing children—Press coverage—United States. |
Children and strangers—United States. | Moral panics—United States—History. |
Children—Legal status, laws, etc.—United States—History. |
Crime and the press—United States—History.
Classification: LCC HV6598 .R45 2020 (print) | LCC HV6598 (ebook) |
DDC 364.15/40973—dc23
LC record available at https://lccn.loc.gov/2019034331
LC ebook record available at https://lccn.loc.gov/2019034332

1 3 5 7 9 8 6 4 2

Printed by Sheridan Books, Inc., United States of America

Some material in earlier form appears in "Lost in the Heartland: Childhood, Region, and Iowa's
Missing Paperboys," *Annals of Iowa* 74, no. 1 (Winter 2015): 29–70. Used with permission of the
publisher; "Keeping Children Safe is Good Business: The Enterprise of Child Safety in the Age of
Reagan," *Enterprise & Society* 17, no. 1 (March 2016): 151–187. © The Author 2015. Published
by Cambridge University Press on behalf of the Business History Conference. All rights reserved;
"'The City Too Busy to Care': The Atlanta Youth Murders and the Southern Past, 1979–81,"
Southern Cultures 21, no. 4 (Winter 2015): 43–66; "Milk Carton Kids: Endangered Childhood and
the Carceral State," in *Growing Up America: Youth and Politics since 1945*, edited by Susan Eckelmann
Berghel, Sara Fieldston, and Paul M. Renfro. University of Georgia Press, 2019, 244–261.

To Mom and Dad

For the lost

CONTENTS

ABBREVIATIONS

ABMC	US Attorney General's Advisory Board on Missing Children
ACLU	American Civil Liberties Union
AMBER Alert	America's Missing: Broadcast Emergency Response
BDSM	bondage, domination, and submission (or sadomasochism)
CDC	Centers for Disease Control
CPS	Council for Public Safety (New York City)
CPTF	Child Protection Task Force (Moral Majority)
DARE	Drug Abuse Resistance Education
DCI	Division of Criminal Investigation (Iowa)
DOJ	US Department of Justice
FBI	Federal Bureau of Investigation
GCN	*Gay Community News*
HOPE	Homes Offering a Protective Environment (Iowa)
ICE	US Immigration and Customs Enforcement
JJDP Act	Juvenile Justice and Delinquency Prevention
KKK	Ku Klux Klan
MCA	Missing Children Act
MCAA	Missing Children's Assistance Act
NAACP	National Association for the Advancement of Colored People
NAMBLA	North American Man/Boy Love Association
NCIC	National Crime Information Center
NCMEC	National Center for Missing and Exploited Children
NCNW	National Council of Negro Women
NCPC	National Crime Prevention Council
NCSC	National Child Safety Council
NISMART	National Incidence Studies of Missing, Abducted, Runaway, and Throwaway Children

NOW	National Organization for Women
NYPD	New York Police Department
OJA	Office of Justice Assistance
OJJDP	Office of Juvenile Justice and Delinquency Prevention
PCSP	President's Child Safety Partnership
PFLAG	Parents, Families, and Friends of Lesbians and Gays
PROTECT Act	Prosecutorial Remedies and Other Tools to End the Exploitation of Children Today
PRWORA	Personal Responsibility and Work Opportunity Reconciliation Act
PTA	parent-teacher association
ROTC	Reserve Officers' Training Corps
SCLC	Southern Christian Leadership Conference
SOR	sex offender registry
STOP	Committee to Stop Children's Murders
SWAT	special weapons and tactics
TANF	Temporary Assistance to Needy Families
UVVA	Unborn Victims of Violence Act
VCA	Vanished Children's Alliance
VCCLEA	Violent Crime Control and Law Enforcement Act

Stranger Danger

Introduction

It was July 27, 1981, and Revé Walsh had some errands to run. First, the Hollywood, Florida, mother needed to stop by St. Mark's Lutheran School to pay her son Adam's $90 tuition. She then planned to buy a lamp at the Sears department store in the Hollywood Mall before heading to the gym for an afternoon workout. Since six-year-old Adam was on summer vacation, he joined his mother as she ran these errands. After dropping by St. Mark's, the pair arrived at Sears around 12:30 p.m. Revé set out for the store's lighting and home furnishings section, allowing her son to watch a video game demonstration in the toy department just a few aisles away. "I said, 'I'm going right over here to the lamp department,'" Revé recalled, "and he said, 'Okay, Mommy, I know where that is.'" After making her purchase, Revé returned to the toy section to collect her son, but he was nowhere to be found. A frantic search of the store was followed by what some called "the largest manhunt in the history of Florida."[1]

Over the coming weeks, Adam's parents Revé and her husband John brought local and national attention to their son's presumed abduction and to their efforts to recover him. The couple traveled to New York City on August 10 to appear on the nationally televised ABC program *Good Morning America*. That evening, John Walsh learned that two fishermen had come across the decapitated head of a young boy in an Indian River County canal, some 125 miles north of the Walshes' hometown. Local officials asked John for the name of his son's dentist, so they could compare Adam's dental records with the corpse's teeth. John hid this news from Revé and soldiered ahead with the couple's scheduled appearance on national television the following morning. In John Walsh's rendering, he did this not only to disseminate to a national audience information about his own son—who, considering the evidence available at the time, might have still been alive. At the urging of Julie Patz, whose son Etan had been missing since 1979, John Walsh also felt compelled to raise awareness about other missing children. "No one was listening" to Julie Patz and other mourning mothers, Walsh wrote later. "And I was a man, wearing a suit." On the August 11 broadcast of *Good Morning America*, John Walsh, alongside his wife and Julie Patz, conveyed masculine (and paternal) strength as he informed viewers across the country of his son's disappearance and of a larger child safety crisis.[2]

Soon after John and Revé stepped off the *Good Morning America* set, they received word that the boy in the canal was Adam. Despite his manly resolve and his self-image as "the guy with the stiff upper lip," John Walsh and his wife were "destroyed human beings" following their son's murder. Worse still, perhaps, their very destruction had unfolded before the entire country. Their panicked search and, later, their expressions of grief were beamed to television sets nationwide. Clips of Adam's funeral and of John Walsh weeping aired on NBC's *Nightly News*. The Walshes, and especially John, channeled their highly publicized sorrow into the burgeoning child safety campaign. "Maybe we can help this cause," John Walsh explained in a press conference held after the discovery of Adam's remains. "We will continue, Revé and I, to try to make people aware of the lack of concern for missing children." Revé concurred, appealing to all American parents. "We *all* have to help. Don't wait until it happens to you."[3]

John Walsh quickly became the de facto leader of the child safety cause, cultivating a compelling public persona as a bereaved father thirsty for justice. Through two made-for-television movies centered on Adam's case and his parents' subsequent advocacy—*Adam* (1983) and *Adam: His Song Continues* (1986), both airing on NBC—John Walsh further solidified his place in the national spotlight. In 1988, Fox tapped him to host the weekly reality television program *America's Most Wanted*, which ran for twenty-four years. He starred in a similar show, *The Hunt with John Walsh*, on CNN from 2014 to 2017, and in 2019 he and his son Callahan began hosting another program, *In Pursuit with John Walsh*, on the Investigation Discovery channel. Since the early 1980s, when "victims' rights crystallized as a national discourse," Walsh's celebrity has depended largely on his vigilantism, "tough guy" image, and criticism of conventional law enforcement strategies.[4]

In many ways, the Walshes' crusade for child safety culminated in 2006 with the passage of the federal Adam Walsh Child Protection and Safety Act. Even though there is no evidence to suggest that Adam was sexually

Figure I.1 Lawmakers applaud John and Revé Walsh at the Rose Garden signing ceremony for the Adam Walsh Child Protection and Safety Act (HR 4472), July 27, 2006. Photograph by Paul Morse. Courtesy of the George W. Bush Presidential Library and Museum, Southern Methodist University, Dallas, Texas.

molested, the law bearing his name targeted sex criminals, particularly those who ostensibly pose threats to American children. The Walsh Act enhanced the federal penalties for failure to register as a sex offender, allowed for the federal prosecution of state sex offenders for failure to register pursuant to interjurisdictional or foreign travel, widened the range of offenses for which adults could be forced to register to include possession of child pornography, and standardized the information to be obtained from offenders for online publication and dissemination. Upon signing the bill into law on the twenty-fifth anniversary of Adam's abduction, President George W. Bush applauded John and Revé's "tireless crusade" to "combat child abduction and exploitation across the country." The president also touted the Walsh Act as "a good piece of bipartisan legislation," one that "makes an important step forward in this country's efforts to protect those who cannot protect themselves," chiefly young children.[5]

As justifiable as the 2006 Walsh Act might appear, and as tragic as the case that inspired the law was, they both foregrounded kidnappings of children by strangers, which are extremely rare in the United States. Studies indicate that, annually, some one hundred to three hundred minors are taken by individuals they do not know. Though heartrending, stranger abductions of children occur far less frequently than those perpetrated by family members and acquaintances, which account for 100,000 to 200,000 cases each year in the United States. A 2002 Department of Justice (DOJ) study found 117,200 reports of child kidnapping by family members in 1999 and 33,000 cases of nonfamily abduction, approximately 115 of which qualified as "stereotypical" stranger abductions like Adam Walsh's. According to the DOJ, 105 of such stereotypical stranger kidnappings occurred nationwide in 2011, and no more than ten of these cases ended in homicide. (Runaway or "thrownaway" children comprise the overwhelming majority of missing youths, with an estimated 628,900 cases in the United States in 1999.) Furthermore, data compiled between 1991 and 1996 suggest that family members constitute nearly half of those who sexually victimize children under the age of six and 42 percent of those who sexually assault youths between the ages of six and eleven. All told, an estimated 93 percent of those who sexually abuse young people in the United States are acquaintances or relatives.[6]

Yet "stranger danger" remains a pervasive fear, an enduring consequence of the eighties child safety scare. Beginning with the Etan Patz disappearance in 1979, a spate of high-profile cases of missing children fueled Americans' anxieties about child kidnapping and exploitation. Publicized through an emergent twenty-four-hour news cycle, these cases supplied evidence of what some commentators dubbed "a national epidemic" of child abductions and disappearances.[7] The bereaved parents of missing or slain children—people like John and Revé Walsh—turned their grief into a movement and helped to propel a moral panic, warning Americans of a supposedly widespread and worsening child kidnapping threat. These child safety crusaders claimed that as many as 50,000 American children fell victim to stranger abductions annually, though the actual figure was (and remains) somewhere between one hundred and three hundred.

Nonetheless, these exaggerated statistics—and the "emotionally resonant child-centered" images and narratives marshaled behind them—convinced policymakers, media figures, and everyday Americans alike that stranger danger represented a grave and growing problem.[8] "Each day someone's getting kidnapped, and they can't find them," a Maywood, Illinois, girl told an NBC *Nightly News* reporter in 1985. "You hear it almost every day on the news. 'This child is missing,' and so on and so on," proclaimed another girl. By 1987, 76 percent of children surveyed by Roper noted that "they were 'very concerned' about kidnaping," making it the most common fear in that poll—edging out "nuclear war and the spread of AIDS." Of 315 Midwestern fifth-graders polled in another 1987 study, about half "ranked someone grabbing them as their primary concern," while 44 percent indicated "it was likely or highly likely that they would become missing children." In a 1991 Mayo Clinic study, 72 percent of parents "said they feared their children might be abducted," and over one-third identified stranger kidnapping as a "frequent" worry, "a degree of fear greater than that held for any other concern"—including automobile accidents, from which far more children die each year. A 1997 *Newsweek* poll also found child abduction and murder to be parents' principal fears, ranking above serious accidents and illness.[9]

Before the early 1980s, the isolated kidnapping or disappearance of a child did not regularly generate national interest or gesture toward a broader social problem. This began to change with the Patz case, and by the early eighties a distinct discourse had congealed around "missing children" or "missing and exploited children." Indeed, only in 1981, when the US Congress convened the first hearings on the child safety scare, did the term *missing children* come to refer to a large-scale social problem. As ABC reporter Al Dale explicated in 1981, "usually our attention is drawn to missing children only after they are found dead." To support this claim, Dale pointed to the 1970–1973 "candy man" slayings in the Houston area and the John Wayne Gacy murders, which took place in the greater Chicago area from 1972 through 1978. Dean Corll, Houston's "candy man," had kidnapped, mutilated, and killed at least twenty-eight teenage boys and young men, while Gacy had abducted, sexually abused, and murdered thirty-three, burying many in the crawlspace of his Norwood Park Township home. In both instances, however, authorities did not link related cases of missing youths until they had discovered Gacy's and Corll's respective mass graves.[10] By contrast, the individual cases of Etan Patz, Adam Walsh, and other children (mostly boys) in the late seventies and early eighties brought national attention to child safety and victims' rights, inciting a moral panic.

The concepts of moral panic and, relatedly, sex panic emerged from the fields of sociology, criminology, and gender and sexuality studies in the 1970s and 1980s. Over the years, scholars have generated many different definitions for these terms.[11] For the purposes of this book, a moral panic represents a campaign (or, more aptly, a crusade) waged by aggrieved parties and "moral entrepreneurs." They launch this crusade in the wake of a perceived epidemic or crisis, which they substantiate through emotional accounts and embellished or fabricated statistics. "Moral crusaders" often scapegoat "marginal cohort[s]" or "folk devils" whose behavior has engendered the "apparent fragmentation or breakdown of the social order." Accordingly, "panics emerge during times of uncertainty" and "provide a forum in which 'moral boundaries,' the dividing lines between good and evil, can be highlighted and drawn anew." Political leaders and certain segments of the news media enthusiastically support the crusade and feed the discourse around it, petitioning for measures "that they claim would suppress the threat." With varying levels of success, academics, medical professionals, and reporters try to challenge and tamp down the panic. Sex panics follow much the same "cycle of putative threat, collective outrage, demonization, and state repression" evident in moral panics, albeit with sexual minorities cast as folk devils. In both moral and sex panics, theorists hold, order is eventually restored, and the panic dissipates.[12]

The late twentieth-century frenzy over stranger kidnapping bore many of these hallmarks. Through a receptive news media, bereaved parents like Julie and Stanley Patz and John and Revé Walsh, alongside moral entrepreneurs like self-styled child safety expert Kenneth Wooden, alerted policymakers and the general public to the plight of "missing children" or "missing and exploited children." Because the most prominent and widely discussed missing child cases focused on stranger kidnappings of young children, vague terms like *missing children* conjured vulnerable, prepubescent kids snatched by nefarious strangers, while obscuring more statistically common cases. The vast majority of minors outside of legal parental or institutional custody were (and remain) either teenage runaways or the teenage victims of familial or acquaintance abduction.[13] This slippage between young children kidnapped by strangers, older runaway youth, and other kinds of missing and exploited kids exacerbated the statistical confusion surrounding issues of child protection. Such confusion enabled grieving parents to suggest, with little resistance, that tens of thousands (if not millions) of American children were abducted by strangers annually. Television and print media propagated such myths and helped to manufacture a strong bipartisan consensus around issues of child protection. Politicians like US senator Paula Hawkins (R–Florida) and congressman (and later US senator) Paul Simon (D–Illinois) shored up this consensus. Together with grieving parents, moral entrepreneurs, and journalists, these officials promulgated the stranger danger myth in the service of new legal and cultural mechanisms designed to keep children safe.

This campaign, of course, grew out of unfathomable devastation and uncertainty, as the parents of missing and exploited children generally had no sense of where to turn following their respective losses. "There is no structure to tell you what to do," one parent of a missing child told ABC News in 1981, "who to get in touch with, how to look for the person that you're missing, whether it be a mother, or a child, or a husband, or a wife, or whatever. You just—you sit there, and you don't know where to go from there." Another nationally televised ABC News report insisted that "nobody knows" about this lack of government and private sector assistance more than Etan Patz's parents, Stanley and Julie, who had "been virtually on their own ever since" their son vanished two years prior. "Somehow," Julie Patz asserted, "if the police don't have [a system] set up" to search for the missing and the lost, "and the federal or state government don't have it set up . . . our son is missing; we have to do it." Seemingly abandoned by their elected representatives, these activists leveraged their newfound identities as bereaved parents and "secondary victims" to advocate for new measures to protect kids and punish those who purportedly threatened them.[14]

To this end, child safety crusaders and their news media allies pioneered a new visual grammar through which Americans could understand the problem of stranger danger and, more broadly, the politics of childhood. *Stranger Danger* calls this visual language the image of endangered childhood. Through a torrent of pictures featuring missing or slain white children like Patz, Walsh, and Iowa paperboy Johnny Gosch, the image of endangered childhood announced to the American public the supposed ubiquity of the stranger danger threat, as well as its ability to shatter the racialized and classed idyll of childhood innocence. The power of these pictures derived not only from the beautiful young people they depicted, but also from what remained conspicuously absent from such images—to wit, the unspeakable suffering that these lost innocents might have endured.

Joyful scenes of Etan Patz noshing on an apple or playfully flashing a mischievous grin trembled with the painful, paradoxical knowledge that the six-year-old may very well have been executed by a sadistic killer.[15] Transmitted via television news broadcasts, films, "MISSING" posters, milk cartons, and other media, pictures of imperiled childhood saturated the cultural landscape beginning in the late seventies. These visuals suggested to the public that cases like Patz's or Walsh's were commonplace and enlisted everyday Americans in the protection of young people who resembled these lost boys. The imagery of endangered childhood also reified the idea that young Americans—specifically the photogenic, middle-class, white bodies to whom childhood innocence is so readily assigned—faced new or intensifying threats from deviant strangers emboldened by sexual liberation. Through such affective imagery and rhetoric, the child protection campaign and its attendant logic of sexualized stranger danger became virtually unassailable in the early eighties. Few dared to challenge the movement or the faulty statistics animating it. Policymakers from across the political spectrum proved all too willing to join the cause, which they planted within interlocking "family values" and "law and order" frames. Accordingly, the movement to protect American kids sought to reassert social and institutional control over young people and turned to an expanding carceral field to do so.

Figure I.2 A smiling Etan Patz clutches an apple. Photograph by Stanley Patz. Courtesy of Stanley Patz.

From the outset of the child safety scare, though, there was pushback. In the early 1980s, Justice Department officials (with minimal success) contested efforts to increase DOJ involvement in matters of child protection. DOJ leaders identified state and local agencies as those best suited to address cases of missing and exploited children. By the mid-eighties, journalists, academics, and child welfare advocates had begun to question the assumptions on which concerns about child endangerment rested. The *Denver Post* earned a Pulitzer Prize in 1985 for its takedown of the "exaggerated statistics" undergirding claims of a child kidnapping "epidemic." For their part, famed pediatricians Benjamin Spock and T. Berry Brazelton maintained that fingerprinting children and surrounding them with pictures of their missing peers ultimately proved counterproductive.[16]

But the late twentieth-century child protection scare never truly died. While the most grotesque elements of this panic did subside in the final years of the 1980s, its governing logic did not. The "state of panic" that took hold in the late seventies and early eighties continued to structure policy and practice long after the apogee of the child kidnapping scare. Panic, at least as it related to the stranger danger threat, became "a way of life."[17] Across the 1980s, 1990s, and 2000s, as the illogic of stranger danger became increasingly engrained, those campaigning for child safety assembled a new legal and cultural system through which perceived threats to children would be understood and handled. *Stranger Danger* calls this the child safety regime.

REGIME CHANGE

Consisting of everything from new federal laws to cultural tools like the milk carton campaign—which plastered missing children's images on widely circulated dairy products—this regime emerged directly from the 1980s child kidnapping scare and remains firmly entrenched in the third decade of the twenty-first century. Since it congealed in the late twentieth century, the child safety regime has widened the reach of the carceral net and placed more Americans under some form of penal control—whether through conventional imprisonment or panoptic practices of public shame and surveillance. The proliferation of sex offender registries and civil commitment protocols has subjected more and more convicted offenders to indefinite detention, intense supervision, and social death.[18] The regime has also facilitated the development of products and practices intended to safeguard kids from stranger danger. Ranging from the commonplace child fingerprinting drives of the early 1980s to AMBER Alerts, these mechanisms have rendered normative and commonsensical the heightened surveillance of children, both by family and community members—and abetted by the state. Such surveillance seeks to neutralize the moral threats confronting young Americans and their families rather than the material threats, such as hunger, poverty, educational inequality, and other structural problems.[19] Stranger danger represented perhaps the most severe and existential of these moral threats in the late twentieth century, and it is the subject of this book.

But stranger danger joined with other moral concerns that received ample political, media, and public attention in the late twentieth century and worked to bolster the child safety regime. These causes derived from a growing victims' rights sensibility sanctioned by the Reagan administration and a tabloidized news media increasingly invested in "infotainment."[20] In 1984, President Reagan signed the Victims of Crime Act, thereby establishing the Crime Victims Fund, which offers compensation to victims of federal crimes. That same year, in response to the victims' rights campaign waged against underage drinking and drunk driving, Reagan yoked federal highway funding to the revision of state alcohol laws and thus set a de facto national drinking age. A moral/sex panic over ritualized child abuse ostensibly carried out by "Satanists" generated significant news coverage through much of the eighties. The "Just Say No" initiative, overseen by First Lady Nancy Reagan, discouraged children from using illicit drugs and functioned as the softer public outreach component of the so-called war on drugs. Formulated by Los Angeles police chief Daryl Gates and the Los Angeles Unified School District, the DARE (Drug Abuse Resistance Education) program buttressed Nancy Reagan's efforts, teaching "elementary and junior high school children to develop self-esteem and to resist peer pressure in order to 'just say no' to drugs and gangs." The Parents Music Resource Center, launched in 1985 and headed by Senator Al Gore's wife Tipper, railed against explicit lyrics in popular music. The Reagan administration also couched its antipornography agenda, on display in the Attorney General's Commission on Pornography, in the language of child safety. All these undertakings—particularly those intended to protect American youths from predatory abduction, cultural rot, and sexual abuse—bespoke a growing political and cultural interest in burnishing the American family and child through moral purification and an anticrime populism.[21]

The initial successes of the child protection movement were modest, with activists focused primarily on cutting the "red-tape," as one Oklahoman writing to her congressman put it, "not to mention the unfair bureaucratic procedures, which accompany the reports of these missing children." In the early and mid-1980s, parents like Noreen Gosch, the mother of paperboy Johnny Gosch, drafted or supported legislation blocking law enforcement from observing a waiting period before investigating reports of a lost or missing child. They also petitioned for a consolidated national database, accessible to law enforcement agencies across the country, that would list missing youth. To this end, child safety activists found a friend in Ronald Reagan, who signed into law the Missing Children and Missing Children's Assistance Acts (MCA and MCAA) in 1982 and 1984, respectively. The MCA formed the missing child database for which child protection crusaders had appealed, and the MCAA created the National Center for Missing and Exploited Children (NCMEC), a "resource center and clearinghouse" intended "to provide technical assistance to local and State governments, public and private nonprofit agencies, and individuals in locating and recovering missing children."[22]

The Reagan administration portrayed the missing child "epidemic" and a perceived (though unfounded) spike in juvenile crime as logical, lamentable consequences of youth liberation and cultural permissiveness. Reagan and other policymakers set out to rectify these youth-oriented social problems by guaranteeing children's placement in either parental or state custody. Reagan's Office of Juvenile Justice and Delinquency Prevention (OJJDP) took a hardline approach to (nonwhite) "serious juvenile offenders" and a more nurturing approach to missing, vulnerable (white) youths through NCMEC messaging, programming, and grants. The nonwhite youth disproportionately ensnared in the juvenile justice system faced an increasingly punitive OJJDP in the Reagan years. Officials like Alfred Regnery, head of the OJJDP from 1983 to 1986, endorsed the long-term incarceration of "chronic" juvenile offenders—who, in his formulation, were largely nonwhite and irredeemable. Such OJJDP action, alongside changes in state-level juvenile justice policy in the early to mid-eighties, led to elevated juvenile incarceration rates through the mid-nineties. Conversely, the child safety scare reinforced the same notions of white innocence and vulnerability that structured Reagan's "family values" politics and the war on drugs. By stressing "the historic notion that children have a right to be in the custody of their parents or legal guardians" and rejecting "the premise that children have a right to freedom from custody," the Reagan administration depicted the heteropatriarchal (white) dual-parent family as an antidote to stranger danger and the broader "horrors of life on urban streets." Unlike their nonwhite counterparts, then, white youths were vulnerable, innocent, and deserving of "a family in a stable home environment."[23]

Reagan and his acolytes also sanctioned a crop of public and private sector child safety exercises and products that helped to form the contours of the child safety regime. Fingerprinting programs popped up around the country in the early 1980s, as parents recorded their children's vital information in the hopes of easing the investigative and search processes should their kids ever vanish. "It's about fear," one 1983 *Chicago Tribune* article read. "[It's about] parents who can't forget Etan Patz, the New York boy whose face still grins from tattered 'Missing' posters more than three years" after his disappearance, "or little Adam Walsh, led by an abductor from a crowded Hollywood, Fla., mall and murdered soon after. These are the parents who are fingerprinting their children, then—just in case." School districts, law enforcement agencies, community groups, and other entities backed such fingerprinting initiatives. With federal support, the business sector got involved, too. Blue-chip companies like K-Mart and Mobil raised awareness about stranger danger, while more dubious startups (which one critic derided as "an army of child saving charlatans") hawked items purported to alleviate the threats of abduction and exploitation. Companies sold leashes and other restraint devices for children, home fingerprinting kits, and "electronic monitoring system[s]" that sounded an alarm if a child wandered too far from a designated area. Dairies, supermarkets, pizza shops, and various manufacturers put missing kids' photographs on their product packaging. Media conglomerates ran public service programming like the made-for-TV movies about Adam Walsh. President Reagan appeared on one of NBC's broadcasts of *Adam*, reading the names of missing children as their faces flashed on the screen. Through an April 1985 executive order, Reagan also created the President's Child Safety Partnership, which would "encourage the development of public/private sector initiatives to prevent and respond to the victimization of children." These public–private ventures spoke to Americans' growing faith in the business sector, amidst their waning confidence in the state. Further, they operationalized a logic of mass vigilantism that enlisted the "non-deviant" American public in the project of saving young people.[24]

Though the Reagan administration proved instrumental in assembling the child safety regime, this regime grew most rapidly and intensely in the 1990s and 2000s. Laws implemented in these decades had a dramatic effect on the expanding carceral and surveillance states. Frequently inscribed with the names of missing or murdered (white) children, laws like the Jacob Wetterling Crimes against Children and Sexually Violent Offender Registration Act—part of the 1994 federal crime bill (VCCLEA)—and the 2006 Adam Walsh Act found new and ever more daunting ways to criminalize, incarcerate, and supervise those deemed sexually dangerous, particularly to children. For one, the Wetterling Act—named for an eleven-year-old St. Joseph, Minnesota, boy who was abducted, sexually assaulted, and killed by a stranger in 1989—"formed the basis of federal sex offender laws" by requiring states to establish and maintain sex offender registries (SORs). While some states had launched such registration systems before 1994, the Wetterling Act mandated the nationwide adoption of SORs and thus dramatically increased the number of Americans under correctional or community control. Moreover, the VCCLEA's "three strikes, and you're out" provision, motivated in part by the 1993 kidnapping and slaying of twelve-year-old Polly Klaas, imposed "a minimum sentence of 25 years to life for three-time repeat offenders with multiple prior serious or violent felony convictions."[25]

While states, and not the federal government, mete out punishment for most sex offenses, the federal government could withhold funding from states that failed to comply with the VCCLEA and similar laws.[26] The Wetterling Act and its 1996 amendment Megan's Law—named for seven-year-old Megan Kanka, who was raped and murdered by a stranger in 1994—articulated such compliance requirements. Megan's Law required "the release of relevant information . . . to protect the public concerning registered [sex] offenders," and, like the Wetterling Act, it stipulated that states refusing to follow its directives would face a 10-percent garnishment of federal funds. These provisions corresponded with a swell in state incarceration rates for sex crimes, which in turn produced more and more individuals required to register as sex offenders. Incarceration rates, in general, boomed from the 1970s through the 2000s, but incarceration rates for sex offenses rose even more precipitously across the same period. The state prison population increased by 206 percent, while the number of state inmates imprisoned for sex crimes grew 330 percent from 1980 to 1994. Between 1980 and 2010, the rate of commitment to state prison for sex offenses rose 275 percent. Across both state and federal prisons, incarceration rates for sexual assault increased by about 300 percent from 1980 to 1996.[27]

Federal prosecutions of child sex offenses also exploded after the early 1980s. New programs coordinated through the US Department of Justice, NCMEC, and Federal Bureau of Investigation addressed the sexual exploitation of minors and the production and dissemination of child pornography—while also formally and informally broadening definitions of "exploitation," "harm," and "pornography." The Child Protection Restoration and Penalties Enhancement Act of 1990, the 1996 Child Pornography Prevention Act, the 2003 PROTECT Act, the Adam Walsh Act, and the 2008 PROTECT Our Children Act, among other laws, escalated penalties for child sexual abuse, child sex trafficking, and the transmission of child pornography. As an expanding World Wide Web facilitated the flow of illicit material online in the 1990s and 2000s, it also activated new federal prosecutorial strategies which have toughened penalties for child exploitation and pornography, even when such content features no "flesh-and-blood children" whatsoever.[28] Under President George W. Bush, for instance, Justice Department officials aggressively pursued individuals who produced and consumed computer-generated imagery depicting imaginary minors engaged in sexual activity. Such developments increased the number of child sex offense charges filed by the government in the 1990s and 2000s. Though such cases make up a relatively small percentage of the federal caseload, the number of child exploitation suspects referred to US Attorneys jumped from a total of 774 in 1994 to 3,661 in 2006, a 466 percent surge.[29]

Working within a metastasizing carceral state, the ideology of stranger danger helped expand state and federal supervision of those branded as sex offenders. Indeed, the very concept of monitoring sex offenders in a broad, systematized manner ensued from the 1980s kidnapping "epidemic." With the implementation and enforcement of a sprawling system of sex offender registration, a project undertaken primarily through the Wetterling Act, Walsh Act, and other federal tools, the number of listed offenders rose from a few thousand (at most) in the early 1990s—when only a dozen or so states operated SORs—to over half a million by 2005. Even since the NCMEC began compiling comprehensive statistics on sex offender registrants in the mid-2000s, the rolls have grown considerably. In 2005, some 551,987 were registered in the United States (and in US territories that keep statistics). That number had climbed to over 900,000 by 2018. Further, anyone with an Internet connection can now see the convicted sex offenders who live around them—or who live anywhere in the country. Americans seem mostly comfortable with this massive project of social death and banishment. A 2005 Gallup survey found that some 94 percent of Americans support the existence of sex offender registries, no doubt in the service of protecting the idealized child. And for many Americans, the humanity of convicted sex criminals remains an open question.[30] The creation of this sizable population of pariahs has flowed directly from the moral panic at the center of this book.

FAMILY VALUES IN PERIL

Although the child safety regime has its immediate origins in the late 1970s and early 1980s stranger danger panic, child kidnapping and exploitation (both real and imagined) have deep roots in the American past. From the late seventeenth through the late nineteenth centuries, Indian captivity narratives enjoyed tremendous popularity and served a distinct ideological purpose. Regularly embellished by publishers for effect, these tales often portrayed white women and youngsters as victims while vilifying their Native American captors. Captivity narratives remained a staple of the American literary canon until the 1870s or so, when stories about ransom kidnappings began to appear in print media and particularly in serialized crime stories.[31]

The 1874 ransom abduction of four-year-old Charley Ross heralded the arrival of this new type of captivity story. The first such case to draw widespread media attention, Ross's disappearance elicited sympathy nationwide, as Americans conducted massive searches for the boy and turned him into a national icon. Responses to the Ross case reflected larger transformations in cultural understandings of childhood. Conceptions of young children as economically "worthless" yet emotionally "priceless" had started to solidify in the mid- to late nineteenth century. The denial of children's economic value and assertion of their sentimental value not only informed Progressive efforts to insulate American children from the ills of poverty and industrial society. This new sensibility also shaped Americans' cyclical fascination with tales of child kidnapping and abuse in the late nineteenth century and throughout the twentieth, as seen in the 1932 abduction of famed aviator Charles Lindbergh's baby.[32]

Intermittent sex panics across the twentieth century also cast certain women and children as victims. Victorian concerns about "white slavery"— the kidnapping, interstate trafficking, and despoliation of chaste white women and girls by men of color—led to the passage of the 1910 White-Slave Traffic Act. Also known as the Mann Act, the law enhanced the powers of federal law enforcement, particularly with respect to surveilling and penalizing nonnormative and antinormative sexual behaviors. Scares over "sexual psychopathy" in the 1930s and after the Second World War prompted new laws and "treatment" practices which consecrated the bonds between criminal justice and psychiatry in the regulation of "sex crime." For historian Regina Kunzel, "psychiatric authority" and "the language of illness, treatment, and cure" conspired to "mystif[y]" the "sexual psycho-path laws" of the mid-twentieth century "in ways that made them difficult to challenge, both at their moment of origin in the 1940s and 1950s and in their later incarnations as sex offender legislation after 1990."[33]

This series of midcentury sex panics eventually dissipated, but another, more potent scare over sexualized stranger danger would emerge in the post-liberationist 1970s and 1980s. Just as earlier panics over the abduction and exploitation of women and children had articulated anxieties about shifting mores, so too did the stranger danger moment touched off in the late seventies. This late twentieth-century panic, though, had more far-reaching effects, as it fed off and fed into "a late-modern media-saturated world where everyday experience has been rendered increasingly full of simulations" *and* stimulation. Cable news and the twenty-four-hour news cycle breathed life into the discourse of missing children and child protection. Rare, isolated cases of missing and endangered youth—news of which traveled via television, newspapers, and political rhetoric—together generated an easily digestible composite image of imperiled (white) childhood that confirmed fears of familial and national decline.[34]

The dislocations and failures of the 1960s and 1970s had left many white American families disillusioned, uncertain of what the future might hold for their children. For some observers, these developments seemed rooted in, or at the very least related to, a perceived moral rot unleashed through sixties and seventies liberationism. Economic and political instability, alongside the reconfiguration of cultural and sexual norms, had supposedly disrupted the idealized white American family and the child upon which it hinged. The late twentieth-century moral panic over child kidnapping and exploitation took hold in this "age of fracture." Following Watergate, a disastrous war in Vietnam, and the abuses of power uncovered by the Frank Church Committee, Americans had lost faith in their government and its institutions. In 1964, fully 77 percent of Americans had reported that they trusted the federal government; by 1980 that figure had dropped to 26 percent. A series of economic crises in the 1960s and 1970s underwrote "a politics of frustration, reaction, and division," as the Fordist social contract and the masculine ideal of "breadwinner liberalism" fell by the wayside.[35]

With the dissolution of the Fordist family wage, the Americans who had benefited most handsomely from its protections now found themselves exposed—not only to the vagaries of the market but also to a broader "permissive society," one presumed feature of which was widespread criminal depravity. Accordingly, American fears of crime (to the extent that they can be quantified) increased in the 1960s and 1970s before reaching record levels in the early 1980s. While 35 percent of those polled in 1968 indicated they "would be afraid to walk alone at night" in some areas within a mile of their home, an all-time high of 48 percent expressed this same fear in 1982. Fully 54 percent of respondents in 1981 reported "more crime" in their neighborhoods "than there was a year ago," tied for another record high. (Fifty-four percent of those surveyed in 1992 also claimed that their neighborhoods had seen an uptick in crime over the previous year.) In another poll, conducted in 1980, 40 percent of Americans declared "that they were 'highly fearful' of assault," even though one's chances of being victimized by violent crime in the early eighties stood at just 0.6 percent.[36]

A series of constitutional victories secured on behalf of criminal defendants in the sixties and seventies further stoked fears of legal and cultural permissiveness. Rulings in favor of "defendants' rights" and the rights of the convicted—including 1972's *Furman v. Georgia* decision, which placed a moratorium on the death penalty—galvanized activists in the ascendant victims' rights movement. According to these advocates, the US criminal justice system had strayed from its key mission of protecting victims and "secondary victims," the friends and family members left to pick up the pieces. By coddling the accused, the convicted, and the damned, these critics charged, law enforcement officials and the courts had stymied victims and their loved ones in their pursuit of justice.

This "due process revolution," in legal scholar Barry Feld's formulation, spread to the juvenile court. Starting in the sixties, a spate of US Supreme Court decisions and legislative developments expanded the rights of accused juveniles. The *In re Gault* and *In re Winship* decisions of 1967 and 1970, respectively, affirmed the Fourteenth Amendment due process rights of juveniles.[37] The 1974 Juvenile Justice and Delinquency Prevention (JJDP) Act set out to remove, or "deinstitutionalize," runaway youths and "status offenders" from secure adult facilities such as county jails. At least implicitly, then, the JJDP Act permitted American youngsters to run away from home without fear of incarceration.

The same liberationist principles which underpinned the "due process revolution" in juvenile justice also precipitated changes that applied to a wider swath of the youth population, not just those entangled in the juvenile system. The US Supreme Court affirmed the First Amendment rights of young people in *Tinker v. Des Moines*, decided in 1969. College students nationwide petitioned for free speech rights, and many became involved in antiwar organizing. As adults in the nation's capital shipped their peers off to Southeast Asia, young people became increasingly disenchanted with adult authority—objecting to the notion that they could fight and die in Vietnam (frequently through conscription), yet they could not vote or legally consume alcohol. Hoping to placate antiwar activists, especially those of draft age, Richard Nixon campaigned on ending the draft in 1968, and the Department of Defense stopped issuing conscription orders in early 1973. Further, youth-led mobilization efforts prompted the introduction and ratification in 1971 of the Twenty-sixth Amendment, which extended the franchise to citizens eighteen years of age and older. States also set out to lower their minimum legal drinking ages, usually from twenty-one to eighteen, in alignment with the new voting age.[38]

It should come as little surprise, then, that the white family—and the idealized child around which it revolved—became political focal points starting in the mid- to late 1970s. As hierarchies of gender, sexuality, race, class, and indeed generation looked destined to collapse, public figures rushed to salvage the "besieged" American family, which had long reflected and reinforced these hierarchies. Commentators as ideologically estranged as Phyllis Schlafly and Christopher Lasch lamented the family's diminishing position as a "haven in a heartless world." In one critic's words, Lasch took the nuclear family as "an indispensable feature of social life," "the agency to which society entrusts [the] complex and delicate task" of socializing and rearing children. From Lasch's ambivalent liberalism to the vitriolic "family values" conservatism of "Save Our Children" founder Anita Bryant and "Moral Majority" leader Reverend Jerry Falwell, cultural commentators and policymakers increasingly focused on the normative, patriarchal, procreative family as a "disciplinary matrix"—a site of social control and a guarantor of social order.[39]

Because they seemed to pose an existential threat to the white, heteronormative, male-breadwinner family, gay men shouldered much of the blame for the crises buffeting the family and the child in the 1970s and beyond. Accordingly, they often emerged as suspects in the initial cases fueling the stranger danger panic, which involved Patz and other young boys. In this climate, antigay activists opposed antidiscrimination measures and pushed for new prejudicial ordinances intended to limit gay men's "access" to young people. Since "homosexuals cannot biologically reproduce children," Anita Bryant infamously postulated, "they must recruit our children." This idea colored 1978's proposed Briggs Initiative, which aimed to bar LGBTQ people from working in California public schools. Though this effort foundered, its governing logic endured, looming over the Patz saga and other cases of missing and murdered boys. Such cases lent themselves to speculation about homosexual pedophilic predation, even though there is no evidence that gay men are more likely to sexually abuse children or that boys are more likely than girls to fall victim to stranger kidnapping or sexual abuse. On the contrary, some 70 to 81 percent of children in "stereotypical" abductions are girls.[40]

Yet in the child safety panic of the late twentieth century, the young photogenic white boy served as the prototypical victim, at least at first. Boys were the child-victims most commonly featured in press accounts during the late 1970s and early 1980s stranger danger scare, but the gender dynamics of child safety narratives changed in the 1990s, when cases involving girls began to attract significant media and political attention. Though it is difficult to fully explain this shift, it stands to reason that the feminist sexual empowerment and virulent antifeminism of the 1970s and 1980s undermined conceptions of girlhood innocence. Only with the solidification of a "postfeminist" ideology in the late 1980s and 1990s did girls and young women reclaim the mantle of innocence—this time as liberated subjects, ostensibly with equal standing in the marketplace and workplace, who could elect to be shielded by a growing carceral and national security state.[41] Therefore, the most widely circulated stories of missing persons since the early 1990s have involved photo/telegenic, white, middle-class girls, such as Polly Klaas, Megan Kanka, JonBenét Ramsey, and Natalee Holloway.[42] Still, out of the anxious, homophobic, "profamily" climate of the 1970s and 1980s emerged a stranger danger panic initially fixated on young male victims. Abetted by child safety activists, receptive lawmakers, and an eager news media, this moral panic remade American childhood and the carceral state.

CONSERVATISM, CARCERALITY, AND THE CHILD

By demonstrating how a late twentieth-century moral panic constructed a new child safety regime, *Stranger Danger* illuminates, in ways that have been overlooked, how the politics of family values and child protection facilitated America's turn toward punishment since the 1960s and 1970s. In so doing, the book also makes a case for the primacy of childhood in recent US political history. *Stranger Danger* locates children and their figurations at the heart of some of the major political, cultural, and economic transformations in the United States since the 1970s. In its treatment of mass incarceration, the diminishing autonomy of young people, the intensifying "war on sex" (especially underage sex), and the bipartisan fetishization of family values and child protection, this book shows that childhood is political. *Stranger Danger* thereby troubles assumptions of adults' political agency and children's "apolitical" nature, complicating the ageist dynamics at play in virtually all work on American political culture and "high politics."[43]

This is a political history, then, though not one that resolves neatly into overdrawn binaries of red and blue, Republican and Democrat, right and left. *Stranger Danger* moves beyond the historiographical framework of the right-wing ascendency while shedding much-needed light on the very moment that conservatives supposedly reached the mountaintop: the Reaganite 1980s.[44] Curiously enough, for all the ink spilled on conservatism and the GOP, few histories—with the exception of a growing historiography on HIV/AIDS—have actually grappled with the eighties and its echoes.[45] This book begins in 1979 and focuses significant attention on the Reagan White House, its Department of Justice, and the conservative movement. Yet it also explores the continuities between late twentieth-century conservatives and liberals—not just those in the halls of power but also the ordinary parents concerned about stranger danger. As with the construction of the carceral state more broadly, the child safety regime found support across the political spectrum. Not only did white, suburban, and rural silent-majoritarians like Johnny Gosch's mother and Jacob Wetterling's parents petition for swifter police intervention in missing children's cases and harsher penalties for a range of sexual offenses; so too did many liberal feminists, gay rights advocates, journalists, African American activists and leaders, businesspersons, and other actors concerned about the potential excesses of liberation. A rigid "red–blue divide" cannot explain the carceral agendas shared by liberals and conservatives in the last decades of the twentieth century, nor can it account for the bipartisan authorship of the child safety regime.[46]

Stranger Danger documents the birth of the missing child scare in the late 1970s and 1980s and reveals how this panic formed a new legal and cultural system through which Americans would understand and manage threats to children. The first part, called "The Stark Terror of a Unique Tragedy," concentrates on three cases of missing and exploited youth. Each seized national headlines and implied a pervasive (and worsening) stranger danger threat. By stoking panic and fear, these cases helped launch local, regional, and national child protection efforts that would build the child safety regime.

Chapter 1 assesses Etan Patz's 1979 disappearance and its after-math. Unlike earlier cases of missing children, Patz's appeared to signal a growing child safety problem. Photographs of Etan gave rise to the image of endangered childhood. The boy's pictures oriented the emergent child protection campaign around visuals and around the myth of gay preda-tory pedophilia, as investigators, activists, and the news media implicated the North American Man/Boy Love Association (NAMBLA) in Patz's ab-duction. Accordingly, the first chapter situates reactions to the Patz case within an antigay political project undertaken by conservative culture warriors and within the increasingly normative LGBTQ and feminist movements of the 1980s.

The second chapter focuses on the 1979–1981 kidnappings and murders of some twenty-nine black youths in Atlanta. These abductions and killings, which primarily targeted young males from Atlanta's poor and working-class neighborhoods, exacerbated African American anxieties about anti-black violence and raised the specters of southern racism and the myth of gay pedophilia. Public, political, and media responses to the Atlanta murders emphasized the young victims' "street smarts," "hustling," and even their alleged same-sex sex work, often depriving them of the individ-ualized innocence so readily lavished upon Etan Patz and other missing or murdered white youth. Moreover, in an effort to preserve Atlanta's reputa-tion as progressive and business-friendly, the city's biracial political and ec-onomic establishment sought to downplay the racial and class dimensions of the abductions and slayings. The Atlanta tragedies thus exposed the ra-cial and class limitations of the image of endangered childhood and dem-onstrated how notions of white child-victimhood grounded the child safety regime.

Chapter 3 centers on the disappearances of *Des Moines Register* paperboys Johnny Gosch and Eugene Wade Martin in 1982 and 1984, re-spectively. These incidents challenged white Midwestern ideas about child-hood and regional innocence, as locals took the paperboy cases as signs of regional and national decline. White Iowans responded by demanding state protection for their children, who supposedly faced new threats from strangers emboldened by moral relativism and sexual liberation and impervious to the symbolic power of an innocent and secure Midwest. Many of the legal and cultural mechanisms adopted in the service of protecting young Iowans were replicated in the construction of the national child safety regime.

The book's second part, titled "The Battle for Child Safety," explores the political and policy implications of the 1970s and 1980s child safety scare. Chapter 4 recounts how the DOJ obstructed missing child legislation in the early eighties but eventually buckled under pressure from activists, who deployed an affective politics of child safety to paint the DOJ as cruel and obstinate. The DOJ subsequently transformed into the federal entity most committed to the child safety cause, working to publicize and combat the problems of child abduction, exploitation, sexual abuse, and pornography. The Department's "conversion" proved vital to the making of a punitive child safety regime in the late twentieth and early twenty-first centuries.

The fifth chapter shows how the child safety issue further splintered federal juvenile justice and youth policy along racial and class fault lines.[47] Tracing the movements of rightwing luminary Alfred S. Regnery, chapter 5 illustrates how Reagan conservatives embellished the severity of moral threats facing "innocent" children (coded as white and middle class) in the service of "toughening" juvenile justice policies targeting poor, working-class, nonwhite youth.

Chapter 6 chronicles how the Reagan administration lauded the role of the private sector in protecting American children. The celebration by Reagan, other conservatives, and neoliberals of private sector (and especially business sector) efforts to "save" certain American youngsters and promote "family values" cleared the way for a more expansive child safety regime pieced together at the turn of the twenty-first century.

Finally, chapter 7 uncovers how the so-called New Democrat Bill Clinton seized upon the stranger danger myth and hitched it to his racialized "law and order" and "family values" policy programs. As president, Clinton underwrote the passage of the Wetterling Act, the federal "three strikes" law, and Megan's Law, which together federalized systems of sex offender registration and community notification. Imprinted with the names of white child-victims and awash in the imagery of endangered childhood, these laws enlarged and formalized the child safety regime, thus augmenting a carceral and surveillance state that disproportionately ensnares queer Americans, people of color, and youth.[48]

From the AMBER Alerts that periodically rattle smart phones nation-wide to the unnerving sprawl of sex offender registries, the child safety regime has shaped the lives of Americans young and old. Yet Americans have not grappled with the origins of this regime—or the indelible imprint it has left on their society and culture. *Stranger Danger* takes up this torch to illuminate perils and predators both real and imagined.

PART I

"The Stark Terror of a Unique Tragedy"

CHAPTER 1

✧

"He Was Beautiful"

Etan Patz, Queer Politics, and the Image of Endangered Childhood

E tan Patz was dead. On June 19, 2001, more than twenty years after the six-year-old's disappearance, a Manhattan surrogate court judge declared the boy officially deceased. That evening, the judge's ruling was the lead story on *CNN Tonight*. Etan Patz's beaming face opened the CNN feature, a testament to the enduring visual appeal and symbolic resonance of his image. "It's hard to fathom that such a joyful face could have inspired such a sad movement," CNN correspondent Maria Hinojosa mused as Etan's visage appeared on screen. "But the disappearance of Etan Patz is credited with starting the national missing children's movement in this country." In February 2017, after a Manhattan jury found fifty-six-year-old Pedro Hernandez guilty of kidnapping and murdering Etan, news media accounts similarly fixated on the young boy's face, forever frozen in the 1970s. "The mystery of what happened to Etan shook New York and the nation," the *New York Times* wrote following the Hernandez verdict, "with photographs of the smiling, sandy-haired boy ubiquitous on milk cartons, 'missing' posters, newspaper front pages and television newscasts." The unspeakable loss these visuals signified caused "alarm . . . across America," the *Times* observed, and helped initiate the late twentieth-century stranger danger panic. "It was an age of innocence," Patz family attorney Brian

O'Dwyer recalled in 2001. "May 25, 1979, represented the death of innocence of New York."[1] Etan Patz was killed that day.

Never before had Etan walked the two blocks to the school bus stop by himself, without parental or adult supervision. But on that Friday morning, just before the long Memorial Day weekend, Etan ("a Hebrew name to which he answers as Ai-tan," the *New York Times* noted days after the disappearance) set out to do just that. Despite her reservations, Julie Patz had allowed her son to make the trek alone, after Etan's constant appeals for greater autonomy. In the morning rush, as Julie Patz readied her other children for the day, Etan eagerly prepared for his jaunt to the bus stop. He donned blue pants, a jacket, sneakers, and a pilot hat stamped with the words "Eastern Air Lines Junior Pilot." Carrying "a small blue tote bag imprinted with cartooned red and white elephants," Etan departed his home about five minutes before eight o'clock. From the fire escape of the family's third-floor loft in SoHo, Julie Patz watched her son walk toward the bus stop, alone, for the first and last time. She saw him pass Wooster Street, the next street over from the bus stop at Prince and West Broadway. On that block, Etan had planned to visit a bodega to buy a soda for lunch. Another mother, keeping a lookout over the bus stop, waited for Etan until 8:20, twenty minutes after the school bus left. Etan never arrived.[2]

At the time, eighteen-year-old Pedro Hernandez was working as a bodega clerk in SoHo. By his account, Hernandez lured Etan Patz into the basement of the bodega with the promise of a soda. Once they entered the basement, Hernandez claimed, he began to choke the boy. According to Hernandez, Etan may have still been alive when he shoved him into a plastic bag, placed the bag into a box, and tossed the box into a dumpster. After news of Etan's disappearance broke, Hernandez began to tell family members and acquaintances that he had killed a boy in Manhattan, and he continued to share this story into the twenty-first century. Questions about his mental health and intellectual capacity loomed over these confessions and forestalled prosecutorial action until 2012, when Hernandez formally confessed to abducting and killing Etan Patz. To certify this confession, Hernandez signed one of the millions of "MISSING" notices imprinted with Etan's picture that swirled around Manhattan and beyond after May 25, 1979.[3]

Just five days after Patz vanished, the *New York Times* observed, "Thousands of circulars with Etan's pictures" on them had been "affixed to lampposts and store windows, distributed by neighborhood children and adults and posted by transit police." Taken by Etan's father Stanley, a professional photographer, these pictures came to represent a national trauma: a supposed epidemic in child kidnapping, molestation, exploitation, and

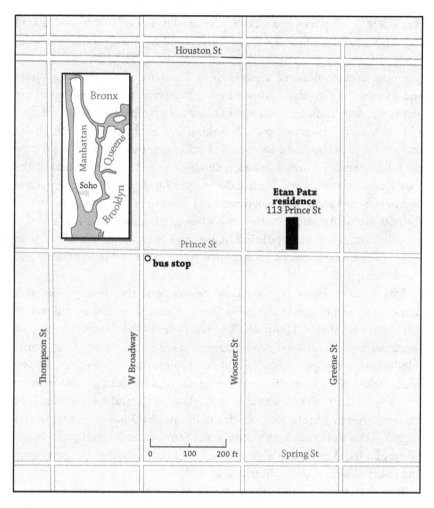

Figure 1.1 The Patzes' residence in SoHo and Etan's bus stop. Map by Erin Greb Cartography.

murder. According to one CBS *Evening News* story airing in December 1982, Etan had "become a symbol of all the children—perhaps fifty thousand— who are kidnapped by strangers each year."[4] These figures were wildly in- flated, as journalists, social scientists, and government officials had made clear by the mid-1980s. But Etan's photographs helped buttress such exag- gerated claims and the broader child safety cause by inaugurating a new cultural form: the image of endangered childhood.

Such imagery generally spotlighted young, white, photogenic, middle- class children and explicated the dangers that ostensibly confronted them in a moment of national uncertainty. Beginning with Etan's photograph, the image of endangered childhood—delivered via consumer products and through texts like news broadcasts, popular novels, and films—articulated the message that "stranger danger" threatened American childhood innocence. Announcing that particular children were "MISSING" or "LOST," these pictures encouraged viewers to look out for the featured subjects and to ruminate on their fates. At no other point in the American past had visual depictions of so many healthy young people been dispatched to address a moral threat supposedly lurking within the republic. Patz quite literally became the face of a specific kind of child-victimhood in the late twentieth-century United States, one that perfectly complemented the narratives of national and familial decline proffered by social conservatives and neoliberals alike. The proliferation of these pictures gave credence to the notion that American children were being kidnapped en masse and also provided ammunition to political figures and "moral entrepreneurs" who located the missing child scare within a wider crisis facing the family and the nation.[5]

Etan's photographs circulated via newspapers, the nightly television news, and twenty-four-hour cable news stations, reaching millions of American households. Many New Yorkers no doubt saw Etan's face daily on handbills papered across the city. Images of a contented, photogenic, white, middle-class boy ripped from his safe and comfortable two-parent household worked to tighten the tangle of grievances knotted around matters of family, childhood, and sexuality in the late 1970s and early 1980s. That Patz went missing in the journalistic, financial, and (some would say) queer capital of the world; the largest city in the country; and a metropolis in the midst of a fiscal crisis and a panic over crime only added to the emotional and political weight of his disappearance.[6]

The ubiquitous, captivating pictures of photogenic young Etan also served to substantiate a sexual motive for his kidnapping, as did the larger antigay context. Beth Gutcheon's popular 1981 novel *Still Missing* (based on Etan's case) and its 1983 film adaptation *Without a Trace* gave credence to the theory that the six-year-old boy had been snatched for sexual purposes. This theory gained currency beginning in late 1982, when members of the North American Man/Boy Love Association (NAMBLA) emerged as prime suspects in the Patz abduction. A December 1982 police raid on a cottage reportedly affiliated with NAMBLA turned up a photograph of a boy who resembled Etan. Though investigators later confirmed that the image came from a nonpornographic "boyhood" calendar published in 1968 (four years before Etan was born), this discovery appeared to provide a logical rationale for the Patz kidnapping: One or more queer men had kidnapped and sexually exploited the handsome young boy. That a photograph would prompt such suspicions reinforces the centrality of Patz's image to conceptions of his innocence and appeal. Given its promotion of endangered child imagery, and the sexual anxieties embedded therein, the Patz case also revealed some of the key fissures within late twentieth-century LGBTQ and women's activism, as antirape feminists, mainline "homonormative" gay rights activists, and proponents of "man/boy love" battled over the boundaries between sexual freedom and sexual exploitation.[7]

Though earlier incidents of youth abduction and murder—such as the saga of Richard Leopold and Nathan Loeb; the 1955 sexual assault and slaying of fourteen-year-old Stephanie Bryan in California; the 1970s "candy man" murders in Texas; and the John Wayne Gacy Jr. killings—had stirred anxieties about homosexuality, none of these individual cases had sparked larger, sustained discussions about child kidnapping or sexual abuse. Of course, Americans have long agonized over the sexual victimization of children, but only with the Patz case and those that followed in the early 1980s did pedophilia—and specifically "pederasty," or relations between adult men and males under the legal age of consent—become the clearest suspected motive in high-profile child abductions. As one *New York Times* headline explained: "Etan Patz Case Puts New Focus on a Sexual Disorder, Pedophilia." Because, as historian Paula Fass contends, American child abduction stories became "much more explicitly sexual" in the late twentieth century, the child safety campaign and the images at its core took on sexual meanings. The deluge of endangered children's photographs that arrived in the 1980s and 1990s—conspicuous in post offices, on milk cartons, on billboards, on Walmart store bulletin boards, and on direct-mail leaflets—conflated "missing" and "exploited," with the latter term connoting sexual abuse. This visual and symbolic connection, manifest in the name of the federally subsidized National Center for Missing and Exploited Children, originated with Etan Patz.[8]

The tension between widely disseminated "pictures of innocence" (like those depicting Etan) and the nefarious forces that putatively threatened the innocence displayed therein motored the 1980s child safety campaign. For art historian Anne Higonnet, such images "guard the cherished ideal of childhood innocence" yet also "contain within them the potential to undo that ideal." In the stranger danger panic, the sheer breadth of images spotlighting photogenic missing youngsters (especially boys, at least initially) suggested that stranger abductions constituted a grave and growing problem and that (homo)sexual motives underlay the majority of these incidents. Though data indicate that reports of child sexual abuse—along with other forms of mistreatment—did increase from the mid-1970s through the 1990s, experts interpreted this uptick as "the result of a new public and professional mobilization to identify and report cases." There was no verifiable spike in child sexual assaults perpetrated by strangers during this period. Still, overlapping late twentieth-century fears concerning child abduction and child sexual abuse found a common host in the racialized image of endangered childhood. This image helped construct the child safety regime.[9]

PICTURING CHILDHOOD

It would be difficult to identify a moment in recent human history when images of children did not perform vital political work. Generally such visuals have rested upon Victorian-era conceptions of the child as "'economically worthless' but 'emotionally priceless.'" Late nineteenth- and early twentieth-century reformers like Grace Abbott, Lewis Hine, and Jacob Riis marshaled symbolic and flesh-and-blood children in the service of various Progressive causes—chief among them the abolition of child labor and the end of child poverty and hunger.

For their part, Hine and Riis captured in their photographs scenes of children toiling in factories, of newsboys (or "newsies") hawking papers, and of young farmhands tilling the soil. Such images ginned up public

Figure 1.2 A seven-year-old Mobile, Alabama, "newsie" appears in this October 1914 photograph, which epitomizes the Progressive "muckraking" impulse. Photograph by Lewis Hine. Courtesy of the Library of Congress, LC-DIG-nclc-03945.

support for "saving" young Americans from the ills of industrialization, modernization, and poverty. The "emotionally priceless" child has also long operated "as a means to rally populations to war." In the 1920s and 1930s, global economic insecurity and the rise of fascism popularized images of needy, waifish children, sometimes flanked by their stoic mothers: a hysterical infant sitting amidst the rubble of a Shanghai railway station during the Sino-Japanese War in 1937; Jewish refugee children escaping Nazi Germany in the *Kindertransport*; Dorothea Lange's *Migrant Mother*; and other dispossessed women and children. These widely distributed examples of "gritty photographic realism" evinced the reformist and revolutionary sensibilities guiding the era's populist and radical movements.[10]

American propaganda disseminated during and after World War II centered on images of idealized white children and their families. Conjured by Franklin Delano Roosevelt's "four freedoms" and perfected in Norman Rockwell's paintings, such representations called upon the public to "fight . . . for the American family" and to fulfill private obligations by mobilizing in defense of the nation. These pictures of cheerful (white) American children jarred with the waif and Madonna-and-child iconography that had become "part of the architecture of Cold War liberalism." Emaciated children in breadlines, their photos often taken by US army personnel stationed abroad, offered a cultural shorthand for "hunger" and whipped up enthusiasm for American interventionism. Postwar institutions like the United Nations and its Children's Fund (UNICEF) trafficked in such imagery "to raise money and build support for their mother-and-child health and child-feeding programs." The Cold War also curated an imagined child who faced new perils characterized "not by bayonets and storm troopers but rather by ideological infiltration and weakness." By the 1950s, images of jubilant white youth cropped up on both sides of the Cold War binary. Propagandists relied heavily on romanticized pictures of children that at once explained the superiority of Soviet or American childhood (depending on the audience) and underscored the ideological threats confronting impressionable young people.[11]

Countervailing images of childhood gained purchase during the American civil rights, antiwar, antipoverty, and student movements of the sixties and seventies. Transmissions from Birmingham, Alabama, in 1963; Watts, Los Angeles, in 1965; or Madison, Wisconsin, and Kent, Ohio, in 1970 shed light on the divergent experiences of young Americans. Reappropriating the violent images emanating from Alabama and elsewhere, Soviet propagandists sought to win the "hearts and minds" of black and brown peoples in the global south by exposing the persistent paradox of race in American democracy. Far removed from Rockwell's representations

The best Santa of all...

WHEN YOU BUY a gift for a child at Christmas, or any other time, make it a toy—an American toy. For American toys are designed with the American child in mind. Nobody else. These are toys that develop initiative, imagination, dexterity. Toys the child prefers. Toys that aid in his or her growing up.

To further the scientific development and improve-

ment of toys for the American child, the Toy Manufacturers of the United States formed the American Toy Institute. The American Toy Institute gives standards of safety to American toy manufacturers, as well as the services and advice of leading child psychologists.

That's why we know—the best gift of all, from the best Santa of all, is the American toy.

The American Toy Institute
of Toy Manufacturers of the U.S.A., Inc. · 200 FIFTH AVENUE, NEW YORK CITY 10

Figure 1.3 By Americanizing Santa Claus and spotlighting contented (white) American children, this early Cold War advertisement designates capitalist consumption as the best means by which to "develop initiative, imagination, dexterity" in young people. From *Saturday Evening Post* 220, no. 20 (November 15, 1947), 51.

of American affluence, moreover, the stagecraft of Lyndon Johnson's War on Poverty operationalized scenes of Appalachian dispossession, replete with barefoot white children in lowly log cabins. Late twentieth-century resistance to the midcentury rights revolutions also commissioned new images of youth along racial lines: those deserving of protection and those deserving of punishment. With respect to the latter, antiwelfare and "law and order" sentiments expressed by conservatives and neoliberals alike— reinforced through sensationalized magazine covers, newspapers, and television programming—took black teenagers as drug peddlers, African American fetuses and infants as "crack babies" (and potential public charges), and nonwhite juveniles as "superpredators," a "new breed of predatory street criminal."[12]

In this late twentieth-century moment, images and accounts of lost, missing, or exploited photo/telegenic middle-class white children fed a burgeoning moral panic over stranger danger. Anxieties about feminism, gay rights, and sexual permissiveness nurtured the idea that children within the American family household faced intensifying threats from strangers and other malevolent actors outside the home. Concerns about crime and moral decay, exacerbated by the mid- to late twentieth-century rights revolutions, pivoted on the image of endangered white childhood. That Patz went missing as New York City confronted interlocking crises regarding "street crime" and fiscal policy only heightened the allure of his case.[13]

"WELCOME TO FEAR CITY"

Americans' fears of crime remained at historic highs throughout much of the late twentieth century. These fears corresponded with a national panic over urban spaces—and the inhabitants of these spaces—in the civil rights and "post–civil rights" eras. Etan Patz went missing in a moment of unrest and uncertainty in New York City. In the 1970s especially, the city's economic woes exacerbated crime, white flight, declining population figures, and a racialized war on drugs. Together, these phenomena reinforced understandings of New York as a city in chaos. While news media dispatches from, and cultural renderings of, New York City during this period often bordered on the sensational, they nonetheless reflected a larger sense of danger and despair. "I remember the New York of that era well, having arrived to start college there in 1976 and never left," one New Yorker recalled. "The city was compelling in its contradictions: a vibrant and very cheap place to live, it attracted talented young people in droves. It was also coming apart at the seams."[14]

Like much of the country, New York City had experienced a sustained postwar economic boom followed by a slowdown and stagflation in the seventies. From 1970 through 1976, the city lost over six hundred thousand jobs, or about one-sixth of its employment base. It teetered on the verge of bankruptcy in 1975; the city's outside counsel had even prepared a petition for bankruptcy and delivered it to the state supreme court that October. The economic picture improved slightly beginning in the late seventies, as the city added more than four hundred thousand jobs from 1976 to 1987. Yet these job gains appeared primarily in the service, construction, and financial sectors, in keeping with broader patterns of economic neoliberalization. Deindustrialization battered New York City with an enduring intensity. While job losses in manufacturing occurred gradually, they ultimately devastated many of the city's once-thriving industries, from apparel and home furnishings to metals and rubbers. In 1966, nearly a quarter of Gotham's employment base worked in manufacturing. By 1993, that figure had dropped to 9 percent. Some industries operating in the city lost more than 70 percent of their workforce across this twenty-seven-year period.[15]

The displacement and elimination of New York City's blue-collar manufacturing jobs—along with an increasing flow of real estate and financial capital toward the suburbs, abetted by federal mortgage subsidies and highway funding—drove many white residents out of the city, diminishing its income tax base. Between 1970 and 1980 alone, some two million white New Yorkers bolted for the suburbs, leaving in their wake "a checkerboard of ethnic enclaves"—particularly in the city's outer boroughs—"fraught with explosive racial and class tensions." This demographic realignment helped elevate a volatile politics of white ethnic nationalism. Politicians like the "Reform Democrat" Ed Koch seized upon the racial and class resentments coursing through the city, using flashpoints like the 1977 blackout and the December 1984 subway shooting by *"Death Wish* vigilante" Bernhard Goetz to promulgate "racially laced antiwelfare and law and order rhetoric" and policy.[16]

New York City's violent crime rates rose dramatically across the seventies and eighties, a direct result of the city's financial crisis. In 1966, the city registered 654 homicides. By 1970 that figure had climbed to 1,117, and in 1980 the city saw more than 1,800 murders. Reports of theft, simple assault, sexual assault, and robbery similarly increased across this period. These conditions stemmed, in large part, from the neoliberal austerity measures put in place by the city and state governments beginning in the mid-1970s. Saddled by severe budget deficits, the city government, in collaboration with New York State's Emergency Financial Control Board, laid off some fifteen thousand city employees, including five thousand police officers. A hiring freeze prevented the New York Police Department (NYPD) from recruiting or training new officers from July 1975 through November 1979.[17]

The city's neoliberal social policy revolution plunged many of its residents into poverty. From 1969 to 1979, the share of New Yorkers living in poverty rose from 14.5 percent to over 20 percent. Many in the city's poorer areas became untethered from the formal labor market and moved instead toward alternative, occasionally illicit, economic networks and practices. These same neighborhoods also bore the brunt of the crack-cocaine and HIV/AIDS crises. Cuts in city services, from police and fire to sanitation and transportation, magnified misery throughout the city—as trash piled up, the subway deteriorated, fires raged, and authorities failed to maintain "order" in the 1977 blackout, the 1988 Tompkins Square Park riot, the 1989 "Central Park Five" case, and the Crown Heights rebellion of 1991.[18]

New York's "crime epidemic" carried tremendous symbolic and cultural meaning.[19] For historian Jonathan Soffer, the city's relationship with crime "flits between real tragedy and the world of myth and legend." Indeed, commentators easily exploited the tragic fact that the journalistic and financial capital of the nation (if not the world) struggled to contain fires both literal and figurative in the last decades of the twentieth century. President Gerald Ford, for one, leveraged New York's financial troubles in the service of his hyperbolic antiurban politics. His hostility toward the city spawned the infamous *New York Daily News* front page headline, "FORD TO CITY: DROP DEAD." For their part, hip-hop, punk rock, postpunk, and neoexpressionist artists in the 1970s and 1980s found aesthetic inspiration in the grunge, grit, and graffiti of the New York City streets. But in films, TV news programs, and other texts, these flourishes often served to signal urban decay and youth degeneration. From *Taxi Driver* to *Escape from New York*, for example, American cinema in the seventies and eighties depicted New York City as a veritable hellscape stained by the visual and sonic refuse of punk, hip-hop, and street art.[20]

Tensions between the NYPD, communities of color, and high-ranking city officials exacerbated crime and stoked the cultural anxieties undergirding New York's "urban crisis." The mass firings of NYPD officers during the mid-1970s fiscal crisis, along with the subsequent four-year hiring freeze, led to rising crime rates and impeded the NYPD's basic operations for at least a decade. As one *New York Times* article explained in 1985, those "difficult days" sat "at the root of a severe problem the department is struggling with today. For there is a missing cadre in the New York City Police Department—a gap in the thin blue line." This gap, the story continued, "hampers the operations of the Police Department every day, making it just that much more difficult to do a difficult job." Outraged by the austerity measures imposed upon the NYPD in a moment of tumult, unions comprising firefighters, law enforcement officials, and other public sector employees published terrifying, largely embellished accounts of New York City crime in 1975. Calling themselves the Council for Public Safety, these unions produced the salacious *Welcome to Fear City: A Survival Guide for Visitors to the City of New York*, followed by two other pamphlets called *If You Haven't Been Mugged Yet . . .* and *Who's Next?*[21]

Welcome to Fear City preyed on widespread fears of crime and of urban environments generally. On its cover appeared a figuration of Death, a black hood draped over his skull, his eye sockets menacingly deep and dark, his teeth rotting and chipped—a perverse mascot for the crime-infested city. The leaflet directly rebuked Abraham Beame, New York's mayor from 1974 through 1977, who shouldered much of the blame for the crises confronting the city. "By the time you read this," *Welcome to Fear City* warned, "the number of public safety personnel available to protect residents and visitors may already have been still further reduced" by Mayor Beame. "Under those circumstances, the best circumstances we can give you is this: Until things change, stay away from New York City if you possibly can." But, the pamphlet advised, "some New Yorkers do manage to survive and even to keep their property intact." To last in Fear City, as these lucky locals had, tourists would be wise to avoid the subway, keep "off the streets after 6 p.m.," and never venture beyond Manhattan. Some one million of these circulars were printed, meaning the striking image of Death cropped up throughout the city, alerting visitors and residents alike to the perils purportedly lurking around them.[22] While *Welcome to Fear City* and its sequels clearly exaggerated the threat of crime, the pamphlets nonetheless confirmed prevailing conceptions of New York City as unspeakably dangerous—precariously positioned between calamity and collapse.

THE IMAGE OF ENDANGERED CHILDHOOD

Against this backdrop, Etan Patz's 1979 disappearance provided further material, symbolic, and visual evidence of New York's depravity and decay. Etan's presumed abduction appeared to deliver the worst of Fear City to the Patzes' close-knit neighborhood, although the SoHo of the late seventies was a far cry from the hypercommercialized, affluent, and gentrified SoHo of the twenty-first century. Deindustrialization and capital flight had hit the area particularly hard in the 1950s and 1960s. Its vacant cast-iron buildings, once occupied by garment and print manufacturers, enticed artists seeking "sun, light, and open space" in which to pursue the ambitious, large-scale projects that defined the modernist period. SoHo's proximity to Greenwich Village further appealed to artists and bohemians. By the late sixties, SoHo housed an eclectic mix of individuals and families enamored of the neighborhood's ambiance, architecture, and relative affordability. Nevertheless, the neighborhood was hardly insulated from the convulsions felt throughout the rest of the city.[23]

Still, press coverage of the Patz case treated SoHo as more of a small town or suburban community than a neighborhood in the nation's largest city. "What makes SoHo a small town," a 1980 *New York Times* profile of the Patz family read, "is the friendship and a shared sense of survival that links its early settlers" like the Patzes. "They were in the trenches together." As a *New York Daily News* writer explained in 2001, "I think a lot of the people who moved down [to SoHo] knew each other really well, because there weren't that many of them, and I think a lot of them felt apart from any other issues of crime, so that a mother might feel, especially down there at that time, that it was okay to let your six-year-old walk the two blocks [to the school bus stop]." Just a few days after the disappearance, one SoHo resident participating in the search for Etan told the *New York Times*, "People who think of SoHo don't realize what a community this is." For this volunteer, the fact that her neighbors were "writing descriptions of Etan in Spanish and Italian" and "putting up signs and knocking on doors" exemplified the ties that bound the neighborhood together. A key investigator in the Patz case remembered how "parents would leave baby carriages outside of bakeries or a candy store just to run in for a moment to get something," but this practice came to a halt after Etan's disappearance. The Patzes' lawyer expressed a similar sentiment. "Up until that time," he said, "all of us felt that our children had free rein of the streets." As author and longtime television news producer Lisa Cohen later recounted on the CBS *Evening News*, "I can't tell you how many times people have said to me, 'How could [Etan's mother Julie Patz] let him walk to the bus stop by [himself]?' That was what people did back then. That was absolutely a standard." Amidst heightened anxieties over crime, the Patz case and its associated imagery came to signify a new kind of threat confronting SoHo, New York City, and the country.[24]

Photographs of Etan blanketed New York City after the boy disappeared in May 1979. "His impish face, all bangs and baby teeth, seemed to be everywhere," one 1980 *New York Times* article observed. The fact that Etan disappeared from the streets of SoHo, not far from some of the world's most powerful media and financial institutions, allowed his face and his story to travel swiftly and widely across the country. Soon after news of the presumed abduction broke, NYPD officers handed out flyers on Manhattan sidewalks and informed passersby of Etan's physical description via bullhorn. Two months after Patz went missing, NBC's nationally televised

Nightly News program reported, "There are posters like this one all over New York City, all of them asking for help in locating six-year-old Etan Patz." The poster appearing alongside the anchor in the newsroom showed Etan smiling into the camera with bold, red, capitalized text around him, reading: "STILL MISSING: LOST CHILD ETAN PATZ." The newscaster went on, "A little over two months ago on his way to the school bus stop two blocks from his home, Etan simply disappeared, and his disappearance has led to the most extensive search for a missing child in New York City in decades."[25]

Julie Patz identified "publicity" and "posters," respectively, as the second and third most important components of her family's campaign to find their six-year-old. ("Police" came first.) She estimated that "[a]s many as half-a-million posters" featuring her son's face and descriptive information may have been distributed between May 1979 and October 1981. "The saturation of our neighborhood," Patz indicated in 1981, "was an effective way of alerting people to an immediate and local problem. We still rely on posters for first contacts with other police departments, and for relaying information to people with leads. We have mailed posters to individuals all over the country, thus reaching areas even the police and media failed to reach." The project had a global scope, too, as "[f]riends and concerned persons distributed posters in parts of Europe and the Middle East," especially Israel. Although Etan's relatives had failed in their efforts to place "'Missing Child' posters [in] every public and private school in the country," they had successfully included "Etan's photograph in several educational journals which reach many teachers and school superintendents"—all with the assistance of US congressman Peter Peyser (D–New York).[26]

This kind of large-scale distribution of a previously unknown missing child's image was unprecedented. Public interest in the Lindbergh baby kidnapping can be largely attributed to aviator Charles Lindbergh's popularity, and until the late 1970s and early 1980s public attention usually concentrated on "missing children only after they are found dead," according to one ABC reporter. By contrast, Julie Patz saw "publicity" as the "second most important element" in the search for her son, publicity that largely hinged on the use of Etan's photos. "The communications media has been invaluable in the rapid and extensive broadcasting of information pertinent to our missing child," she claimed. "The media operates at it's [sic] best on such sympathetic stories as ours, where it can provide a real service." Julie Patz recognized the sentimental power of her son's photographs, as well as the news media's ability to harness that power in the name of public service.[27]

By the early 1980s, Etan's photographs sat at the forefront of a wider national conversation about child abduction and endangerment. In news segments on "the growing problem of missing children," as one ABC *World News Tonight* story termed it, the young Patz stood in for the putative

STILL MISSING

POLICE DEPARTMENT CITY OF NEW YORK

LOST CHILD ETAN PATZ

Missing Since Friday May 25th, 1979. Last seen 8 a.m., at Prince St. & West B'way.

DESCRIPTION:
Date of Birth: October 9, 1972   Male, White, 6 yrs.
Height: 40 Inches   Weight: 50 lbs.
Blond Hair, Blue Eyes, Wearing Black Pilot Type Cap, Blue Corduroy Jacket, Blue Pants, Blue Sneakers with Fluorescent Stripes; Carrying Blue Cloth Bag with Elephants Imprinted.

Persons Having Any Information Are Requested To Call

(212) 374-6913

Figure 1.4 Two of the "MISSING" notices circulated throughout New York City and disseminated nationally via television news broadcasts. Photograph by Stanley Patz. Courtesy of Stanley Patz.

POLICE DEPARTMENT
CITY OF NEW YORK

LOST CHILD

ETAN PATZ

113 PRINCE STREET

Missing Since Friday May 25th, 1979. Last seen 8 a.m., at Prince St. & West B'way.

DESCRIPTION:
Date of Birth: October 9, 1972   Male, White, 6 yrs.
Height: 40 Inches   Weight: 50 lbs.
Blond Hair, Blue Eyes, Wearing Black Pilot Type Cap,
Blue Corduroy Jacket, Blue Pants, Blue Sneakers with
Fluorescent Stripes; Carrying Blue Cloth Bag with
Elephants Imprinted.

**Persons Having Any Information
Are Requested To Call**

(212) 374-6913

Figure 1.4 (Continued)

thousands snatched by strangers each year. Airing in 1982, the *World News Tonight* piece opened with a photograph of Etan, smiling at the camera with an angular grin. "Three years ago tomorrow," reporter Al Dale narrated, "six-year-old Etan Patz disappeared while on his way to school in Manhattan. Despite a door-to-door canvas by police, posters sent nationwide, and the offer of a reward, the parents have received no hint of his fate." The camera focused on one of the famed "LOST CHILD" signs, which featured two photographs of Etan with the words "STILL MISSING" and "$25,000 REWARD" stamped alongside them in red ink. In the *World News Tonight* story, the six-year-old played the role of "everychild." "It is a national problem," Julie Patz told those watching. "It can happen to anyone, anywhere, anytime." In closing, the ABC report displayed a "wall of missing children" in an unknown location, most likely the office of a private child safety advocacy group. Onscreen a woman added new photographs of young people to the wall, exhibiting the supposed scope of the child abduction threat and the seeming regularity with which children went missing. Among these images were two of Etan: one of his iconic "MISSING" leaflets and another poster showing the headshots of at least fifteen youths, one of whom was Etan.[28] These signs served as templates for the flyers, milk cartons, billboards, television spots, and other materials that abounded during the 1980s missing child scare and its afterlives. By trafficking in the image of endangered childhood, they supplied visual testimony of "stranger danger" as a pervasive and horrifying threat, fueling fears of child abduction and exploitation and generating the affective capital necessary to crack down on these putative threats.

News media outlets have ascribed great importance to Patz's photographs since the late seventies, oftentimes identifying his image as the one that launched the "missing children movement." As the national child safety campaign gained steam, journalists cast Patz as the literal poster boy for this broader effort. Beginning with a shot of one of Etan's posters, a CBS *Evening News* broadcast airing in December 1982 reminded the national audience of "Etan Patz, a New York City youngster missing without a trace since 1979. Because of national publicity, he has become a symbol of all the children—perhaps fifty thousand—who are kidnapped by strangers each year." The report explicitly hitched the exaggerated statistics of the child safety panic to Etan's image. In 1985, another CBS *Evening News* segment affirmed that Etan Patz's "photograph has come to symbolize *all* missing children." In the twenty-first century, journalists like Dan Harris and David Muir have identified Etan "as a poster boy" and opined, "His was the case— and the face—that made missing children a burning national issue" and "ignited a movement."[29]

It is not surprising that Etan's photos captivated the public and have accrued such explanatory value since the late 1970s. Stanley Patz amassed a stunning collection of images depicting his son. This archive supplied news outlets, police investigators, and the general public with high quality, beautifully composed, well-lit photographs that were ready for primetime. Most of these pictures display Etan smiling radiantly or inquisitively staring into the camera as he clutched a bouncy ball or posed in his football pajamas. Such photographs embody the cultural tension between desiring and protecting children. Those who celebrate these kinds of images actually cherish and "seek to safeguard at all cost" the childhood innocence that they showcase. In their portrayal of a "young . . . beautiful . . . white . . . blue eyed, blond haired boy," in producer Lisa Cohen's formulation, images of Etan Patz presented a seemingly perfect American child, one who checked all the boxes. "[T]here were a number of things that made this a story that people could not walk away from," Cohen explained in a 2012 appearance on PBS, including the fact "that [Etan] was so young . . . [and] that he was beautiful."[30]

Stanley Patz acknowledged as much in a 1991 *Vanity Fair* piece. "One of the things you should explore in your article," he advised the interviewer, "is the unusual popularity of our case. It happened to middle-class people with a father who was a photographer and who just happened to have an unusual cache of interesting kiddie pictures." He posited, "If I hadn't been a photographer with those pictures—if we had been a poor, black family with blurry Polaroids—this case would have come and gone with the rest of them." Stanley Patz's shrewd assessment of public and press interest in the case evinced a kind of racial liberalism and class consciousness that belie reductive characterizations of child protection politics as purely reactionary or silent-majoritarian. For Patz, a self-described "knee-jerk liberal," the enduring, large-scale appeal of his son's case had as much to do with race and class as with the quality of Etan's photographs, but together these factors worked to propel his young child into the national spotlight. In offering up a narrow vision of endangered late twentieth-century childhood—and especially boyhood—these pictures spurred efforts to protect the vulnerable by punishing the perverted.[31]

"RUMORS ABOUT ETAN PATZ"

The impressive quality of Etan's photographs, and the visual allure of the boy shown within them, prompted speculation about a possible sexual motive for the kidnapping. The theory that one or more "pederasts" had abducted, molested, and possibly murdered young Etan generated some interest following the boy's disappearance but did not receive significant attention until late 1982, when police executed a search on a Wareham, Massachusetts, cottage reportedly affiliated with NAMBLA. During this raid on the waterside Cape Cod–style house, authorities found a photograph of a boy who resembled Etan Patz. As a result, NAMBLA—a fringe group formed four years earlier to advocate for the elimination of age of consent laws—came under intense investigative and public scrutiny. The organization's alleged role in snatching and exploiting Etan Patz also strained alliances within New York City's LGBTQ movement. Gay, lesbian, and feminist activists had clashed over the question of "man/boy love" since before NAMBLA's founding. But the picture unearthed in the Wareham raid raised the group's profile and jeopardized its already tenuous position in various coalitions for women's and LGBTQ rights. The accusations levied against NAMBLA, though false, encouraged many feminist and LGBTQ advocates to distance themselves from the man/boy love organization.[32]

A homophobic climate kindled these sorts of allegations in the Patz case and the larger child safety panic. Specifically, the myth that gay men are predisposed to lust after and prey upon young boys proved central to antigay mobilization efforts in this period. Employing to great effect "the purported threat to children posed by gay visibility"—in particular, "the stereotype of gays as recruiters of children"—Anita Bryant's 1977 "Save Our Children" campaign pushed voters to repeal a local gay rights ordinance in Miami–Dade County, Florida. The following year, California voters narrowly rejected a referendum that would have barred gays and lesbians from teaching in the state's schools. In this same moment, many feminist and LGBTQ activists sought to "mainstream" their movements by shedding their more radical contingencies. A politics of respectability and personal empowerment, indicative of "postfeminist" and "post–gay rights" sensibilities, concealed (and, in some ways, widened) the most glaring inequalities among women and LGBTQ Americans.[33]

Indeed, the LGBTQ and women's movements have helped expand the carceral net in ways that disproportionately ensnare queer Americans and people of color. Social conservatives and feminists came into increasing alignment in the seventies on matters of sexual abuse and exploitation. From both the right and the left, mobilization efforts against adult and child sexual assault, and against pornography depicting adults and minors alike, made the criminal justice system more responsive to sex offenses. In the eighties, white, middle-class gay rights advocates retreated from the criminal justice concerns on which they had mobilized since World War II—and on which they had forged alliances with many black and Latinx people. The LGBTQ movement had long militated against police harassment of sexual and racial minorities, as "vice" squads in urban areas often targeted establishments frequented by LGBTQ and nonwhite individuals alike. Over time, activists proved remarkably successful in safeguarding gay bars, bookstores, and other spaces from police incursion.[34]

In the wake of these accomplishments, the relationship between the gay rights movement and the carceral state shifted. Mainstream activists increasingly embraced carceral logics as they settled and fortified "gayborhoods" and cast off their more sexually "perverted" compatriots, who were subject to heightened policing and punishment within the "war on sex offenders." The so-called New Democrats of the 1980s and 1990s folded normative gay, lesbian, and feminist activists into their coalition while promoting proposals for incremental (oftentimes symbolic) change in the realms of women's and LGBTQ rights. While it would be difficult to overstate the successes of the women's and gay rights movements with respect to social acceptance and the attainment of marriage equality, these gains have come hand-in-glove with the rise of mass incarceration and a child safety regime that disproportionately surveils and disciplines queer people and nonwhite Americans.[35]

From the outset, investigators in the Patz case viewed sexual exploitation as a plausible motive for the boy's kidnapping, though this line of inquiry received minimal attention in initial press accounts. Until the Wareham raid, newspaper and television reports on Etan's disappearance seldom mentioned sex or sexuality. Instead, they tended to concentrate on the frustrating search for clues and the trauma inflicted upon the Patz family and their SoHo community. The *New York Times*, in 1980, did note that the arrest of "a child pornographer in Etan's neighborhood" had caught the attention of investigators working on the Patz case. Detectives rifled through the suspect's cache of illicit photographs and films under the suspicion that they might find evidence of Etan ("our little boy," as detectives referred to him), but they did not. Such investigative action turned on the imagery of endangered childhood and the notion that one or more pederasts may have snatched Etan for sexual purposes. However, this assumption remained mostly unwritten and unspoken in news coverage in the years immediately following the disappearance.[36]

Only with the December 1982 Wareham raid did NAMBLA and pedophilia take center stage in the Patz case. Purchased by Rupert Murdoch's News Corporation on the same day as the raid, the *Boston Herald American* seized upon news of the photograph which, according to the FBI, portrayed a child who bore "a striking resemblance" to Patz. On the front page of its December 20 issue, the *Herald American* ran a picture of Etan and asked, "DID SEX CLUB TRAP THIS BOY?" The jumpline read, "Photos seized in Wareham raid are look-alikes of vanished New York 6-year-old." The tabloid's coverage of the bust bordered on the sensational and homophobic. Its headlines dubbed NAMBLA a "sex ring" that "recruited with gifts"; a "gay group [with] chapters world-wide"; and an organization whose "literature defends homosexuality." Other tabloids ran similar stories. The December 20 cover of the *New York Post* mirrored that of the *Herald American*. Beside a picture of a barechested Etan beaming and staring at the camera, the *Post* printed the headline: "SEX CLUB CLUE IN HUNT FOR SOHO BOY." A subheading in smaller print read, "Porn pix found—are they Etan Patz?" The juxtaposition of Etan's innocuous image with the salacious text no doubt troubled readers and rendered the boy's alleged kidnapping and abuse simultaneously unspeakable and explicable. Readers might reckon that Etan's beauty subjected him to sexual predation, especially considering that the *Post* headline was just one example of the homophobic muckraking seen after the Wareham bust.[37]

The raid on the cottage purportedly associated with NAMBLA laid bare the fault lines in early 1980s LGBTQ and feminist politics. Emulating the trajectories of other American social movements, the gay and lesbian rights movement sought to enter the mainstream in the late twentieth century, an era characterized by the growing politicization of sexual identity. The practice of "coming out" to friends and family served to demystify homosexuality in the twentieth century's final decades. This rite of passage brought queer individuals out of "the closet," while the family and its auxiliaries—such as Parents, Families, and Friends of Lesbians and Gays (PFLAG)—became sites upon which queer youth negotiated and came to terms with their sexualities. In the shadow of the HIV/AIDS epidemic, as more and more gays and lesbians began to raise children in two-parent, same-sex households, activists increasingly eschewed matters of sexual freedom and behavior, fighting instead for inclusion within the pronatal, dual-parent familial ideal. This approach, perhaps most evident in the fight for marriage equality, marked a departure from a more radical queer organizing tradition that embraced antinormative and nonnormative forms of kinship while seeking "the redistribution of economic resources and the protection of sexual freedoms."[38]

NAMBLA's very existence undermined the prospect of "mainstreaming" gay and lesbian people. The "NAMBLA question" dated back to the late 1970s, when longtime gay activist and NAMBLA cofounder David Thorstad began to publicly endorse the abolition of "all age of consent laws." His "Statement to the Gay Liberation Movement on the Issue of Man/Boy Love" made the rounds at the Conference on Man/Boy Love and the Age of Consent in December 1978 and wound up in Boston's influential *Gay Community News* in early 1979. Its publication spurred considerable debate in the paper and set the stage for several disputes regarding NAMBLA's place in the LGBTQ movement. In spring 1980, for instance, a gay and lesbian rights rally in Albany, New York, splintered over NAMBLA and the age of consent. The New York State chapter of the National Organization for Women boycotted the event after Thorstad landed a slot as a keynote speaker. Such disputes revolved around notions of patriarchy and the stereotype of gay male pedophilia, since feminists and many mainline gay and lesbian activists saw in NAMBLA the male chauvinism, sexual predation, and power asymmetries they abhorred.[39]

The Wareham bust intensified the debate unfolding within the gay and lesbian rights movement over "man/boy love." In the main, normative LGBTQ activists rejected NAMBLA and its calls to repeal age of consent laws in the name of "sexual freedom for all." These mainline activists also recognized the potentially catastrophic political costs of including NAMBLA in the gay rights coalition. As A. Damien Martin noted in the pages of the *New York City News* in March 1983, NAMBLA "irritates and disturbs most of us" in the LGBTQ struggle. Martin, a communication professor at New York University, claimed that NAMBLA "publicly advocates the most dangerously effective charge brought by the Far Right, that gay people and the Gay Liberation Movement promote sexual relations between adults and children." Another activist named Mitchell Halberstadt sent much the same message less than a month after the Wareham scandal broke. "Despite attempts by much of the gay community to separate itself from the 'man-boy love movement,'" Halberstadt insisted, "irresponsible elements in the straight media have again been tarring gay people as child molesters, using contrived scandals involving the North American Man-Boy Love Association . . . as launching pads." He called NAMBLA's "brash stance" on age of consent laws "suicidal" for the gay rights movement, since it "play[ed] into the hands of our enemies (for instance, giving new life to fear of gay teachers)." NAMBLA was perfecting "a recipe for martyrdom," Halberstadt charged, and "demand[ing] that the whole gay and lesbian movement follow it on a course to oblivion."[40]

Yet Halberstadt and others in the "establishment" wing of the gay and lesbian movement also came to NAMBLA's defense, albeit timidly and perhaps cynically, following the Wareham raid. According to Halberstadt, gay rights activists "should be wary of ostracizing unpopular minorities, especially when they are besieged," since "*we* have been the victims of such fear and 'expediency.'" Grotesque caricatures of a (homo)sexual underworld, which surfaced frequently in the child safety scare, fostered "gross, unreal stereotypes of 'chickenhawks' preying on vulnerable youths, of super-virile beasts pummelling [*sic*] sobbing infants." Halberstadt argued, then, that NAMBLA's posturing certainly warranted scrutiny and scorn, but that critics ought to focus on the organization's actual platform instead of weaponizing homophobic stereotypes. Harold

Pickett, a gay activist who had previously expressed hostility toward
NAMBLA, protested the group's treatment at the hands of law enforcement and the news media, especially following the Wareham raid. "[W]hy
the sudden media blitz of sensationalism?" asked Pickett. "Is it part of
an ongoing police–FBI campaign against the [North American] Man/
Boy Love Association? Or is it a broader campaign against the entire gay
community, continuing to stereotype us as dangerous child molesters?"
David Rothenberg, another activist closely aligned with the more moderate elements of the New York City LGBTQ movement, concurred with
Pickett. "There is little question," Rothenberg declared, "that the press
and FBI's treatment of NAMBLA—and the entire gay community—has
been atrocious. Trial-by-innuendo, concerning the missing Soho [sic]
youth, Etan Patz, served as the catalyst for the false charges directed at
NAMBLA." Such "rumors about Etan Patz," Rothenberg continued, "were
headlines. Unsubstantiated stories and political charges with gay tones
get printed. Reality does not."[41]

But while Rothenberg situated the "false charges" against NAMBLA
within a larger antigay project undertaken by some "local newsrags," he
also placed NAMBLA firmly outside the LGBTQ movement. "[S]exual attraction to youth is not a gay issue," Rothenberg wrote, suggesting that
debates over the age of consent or more "deviant" sexual behaviors were
largely immaterial to the struggle for gay and lesbian rights. "The gay movement is about the right of sexual relations between consenting adults,"
he contended. "There is some room for discussion on the rights of post-
pubescent sexuality but the insistence that it be inter-generational is self-
serving and controlling." By insisting that the "political charges" against
NAMBLA had tarnished "the entire gay community," Halberstadt, Pickett,
Rothenberg, and other moderate gay rights activists could dispute the gay
predator myth while distancing NAMBLA from the mainstream gay and
lesbian movement. This sort of maneuver enabled the criminalization of
more radical and subversive sexual behaviors and identities in the late
twentieth-century United States.[42]

Beyond the formal boundaries of the gay rights movement, liberals and
conservatives alike characterized NAMBLA and the photograph discovered
in Wareham as lamentable but logical consequences of sexual liberation.
"Thousands of young boys," read the "Conservative Forum" section of the
January 8, 1983, issue of *Human Events*, "some no more than eight or nine
years old, have been lured into sexual activity with adult males by a bizarre
'international man-boy sex club.'" More disconcerting for the "Conservative
Forum" authors, the Wareham photo "bears a 'remarkable resemblance'" to
Etan Patz," and NAMBLA members "have refused to cooperate with police

on the Patz investigation." The "Forum" also warned that NAMBLA and similar groups were more widespread than readers might realize.[43]

Elsewhere on the political spectrum, Pulitzer Prize-winning journalist Sydney H. Schanberg too blamed NAMBLA and a wider climate of sexual permissiveness for Etan's abduction. "In the name of what twisted idea of sexual freedom," he wrote in a *New York Times* editorial, "can anyone justify as 'benevolent' the criminal taking of a first-grade boy from his parents?" Here, Schanberg suggested that NAMBLA's alleged role in Patz's abduction pointed to a larger culture of sexual perversion ostensibly cultivated by the women's and gay rights movements. "And if Etan," Schanberg wrote, "who would now be 10 [years old], has been drawn underground, as is suspected, into a homosexual organization known as the North American Man/Boy Love Association (NAMBLA), he could have been moved clandestinely by now to any city or town in the country." Schanberg also derided those with possible knowledge of the case who refused to intervene on Etan's behalf: "And are there homosexual members of NAMBLA, an organization that says it does not condone kidnapping, who have seen Etan and are, criminally, remaining silent?" Sympathizing with the "decent homosexuals" burdened by "the link of NAMBLA with Etan Patz," Schanberg pressured "responsible homosexual organizations" to denounce "this aberrant group."[44]

In a CBS *Evening News* segment airing several weeks after the Wareham bust, the liberal journalist Bill Moyers decried "a culture which indulges in the erotic use of children for commercial purposes." Anchor Dan Rather introduced Moyers's televised editorial. "Police released this photograph today," Rather remarked, directing viewers to the graphic hanging over his left shoulder. "It may be that of Etan Patz, a ten-year-old New York City boy who has been missing since 1979. The photograph was seized in a raid on a group promoting sexual relations between men and boys, and that's the subject of Bill Moyers's commentary tonight." Taking the baton, Moyers fumed:

> If that little boy in the photograph is not the missing child from New York, who is he? Has he too been kidnapped? How did he arrive at this exploitation? And if it could happen to him, could it not happen to your child? Earlier this year the Supreme Court [in *New York v. Ferber*] upheld a law barring the use of children in sexually explicit films. But the practice goes on. The government recently indicted twelve persons in nine states for alleged child pornography. The practice goes on because there is a market for the abuse of children. It's aided by an underground network of adults, some with links to organized crime. They even have their public apologists. An organization surfaced in one city espousing the

rights of children. Their rights included a sexual relationship with an adult. The argument was that sexuality begins these days at an earlier age. But . . . sexuality should be defined as sharing between equals—two people who can consent in mutual give-and-take. There is no way that a forty-year-old man can have a mutual give-and-take with a six-year-old child. Once I even heard child pornography referred to as a "victimless crime." That's nonsense, too. There are, by one count, over half a million children in this country used in sex-for-sale activities. . . . There is indeed a market for the abuse of children—more than one market. And I wonder if the values of a society are not alone to be measured by the price it pays for what it buys, but by its tolerance for what sells.[45]

Like NAMBLA's feminist critics, Moyers avoided the homophobic language deployed by some of the group's other opponents. He also articulated some of the main tenets of mid- to late twentieth-century feminism, concentrating on sexual consent and the eradication of sexual objectification. Yet Moyers imbued the image reportedly depicting Patz with tremendous symbolic value, surmising that the picture typified a troubling cultural tendency to sexualize youth. Once again Etan served as "everychild," the photogenic white boy whose presumed abduction and molestation raised the question, "could it not happen to your child?" Though Moyers surely did not intend to inflame antigay sentiment with these remarks, he nonetheless advanced the image of endangered white childhood and the problematic assumptions embedded within it.[46]

The embattled NAMBLA responded to what its leaders called unfair "ATTACKS BY [the] D.A., FBI & PRESS." In Boston's *Gay Community News*, one gay rights activist wrote, "Since December 3rd," the day of the Wareham raid, "NAMBLA and the gay community have been the object of the most vicious media attack since the communist witchhunt days of the 1950's [sic]." NAMBLA cofounder David Thorstad discussed the "cruel and cynical hoax . . . perpetrated upon the public by the FBI, various police forces, and the media." According to Thorstad, "police know that any allegation of a connection between Etan Patz's disappearance and NAMBLA is a lie, and yet they are deliberately feeding this false information to the media." Thorstad therefore cast law enforcement and the press as co-conspirators in a disinformation campaign waged to propagate an antigay moral panic, leverage the Patzes' grief, and ramp up the surveillance of NAMBLA and the gay community. "The media have functioned as an adjunct of the police," he charged, "rather than as an independent news-gathering and investigative institution." To this end, Thorstad accused the police and FBI "of deliberately and cynically covering up this information in order to grab headlines and vilify NAMBLA."[47]

According to Thorstad, this purported smear campaign pointed to large-scale anxieties over sociocultural change and economic restructuring, anxieties that often centered on young bodies. Unemployment and antigay prejudice, he indicated, had forced many young Americans out of their homes to seek jobs and alternative kinship networks. "Hundreds of thousands of young people, many of them gay, are fleeing the stifling environments and physical abuse of their homes," Thorstad declared. "Men who love boys are being made into scapegoats for social problems for which they are not responsible." For the NAMBLA cofounder, the furor over Etan Patz—and, more broadly, over the vulnerability of white youth—erupted out of interwoven crises concerning the family and the economy. Journalists and law enforcement officials could easily blame his "unpopular" organization for these crises, especially when equipped with compelling images of young people purportedly preyed upon by perverts.[48]

Indeed, that the allegations against NAMBLA hinged upon a photograph reveals the centrality of the imagery of endangered childhood to the moral/sex panic over child kidnapping and exploitation in the late 1970s and 1980s. As Thorstad noted, authorities had claimed "that NAMBLA air-brushed the photo to add a cleft chin, allegedly to make the boy more 'appealing' to NAMBLA members."[49] Again, Etan's physical attractiveness rendered plausible the notion that NAMBLA, or perhaps gay men unaffiliated with the organization, had kidnapped the six-year-old for sexual purposes. Investigators apparently sought to reconcile the fact that Etan did not have a cleft chin with the reality that the boy in the Wareham photograph did. Rather than concede that the boy in the picture was not Etan, law enforcement officials appeared to stretch the available visual evidence solely to incriminate NAMBLA in Patz's abduction.

"LITTLE BOYS WITH MEN"

The Wareham raid and responses to it reflected the larger antigay context. Polling data bear this out. In July 1978, Gallup asked Americans if they would vote for "a generally well-qualified man for President" if their political party nominated him and "if he happened to be a homosexual." Sixty-six percent of respondents said no, while only 26 percent responded in the affirmative. A CBS News exit poll, taken as voters left their polling stations during the November 1978 elections, found that two-thirds of respondents opposed "[p]ermitting homosexual school teachers to work in [their] public schools." In an October 1979 survey sponsored by Virginia Slims cigarettes, 74 percent of men and 70 percent of women declared they would "not accept" a daughter's hypothetical "homosexual relationship" and would "have [a] strained relationship" with their child as a result. Seventy-two percent of respondents in a 1980 Connecticut Mutual Life Insurance poll said they considered homosexuality "morally wrong." Although some polling data from the late seventies and early eighties hinted at a libertarian ambivalence toward gay rights, more evidence supports the idea of extensive homophobia during this period.[50]

Such homophobia permeated pop culture. Released theatrically in February 1980, in the midst of the John Wayne Gacy Jr. trial, the feature film *Cruising* drew protests from the LGBTQ community. The movie follows a detective, played by Al Pacino, who goes undercover to investigate the serial murders of gay men in New York City's bondage, dominance, and sadomasochism (BDSM) scene. One organizer, who had helped assemble an "ad hoc coalition" of eighteen gay, feminist, and radical groups in a demonstration against the film at Chicago's Carnegie Theater, objected to *Cruising*'s facile fusion of homosexuality and violence. For him, the motion picture and the Gacy trial, taken together, distorted the queer experience. "The press seems to be implying that part of Gacy's guilt is that he may or may not be homosexual, that the crimes are homosexual," he stated. In his interpretation, *Cruising* and the Gacy trial dehumanized gay men and normalized violence committed both by and against them. Likewise, the thriller *Windows*, also released in early 1980, raised the ire of activists who were offended by the film's depiction of lesbian desire.[51]

In this conjuncture, a popular book and film based on the Patz disappearance revealed the affinities between antigay and child safety politics. A neighbor of the Patzes for at least a decade, Beth Gutcheon based her 1981 novel *Still Missing*, as well as the screenplay for its 1983 film adaptation *Without a Trace*, on Etan's case. *Still Missing* and *Without a Trace* focus on the kidnapping of six-year-old Alex Selky, who vanishes on his way to the school bus stop. Both emphasize the salience of "pictures of innocence" and enunciate the concerns about homosexual predation that lived within such images. In *Still Missing*, Jocelyn, a friend of Alex's mother Susan, undergoes hypnosis to determine if she remembers anything about the Selky disappearance. She recalls seeing, on the day Alex vanished, "these two joggers, matching faggots in their color-coordinated sweatsuits, one blue and one green. They had white towel sweatbands on, and matching mustaches," she tells a friend. "They're the same height and same weight and same build and same haircut—they're so cute. Being in bed together must be like masturbating. So now the police are looking for them, and I might have to go down and look at mug shots to see if they're known for anything."[52] The ease with which Jocelyn ties the "matching faggots" to the apparent abduction illustrates the causative weight assigned to the gay predator myth in the Patz tragedy and its fictional analogue.

The novel also maps the supposed extent of child sex networks and pornography rings in the United States. Alex's disappearance alerts his mother Susan to the presumed perils confronting American boys in the late twentieth century. She learns of "a loosely organized ring of men from Baltimore to Portsmouth, New Hampshire, who produced por-nographic photographs and films of little boys. Little boys in seduc-tive poses, little boys in apparent terror bound and gagged, about to be anally raped, groggy little boys with drugged smiles looking naked and willing, little boys dressed as little girls. Little boys doing things with other little boys, and especially little boys with men." Others, Susan discovers, did not even bother with pornography. They simply "drugged and tortured, and sometimes killed" their victims—as Houston's candy man did, "with his dozens of pubescent male bodies buried along the beach." Likewise, Chicago's John Wayne Gacy, Susan notes, had "mur-dered at least thirty-three young men and boys and buried them around his house and yard, in pits and trenches, covered over with quicklime to speed deterioration."[53]

While none of the major cases of individual missing boys in the late 1970s and early 1980s were confirmed to be sexually motivated, Gutcheon's novel, newspaper articles, congressional hearings, and child safety activists often imagined, almost obsessively and in excruciating detail, the sexual abuse of young people. As John Walsh counseled a friend over breakfast, "Just envision it for a minute, a 200-pound man raping your [eighteen-month-old] daughter. . . . I mean it. Envision it. It could happen."[54] Though sexual violence against children and adolescents is very rarely perpetrated by strangers, descriptions of such exploitation in the stranger danger panic made it all the more visible, all the more threatening. Such descriptions worked to validate sociocultural fears regarding homosexuality, feminism, and sexual liberation—fears that undergirded the fictional Selky case and its real world counterparts.

Accordingly, Gutcheon tries to fool readers of *Still Missing* by directly implicating in Alex's abduction Philippe Lucienne, the forty-two-year-old gay "houseboy" who helps out around the Selky residence. On Labor Day, about four months after Alex's disappearance, Lucienne goes to meet up with a friend but instead encounters a boy "cruising" for gay sex. Though the youngster claims he is sixteen years old, Lucienne assesses his "slender small body and the smooth face without a shadow of beard, and sincerely doubt[s]" it. Nevertheless, the two decide to go on a stroll together, and the boy soon leads Lucienne into a dark alley where "a big Dodge van" awaits.

They crawl into the back of the Dodge and begin to engage in foreplay. The boy asks to be bound with rope, and Lucienne obliges.[55]

Suddenly the back door of the van swings open, and police officers conducting a sting operation descend upon the pair. The undercover vice squad arrests the boy and Lucienne, all while denigrating them with antigay slurs and physical violence. Upon frisking Philippe, the police officers discover a bloody pair of white underwear in his jacket, which he had not worn since the previous spring. The nametape on the waistband, also "soaked with stiff brown dried blood," reads "Alex Selky." The two officers who find the undergarment, no doubt acutely aware of the Selky disappearance, glare at Philippe "with icy murder in their eyes." One officer shouts, "You filthy shit!" before kicking Philippe in the groin. After Lucienne's arrest, investigators declare the Selky case all but resolved, and the news media crucifies the "houseboy." "POLICE BREAK SELKY CASE," one headline reads, recalling the real-life cover pages of the *New York Post* and *Boston Herald American* following the Wareham raid. Lucienne's 1959 conviction for "sodomy, homosexual rape, and impairing the morals of a minor" in Salt Lake City comes to light. One news story calls Lucienne "a self-confessed homosexual and a convicted child molester who has worked as a houseboy in the Selky home for over two years." These developments unleash "a wave of homophobia" in the city, with seventeen men "savagely beaten on successive dark nights by a gang of teenagers." Gay activists in the book, not unlike those who came to NAMBLA's defense in late 1982 and early 1983, carry signs reading: "Philippe Lucienne is a political prisoner" and "No witch hunts."[56]

For all this antigay violence, yellow journalism, and police posturing, readers learn that the presumed break in the case is nothing more than a misunderstanding. Lab tests determine the blood on the underwear to be Lucienne's, not Alex's. The conviction in Utah resulted from Lucienne's affair with a fifteen-year-old high school freshman. Lucienne maintains that he did not know the boy's age, and when the freshman's father—a prominent leader in the Mormon church—caught wind of the relationship, he convinced his son to "claim rape." Even though Lucienne did not kidnap, sexually assault, or murder Selky, his status as a "convicted child molester," his "extensive collection of photographs of naked boys and men," and his dalliance with the underage boy in the "big Dodge van" all underscore his presumed perversion—and maybe that of all gay men. One gay rights activist in *Still Missing*, while sympathetic to Lucienne's plight, situates the Selky suspect outside of the mainstream LGBTQ movement, just as some real-life queer activists had publicly renounced NAMBLA during the Patz saga. "All we need," he groans, "is a big splashy nationwide murder case about a swell guy who . . . screws teenage boys but who may be innocent of this particular crime, and gay rights go back to the Dark Ages." Although not guilty in the Selky case, a gay man with a questionable past seemed a logical suspect. When, following Lucienne's arrest, Susan Selky stops by neighborhood stores to post new "MISSING" flyers of her son, one shop-keeper declares, "I heard they solved that[;] the kid was murdered by some gay guy."[57]

Similar anxieties about homosexuality structure *Without a Trace.* Menetti receives a phone call from Officer Fred Coffin, who informs him of Philippe Lucienne's arrest for picking up a fourteen-year-old prostitute. Coffin notifies Menetti that a search warrant executed on Lucienne's apart-ment turned up whips, handcuffs, and other BDSM items. Menetti seems quite alarmed by Lucienne's collection, calling it "the kinkiest shit [he's] ever seen." Just as in *Still Missing*, Susan visits Lucienne in jail, at his re-quest. The "houseboy" again blames the punitive culture of Mormon Utah for his rape conviction there, and he pleads for sympathy, calling himself "a faggot with a record." Convinced, Susan meets with Menetti and insists that he and his investigative team "made a mistake." "Have you got motive, Al? What motive did he have for hurting Alex?" she petitions. "He *loved* him." Menetti fires back: "Yeah, that's what we were afraid of," vilifying Lucienne as a pedophile whose "love" can only be sexual, never platonic. Further, Menetti intimates that he and his fellow investigators suspected the "houseboy" to be a predator all along. In an effort to persuade Susan of Lucienne's guilt, the detective reads from Lucienne's psychiatric evalua-tion, which accuses him of having "no normal sexual contact with women." Unlike the novel, *Without a Trace* offers little absolution for its only openly gay character or for the marginalized community to which he belongs. In her heated exchange with Menetti, Susan reminds the investigator that most child molesters are classified as heterosexuals and that "a gay man was the least likely candidate" in Alex's kidnapping. But the detective dismisses Susan's objections. Moreover, viewers never hear from other voices in the LGBTQ movement, only from those in the news media intent on incrim-inating Lucienne as "an avowed homosexual" and from Lucienne himself, who presumably languishes behind bars even after Menetti triumphantly returns Alex to his mother.[58]

Still Missing and *Without a Trace* portray Alex Selky as "the imper-iled white child who was imagined to be [the] victim, not [the] benefi-ciary" of sexual liberation.[59] Emblematic of the antigay milieu in which they were produced, *Still Missing* and *Without a Trace* gave credence to the gay pedophile myth which would prove central to the late twentieth-century stranger danger scare. These texts took "pederasty" as a plausible explanation for the fictional kidnapping of Alex Selky and the real-world disappearances of Etan Patz and other boys. Additionally, the novel and its film adaptation both policed counternormative sexual behaviors, stigmatizing those who identified as queer and those engaging in BDSM activity. In so doing, Gutcheon and the producers of *Without a Trace* unfairly pitted sexual liberationists against those seeking a safe and contented childhood for young Americans.

AFTER ETAN

Etan's disappearance helped to build a nationwide moral/sex panic around the kidnapping and exploitation of minors by strangers. The Patzes' crusade merged with those undertaken by other bereaved parents and "moral entrepreneurs" to form a consolidated movement for child protection. By 1982, Etan Patz had become "a symbol of all the children," one CBS *Evening News* story proclaimed, "who are kidnapped by strangers each year." Ronald Reagan recognized Etan as the formal poster boy of the missing child campaign in 1983, when he declared May 25, the day of Patz's disappearance, to be National Missing Children Day. For their part, Stanley and Julie Patz "received an unusual amount of attention," the *Chicago Tribune* observed in June 1981, "because they are so articulate and have chosen to help lead a crusade" by speaking out and "organiz[ing] other parents of missing children." One HBO program broadcast in 1983 even dubbed the Patzes "unfortunate celebrities in the world of missing kids."[60]

Joining forces with John and Revé Walsh, parents of six-year-old Adam, and Camille Bell—mother of Yusuf Bell, abducted and murdered in fall 1979—Stanley and Julie Patz petitioned for federal assistance in protecting American children. They each testified before Congress in October 1981, in the nation's first hearings on "missing children." Pictures of Etan taken by his father bolstered these mobilization efforts. The visual appeal and emotional resonance of these photographs captured public attention and encouraged speculation about young Etan's fate. As images of missing children proliferated on milk cartons, billboards, grocery bags, and energy bills, so too did the stranger danger myth and the sexual anxieties at its heart. In ways that probably would not have been recognizable ten years earlier, such pictures—especially when presented together—announced a child safety crisis with a decidedly sexual tinge.

This sort of imagery called for vigilance, protection, and punishment. As the image of endangered childhood became ubiquitous in spaces of consumption, governance, community, and family, it supplied the visual, affective capital necessary to build the core components of the child safety regime. Emerging directly from the stranger danger panic, mechanisms like the Missing Children and Missing Children's Assistance Acts of 1982 and 1984, respectively; the National Center for Missing and Exploited Children; the iconic milk carton program; sex offender registries; and AMBER Alerts took as their raison d'être the endangered, white, photogenic child. Reflecting neoliberal and social conservative anxieties centered on the family, these instruments have mistakenly targeted "perverts" and "strangers"—not acquaintances and family members, who perpetrate the overwhelming majority of child kidnappings and sexual assaults. The image of endangered childhood, then, has helped to expand a carceral net that disproportionately ensnares people of color and LGBTQ Americans and locates the moral and sexual threats facing American children and families outside the walls of the idealized home.

CHAPTER 2

☙

"Save Them or Perish"

Race, Childhood, and the Atlanta Abductions and Murders

On May 25, 1981, over three thousand people convened at the Lincoln Memorial in Washington, DC, to protest the slayings of black youths in Atlanta.[1] Event organizers framed the demonstration as part of the March on Washington tradition. Promotional materials urged attendees "TO HELP PAVE THE WAY TO LIVING A REALITY THAT ONCE WAS A DREAM," evoking the famous speech delivered by Martin Luther King Jr. at the Lincoln Memorial. There, in 1963, King had shared his vision of an egalitarian society, one in which his and other children would be un-encumbered by racial prejudice or hatred. But speakers at the rally held eighteen years later seemed less hopeful and more fearful for their children. "Across this country our children are being killed in many ways," Camille Bell, a victim's mother, lamented in her remarks. "And our future is being wiped out."[2]

Between July 1979 and May 1981, twenty-nine young, poor, and working-class African Americans, almost all males, were abducted and murdered in the self-anointed "city too busy to hate."[3] For a year following the initial kidnappings and killings—despite the mobilization efforts of Camille Bell and the family members of other victims—local investigators refused to link the incidents. Bell, a civil rights veteran whose nine-year-old son Yusuf had been snatched and slain in the fall of 1979, helped establish

Figure 2.1 In the spirit of A. Philip Randolph and Martin Luther King Jr., activists converged on Washington, DC, in May 1981 to protest the killings of black Atlanta youth. In this image, Joseph E. Lowery delivers remarks to those gathered. Jesse Jackson appears behind him. Photograph by Elaine Tomlin. Save Our Children pilgrimage, Washington, DC, May 7, 1981, box 880, folder 47, photographs of events (1950s–2004), Southern Christian Leadership Conference records, MSS 1083, Stuart A. Rose Manuscript, Archives, and Rare Book Library (MARBL), Emory University, Atlanta. Courtesy of MARBL and the SCLC.

the Committee to Stop Children's Murders (STOP) in the spring of 1980. On some of its letterhead, STOP printed the phrase "Save Them or Perish," which not only spelled out the group's acronym but also expressed its members' trepidations about the African American future. Comprised of victims' relatives and other Atlanta residents, STOP generated media and public interest in the youth slayings, ultimately pressuring police to create an official investigative task force in July 1980. While the exact reasons for the delays in the investigative process remain unknown, critics argued that Atlanta's biracial power structure valued the preservation of the city's reputation as a peaceful, racially progressive, and "business-friendly" Southern site over the security of its embattled young residents.[4]

As national attention fixed upon the slayings beginning in mid- to late 1980, city officials scrambled to identify those who were preying on Atlanta's black youth. In May 1981, investigators apprehended a twenty-three-year-old African American man named Wayne Bertram Williams in

Table 2.1 "THE LIST": ATLANTA'S TWENTY-NINE VICTIMS LINKED
TOGETHER BY INVESTIGATORS

	Name	Age	Date disappeared	Date body discovered
1.	Edward Smith	14	July 21, 1979	July 28, 1979
2.	Alfred Evans	13	July 25, 1979	July 28, 1979
3.	Milton Harvey	14	September 4, 1979	November 16, 1979
4.	Yusef Bell	9	October 21, 1979	November 8, 1979
5.	Angel Lanier	12	March 4, 1980	March 10, 1980
6.	Jeffery Mathis	10	March 11, 1980	February 16, 1981
7.	Eric Middlebrooks	14	May 18, 1980	May 19, 1980
8.	Christopher Richardson	12	June 9, 1980	January 9, 1981
9.	Latonya Wilson	7	June 22, 1980	October 18, 1980
10.	Aaron Wyche	10	June 23, 1980	June 24, 1980
11.	Anthony Carter	9	July 6, 1980	July 7, 1980
12.	Earl Terrell	11	July 30, 1980	January 9, 1981
13.	Clifford Jones	13	August 20, 1980	August 21, 1980
14.	Darron Glass	10	September 14, 1980	Never found
15.	Charles Stephens	12	October 9, 1980	October 10, 1980
16.	Aaron Jackson	9	November 1, 1980	November 2, 1980
17.	Patrick Rogers	16	November 10, 1980	December 7, 1980
18.	Lubie Geter	14	January 3, 1981	February 5, 1981
19.	Terry Pue	15	January 22, 1981	January 23, 1981
20.	Patrick Baltazar	11	February 6, 1981	February 13, 1981
21.	Curtis Walker	15	February 19, 1981	March 6, 1981
22.	Joseph Bell	15	March 2, 1981	April 19, 1981
23.	Timothy Hill	13	March 13, 1981	March 30, 1981
24.	Eddie Duncan	21	March 20, 1981	March 31, 1981
25.	Larry Rogers	20	March 30/April 1, 1981	April 9, 1981
26.	Michael McIntosh	23	April 1, 1981	April 20, 1981
27.	Jimmy Ray Payne	21	April 21/22, 1981	April 27, 1981
28.	William Barrett	17	May 11, 1981	May 12, 1981
29.	Nathaniel Cater	27	May 21, 1981	May 24, 1981

connection with two of the twenty-nine cases. The following May, Williams was convicted of the two killings and sentenced to two consecutive life terms in prison. After the trial, investigators announced that they had accrued enough circumstantial and physical evidence to link Williams to nearly all of the other abductions and killings. Weeks later, the task force convened to investigate the murders disbanded, and Atlanta public safety

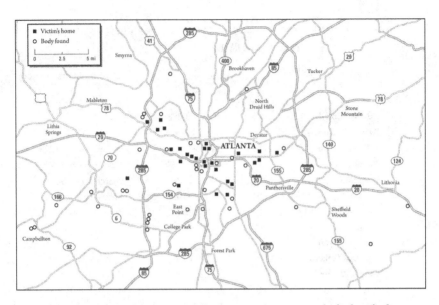

Figure 2.2 The locations of the victims' homes and the sites at which their bodies were recovered. Map by Erin Greb Cartography.

commissioner Lee P. Brown disclosed that he had accepted a position as the police chief of Houston, Texas.[5] The case was closed.

Nonetheless, doubts about Williams's guilt remained. Some speculated that he had been railroaded to alleviate anxieties and salvage the city's reputation. Many black Atlantans, especially residents of the low-income areas from which the young victims had hailed, remained convinced that a white supremacist individual or group bore responsibility for the abductions and killings. After Williams's conviction, Camille Bell declared "that there is no justice in America" and designated Williams "the 30th victim of the Atlanta slayings." Another victim's mother, Annie Rogers, asked, "Are they just going to forget about our black children?" One twenty-six-year-old Atlanta resident claimed that "most people think the verdict was predetermined. . . . Pressure was on the city to do something. Williams may have been the one, but the proper process wasn't used." Williams's father went so far as to deride Clarence Cooper, the African American judge who presided over his son's case, as an "Uncle Tom," a traitor to the race. "Fear doesn't die all that easily," ABC's Ted Koppel told a national television audience after the Williams verdict.[6]

Amidst a resurgent white power movement, a rise in antiblack hate crime activity, and a new president willing to indulge racist "states' rights" voters, African American observers also had ample reason to view the Atlanta kidnappings and killings as part of a white backlash to the black freedom struggle. Yet Atlanta's black establishment, which had recently consolidated control of some of the city's most powerful institutions, downplayed the racial and class dimensions of the slayings and largely dismissed the possibility of a racist motive. Instead, these leaders opted to emphasize citywide unity in a moment of distress. Maynard Jackson, the city's first African American mayor, insisted that the Atlanta tragedy "transcends race, age and class and afflicts us all." Lee P. Brown struck a similar chord when he noted, "I think the issue transcends race. I think the children are colorless." These sorts of rhetorical flourishes obscured the racial and class homogeneity of Atlanta's missing and slain, as well as the structural circumstances that enabled their victimization.[7]

Indeed, some of Atlanta's victims were out running errands to earn small amounts of cash at the time they were snatched. Like many young black Atlantans, these victims lived in material privation and some- times ran such errands to bring money home to their families. According to the 1980 census, 27 percent of Atlanta's population lived in poverty. Some commentators shrewdly identified the kidnappings and murders as products of poverty and want. "Blacks are coming to perceive the vulnera- bility of their children," a CBS reporter explained in March 1981, "as being a direct result of deplorable inner-city living conditions." For civil rights ac- tivist Charles King, a former member of the National Advisory Committee on Civil Disorders (colloquially known as the Kerner Commission), the young African Americans slain in Atlanta never stood a chance. "We handle our children in this society," he intoned in 1981, "without the proper kind of undergirding—economically or educational[ly]—that would give them a chance in life. This, my friend, is murder—before they die." King con- tinued, "We slay them before they have a chance. And if you really want to know who the real killers are—it's not just the one or two people that we're searching for. The real killers are the whites who condone it [and] black politicians who don't give a damn anymore about what happens to black people because they're fighting each other to gain office."[8]

Some media outlets tacitly acknowledged these structural inequalities yet employed racialized and classed designations such as "street hustlers" to describe the victims. On one hand, such terminology shed light on the poverty that stalked the residents of the predominantly black, working- class neighborhoods of eastern, southeastern, and downtown Atlanta. On the other, such portrayals occasionally bordered on caricature, deprived the abducted and slain of the innocence so readily assigned to white child- victims, and (intentionally or not) implicated young Atlantans in their own deaths. Some press accounts seemed to treat the young victims as adults and criminals. The *Atlanta Journal-Constitution*, for one, claimed that eleven-year-old victim Patrick Baltazar was "[a]ll grown up" and "already leading a man's life." The youngster had "learned to make his own way in the world of adults." For his part, a local public safety official even called Baltazar "a hustler from the word go."[9]

The "street hustler" appellation proved particularly insidious in discussions of a possible sexual motive behind the slayings. Rumors of homosexual perversion and predation loomed large in the Atlanta saga, much as they did over other cases of missing or slain youths. But while youngsters like Etan Patz or Johnny Gosch were allegedly forced into sexual contact with adult men, some commentators intimated that Atlanta's victims (as "street hustlers") had *chosen* to participate in such activities. Brown, Camille Bell, and others dismissed the prospect of a pedophilic motive, but the news media did not. Despite a lack of physical evidence, reportage highlighted circumstantial evidence (allegedly supplied by police) which suggested that some of the young victims "were known to travel with adult homosexuals" and had "exchange[d] sex with men for money."[10]

Just as certain media and investigative narratives appeared to blame Atlanta's victims for their own abductions and murders, family members of the missing and slain also drew suspicion and criticism. Depictions of the victims as "streetwise" children with "ghetto chutzpah," in the words of one *Washington Post* staff writer, served to paint their families and communities as negligent and dysfunctional. One FBI agent even accused some of the victims' parents of murdering their children, eliciting the ire of Camille Bell and other STOP members.[11]

At first blush, the Atlanta abductions and killings may seem to fit neatly alongside other late twentieth-century missing child cases. Like Stanley and Julie Patz, John and Revé Walsh, and other grieving parents, Camille Bell and other STOP members took aim at familiar targets: politicians, law enforcement authorities, and criminal deviants. Bell joined the Patzes and Walshes at the initial congressional hearings on missing children and penned a 1981 *Washington Post* editorial situating the Atlanta abductions and murders within a larger child safety crisis.[12]

But the Atlanta abductions and murders diverged sharply from other widely publicized incidents of missing children in the late 1970s and 1980s. These were the only stranger danger cases involving children of color that captured considerable national attention. Moreover, the organizing efforts undertaken in Atlanta grew out of the African American civil rights struggle, not out of a sense of aggrieved whiteness or an ascendant family values neoliberalism. The Atlanta youth murders also demonstrated the racial and class limitations of the image of endangered childhood. Indeed, it was almost exclusively white, middle-class children who populated such pictures—not black, brown, or poor youth. By the mid-1980s, the Atlanta saga had moved to the margins of the national child safety discourse, crowded out by emotionally resonant images and tales of individual missing and slain white children.

"THE CITY TOO BUSY TO CARE"

Since the late nineteenth century, New South boosters had characterized Atlanta as a progressive, cosmopolitan oasis in an otherwise retrograde region. Regardless of the reality on the ground, Atlanta's self-image as a racially moderate, business-friendly southern metropolis animated its remarkable transformation across the twentieth century. After the close of Georgia's white-only Democratic primary in 1946, a biracial leadership coalition gradually took hold in Atlanta and helped mediate the struggles of desegregation and white flight. As white families relocated to the city's burgeoning suburbs—some 160,000 whites left during the sixties and seventies—they opened the door for African Americans to assume leadership positions in the city core. By 1973, Atlanta was a majority-black city and had elected its first-ever black mayor. Yet the city's focus on optics and public relations oftentimes forestalled deeper, more meaningful change. As historian Matthew Lassiter points out, "The politics of racial moderation in postwar Atlanta always sought peace and progress, never justice or equality." During the classical civil rights era, for example, Atlanta's political and business elite refined a rhetoric of colorblindness while simultaneously reproducing "national patterns of metropolitan development and spatial segregation."[13]

As Atlanta wrestled with violent crime throughout the 1970s and into the 1980s, political and business leaders worked to counteract unfavorable portrayals of the city in the press. Even before the youth killings seized national headlines, Atlanta had been designated the nation's "murder capital." Its murder rate sat at a staggering 45.3 per 100,000 in 1979. Television and newspaper reports from across the country described downtown Atlanta as a "war zone." Some media outlets speculated that violent crime in the city might "hurt Atlanta's lucrative convention business"—which, together with its tourism industry, hauled in about $250 million annually in the late 1970s. Responding to pressure from a "business community . . . on edge," as one ABC *World News Tonight* report put it, elected officials like Mayor Maynard Jackson downplayed the severity of violent crime in Atlanta and sought to deflect media attention from the "crime wave" engulfing the city. Even as news outlets captured scenes of chaos and carnage in Georgia's capital city, Jackson reassured prospective visitors, insisting that "Atlanta is still as safe as or safer than other major urban centers in the US." To Susan Harrigan of the *Wall Street Journal*, though, the mayor's pleas seemed pathetic. "Like a desperate Scarlett O'Hara fashioning her gown from faded drapes," Harrigan wrote, "Atlanta still tries to sell herself to the outside world as a city of Southern hospitality and downhome charm. But the act may be wearing thin," as entrepreneurs and potential convention-goers thought twice about bringing their business to the city.[14]

A similar emphasis on public relations, on anodyne "peace and progress," appeared to shape the city government's response to the 1979–1981 youth abductions and murders. The sluggishness of the investigation, and the seeming hastiness with which it concluded, widened existing chasms between Atlanta's black working class and its biracial power structure. At the outset, investigators seemed reticent to connect the kidnappings and slayings. Authorities took minimal investigative action on the youth murders before the summer of 1980. In March 1980, officials had assessed "records involving the homicides of children over the last five years" and identified no "similarities, patterns or trends" among the current cases or between the present cases and earlier ones. That same month, the Atlanta Bureau of Police Services had requested the assistance of the FBI's Behavioral Science Unit in analyzing "all pertinent data related to the cases." In July, nearly a full year after the disappearance of fourteen-year-old Edward Hope Smith—the first of the twenty-nine victims eventually added to "the list" of missing Atlanta youths—authorities finally assembled a task force devoted to investigating the kidnappings and slayings. Only after months of petitioning by STOP, and after a slew of abductions and murders in June and early July 1980, did the city establish this task force.[15]

By that point, eleven children had already been added to "the list" of missing and murdered in Atlanta. Among them were Aaron Wyche, an ebullient ten-year-old with an artistic streak, and nine-year-old "math and science whiz" Yusuf Bell. Effortlessly handsome and "quick to smile," Wyche had a knack for art projects, often repurposing pine and plastic to create bird sculptures. He earned good grades at Thomasville Heights Elementary, a ten-minute walk from the southeast Atlanta apartment he shared with his mother and two younger brothers. Wyche also took pride in mowing lawns using his grandmother's mower, earning $5 per yard. He went missing on June 23, 1980, and his body was recovered beneath a railroad trestle the following day. Wyche had died of "positional asphyxiation" after falling from the twenty-five-foot trestle. Yusuf Bell was in a fifth-grade class for gifted students at Dunbar Elementary School, just south of downtown Atlanta. Adults residing in Yusuf's low-income housing project often asked the nine-year-old for assistance in balancing their checkbooks. He vanished on October 21, 1979, and his body was discovered three weeks later in an abandoned schoolhouse a few blocks from the Bell household.[16]

While Etan Patz's disappearance had promptly mobilized authorities in New York City and garnered media and public attention across the country, the same did not occur in Atlanta. Some observers speculated that the racial and class identities of the Atlanta victims rendered them less valuable than photogenic white children. Riled by this perceived double standard, many black Atlantans advocated for an increased police presence in their neighborhoods and heightened federal investigative interest in the city's missing and slain youth. They did this in spite of the historically adversarial relationship between African Americans and law enforcement—especially federal agencies like the FBI, which had infamously persecuted members of the Black Panther Party and others in the civil rights and Black Power movements. In the words of Camille Bell, "It takes a little bit more to get people concerned about a child out of the ghetto." This view was widespread among bereaved Atlanta parents, civil rights activists, and African American communities nationwide. Fully 79 percent of black Americans polled in 1981 agreed that the Atlanta killings "would be receiving more attention from the media and national leaders if white children were involved." Seventy-three percent of African Americans surveyed indicated that the cases had received inadequate attention from law enforcement. Reba Harrington—a self-identified black woman, mother, and "active duty officer in the United States Air Force"—concurred. In a February 1981 letter to Mayor Jackson, Harrington pleaded for "federal authorities [to] step up their investigation into this barbarous criminal act" and mused, "I only wonder what the reaction would be if the children were white." The Reverend Ralph David Abernathy, a renowned civil rights veteran who had frequently collaborated with Martin Luther King Jr., took a similar tack in a February 1981 sermon, excerpts of which appeared in an NBC *Nightly News* story. "If twenty-one white children had been murdered in Atlanta, Georgia," Abernathy hypothesized, "the federal government would be down here." Audience members loudly voiced their approval. "But they feel that these black children are not important!" he exclaimed. "I firmly believe, at the root of it all, is racism." To accentuate his point, Abernathy wagged his finger in the air.[17]

Even after Williams's capture and conviction, Mildred Glover, an African American legislator representing parts of Atlanta in Georgia's House of Representatives, followed this same line of criticism. In a letter to assistant attorney general William Bradford Reynolds, who led the US Department of Justice's civil rights division from 1981 through 1988, Glover lamented, "Parents [of the victims] contend that the establishment of the special Task Force was a much delayed reaction. . . . They could not understand the obvious limited value that was being placed on investigating such a terrible string of murders of their children." Glover pressed on: "The questions now on the parents' minds—and certainly valid ones—[are:] 1) Were our dead black children from Atlanta's ghettos subject to the same equal rights of the law as an influential white male lawyer from Atlanta's affluent Northside? 2) Had the children been white would the establishment of the Task Force taken place much quicker? I, too, am bewildered. . . . Is it because of color?" Glover juxtaposed the case of Hirsch Friedman, a prominent white attorney in Atlanta, with the city's cases of missing and slain black youth. Friedman had been seriously wounded in 1982 after a car bomb detonated in his driveway. Just two days after the blast, the Georgia Bureau of Investigation and the Fulton County Police Department had formed a task force to investigate the case, and within seventy-two hours the FBI had joined the investigation.[18]

Despite the similar backgrounds of Atlanta's young victims, those within the city's biracial power structure minimized the racial and class significance of the slayings. These leaders instead stressed Atlanta's solidarity amidst the crisis, even as they took steps to avert any potential civil unrest. In his 1981 "state of the city" remarks, Maynard Jackson identified the Atlanta killings as "*our* burden to bear, *our* lament, *our* great challenge" and claimed that "[e]veryone . . . feels the frustration, anxiety and uncertainty born of the cases of the missing and murdered children." For Jackson, Brown, and others, the murder saga "transcends race, age and class and afflicts us all," whether in "Buckhead or Beaverslide [*sic*], Peachtree Hills or Perry Homes, Cabbage Town or Collier Heights, Carver Homes or Cascade Heights."[19] Media outlets repeated these kinds of assertions. But such colorblind, postracial rhetoric masked the profound economic and demographic differences between places like Buckhead, a wealthy white enclave, and Beaver Slide, a historically African American slum where several of the young victims had lived. By papering over the structural and spatial inequalities that had enabled the murders, Jackson could conceal their racial and classed significance and burnish Atlanta's image as a "black mecca," in historian Maurice Hobson's formulation. After all, Hobson writes, the youth abductions and killings "were bad publicity for a striving city."[20]

At the same time, Mayor Jackson, in concert with white civic leaders, pursued peacekeeping plans to thwart any violence that might arise in response to the killings. Cecil Alexander and Rabbi Alvin Sugarman, two prominent Jewish civic leaders in Atlanta, secretly coordinated with

Mayor Jackson to develop a contingency plan in order to prevent "a wave of angry violence . . . if the murderer is black" or, worse yet, "a crisis of major proportions" if police apprehended a white suspect. A civil rights ally, Alexander encouraged black leaders "to take the lead" with the assistance of an "interfaith bi-racial group" that should "convene . . . very quietly to devise a strategy for the situation." Alexander apparently modeled his recommendations after plans drafted during the classical phase of the civil rights struggle. The mayor endorsed Alexander's proposals, forwarded them to his Community Relations Commission, and called for "a major mobilization of community/religious/educational/business resources to insure that our city remains positive, orderly, and improving its race relations." Through such efforts, elites hoped to maintain "law and order" within nonwhite, working-class spaces and to shore up Atlanta's image.[21]

To this end, Maynard Jackson, Lee Brown, and other establishment figures emphasized Atlanta's resiliency in the face of the serial slayings, and local and national news media reiterated the leaders' talking points. "How is Atlanta faring under the pressure?" Jackson inquired during his 1981 "state of the city" address. "'Remarkably well' is my answer. There are the understandable jitters, the rumors, the anger at the criminals, the expected impatience with the pace of things, the intense frustration. Some of our people are afraid[;] many are not: But *all* of Atlanta's people are concerned. I am proud of Atlanta's people." Around the same time, a story on ABC's *World News Tonight* applauded the racial harmony purportedly on display in Atlanta. "[W]hat could have easily become an explosive racial issue in this city," reporter Bob Sirkin opined, "continues to be met with patience and brotherhood." Designating it "a city that has long enjoyed good race relations," CBS journalist Sam Ford glossed over Atlanta's long history of racial inequality. For Ford, city officials had diagnosed "the potential for racial violence" and endeavored to "attack the child murder problem with community spirit." Biracial canvasses for bodies and clues, Ford asserted, had "eas[ed] black suspicions that whites did not care because their children are not being killed." Still other media outlets commended the city's "solidarity," its "grace under stress," and the fact that its residents were "coming together . . . to quell violence against black children."[22]

Developments in the city's most vulnerable communities told a different story. Even as Atlanta's black leaders worked to prevent a potential "crisis of major proportions," they hesitated in deploying police and other resources to solve the abductions and murders or to fortify the city's besieged communities. In response, residents of these communities took matters into their own hands. Vigilantes formed armed self-defense groups that policed Techwood Homes, the largest housing project in the city, and other

Figure 2.3 Launched in 1981 in response to the youth abductions and slayings, the "Let's Keep Pulling Together, Atlanta" campaign served to rehabilitate Atlanta's reputation as a "business-friendly" city that was "too busy to hate." "Let's Keep Pulling Together, Atlanta" poster, Jaci Mays Vickers to Lee P. Brown, July 23, 1981, box 177, series I: office files (1960–2004), MS 509, Lee P. Brown Papers, Benjamin N. Woodson Research Center, Walter W. Fondren Library, Rice University, Houston. Courtesy of the Woodson Research Center.

low-income housing developments. A crew calling itself the Bat Patrol carried a range of weapons—from baseball bats to firearms—and publicly condemned the law enforcement response to the kidnappings and killings. A black veterans group also vowed to protect Atlanta's black working-class communities. According to its leaders, as many as eight hundred African

American war veterans "could be called to arms in Atlanta" if needed. "If it takes our blood to run in the streets," one group member announced, "let it be." Such organizations undermined claims of Atlanta's "solidarity" and "grace under stress."[23]

"STREET HUSTLERS"

For all the talk of citywide unity and of the murders "transcend[ing]" race and class, depictions of the Atlanta victims fixated on their racial and class identities. Some commentators took to using terms such as *streetwise* and *street hustlers* to describe those kidnapped and killed in Atlanta. Such designations incriminated the victims, collapsed them into overly broad analytical categories, and denied them the innocence ascribed to white missing and murdered youths. Many of the young victims in Atlanta had disappeared while performing chores or running errands for small amounts of cash. Some journalists rooted such acts within a culture of "hustling" that purportedly pervaded Atlanta's black, working-class neighborhoods. Though this narrative concerning "streetwise" youth in Atlanta acknowledged the material privation in which the victims lived, it also drew upon harmful stereotypes concerning black criminality, inferiority, shiftlessness, and familial dysfunction. These renderings therefore denied Atlanta's black youth the agency and individuality lavished upon young whites during the late twentieth-century child safety campaign.

Whereas other cases spotlighted individual white child-victims, the situation in Atlanta involved a collection of young people from similar racial and class backgrounds. Whether out of necessity or negligence, media narratives conflated Atlanta's young victims, and thus labels like street child or street hustler loomed over the entire saga. Further, the street hustler narrative concentrated on the localized experience of poverty rather than its structural bases while nonetheless depriving the Atlanta youths of personhood. Press accounts largely neglected, say, Alfred James Evans's obsession with professional wrestling, Angel Lanier's love of *Sanford and Son*, Eric Middlebrooks's strong moral convictions, and other details that might have countered conceptions of the Atlanta victims as a monolithic bloc. Moreover, the street hustler interpretation did not take hold following the disappearances of Johnny Gosch and Eugene Wade Martin, who had both been delivering newspapers for cash when they vanished.[24] Race and class colored this distinction.

That photographs of Atlanta's missing and murdered hardly appeared in media dispatches or in political stagecraft illustrates how race and class circumscribed the image of endangered childhood. In stark contrast to the Etan Patz case, photographs of Atlanta's kidnapped and slain went largely unused and failed to generate much interest. Indeed, for one *Washington Post* story profiling each of the Atlanta victims (one of only a few such pieces), the *Post*'s writers and editors could not find pictures for three of the victims: Aaron Jackson, Patrick Rogers, and Terry Pue. Others, such as thirteen-year-olds Clifford Jones and Curtis Walker, were represented only through low-quality images, and the *Post* printed what seems to be a booking mugshot to represent twenty-three-year-old Michael Cameron McIntosh. Another article on the Atlanta youth victims, published in *LIFE* magazine in April 1981, featured photographs of only eighteen of the twenty-one missing and slain (at that point). This discrepancy—between uses of photographs featuring white child-victims and the dearth of images depicting Atlanta's missing and murdered—might be explained in two ways: First, investigators in Atlanta recovered most of the victims' bodies shortly after their abductions, meaning the periods in which most were "missing" proved relatively brief, and therefore there was no need to distribute their images in the hope of finding them. Yet even after police had identified the bodies of missing white children or declared them dead—in the cases of Adam Walsh, Polly Klaas, Megan Kanka, JonBenét Ramsey, and others—their pictures continued to circulate through formal channels as memorials and clarion calls for justice and protection. Second, and more likely, few photographs of the impoverished Atlanta youths existed at all.[25]

Rather than endowing victims with "innocence," as the image of endangered childhood did in Patz's case and others, pictures of Atlanta's missing and murdered often accompanied news media accounts which advanced the pernicious street hustler narrative. The aforementioned *Washington Post* story, for example, failed to problematize worrisome remarks from "a detective familiar with [eleven-year-old victim Christopher Richardson's] case." This detective characterized Richardson—whose skeletal remains were discovered in January 1981—as "a quiet, sensitive child who lacked the streetwise toughness many of the other victims wore on their sleeves." In his view, Richardson "was a straight good kid," not "streetwise or a hustler." Without any clarification from *Post* writer Art Harris, a reader might infer that Atlanta's other "streetwise" victims were not "good"—a judgment made all the more troubling given that the *Post* story referred to nineteen of the other twenty-six missing and murdered (at that point) as "hustlers" or "street children" who ran errands for pocket change.[26]

Other reportage grafted adult and criminal traits onto Atlanta's young victims and thereby denied them the very status of childhood. "At 11 years of age," one *Atlanta Journal-Constitution* article began, murder victim

"Patrick Baltazar has learned to make his own way in the world of adults, and he has no fear of approaching them to ask a favor or a job. With his uncanny 'street' sense, he can make a buck faster than some of those much older." According to the *Journal-Constitution*, Baltazar maintained the appearance and disposition of an eleven-year-old. "On the surface, Patrick Baltazar's interests are like those for any 11-year-old youngster. He is the owner of a dressed-up bicycle with mirrors, headlights and a horn." But he "is used to making his own way and his own money. . . . Perhaps driven by his poverty, young Baltazar has developed a talent for spotting odd jobs and especially likes to sell things to make money." In these ways, Baltazar apparently resembled his fellow "street smart," "streetwise" victims. According to the *Atlanta Constitution*, acquaintances of thirteen-year-old Timothy Hill described him as "[c]onstantly hungry, preoccupied with money and easily influenced." In the last days of Terry Pue's life, the fifteen-year-old reportedly "prowled Atlanta on a looping, seemingly aimless path," "hustling money in DeKalb" County (west of downtown Atlanta) one day and "continu[ing] to hustle as he worked his way back to Atlanta" proper. In sum, the *Journal-Constitution*, Atlanta's newspaper of record, characterized the victims as "slightly older, street-wise kids who spent their afternoons hustling odd jobs for loose change at grocery stores and shopping centers." Televised national news programs supplied similar descriptions.[27]

Though such news stories documented the material conditions in which many of the Atlanta victims lived, they took poverty as a largely cultural and individualized phenomenon rather than the result of historical processes. This coverage, then, endorsed the notion of a "culture of poverty," an idea enunciated most famously in the Moynihan Report. Issued in 1965 by the US Department of Labor, the Moynihan Report (formally titled *The Negro Family: The Case for National Action* but colloquially referred to by the name of its author, Daniel Patrick Moynihan) argued that a "tangle of pathology" ensnared many African Americans. This "tangle" (which Moynihan believed was "tightening" in the mid-sixties) comprised, most generally, "broken families." If African Americans could simply model their families after white, patriarchal, heteronormative ones, Moynihan held, their life chances would improve dramatically. The Moynihan Report thus implied that African Americans' perceived cultural defects, not structural racism or sustained inequality, perpetuated the cycle of poverty. The most glaring of these defects, from Moynihan's vantage, included "a 'Black Matriarchy' that emasculated sons," as Laura Briggs has put it; a penchant for juvenile delinquency; isolation and alienation; and a general "failure of youth."[28]

Similar language surfaced in treatments of the Atlanta crisis. "The tragedy of the children of Atlanta," *Washington Post* staff writer Art Harris noted, "has focused the nation's attention on something many would rather not think about: the pathology of poverty and the ugly things it does to children." According to Harris, poverty had *made* young black Atlantans "ugly," but he ignored the phenomena that had *made* that poverty in the first place: the city's asymmetrical development, white and capital flight, an evaporating tax base, redlining and other forms of housing discrimination, and educational inequality. For his part, Ed Bradley, an African American journalist for CBS, also failed to penetrate the structural foundations of Atlanta's poverty. Like other newspersons, Bradley saw the city's "street hustlers" mainly as products of individual failure and pathology—specifically, "[t]he apathy, parental neglect, poor education, and social burden" evident in certain Atlanta neighborhoods. To his credit, Bradley pointed to educational inequality as a cause of poverty, yet his litany skewed toward personal and community failings rather than the systems that all but guaranteed those failings. "Many of the children in these neighborhoods have been called 'hustlers,' and that shouldn't be taken in a negative sense," Bradley affirmed. "Only a handful of the murdered kids had what's been called 'minor brushes with the law.' Those kids and others still alive found ways to hustle a dollar: running errands, carrying groceries, doing odd jobs. In other neighborhoods they might be called kids with 'get up and go.' But around here there's no place to go for most. These poverty-lined streets are like barriers to [the] downtown world and the rest of Atlanta." Even a relatively sympathetic national news story like this one could not shake the "culture of poverty" thesis and the attendant trope of streetwise children. Media outfits as far away as San Antonio, Texas, adopted the seductive "street smart" appellation. Camille Bell, for her part, lamented the "active effort" undertaken by news outlets "to imply that [the slain youths] were criminal or at least neglected, unsupervised and incorregible [*sic*] children."[29]

Others apart from Camille Bell militated against these perceptions of the young victims as "hustlers" or "grunchins." "There have been rumors that the kids were hustlers," Lee P. Brown noted in the National Association for the Advancement of Colored People (NAACP) periodical *Crisis*. "That is inaccurate. What we have, in effect, are some enterprising young people who were trying to earn a buck. Picking up aluminum cans, selling [goods] in the shopping centers and taking groceries from the store to the vehicles [of adult shoppers]." Paraphrasing Brown, another *Crisis* article read, "The victims were ambitious, enterprising, streetwise youngsters, says Public Safety Commissioner Lee Brown. But they were the poorest of the poor, not much interested in 'wicked witch' games, but interested in 'making it.' They could have come from any economic group."

Former NPR correspondent Charlayne Hunter-Gault detected a slippage between "at risk" and "culpable" in some media coverage. "They are what the sociologists called the 'at risk' population," she asserted. "And they are children who grow up on the streets. There is a presumption that children like that are strong and independent and can take care of themselves. But underlying all that . . . they are just children, and they are being abused by the streets. In this case, they are being abused in the most extreme way—they are being killed." It is not unreasonable to assume that Hunter-Gault emphasized the victims' identities as children because, as African American youth, they so commonly appeared in press coverage as "street hustlers" who had outgrown childhood or had never enjoyed its protections. As Robin Bernstein and others have shown, the designations of "childhood" and "innocence" (and their associated perquisites) have historically been withheld from youth of color.[30]

Just as Atlanta's missing and slain faced scrutiny (and at least implicit scorn) for their "hustl[ing]," the victims' parents were publicly accused of perpetrating the killings. In April 1981, after delivering remarks to a civic group in Macon, Georgia, FBI special agent Mike Twibell alleged that "some of these kids" in Atlanta "were killed by their parents." Twibell's comments sparked outrage among STOP members, including Camille Bell. At a press conference at city hall organized in response to Twibell's comments, Bell read from a letter that STOP intended to mail to FBI director William Webster. "As parents and relatives of . . . young Americans either murdered or missing in Atlanta for more than 20 months," Bell proclaimed, "we stand united and dedicated to let Almighty God alone be our judge." She then challenged Webster to follow through on Twibell's charges. "For this reason we urge you, based on alleged available evidence, to place under arrest immediately those parents suspected of mercilessly taking their babies' lives." Tapping into her political capital as a bereaved mother, Bell asked, "Why must we suffer the humiliation of a few misinformed people" like Twibell, "while we must constantly endure the frustration of [not] finding out who is killing our children and throwing them away like garbage?" In the wake of Twibell's comments, at least ten mothers from STOP met with an attorney to discuss the prospect of suing the FBI. But no suits nor arrests ever resulted from Twibell's accusations. Still, that a federal investigative official, without evidence, levied such serious charges against the victims' parents reflected a tendency to pin the Atlanta murders on the victims and secondary victims themselves, in sharp contrast to the treatment of white, middle-class child-victims and their families in the stranger danger panic.[31]

A "MERCILESS AND SAVAGE GENOCIDE"

The racial and class homogeneity of Atlanta's victims and the conservative national political climate in which the kidnappings and murders occurred suggested a racial motive for these tragedies. Accordingly, the Ku Klux Klan (KKK) and other white supremacist groups emerged as lead suspects in the Atlanta cases, despite little evidence to implicate them. A lack of investigative leads exacerbated the racially specific anxieties surrounding the slayings and enabled the spread of conspiracy theories foregrounding the racist motivations behind, and federal complicity in, the events in Atlanta. Republicans' capture of the White House and the US Senate in the 1980 elections, coupled with a spike in hate crime activity, convinced some observers that the Atlanta kidnappings and murders were part of a concerted "Assault on Black Life," in the words of Southern Christian Leadership Conference (SCLC) president Reverend Joseph E. Lowery. Some went so far as to call the serial killings a "genocide" that cast doubt on the very prospect of a "Black Future."[32]

For many African Americans, the murders of Atlanta's black youths fit within a broader national effort to reassert white supremacy, and they thus inflamed African American anxieties—locally, regionally, and nationally—regarding racism and racial violence. An October 1980 boiler explosion at the Gate City Daycare Center in northwest Atlanta further aggravated these anxieties. The blast killed five people, including four African American children. "People took to the streets," Camille Bell remembered. "They believed that the center had been bombed and that racist whites were doing it; they felt that the same people who had bombed the [daycare] center" had abducted and slain some of Atlanta's young. Immediately after the explosion, Mayor Jackson rushed to Bowen Homes, a low-income housing project near Gate City, to reassure the crowd gathered there that police suspected no foul play in the incident. "Based on what our fire and police officials have told us," he told the audience through a bullhorn, "the only evidence we have at this time indicates that this was an accident." Crowd members hissed, and some hollered back, "It was the Klan!" One disgruntled African American woman jeered, "Ain't no gas exploded in there." The KKK's involvement "was pure rumor," Jackson later told an interviewer. "[T]here was zero evidence." At a raucous community meeting the day after the blast, locals pressed public safety commissioner Lee P. Brown for answers. Parents and others in attendance berated Brown, who hoped to defuse the situation through his careful word choice and calls for unity. "We are not adversaries in this problem," he insisted. "We are together, and your concern [that] you have, we also share."[33]

The daycare explosion, though an accident, opened old wounds sustained in the darkest days of the Southern civil rights struggle. Surely many black Atlantans recalled one KKK splinter group's September 1963 bombing of Birmingham's Sixteenth Street Baptist Church, which took the lives of four black girls, and other acts of racial violence directed toward the churches, community centers, schools, and protest sites where young African Americans congregated during the black freedom movement. A man named Tommy Battle wrote to Mayor Jackson in the midst of the Atlanta crisis. "It is impossible to forget the incident in 1963 when Klansmen bombed a church in Birmingham and ended the lives of four black children; if the black race is to exist," Battle argued, "black salvation must be our top priority." One woman likened the "fear and sadness" of Atlanta's children to her own feelings in 1963 when her "friend, Denise McNair, was murdered along with 3 other girls while attending Sunday school at Sixteenth St. Baptist Church in Birmingham." Novelist Toni Cade Bambara drew similar linkages in *Those Bones Are Not My Child*, which concentrates on the Atlanta youth murders. For at least one of her characters, the daycare blast evoked not only the attack on the Sixteenth Street Baptist Church but also the 1964 murders of three young civil rights workers—James Chaney, Andrew Goodman, and Michael Schwerner—by the Mississippi White Knights of the KKK.[34]

The Klan had a long history in Atlanta. Stone Mountain, the Confederate landmark just outside the city, had served as the birthplace for the KKK's second iteration in 1915. The organization called Atlanta's Peachtree Street home in the twenties and thirties, during which it boasted large membership numbers throughout Georgia. It maintained a considerable footprint in Atlanta through the 1960s. Herbert Jenkins, Atlanta's police chief from 1947 to 1972, had even belonged to the KKK. Still, Maynard Jackson blamed the Klan rumors on the "frustration[s] of an economically and racially oppressed black community . . . already upset and tense over the disappearance and murders of 14 black children in . . . 15 months." For the mayor, Atlanta's "paranoia" at the time "was . . . just very, very high," and this "paranoia" helped promote the idea that "the Klan was doing it."[35]

Given Atlanta's racial history and the contemporary political context, African American concerns about racial violence were hardly misguided. Published in 1978, a year before the youth murders began, *The Turner Diaries* exhorted disaffected rightwing extremists and white power activists to incite a race war. In Greensboro, North Carolina, the following year, Klansmen and neo-Nazis attacked an anti-Klan rally convened by Communist Workers' Party members, killing five protesters. An all-white jury in Greensboro acquitted the Nazis and KKK members in 1980.

Racial unrest had also broken out in Buffalo, New York; Miami, Florida; Chattanooga, Tennessee; and Philadelphia, Pennsylvania, in the early 1980s. At the same time, paramilitary and white power groups, taking their cues from *The Turner Diaries* and other materials, began a new phase of organizing. These efforts would spawn entities like The Order, a terrorist group associated with the Aryan Nations and best known for its 1984 assassination of the Denver, Colorado, talk radio host Alan Berg.[36]

Observers tied these developments to the events in Atlanta. In one October 1980 broadcast of ABC's news magazine *Nightline*, anchorman

Figure 2.4 Photograph of a child at a march in East Hampton, New York, March 1981. "This is a Start," *East Hampton Star*, March 12, 1981, 18, box 152, folder 8, Joseph E. Lowery papers, SCLC records, MSS 1083, MARBL. Courtesy of the *East Hampton Star*.

Ted Koppel discussed the presumed connections between "assaults on blacks" nationwide, positing that antiblack violence in Atlanta, Buffalo, and elsewhere came as "the result of an increase in rightwing extremism throughout the country." Just a few days later, ABC aired an edition of *20/20* in which Camille Bell and others vented about whites' supposed indifference to the Atlanta murders. The broadcast then cut to local news footage of the Ku Klux Klan "preparing for guerilla war." This causal linkage, offered up to a national audience in primetime, infuriated Atlanta's biracial establishment. Civic and business leaders denounced ABC for fostering a "false impression" of Atlanta as "a criminal city living in constant fear."[37] Atlanta elites thus focused their outrage not on the forces terrorizing the city but on press portrayals of this terror.

Ronald Reagan also made African Americans nervous. Critics located Reagan's 1980 presidential campaign and electoral victory within the same antiblack "backlash" that had ostensibly engendered the Atlanta abductions and slayings. Reagan's successful appeals to "law and order" and "states' rights"—most notably at the Neshoba County Fair near Philadelphia, Mississippi, where Chaney, Goodman, and Schwerner had been murdered—suggested a rejection by many white Americans of federal civil rights protections. In a press conference preceding a White House "revival" convened by Jimmy Carter less than two weeks before the 1980 election, Reverend Lowery rebuked Reagan for his use of "dog whistles" during the campaign. "I am frightened that the forces of insensitivity, of racism, of militarism, of violence, of negativism are gravitating in and toward the candidacy of Governor Reagan," Lowery declared. "The tone and character of the Reagan candidacy," he continued, "were clearly reflected in the selection of Philadelphia, Miss[issippi], where civil rights workers were buried in shallow graves, as the site to raise the ugly spectre of 'states rights' [*sic*]." Following Reagan's victory in November 1980, NAACP executive director Benjamin Hooks encouraged Reagan to address on national television the "hysterical fear in the black community [that] the Reagan administration is antiblack." Hooks tied this black anxiety to the incidents in Atlanta and Buffalo and an overarching "conservative trend" that he said foreshadowed "a rollback of pure civil rights laws, like the Voting Rights Act." In December, various leftwing groups met at an anti-Klan conference in Greensboro and made plans to picket Reagan's inauguration. Attendees of the anti-KKK meeting drew connections between the Klan, the federal government, and events in Atlanta, Buffalo, Greensboro, and Miami. "[T]he government is trying to stifle the movement against the Klan any way it can," a Teamsters leader from Miami claimed. One panel, titled "Germany

1930's / U.S.A. 1980's [sic]—the Danger of Fascism," explicitly compared Reagan's America to the Third Reich.[38]

Even after committing $1.5 million in federal funds to Atlanta, the administration struggled to combat the perception that the Reagan White House despised people of color. Soon after news of this federal assistance went public, vice president George H. W. Bush traveled to the city to demonstrate the administration's interest in the Atlanta murders and its concern for those affected. In remarks delivered during his March 1981 trip, Bush displayed a keen awareness of optics by trying to deflect potential accusations of political opportunism or grandstanding. "I've wanted to come here since the day I was sworn in as vice president," Bush indicated. "There's a certain *symbolism*. But you don't want to do something that just kind of looks political or try to in any way do something that could be *interpreted* as capitalizing on the failing of the community." An anonymous White House official communicated to journalists the administration's anxieties about federal intervention in local investigative matters. Reagan had achieved electoral success in 1980 by lambasting "big government" and promising to shrink the welfare state. But according to this anonymous source, the White House opted not to address the issue of federal "overreach" at that time, choosing instead to assist the grieving city and, in their words, "to show that we care about black children." Still, public figures such as Washington, DC, mayor Marion Barry argued that federal funding should have come sooner.[39]

Rather than simply sowing distrust and fanning the flames of frustration, the Atlanta abductions and murders also activated rumors and existential fears about the uses and abuses of the young victims' bodies. Grounded in black skepticism of the federal government and the Republicans who controlled it, these rumors often fixated on the Centers for Disease Control (CDC), headquartered in the affluent Atlanta enclave of Druid Hills. African American mistrust of the CDC (and the medical establishment more generally) stemmed in part from the CDC's principal role in the Tuskegee syphilis study. From 1932 to 1972, medical researchers examining the effects of syphilis monitored over six hundred African American men in rural Alabama. A team of mostly white doctors performed extensive experiments on these men, the majority of whom were syphilitic, but failed to share diagnoses with these subjects or deliver suitable care for their ailments. The CDC became the institutional home of the Tuskegee experiment in 1957 and retained administrative control over the study until 1972, when a whistleblower alerted the press to the ethical malfeasance on display within the experiment. While the Tuskegee project was shuttered that same year, in 1972, the damage had been done. Most subjects had already died of causes related to syphilis, and many of their relatives had contracted the illness. News of the Tuskegee study eroded blacks' trust in medical practitioners and institutions, deterred African Americans from seeking medical assistance, and exacerbated existing racial disparities in health outcomes. Scholars have determined that by 1980, the same year that the nation's gaze turned to the Atlanta slayings, the 1972 Tuskegee revelations had helped reduce (by 1.4 years) the life expectancy rate for African American men over the age of forty-five. After learning of the Tuskegee study in 1972, one doctor studying venereal disease at the CDC called it "almost like genocide," an interpretation that resonated in the broader African American community.[40]

Against this backdrop, some conspiracy theorists blamed the Atlanta youth kidnappings on genocidal medical researchers backed by the federal government. In her ethnographic research on race and rumor, folklorist Patricia Turner learned from her interviewees the extravagant theories bandied about in Atlanta during the 1979–1981 slayings. Some interview subjects recalled rumors "which accused anti-black groups of a conspiracy to steal black bodies for medical experiments." As one interviewee told Turner, "I remember hearing that the killings in Atlanta were related to [the] genocide of the black race. The [FBI] was responsible and using the bodies for interferon during research at the Centers for Disease Control." For his part, black comedian and provocateur Dick Gregory claimed that certain federal agencies and the CDC stalked and killed black children and adolescent males as part of a quest to find a cure for cancer. Only by extracting blood from the penises of black males between the ages of six and sixteen, Gregory conjectured, could this experimental cure be produced.[41]

Others subscribed to theories of genocide that were perhaps less elaborate. An African American man from Hyattsville, Maryland, lamented in a letter to Jackson the "genocidal slaying of the young, innocent, trusting Black children in Atlanta." In a press release, a representative from the Hartford, Connecticut, branch of the National Council of Negro Women (NCNW) called the Atlanta kidnappings and slayings a "merciless and savage genocide of Black youths." Representatives from the Williamson, West Virginia, NAACP condemned the "apparent attempt of genocide by some sick individuals" and asserted that "our struggle as a people is far from ended." As Ozell Sutton, the southeast regional director of the US Justice Department's Community Relations Service, noted in 1980, "There is a growing perception among blacks in Atlanta of being attacked. The mysterious murder of 10 black children, while four others are still missing, and the explosion in Bowen Homes that killed four children and one adult have raised the possibility of deliberate and systematic attack in the minds of many blacks." Finally, a Washington, DC, Baptist church arranged a "United for Survival" worship march in February 1981. In print materials promoting the march, church minister Lehman D. Bates portrayed African American mobilization in the wake of the Atlanta slayings as an existential imperative:

> These incidents of Mass Murder on African-Americans (Blacks) are not new. The style and form of our ancestors' assassinations are remembered by lynchings, "vicious and *legal* police killings," contract slaying, military murder on the war front, drugs poisoning our schools and communities, and worst of all the day after day and year after year Mind (Murder) Control through the mass media, text books, movies, and the systematic deprivation of essentially needed things.
>
> White America and the killer or killers of our Children and Men are not our First Problem [or] Priority. If African-Americans (Blacks) will Survive in this sick social system, "We Must Unite" under the "Common Cause" of our Survival before the chattle [sic] slavery of the body is totally converted to the "yes sir boss" slavery of our mind, which accepts everything that white America says as "true" and "right" and "just."

Bates placed the Atlanta killings within the long line of violence perpetrated against African Americans, and specifically black men, while pleading for blacks to fight for the "Survival" of their race.[42]

"SAVE OUR CHILDREN"

As Bates's screed suggests, the anxieties regarding genocide and the black future that emanated from the Atlanta youth killings intersected with concerns about black masculinity, homosexuality, and the state of the African American family. Some of Atlanta's black leaders situated the abductions and murders within a supposed crisis in black manhood, one that undermined the stability of "traditional" family forms and the prospect of heteronormative reproduction in African American communities. As in other cases of missing and murdered boys in the late seventies and early eighties, fears about homosexual predation also suffused the Atlanta saga. In response to this cluster of worries, and to the abductions and slayings more generally, Atlanta's black leaders promoted a type of neoliberal, heteronormative "family values" as an antidote to the killings.

In keeping with understandings of the slayings as genocidal, some African Americans argued that the Atlanta killings threatened the future of black leadership and civic engagement in the "post–civil rights" era.

One man writing to Maynard Jackson advised African American parents to reevaluate their "duties and responsibilities" to their children "in order for us to have a generation of law abiding citizens." In her missive to Mayor Jackson, one mother explained, "Only God knows what part those children would have played in our future. (Blacks)." Dennis McCluster, an African American copywriter, similarly observed in 1981: "Any of [the victims] could have grown up to be another black poet, scientist, doctor, or even a Nobel Prize recipient," a likely reference to Atlanta's most cherished son, Martin Luther King Jr. "These are the faces of our most precious natural resource. Now, all they can be are tearful memories. Don't let this happen again in Atlanta, or anywhere," McCluster implored. "Save our children." Like others writing to Mayor Jackson, McCluster recognized the potential of the slain children and the role they might have played in the African American future.[43]

The Reverend Albert E. Love, national administrator for the SCLC from 1980 to 1988, saw the Atlanta crisis as a chance to initiate a set of programs directed at African American youth, especially young males. "Our thrust," Love wrote to Joseph Lowery in September 1980, "could be *Saving Our Black Youth* or *Tomorrow's Leaders*. Who can object or refuse to get on this ban-wagon [sic]?" To craft a plan through which the SCLC could address the youth murders, Love looked to the fraught political climate, in which conservatives and neoliberals harnessed coded racial language to disparage the welfare state and expand the carceral sphere. "Our pitch can be that blacks know how to deal with blacks," Love's proposal read, "so give us the money and let us deal with black youth who whites claim are doing all of the stealing, loafing, and begging." Love's "pitch" assumed a decidedly masculinist and antigay tone. "You know of my bias to address the problem of the degeneration of Blackdom due to the loss of our black males," Love admitted. "Too many of us are in prison, on dope, homosexuals, and unemployed. This places tremendous burdens on the absurdly overburdened black woman. The net effect is weak black men, insecure black husbands, ill-equipped black leaders, and powerless black people." For Love, the killings in Atlanta had worsened a perceived crisis in African American manhood. He also conflated "leader" and "man," insinuating that women should not lead African Americans in the "post–civil rights" age. Finally, Love's remarks reflected the antigay milieu by implicating "homosexuals" in "the degeneration of Blackdom." Love placed homosexuality in the same company as mass incarceration, drug addiction, and unemployment, blaming each for the deterioration of African American families, the inadequacy of African American leadership, and the dispossession of black people generally.[44]

Worries about homosexual predation pervaded the Atlanta saga. Those involved with the investigation offered inconsistent views on the possibility that one or more pedophilic men had abducted and killed the Atlanta youths. None of the bodies recovered by authorities showed signs of sexual abuse. Yet according to at least two "chicken hawks," some victims frequented two houses near downtown Atlanta that were known to be prostitution dens. As one ABC *World News Tonight* story detailed, these homes "reportedly have been hangouts for young teenage boys who police think came here to exchange sex with men for money." The same ABC report included a soundbite from public safety commissioner Brown, who proclaimed, "As far as factual evidence is concerned, there's nothing to suggest to us that homosexuality is any more involved in the killings any more so than any other conceivable possibility." ABC journalist Bob Sirkin immediately contradicted Brown: "But the FBI and other police agencies working on the cases have long considered sex the most viable motive in a number of the children's murders." A segment on the CBS *Evening News* conveyed much the same idea. "Police sources say the theory that many of the youngsters were recruited by homosexuals for sexual favors is the strongest motive investigators now have for the killings," reporter Bruce Hall indicated. One of the victims, Hall added, "may have been involved in recruiting children for homosexuals." Propelled by such suspicions, authorities employed computer technology "to determine whether any former Georgia prison inmates classified as homosexuals live near the young blacks victimized" in Atlanta.[45]

According to one *Village Voice* article, local Atlanta television affiliates also noted that "two or three of the victims were thought or known to be guilty of petty [sic] theft or burglary, 10 of drug violations, and 10 of homosexual prostitution." In addition, the *Village Voice* specified that "at least three of the [slain] children were known to travel with adult homosexuals" and that one FBI source "agreed that homosexual prostitution could be connected to some of the cases." While the FBI did investigate these allegations, it never blamed the Atlanta abductions and murders on such activities. For Camille Bell, the obsession with "homosexual prostitution" underscored the ease with which policymakers, the public, and the press degraded Atlanta's young victims. This emphasis, Bell maintained, distracted from more substantive matters and represented one of "many attempts at blaming the victims." According to Bell, investigators and media officials "implied that the children were homosexual prostitutes" when "the question was not homosexuality or heterosexuality but MURDER. This," she stated in remarks before the US Senate, "is known as clouding the issue."[46]

A green ribbon campaign initiated to raise awareness about the Atlanta killings aroused criticism for its purported homophobia. Launched by an elderly woman from Philadelphia, Pennsylvania, named Georgia Dean, the "humble little plan" evolved into an impressive fundraising program supported by members of Congress, civil rights leaders, and athletes. Dean had chosen the color green, she explained, because "[i]t symbolizes life . . . the bushes are green, the grass is green in the spring. I said, 'That's it. It'll be green.'" Philadelphia's black community was the first to embrace the ribbons, which benefited STOP by way of SCLC. The campaign quickly caught on among area whites. Soon, people in New Jersey, Delaware, Virginia, Illinois, Louisiana, and elsewhere joined Dean's campaign. After Georgetown University men's basketball coach John Thompson proposed putting green ribbons on the team's uniforms, his players, most of whom were black, "hurried out for needles and thread." One representative from the Hartford section of the NCNW vowed that she and her peers would "display in our homes, on our cars, and on our persons green ribbons . . . until the person or persons responsible" for the atrocities in Atlanta "are apprehended and punished." The NCNW also "implore[d] all other Americans of all races[,] creeds and colors to join in this vigil as a symbolic protest."[47]

Oftentimes the slogan "Save Our Children" accompanied these ribbons. For some, the use of this phrase was neither arbitrary nor innocuous. In 1977, singer Anita Bryant had formed an antigay political coalition by the same name. Bryant and her supporters mobilized to repeal a Miami–Dade County ordinance that had outlawed discrimination against gay men and lesbians. The organization portrayed gay rights as antithetical to child safety, a message that swiftly took hold outside of south Florida. Although the myth of the pedophilic and predatory gay man had long shaped Americans' understanding of homosexuality, only in the late 1970s did a formal political consciousness congeal around this myth.[48] In this conjuncture, critics interpreted the green ribbon campaign as antigay. As Jamaican American author Michelle Cliff observed, "Now the meaning of [the] green ribbon has shifted. They are killing black children in Atlanta—also elsewhere. . . . Each newspaper report seems more clouded than before: today they claimed the children died at the hands of a 'gentle' killer: does this translate as female? homosexual? What are they getting at?" David Thorstad, founder of the North American Man/Boy Love Association (NAMBLA), wrote that the ribbons "had overtones of anti-homosexuality" and asked, "In the Atlanta context, what did ['Save Our Children'] mean? . . . Save our children from what? Murder? Homosexuality? Parental child abuse?

Poverty? Reaganism? How, I wondered, could people sport a button that not so long ago was used as a rallying cry against gay men?"[49]

Concerns about homosexuality also saturated the trial of Wayne Williams, who was charged with murdering two of the older victims on "the list"—twenty-seven-year-old Nathaniel Cater and twenty-one-year-old Jimmy Ray Payne. For Thorstad, "the state was trying to make Wayne Williams into the stereotype of the queer molester–murderer." Throughout the trial, Williams denied being gay ("There ain't no way I'm no homosexual, huh-uh, no," he insisted) or homophobic, even though he had referred to homosexuals as "Hostess cupcakes, gays, faggots and Twinkies," according to two witnesses. While the defense refuted rumors of Williams's homosexuality, the prosecution took a less coherent approach on the matter. "Although two prosecution witnesses have testified that Williams solicited them to perform homosexual acts," one *Journal-Constitution* article recounted, "they never said whether the acts took place. It is unclear if prosecutors are trying to portray Williams as a homosexual, or as someone who taunted and disliked them." Upon Williams's conviction, *Newsweek* magazine celebrated the guilty verdict and pilloried Williams as conniving, a descriptor long applied to gay men, women, and criminals. When Williams took the stand in his own defense, "He said he was not a homosexual," the *Newsweek* story read. "He said he had never held hands with Cater on a downtown street, as a witness charged. In fact, said Williams, he had never met any of the victims." But, the article claimed, this "was a poised performance" by a man with a "Jekyll-and-Hyde personality" and "a violent temper."[50]

The discourse regarding homosexuality during the Atlanta kidnappings and murders beckoned to fears of black familial decline. African American organizational efforts during the killings stressed the virtues of familial cohesion and community protection. The City of Atlanta hosted an "I Love My Family" week at the height of the saga in April 1981. The program cited the "strong and healthy" African American family as a bulwark against the forces threatening the city. Around the same time, STOP called on supporters to travel to Washington, DC, and "revisit the Lincoln Memorial" for a "national unity rally" championing the "revitalization of family unity." Atlanta's black leaders harkened back to a fictive golden age in which community members made up an extended kinship network for African American youth. Also in April 1981, Lee Brown urged Atlantans "to exercise extraordinary parental supervision, to look out for our children, to revert back to the concept which we used to talk about and believe in that we are our brother's keeper. There were times," Brown went on, "when if Lee Brown was down the street, Mrs. Jones would not hesitate to look out for him and take care of him . . . even if he did something wrong." Jondell Johnson, executive secretary of the Atlanta NAACP, echoed Brown's sentiments. Detailing his organization's outreach efforts in Atlanta neighborhoods—which included child safety programs such as Neighborhood Alert against Child Pickup—Johnson pointed out: "We have been trying to get back to the old days when everyone in the neighborhood knew everyone else, and look[ed] after everybody else's kids."[51]

In the 1970s especially, white academicians and politicians fretted over the idea that the white family increasingly resembled the African American household, "shaped by divorce and separation, single parenthood, and dual wage earning." For Christopher Lasch, Phyllis Schlafly, and other white critics from across the political spectrum, the white family required fortification and purification. Otherwise, it risked becoming ensnared in the same "tangle of pathology" that entrapped African Americans.[52] This brand of "family values" politics found a counterpart in Atlanta, as African Americans embraced the patriarchal, heterosexual, dual-parent black family and its extended bonds of kinship as potential deterrents to abduction and murder—and, for some, genocide.

THE COLOR OF CHILDHOOD

The Atlanta tragedies fit imperfectly within the burgeoning national child safety campaign. On the one hand, these abductions and murders—like the disappearances of Etan Patz and Adam Walsh—seemed to provide further evidence of a supposedly new, or worsening, child kidnapping threat. On the other hand, Atlanta's poorest neighborhoods bore little resemblance to SoHo; Hollywood, Florida; or the Des Moines suburbs. The Patz, Walsh, and Iowa paperboy cases fixated on individual, white, middle-class children, in contrast to a group of nearly thirty poor, young African Americans. Incidences of missing white boys generally prompted discussions of innocence lost, of the white family buffeted by sinister, exogenous forces, and of an American childhood idyll under serious threat. Conversely, the discourse surrounding the Atlanta saga denied the young victims the very status of childhood, portraying the missing and slain not as innocents but as sexually depraved "street hustlers" consumed by the decrepit neighborhoods in which they dwelled. Put simply, the black youths snatched and slain in Atlanta did not possess the traits that made Patz, Walsh, Gosch, and Martin "all-American," and the names and faces of Patrick Baltazar, Earl Terrell, and Darron Glass did not populate images of endangered childhood or drive the child safety campaign.

There were continuities, of course, between the Atlanta tragedies and the other cases propelling the stranger danger panic of the late twentieth century. As the Patzes and Walshes had, bereaved parents like Camille Bell and other STOP members expressed skepticism of, and hostility toward, the government—particularly law enforcement. Further, just as white Americans took the abductions of Etan Patz, Adam Walsh, and other white boys as signs of national, familial, and racial decline, black Atlantans pondered the larger meanings of the crimes visited upon their communities. What, they asked, did the seemingly systematic abduction and murder of economically disadvantaged black youth say about African American life in the Reagan-era, "post–civil rights" South? The Atlanta kidnappings and slayings also stoked homophobic fears of pedophilia and helped bolster a heteronormative "family values" politics among Atlanta's black leaders. The Patz and Johnny Gosch cases, among others, similarly played on and played into stereotypes of gay male perversion and predation. Moreover, the Atlanta cases contributed to the national conversation about child endangerment. For her part, Camille Bell helped raise awareness nationwide about stranger danger. Alongside John and Revé Walsh and Stanley and Julie Patz, she participated in the first congressional hearings on missing children in 1981. Elsewhere, Bell instrumentalized the same exaggerated statistics that fueled the broader child protection crusade. "No one knows," she lamented in a 1981 *Washington Post* editorial, "how many of the 50,000 missing children in the United States today are dead, dying or succumbing to the wishes of adults in the back bedrooms and streets in this country."[53]

Despite Bell's initial efforts, she soon faded from the spotlight, as did Atlanta's twenty-nine victims—their names and faces eclipsed by photogenic white children whose cases resolved neatly into narratives of stranger danger and innocence lost. While these white child-victims became the poster children for new child protection laws and practices, black and brown children did not. On the contrary, this historical moment saw the intense demonization of urban, nonwhite youth like Atlanta's "street hustlers," the Central Park Five, and John DiIulio's "superpredators." Though the racialized logic of urban juvenile criminality and suburban childhood innocence did not originate in the late twentieth century, it perhaps proved most influential beginning in the late sixties with the development of a two-pronged criminal justice approach that worked to protect and "rehabilitate" white youths while punishing black and brown "delinquents" and "drug pushers." Much the same dynamic shaped federal justice policy in the 1980s and 1990s. Juvenile incarceration rates rose precipitously across this period, and black and brown youth bore the brunt of the burden. In 1979, the juvenile incarceration rate per 100,000 stood at 251; it had increased to 357 per 100,000 by 1987 before reaching 381 in 1995. Over that same timeframe, the proportion of African Americans in juvenile detention facilities grew from 28 percent of the total population in 1979 to 34 percent in 1987 and 40 percent in 1991 and 1995. Likewise, in 1979, Latinx juveniles comprised 9 percent of the total population in juvenile correctional facilities and 17 percent by 1995.[54]

The Atlanta saga, then, did not mesh with the normative stranger danger narrative, which derived significant power from the image of (white) endangered childhood and a racialized moral panic over the state of US cities. Indeed, the politics of John Walsh and Noreen Gosch hinged on white childhood innocence. Embedded in stories of loss and in photographs of the missing, this emotionally resonant trope helped sanction policies and practices designed to protect white spaces—and the most vulnerable residents of those spaces. These policies and practices, rooted in differential valuations and depictions of white and nonwhite youth, helped make the child safety regime.[55]

CHAPTER 3

☙

Trouble in the Heartland

Region, Race, and Iowa's Missing Paperboys

When *Des Moines Register* paperboy Eugene Wade Martin vanished in August 1984, the newspaper's editor-in-chief James P. Gannon was "mad as hell." Martin was the second *Register* carrier to disappear from the Des Moines area in as many years. Twelve-year-old Johnny Gosch had been kidnapped in September 1982 while delivering papers in West Des Moines. Gannon responded by publishing a searing editorial that took the Martin and Gosch incidents as evidence of regional and national decline. "Here," the editor wrote, "in the normally safe-and-sane heartland of middle America, where clean living, neighborliness and a sense of security are supposed to prevail, a sinister shadow darkens our doorways and our lives." According to Gannon, the losses of these paperboys—whose fates remain unknown, as their bodies were never recovered—"raised questions that violate everything we hold dear about living in this comfortable, contented community: Is it no longer safe to let our youngsters walk our neighborhood streets?" In his mind, the Gosch and Martin disappearances had disproven once and for all "the 'it can't happen here' myth."[1]

The Gosch and Martin cases kindled a specific sort of anxiety in the Midwest. For Gannon and other white Midwesterners, spaces like West Des Moines ought to be exempt from tragedies like these. As one Sioux City resident noted in a letter to Gannon, the paperboy abductions "have stained the city of Des Moines." Another Iowan insisted that "this type of terrorism . . . tarnishes every citizen in this community." That two white, middle-class paperboys were plucked from ostensibly secure surroundings signaled to one suburban Des Moines mother that her "once-quiet 'great-place-to-raise-kids' city may become the crime capital of the world." Other Iowans faulted "wicked, perverted people" for the paperboy crimes.[2]

These concerns about regional and national decline, crime, and sexual deviance flowed from conceptions of white Midwestern innocence—particularly the conviction that the "heartland" constituted an idyllic American setting. For these Iowa residents in the early to mid-1980s, child kidnapping and other undesirable phenomena represented exogenous threats to the white Midwest. Indeed, Gannon urged his fellow Des Moiners not to "cede the streets to the shadowy threat of terror," as had residents of the implicitly nonwhite cities of "Detroit or Newark or Chicago," all sites of asymmetrical metropolitan development and, at various points, profound racial unrest. In their defense of a white heartland and its purportedly imperiled children, Gannon and other "mad as hell" Midwesterners helped shape the burgeoning national discourse on child safety in the eighties. Many observers lamented the sociocultural changes that had presumably undermined the safety of their communities and their young. In their understanding, bureaucratic bloat, libertine excess, and other products of big-state liberalism threatened Midwestern households and the "all-American" paperboys within them. The parents, politicians, and other actors who mobilized in response to the paperboy cases thereby positioned themselves as righteous, tax-paying, law-abiding silent-majoritarians united in defense of a certain way of life.[3]

The American Midwest supplied a fitting stage for this politics, especially amidst the nostalgia of the Reagan years. In the popular imagination, the Midwest has long functioned as America writ small, a region replete with white, heteronormative households in charming small towns set against a picturesque pastoral backdrop. Given Iowa's racial and ethnic homogeneity in the late twentieth century, this portrait contained a kernel of truth; racial and ethnic minorities comprised just 3.1 percent of the state's population in 1980. Test marketers have long flocked to the Midwest because of its reputation as "the most American region." They believe "that if a product will sell in Des Moines or Columbus," one historian writes, "it will sell anywhere." Most insidiously, the Midwest has served as "a floating signifier of progress, closure, whiteness, and the absence of violence."[4] Of course, this regional triumphalism belies the historical record. The American Midwest (like the country's other sections) has played host to massacres, ethnic cleansing, riots, lynchings, and other manifestations of racial and xenophobic animus. While scholars have ably chipped away at notions of Midwestern (and, more generally, northern) racial and historical innocence, others continue to champion the Midwest as a paragon of American egalitarianism, oftentimes by obscuring the region's diversity, urbanity, blight, and blemishes. In the wake of the Gosch and Martin disappearances, romanticized visions of the Midwest helped advance the trope of endangered white childhood and bolstered child safety efforts in the region and nationwide.[5]

Just as the Midwest operates in the political consciousness as a space of American goodness, the region also serves as the normative site of American childhood. Childhood innocence, as a historical construct, has hewn to familiar indicators of privilege along lines of race, class, and gender.[6] As white paperboys from middle-class Midwestern suburbs, Johnny Gosch and Eugene Martin epitomized boyhood innocence and vulnerability. Their disappearances symbolized not just physical losses but also the losses of innocence, childhood, whiteness, middle-classness, and midwesternness. Because Gosch and Martin represented "typical" American youth in media, political, and popular portrayals, their disappearances sanctioned new cultural and policy models for child protection in and beyond the Midwest.

This chapter tells the stories of Johnny Gosch, Eugene Martin, and two boys named Danny Joe Eberle and Christopher Walden, who vanished under similarly suspicious circumstances near Omaha, Nebraska, in 1983. Responses to these cases reified the narrow image of endangered childhood that had grown increasingly visible within the nationwide stranger danger panic. These regionally and racially grounded reactions helped authorize new mechanisms of child protection in the Midwest and augured the rise of a new legal and cultural child safety regime nationwide. For instance, the Johnny Gosch Bill, passed in Iowa in 1984, stipulated that law enforcement officials in the state could not observe a waiting period before investigating a report of a missing child. This law served as a precursor to the federal National Child Search Assistance Act of 1990, which required law enforcement agencies nationwide to immediately input information about missing children into the FBI's National Crime Information Center database. Johnny Gosch and Eugene Martin were also the first missing youths to appear on milk cartons, pioneers in a campaign through which several billion pictures of missing children were eventually distributed. The milk carton initiative and similar mechanisms fortified the visual architecture of endangered childhood—and, by extension, the national child safety regime.

"A SENSE OF PANIC"

Around six in the morning on Labor Day Sunday, 1982, Johnny Gosch and a fellow paperboy picked up their allotments of newspapers from the local United Methodist Church in West Des Moines. Gosch, a husky, freckled thirteen-year-old with a mop of light brown hair, departed the church with the other paperboy, and they diverged on their respective routes. Johnny's dachshund Gretchen walked beside him.

Soon after the boys left the church, "a man wearing a baseball cap and driving a dark blue car . . . asked both boys, in separate conversations" for directions to the same location. The other paperboy, "whose frightened mother asked that his name not be used" in newspaper accounts, saw Johnny speaking to a man near the intersection of Forty-second Street and Marcourt Lane. In the predawn darkness, the young carrier could not determine whether this was the same man who had asked Johnny and him for directions earlier. An adult neighbor corroborated the boy's version of events, confirming that, as the paperboys had, he too had provided directions to a man in a blue car. Witnesses disagreed on what happened

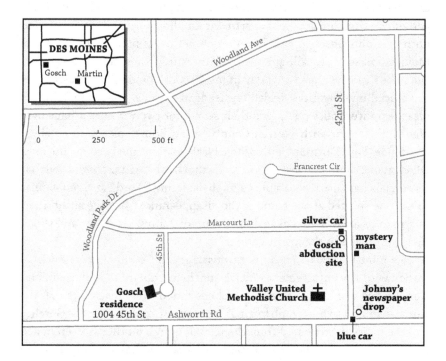

Figure 3.1 The Gosch abduction site. Map by Erin Greb Cartography.

next. Some insisted that a man followed Johnny around a street corner before snatching him. Others claimed they heard a car door slam and tires screech before watching a vehicle run a stop sign and travel northbound toward Interstate 235 "at a high rate of speed." In addition to the blue vehicle, another witness recalled seeing a silver Ford Fairmont around the time of the disappearance. For all of this eyewitness testimony, the presumed abduction generated little physical evidence. Gretchen the dachshund returned home, unscathed, without Johnny, and his father found the boy's wagon still full of newspapers two blocks from the family home.[7]

The Gosches initially applauded the law enforcement response to Johnny's disappearance. One newspaper report indicated that between twenty-five and thirty area law enforcement officials had searched for Johnny within a few hours of his disappearance. A television news segment stated that forty city police officers, Polk County sheriff's deputies, and state highway patrolmen had conducted similar surveys of the area on that Sunday. The following day—Labor Day Monday—Boy Scouts, sheriff's officials, other law enforcement authorities, and approximately one thousand volunteers scoured the area for Johnny's body or any clues that might lead to his recovery. The "[s]omber searchers," as the *Des Moines Register* characterized them, "anxiously" combed through "woods and parks, fields and ditches," vacant lots and apartment buildings—but ultimately found nothing. John Gosch, Johnny's father, nonetheless praised the West Des Moines police force, calling its work "fantastic." "They are working overtime like I've never seen anybody in my life work before," he attested. Yet the official investigation yielded few leads in the days following Johnny's disappearance. Police publicized their search for two vehicles: a "blue over blue" full-size car with Warren County, Iowa, license plates and a silver late-model Ford Fairmont with a large black stripe at the bottom. The Iowa Division of Criminal Investigation (DCI) shortly thereafter announced that its officials had discovered a photograph depicting a Ford Fairmont similar to the one spotted at the scene of the disappearance.[8] But the authorities' failure to locate either vehicle drew the ire of Johnny's parents and shook their confidence in the investigation.

One month after their son went missing, the Gosches expressed frustration with law enforcement officials for their inability to find what John Gosch called two "distinctive" automobiles and for their insistence that the Gosches submit to polygraph testing. The relationship between the Gosches and the police deteriorated from there, as Johnny's mother Noreen honed a harsh, "law and order" rhetorical mode that she has reconfigured and rearticulated since 1982. In October of that year, she called the office of Iowa governor Robert D. Ray and left a message with his administrative assistant. The secretary's handwritten note, which she presumably placed on the governor's desk after she finished speaking with Gosch, read: "There is a 'white-washing' job being done as far as what is being done [sic] . . . considering class action suit because of ways [the case is] being handled. Wants someone with 'clout' to demand their file [sic]." Noreen Gosch phoned Governor Ray at least once more in 1982 to cast aspersions on the police investigation. The Gosches' distrust of authority, coupled with their belief that "the police ha[d] reached a dead end," drove them to seek the assistance of private investigators.[9]

Johnny Gosch's disappearance made Iowa parents and children anxious. Just a few days after Johnny went missing, Noreen observed "how many mothers were stationed along the way, escorting their children home" from school. She claimed that Johnny's case had "created a sense of panic in people, and rightly so." This "sense of panic" revealed itself the weekend after Labor Day, as young paper carriers set out on their routes amidst drastically heightened security. Police established checkpoints around the site where Johnny had vanished, questioning motorists and looking out for any suspicious activity. Many parents accompanied their children as they delivered papers. The *Des Moines Register* kept tabs on its two thousand young carriers, conducting periodic checks on their routes and issuing emergency whistles to each of them. A local television report featured a spokesman from the paper who tried to reassure the public, and especially the families of young carriers, about the safety of the *Register*'s delivery program. "We're very, very concerned about creating some unnecessary panic amongst our carriers, and I hesitate to use the word 'panic,' but, uh, we don't want to unnecessarily scare a carrier." He continued: "Newspaper work traditionally has been a good learning experience for young people, and this is an unfortunate situation. It's the first [child carrier abduction] that I'm aware of in the Des Moines area." The spokesman aimed to restore community members' faith in not only the *Register* but also in the security of young carriers and their tradition of paper delivery. Gosch's presumed abduction was an aberration, he reminded viewers, one that did not warrant any "unnecessary panic."[10] Still, the attention that Johnny Gosch garnered in the state and nationwide suggested to many Iowans that his case was not peculiar but rather part of a national scourge about which they had previously been blissfully ignorant.

To address the "epidemic" of child kidnapping, the Gosches and other Iowa child safety activists hitched themselves to the national child protection campaign. Within two months of their son's disappearance, the Gosch family had established the Johnny Gosch Foundation, alternately called Help Find Johnny Gosch, Inc. Under the aegis of this organization, the Gosches penned letters to elected officials, raised funds to help pay for their private detectives, and hosted bimonthly group gatherings at their home. The couple also created an abduction awareness presentation, called "In Defense of Children," which they delivered hundreds of times across Iowa and the Midwest in the 1980s. With other bereaved parents and child protection advocates, Gosch and her husband found common cause. "I worked alongside John Walsh and some of the other families who were affected by this [issue]," Noreen Gosch recalled in a 2015 interview, to "increas[e] awareness to what is going on in our country concerning the safety of children." As John Walsh and other likeminded activists did, the Gosches regularly lobbed rhetorical "assaults on officialdom," as one *Des Moines Register* article put it. In so doing, they received "widespread media coverage, including [on] the *Phil Donahue Show*" and "angered more than a few people."[11]

Noreen Gosch also employed the figure of the "priceless child" when levying criticisms against the government. During a press conference and seminar held at Des Moines' Savery Hotel some two months after Johnny's disappearance, Noreen Gosch erroneously charged that investigators were required to observe a seventy-two-hour waiting period before pursuing cases of missing children, yet they could immediately search for lost or stolen property. Police would "generally" follow a lead on "a hunk of metal" without waiting, she complained, but not on a child who "is flesh and blood." In actuality, only some local agencies observed waiting periods following each report of a missing child, and no state or federal policies seemed to require police or sheriffs' departments to do so. Misleading statements like this one by Noreen Gosch saturated appeals for stricter child safety laws in the early 1980s. As two of the main architects of such appeals, John Walsh and Noreen Gosch helped foster a national conversation that led to the passage of the Missing Children and Missing Children's Assistance Acts (MCA and MCAA).[12]

While the activism undertaken in Iowa in the wake of Gosch's abduction helped propel the national child safety crusade, these local and statewide initiatives also reflected a distinctively white, Iowan, and Midwestern sense of loss. Johnny Gosch began to serve as a cautionary tale in Iowa, as observers perceived his apparent abduction to be a symptom of the ills seeping into the region. The boy became a base upon which adults taught youngsters about safety and a phantom upon which they projected their fears. "People don't want to believe that these things happen in little Iowa," lamented Candy Gilchrist, who had launched a Des Moines chapter of the national organization Child Find Inc. after Johnny went missing. The Gosch disappearance directly informed fingerprinting campaigns in

Iowa. A 1983 *Register* article, for instance, alluded to the Gosch case as it covered a fingerprinting drive in the college town of Ames. Hosted by the city's police department and the Iowa State University Air Force ROTC, the event successfully fingerprinted some five hundred area children. In March 1983, the small town of Conrad, Iowa, with a population of just 1,133, sponsored the fingerprinting of two hundred kids. A TV piece covering the Conrad fingerprinting initiative took the Gosch incident as evidence of the purportedly "rising number" of youth kidnappings, as well as the notion that such atrocities "can happen anywhere," even in a sleepy town like Conrad. Likewise, the Des Moines police department and the city's PTA council teamed up with local public and private schools in April 1983 "to provide a uniform identification system to assist law enforcement agencies in locating lost, missing, or abducted children." The fingerprinting program, dubbed KIDS ("Kids Identification and Description System"), was offered to approximately twenty-one thousand children enrolled in kindergarten through sixth grade in the Des Moines area. For its part, the *Des Moines Register* started a "carrier safety program" called Homes Offering a Protective Environment (HOPE) that was "designed to tell carriers and parents what they can do to prevent or respond to dangerous situations." The *Register* project designated certain homes as "safe spaces . . . where carriers can seek assistance."[13]

Both statewide and nationally, the Gosches worked to raise awareness about the issues of child kidnapping and exploitation, but on the grassroots level they organized primarily to bring their son home. Even a year after Johnny's disappearance, a local television news report noted, John and Noreen Gosch could still be seen "on any given night" at Des Moines–area shopping malls, grocery stores, or community events dispensing flyers imprinted with their child's face. To raise money to retain their private investigators, the couple sold candy bars, buttons, and raffle tickets for a miniature racecar. Others joined in, as well. Jeanne Wunn, a friend to the Gosch family, walked across Iowa to benefit the Help Find Johnny Gosch fund. In one TV news clip, she wore a "HELP FIND JOHNNY" trucker hat, slowly trudging along a deserted highway in the bleak mist, flanked by her two German shepherds and trailed by her husband in a rusty pickup truck. The pastoral scene evoked Iowa's agricultural tradition, and Wunn's trek across Iowa implied a kind of statewide unity in the wake of the Gosch disappearance. To solicit donations, Wunn sold her dog's puppies and named them after the places through which she passed. In each town in which the Wunns stopped, the couple circulated petitions and screened a documentary about missing children. The walk ultimately netted almost $5,000 for the Gosches' private investigators. Individuals who did not personally know the Gosches also volunteered in the search for Johnny and devoted their time to attend meetings, raise funds, disseminate flyers, and write letters.[14]

Such efforts, and the attitudinal shifts that had activated them, likely exacerbated Iowa children's anxieties about their own security. A 1983 survey of five hundred first, third, and fifth graders in Des Moines elementary schools documented the children's concerns about "[w]hat the future holds," "[d]eath and dying," and other, more mundane matters. Sixty-three percent of respondents "said they worry about the safety of their neighborhood." Local researcher and guidance counselor Jan Kuhl attributed this statistic to Gosch's disappearance and "the attention that case has received" in the press and around dinner tables across the state.[15]

Influenced by the Gosches' mobilization strategies, and in response to local anxieties, Iowa state legislators proposed and passed Senate File (SF) 517, also known as the Johnny Gosch Bill, in 1984. Noreen Gosch played a principal role in petitioning for and crafting the law, which established a legal typology of missing children and required law enforcement agencies to respond "as soon as practicable" to a report of a missing child. Advocates of the bill insisted that it would fortify the Iowa home against the dangers and perversions that ostensibly confronted it in the early to mid-1980s. One state senator diagnosed the "sick[ness]" that legislators sought to counteract with the bill's passage: "We live in a sick and rotten society that is getting sicker and rottener every day. I don't know what's happened to the United States, but it has become more animalistic, not more humanistic in recent years."[16]

Even as public officials helped to advance the Gosches' agenda, Noreen Gosch remained committed to attacking "officialdom." She identified police mismanagement of her son's case as the engine behind the Johnny Gosch Bill, and she whipped up support for her cause through populist pleas to ordinary Iowans. Some local authorities grew weary of her criticisms. In January 1983, the *Des Moines Register* published some scathing remarks delivered by West Des Moines police chief Orval Cooney. "I really don't give a damn what Noreen Gosch has to say," Cooney declared. "I really don't give a damn what she thinks. I'm interested in the boy and what we can do to find him. I'm kind of sick of her." These tensions erupted in a West Des Moines city council meeting held the day after Cooney's remarks appeared in the *Register*. During this meeting, attorneys representing the Gosches and Polk County aired their respective grievances concerning the Johnny Gosch investigation. Afterwards, both sides took the conversation outside. In the bitter January cold, Noreen Gosch entered into a heated exchange with the Polk County attorney. As the lawyer gesticulated, Noreen reprimanded him, "Don't shake your finger at me!" In subsequent letters sent to elected officials and in other writings, Noreen Gosch portrayed Cooney as an inept alcoholic, calling him a "known drunk" and the "town drunk," among other things.[17]

While Cooney and other officials may not have cared for Noreen Gosch's tactics or her tone, her advocacy struck a chord with everyday Iowans. In their correspondence with government officials, these Iowans took Johnny's case—and public servants' seeming inability to reckon with it—as an indictment of their state and an existential threat to their communities and children. They thus built on Noreen Gosch's affective labor, performed on behalf of her missing son. In a letter to Iowa governor Terry Branstad (who had taken office in early 1983), one Iowa mother expressed her disgust with governmental inaction on the matter of missing children. "My daughter Allyson and I attended a meeting last night on child safety," she told the governor. "The speaker was Noreen Gosch. What she said angered and shocked me. Our children are a very special gift and should be protected" through "greater involvement and interest by State and Federal employees." Shirley Frette from Story City told the governor how "fortunate" she was "to hear Mrs. Norene [sic] Gosch speak in our community about the statistics on this problem" of child abduction and molestation. She touted Noreen Gosch as "a Godsend" and found solace in the idea that "God is speaking through her to alert us of the growing operation of molesters and abductors." Frette excoriated public officials while demanding vigilante action: "I was amazed, shocked, and downright furious that this problem is being taken so lightly by the police force, FBI and government officials. . . . If our government officials won't take a stand on this issue then it is up to us, as parents, to protect the innocent victims, our children." Finally, Frette struggled to grasp whether tragedies like Gosch's occurred in tiny towns like her own. "I have never heard of any incidents of this nature in Story City. Could it possibly be that this never happens here? I doubt it." For Frette, the Gosch case had papered over the differences between suburbs like West Des Moines and small towns such as Story City, proving that no community was safe from child kidnappings. Carolyn Heuser from Manson also alerted the governor to the supposed ubiquity of the missing child problem. "I have one question which is really bothering me and I suppose many many other concerned parents and citizens [sic] of Iowa," she wrote. "'How can we make our laws stricter and punishment more severe on child abductors'? As you are well aware this is a very real and severe problem and getting worse all of the time. We are in a small community but very aware that we are not immuned [sic] to such crime."[18] Blaming "State and Federal employees," in part, for the problems of child abduction and exploitation, the authors of these missives bemoaned the declining fortunes of their state and its young inhabitants, while applauding Noreen Gosch's efforts "to protect the innocent victims, our children."

Such populist sentiments, which appeared time and again in Iowans' responses to the paperboy disappearances, derived significant power from the tropes of the imperiled white Midwestern boy, family, and home. In much the same way that Etan Patz had carried the requisite identity markers to garner substantial national attention, Gosch and Martin were both white, middle-class, suburban, Midwestern paperboys—all signifiers of innocence, comfort, vulnerability, and an "all-American" boyhood that Iowans hoped "to safeguard at all cost." As the *Chicago Tribune* explained in mid-1983, "By all accounts, Johnny was indeed the all-American boy." Johnny's father expressed much the same sentiment. "Paperboys symbolize the all-American boy," he told the *Tribune*. "I guess when this happens to these kids, it hits a little too close to home." For John Gosch, his son's status as an "all-American" paperboy made his disappearance all the more troubling. *Des Moines Register* editor James Gannon conveyed a similar idea in the pages of the *Tribune*. "This case sends home the message," he wrote, "that if you're not safe in West Des Moines in a nice neighborhood, you're not safe anywhere." For many observers, then, Johnny's abduction marked a fundamental shift in the lives of middle-class white children in places like West Des Moines.[19]

PERVERSION ON THE PLAINS

The panic that struck Iowans young and old in the 1980s also arrived on the Great Plains. Thirteen-year-old paperboy Danny Joe Eberle went missing in September 1983 while delivering the Sunday *Omaha World-Herald* in the suburb of Bellevue, Nebraska. Given the details of the Eberle disappearance, some reasonably speculated that his case was related to Gosch's. Herb Hawkins, a special agent who oversaw FBI operations in Iowa and Nebraska, thought Eberle might lead to a break in the Gosch investigation. "When I heard the boy [Eberle] was missing, the first thing I thought of was the Gosch case," Hawkins said. "The circumstances and the modus operandi were so close to the Gosch case. They were paper boys. Their looks were almost identical." Hawkins's emphasis on the boys' similar appearances suggested that he suspected a sexual motive such as pedophilia or hebephilia/ephebophilia (the adult attraction to adolescents). The print media also ruminated on the possibility of sexual abuse in these cases, although no evidence of molestation ever emerged to substantiate such claims. Two Iowa DCI agents assigned to the Gosch case joined the Eberle investigation to ascertain whether there was a connection between the two incidents, but no link ever materialized. Just days after Eberle vanished, a search party discovered his body in a ditch "some three miles from where he disappeared." The Eberle case caused four young *Des Moines Register* carriers, likely already shaken by the Gosch incident one year earlier, to quit their jobs. Twenty *Omaha World-Herald* paper carriers left their posts after Eberle's abduction and slaying. Murray, the *Register*'s circulation director, vowed to "step up" the newspaper's carrier safety initiative in the wake of the Eberle tragedy.[20]

The December 1983 kidnapping and slaying of another suburban Omaha boy, twelve-year-old Christopher Paul Walden, invited further comparisons to Gosch, although law enforcement officials denied any such linkage. Still, the *Register* took special interest in both Omaha incidents and underscored, as it had with the Gosch case, the middle-class and Midwestern serenity they had apparently shattered. "In less than three months," one article read, "13-year-old Danny Joe Eberle and 12-year-old Christopher Paul Walden were abducted from the streets of peaceful middle-class Omaha suburbs a few miles apart, and killed." A twenty-year-old US Air Force pilot named John Joubert was charged with and convicted of abducting and murdering Eberle and Walden, but authorities determined the airman had not been in Iowa in September 1982 when Gosch disappeared. Investigators never identified Joubert's motive for these slayings. While Joubert had forced the boys to disrobe before their executions, he claimed to have done so only for "the power and the domination and . . . the fear." Moreover, neither of the boys' bodies exhibited signs of sexual abuse. Although psychiatrists identified Joubert as a latent homosexual, he denied being pedophilic, ephebophilic, or gay and asserted that he had never had sex.[21]

While detectives rejected any relationship between the Gosch and Omaha episodes, ordinary Iowans and Nebraskans imagined them as interrelated incidents that challenged core assumptions about the Midwest's innocence and security. Indeed, Midwesterners interpreted these disappearances as assaults on their very communities. One Goldfield, Iowa, woman told the *Des Moines Register* that her son had previously delivered papers on Eberle's route. "I was angry and concerned at the abduction of Danny Eberle in Omaha," she explained in a letter published in the *Register*. "Needless to say, my family was deeply affected [by the incident] . . . there are so many parents, in Iowa alone, concerned with the problem." She went on to advocate for school programs "to inform our children and the public what they should do to avoid, prevent or reduce the risks they face as potential victims of abduction, molestation and other crimes committed against children." Likewise, staff members at Midlands Community Hospital in Papillion, Nebraska (near Omaha), devised a program "to provide advice to parents dealing with children's fears stemming from the killings of Christopher Paul Walden and Danny Joe Eberle." The lead nurse instructed parents "not to minimize their children's fear" because "[t]heir fears are realistic," despite the infrequency of such stranger kidnappings. Moreover, residents of tiny Carter Lake, Iowa—located along the Iowa–Nebraska border—had first proposed the creation of a youth "protection group" after Gosch vanished, and the Eberle and Walden incidents unleashed an additional "surge of public sentiment" in favor of such a "public patrol program." Gesturing to the Eberle and Walden abductions and slayings, one Carter Lake resident pledged, "We're just not going to stand by and let something like this happen in our community."[22]

Stranger danger fears also encroached upon the lives of Midwestern paperboys outside of Omaha and Des Moines. A Cedar Rapids TV news broadcast airing in October 1983, a month after authorities found Eberle's body, detailed an alleged encounter in Brighton, Iowa, between an eleven-year-old paperboy and a "strange man" in a green pickup truck. The man had reportedly tried to lure the young carrier into his vehicle, but the boy had darted away. While the eleven-year-old continued delivering papers, he admitted that he was "scared," especially when passing the area where he had purportedly encountered the man in the truck.[23]

The Eberle and Walden incidents reinforced two main tropes present in responses to the Gosch case: those of governmental incompetence and of idyllic Midwestern boyhood buffeted by "strange" men. Regarding the former, the Gosches used the Omaha cases to shore up their arguments against law enforcement ineptitude. According to Noreen Gosch, the FBI and local officials had moved far too slowly in their investigation of Johnny's disappearance but had sprung into action in Omaha, first, because of her advocacy; and, second, to make up for their failures in her son's case. "The amount of publicity my husband and I generated brought faster action to the boys in Bellevue," Noreen Gosch claimed in March 1984. "The city of Omaha has just suffered two terrible tragedies. In that case [sic], the police acted immediately. The FBI got involved right away. The reason there was such prompt action was because there had been a great many mistakes in our case. I look at that as progress—taking a bad situation and learning from it." Addressing these claims, a journalist for the Omaha World-Herald wrote that Noreen Gosch "says she was largely responsible for the swift response of law enforcement agencies to the kidnap-murders" in Nebraska, while a headline in Oelwein, Iowa's Daily Register declared, "Mrs. Gosch takes credit for fast police action" in the Omaha cases.[24]

FBI special agent Herb Hawkins dismissed the Gosches' contentions, insisting that the family's publicity tactics may have actually proven detrimental to their campaign. Federal investigators remained "tight-lipped" on the Gosch case, Hawkins maintained, to ensure "[t]he safety of the child." This approach jarred with the strategies endorsed by Noreen Gosch. For Hawkins, disclosing certain details about the case might cause Johnny's abductor or abductors to panic and, in haste, harm the boy. Hawkins also noted that "immediate publicity" in the Gosch kidnapping and in other missing child cases could complicate the investigative process. "It makes our job [ten] times more difficult," he told the *Omaha World-Herald.* "Law enforcement prefers no publicity in a case like this until all the leads have been totally exhausted and to give the abductor an opportunity to make contact with the parents." The FBI did appear to move more quickly in response to the Eberle and Walden cases, but Hawkins argued that this mobilization demonstrated the FBI's active and sustained interest in the Gosch affair. "I thought at that point," he remarked, "we could solve the Gosch case at the same time." To this end, even though the FBI "had no investigative jurisdiction . . . in the Gosch matter," the Bureau continued to assist in the search for young Johnny, collaborating and sharing resources "with the Gosches' Chicago-based private investigators."[25]

A second trope, a fixation on deviance (specifically regarding "strange" or "weird" men), recurred in rhetoric surrounding the Gosch, Eberle, and Walden cases. On the morning Johnny went missing, he had apparently told two witnesses about a suspicious man in a blue car. "That man is really weird," Johnny reportedly said. Another individual, referred to in newspaper reports as the "mystery man," phoned the Gosch parents on November 22, 1982, to inform them that "he gave Johnny a lift from Des Moines to Atlantic," a small town in Cass County, Iowa. Yet authorities soon determined that this "mystery man" had lied about giving Johnny a ride "because he said he felt sorry for the parents." In the early months of the investigation, furthermore, Noreen Gosch had implicated a religious cult in Johnny's kidnapping. She targeted a group called The Way International, which had allegedly mailed literature to the Gosches in the months before Johnny went missing. In Noreen's telling, The Way had triggered a slight personality change within Johnny, who became more of a contrarian in the week or so before his disappearance. The Way denied these charges and resented being called a "cult." One representative of The Way dismissed Noreen Gosch's accusations as "ridiculous" and emphasized the group's adherence to more conventional religious doctrine. "We're not a cult," the spokesman declared. "A cult conjures up thoughts of Jonestown, Charlie Manson, Hitler. . . . We believe that the Bible is where it's at."[26]

The theme of deviance appeared in Noreen Gosch's subsequent criticisms of pornography, child prostitution, and what she called "homosexual groups." In particular, Noreen claimed that unspecified "homosexual groups" had undertaken "a broad-based effort to embarrass her" in the mid-eighties. During a 1984 US Senate hearing, she set her sights on the North American Man/Boy Love Association (NAMBLA)—likely one of the "homosexual groups" to which she had referred—blaming the controversial organization for her son's disappearance. "Information . . . has surfaced during the investigation" into Johnny's presumed abduction "to indicate organized pedophilia operations in this country in which our son perhaps is a part of it [sic]," Noreen Gosch testified. Although the hearings focused on the "effect of pornography on women and children," broadly conceived, much of the witness testimony concentrated on child sex abuse, and media coverage of the proceedings fixated on "man/boy love." An ABC *World News Tonight* segment on these hearings devoted considerable time to NAMBLA and its putative role in the Gosch kidnapping. When asked to explain why she believed NAMBLA might have taken her son, Noreen Gosch pointed to instructional literature distributed within the organization, identified by ABC as one of several "clearinghouses for information on child pornography." Gosch included with her testimony an issue of NAMBLA's *Bulletin* that made several references to her son's disappearance. The publication urged Johnny Gosch to "PHONE HOME!" and encouraged all runaway youngsters to call the National Runaway Youth Hotline in order to "relieve anxiety at home and resolve the question about the conditions under which leaving occurred." The *Bulletin* also bristled at the idea that the public perceived NAMBLA to be "well informed" on the issue of runaway youths, calling this conception "both wrong and being used by the FBI against us." Indeed, the FBI had zeroed in on NAMBLA in the early phases of the stranger abduction panic, as the Patz case demonstrated. The "man/boy love" organization decried the "continuing efforts" of law enforcement "to blame boy-lovers for the disappearance of children, [and] to portray boy-lovers as bad guys and the police as good guys." NAMBLA representatives denied the group's participation in "*any* illegal activities including the production and dissemination of 'kiddie porn' or the transportation of minors across state lines for 'immoral purposes,' or indeed any . . . exploitative operations that may involve young people."[27]

For Noreen Gosch, NAMBLA's seeming refusal to cooperate with investigators focused on Johnny's case meant that the "boy-lovers" deserved scrutiny. Among "a great many other crude articles involving sex with men and boys," she advised, the *Bulletin* instructed NAMBLA "members not to submit to questioning regarding the disappearance, kidnaping of our son Johnny." US senator Arlen Specter (R–Pennsylvania) asked Gosch for clarification: "And in the course of that publication there is a suggestion that your son Johnny is in [NAMBLA's] custody?" Noreen Gosch did not respond directly to Senator Specter's question but alluded again to NAMBLA's noncompliance with the FBI. "They are vehemently opposing any type of questioning, so this did arouse our suspicion," she explained. "We have, through Senator [Charles] Grassley's [R–Iowa] of-fice and Senator [Roger] Jepsen's [R–Iowa] office, requested information from the FBI as to why they visited NAMBLA regarding our case. What was the reason to suspect them in the first place?" Noreen Gosch inquired. "We have not got [sic] that resolved as yet." In a prepared statement deliv-ered to the Senate, Gosch further underscored the problem of pedophilia. "When I was a child the major threat to children was 'POLIO' that has been changed it is no longer that disease [sic], we now have something new which is growing at an alarming rate in this country. The danger is 'PEDOPHILE's' [sic]." Many others involved in the child protection move-ment shared Noreen Gosch's understanding of abduction and pedophilia as "new" and demonstrative of liberationism gone awry. "I think that we must begin to realize," she exclaimed, "that we are living in a society in this country that has been programmed to believe: If it feels good, do it. If you want it, take it." For Gosch, such perversion and depravity jeopardized white, middle-class, Midwestern boyhood. "We lived in a nice quiet neigh-borhood," she recounted at the 1984 Senate hearing, "in which one would least expect this type of tragedy to occur."[28]

These discussions of deviance and nonconformity shed light on the broader sociocultural effects of the Gosch, Eberle, and Walden cases. One Omaha woman writing in 2002 conflated the three incidents and described the terror they inflicted on her Midwestern community. The Johnny Gosch disappearance, author Rainbow Rowell contended, had brought national concerns about stranger danger to the Midwest, while the Eberle and Walden tragedies delivered them directly to her doorstep: "Right here. In Bellevue." Her "parents clamped down tight" and forbade her from en-tering public restrooms alone. Fears of "white slavery," AIDS, nuclear hol-ocaust, and other threats, recalled Rowell, deprived Omaha youngsters of a part of their childhoods. Unsurprisingly, this collection of perceived threats centered on the sexual exploitation of minors and other innocents. "Omaha kids stopped feeling like kids that year," Rowell wrote. "We felt like prey. Scared all the time. Every car—or God forbid, van—that drove by us too slowly. . . . . Our nightly prayers filled up with new anxieties. [']Please God, protect me from kidnappers. And rapists. And people who put AIDS-infected needles in phone booth change slots. And if I am kidnapped and raised in another state, please help me to remember my real name and phone number, so that someday, after the kidnappers start to trust me, I can call 911.[']" For Rowell, neither her childhood nor her previously secure Midwestern environs could insulate her from the dangers that seemed to be gathering around her.[29]

The Martin abduction in 1984 further legitimated these tropes by supplying Iowans and Midwesterners with more evidence of a regional and national crisis—one that illustrated the failures of their civic and political institutions, the disorder unleashed by the sexual revolution, and the loss of white boyhood innocence.

"TERROR IN DES MOINES, OF ALL PLACES"

Eugene Wade Martin went missing on August 12, 1984, just days after Noreen Gosch testified before the US Senate, bringing further unwanted national attention to the Des Moines area. Like Johnny, the thirteen-year-old Martin—handsome, appearing both boyish and mature—had left his home to deliver the Sunday *Register* in the early morning hours and never returned. As in the Gosch case, witnesses shared conflicting accounts concerning "mystery" men who may have orchestrated Martin's abduction. One anonymous caller to the *Des Moines Register* claimed to have seen Martin standing alongside a man and "a 1972 or 1973 green Chevrolet Malibu with gray primer marks at Southwest Fourteenth Street and Highview Drive, where the youngster's papers were found." According to this witness, the unknown man "had his hands on Eugene." Others reported seeing a "clean-shaven mystery man" walking past Martin as he folded newspapers on the day he disappeared.

Right away, Iowans drew parallels between the Gosch and Martin incidents and wondered what they meant for their children, their communities, and their region. In a story on ABC's *World News Tonight*, Eugene's father Donald Martin brooded on camera. "I'm afraid of what I think now," Martin professed. "I think we got another deal like that poor Johnny Gosch setup." Noreen Gosch, in the same news segment, concurred, "They're disappearing rapidly. Our child, the Martin child . . . it's the same story repeated all over the country." The televised account also accentuated the distinctively Midwestern—and, by extension, "all-American"—context in which the snatchings had occurred. Standing before a row of boxy police cruisers in Des Moines, reporter Karen Burnes declared that "it's hit home this time. These are *Iowa's* paperboys." Back in the New York studio, anchor Peter Jennings introduced the story by waxing nostalgic about the craft of

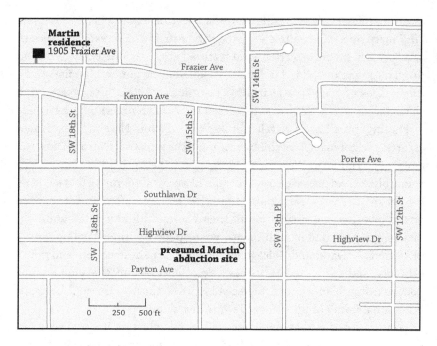

Figure 3.2 The Martin abduction site. Map by Erin Greb Cartography.

paper delivery: "It wasn't so long ago in this country that having your own newspaper route was part of the American dream. It's an early way to learn responsibility and earn a little pocket money at the same time. It has *not* been that way in Des Moines, Iowa."[30]

By casting the paperboy as an avatar of "the American dream," Jennings reified the symbolic power of white Midwestern boyhood innocence. Within Jennings's depiction and others like it resided particular assumptions about race, sex, gender, region, and class. Gosch and Martin were both white, middle-class, presumably asexual veering toward heterosexual, suburban, Midwestern paperboys, all descriptors that rendered them innocent and privileged in the popular imagination. They were "all-American" boys performing an "all-American" pastime, ripped from "all-American" environs by an insidious (perhaps queer) force that threatened "the normally safe-and-sane heartland of middle America."[31]

For *Register* editor Gannon, the Gosch and Martin disappearances had placed the white suburban Midwest in bad company with cities like "Detroit or Newark or Chicago," where unrest (at least to Gannon) seemed ordinary. News media coverage of crime and disorder in these and other cities surely shaped Gannon's thinking on the matter. Reportage on the 1967 Newark uprising, for example, had cast violence against children of color as normative and "predictable." On the cover of its July 28, 1967, issue, *LIFE* magazine referred to the "[s]hooting war in the streets" of Newark as a "predictable insurrection" and featured a picture of a twelve-year-old African American child, Joe Bass Jr., wounded by gunfire. Similarly stirring images of young blacks in 1967 Detroit and 1968 Chicago seemed to characterize violence as a core feature of the African American experience.

Photographer Enrico Natali captured armed white National Guardsmen escorting frightened black children through the streets of Detroit. Likewise, amidst the rubble in West Side Chicago after the April 1968 riots, a very young black child played on a guardsman's knee while donning that soldier's helmet. At the very least, these and other children of color watched the armed invasion and occupation of their communities by police and military forces. And, undoubtedly, many young people within these upheavals in Detroit, Newark, and Chicago witnessed death, destruction, and police brutality and intimidation.[32] These experiences—and the photographs documenting them—bore little resemblance to those of Gosch, Martin, or other inhabitants of the idealized white heartland.

Gannon worried that the white Midwest might lose its privileged position of safety and security. Indeed, national media outlets seized upon the paperboy cases as evidence of decline and disarray. "[T]he television networks and the national press are fascinated with an unlikely tale: terror

Figure 3.3 National Guardsmen escort children down the street during the 1967 Detroit uprising. Photograph by Enrico Natali. Courtesy of Enrico Natali.

in Des Moines, of all places," Gannon wrote. "We are on display, each one of us bit players in a drama that examines what's wrong in a place that's supposed to be so right." Because of this fact, Gannon insisted, "We should be mad as hell." His editorial posited a collective (white) Midwestern trauma engendered by the paperboy disappearances, and he identified an anticrime populism as the appropriate response. The apparent abductions, in this view, had undermined the key tenets of Midwestern identity. "I didn't move my family to Des Moines to live in fear behind locked doors," Gannon continued. "I do not cede the night to shadowy figures who hide by day. I do not accept the notion that my children's freedom of movement is a daytime right only. The sun should never set on freedom and personal security," rights Gannon associated with the American Midwest.[33]

This idea that new threats somehow faced white Midwestern children in the early to mid-1980s was ahistorical. Similar child abductions had occurred in Iowa in the fifties, sixties, and seventies. The abductions and murders of eight-year-old Jimmy Bremmers and twenty-one-month-old Donna Sue Davis in 1954 and 1955, respectively, ignited a sex panic in Sioux City, Iowa. In the wake of these tragedies, local authorities rounded up and institutionalized twenty gay men from Sioux City and surrounding areas. As other states did during this period, Iowa also passed a "sexual psychopath" law in early 1955 following the Bremmers murder.[34]

On Christmas Eve 1968, ten-year-old Pamela Powers was kidnapped from a Des Moines YMCA, raped, and murdered by Robert Anthony Williams, an African American fugitive from an area mental hospital. Police issued a warrant for Williams's arrest on the abduction charge, and he surrendered two days later in Davenport, approximately two-and-a-half hours east of Des Moines. As the authorities transported Williams back to Des Moines, he led them to Powers's body. Defense attorneys argued that the information provided by Williams during the car ride could not be admissible as evidence; the judge disagreed, and the jury at the subsequent trial found Williams guilty of first-degree murder. The Iowa Supreme Court upheld this decision, but the United States Supreme Court did not. In its 1977 *Brewer v. Williams* ruling, the US Supreme Court overturned Williams's conviction on the grounds that detectives had denied Williams his right to counsel, "used psychological coercion," and violated explicit instruction "not to interrogate Williams without his attorney present."[35] The slaying and the judicial wrangling it prompted generated substantial attention in the *Register* and elsewhere. However, the media focused primarily on the legal dimensions of the case, not on the broader threats the tragedy might have represented. Surprisingly, race received little attention in media coverage of the case.

Likewise, the 1973 disappearance of an eleven-year-old Boy Scout from Cedar Rapids named Guy Howard Heckle—Iowa's oldest active unsolved missing persons case—garnered significantly less press than those of Gosch and Martin. Even though Heckle vanished in a year of profound economic and political turmoil, his disappearance did not appear to alert Iowans to a larger national problem. Conversely, media treatments of Gosch's case referred to the boy as "a statistic, one of 150,000 children who disappear each year" in the United States, and a "unique statistic" at that: "the only Iowa child who is believed to have been abducted and who is still missing."[36]

Despite the historical antecedents of Bremmers, Davis, Powers, and Heckle, Iowans approved of Gannon's screed and used it as a rallying cry against a seemingly new assortment of threats. "The citizens of Des Moines and surrounding areas should be mad. We should be mad as hell," Scott B. Neff of Des Moines wrote in a letter to the *Register*, adopting Gannon's language. "This city and this geographical area are supposed to be comfortable, safe places to raise children, work and lead productive lives. This entire situation tarnishes every citizen in this community. Kidnappings, murders, rapes and this type of terrorism should be a call to arms and a call to anger for all law-abiding citizens." Neff saw the Gosch and Martin episodes as blemishes on the Midwest that ought to mobilize the region's residents to combat "this type of terrorism." Paul Jackson of Sioux City agreed. "Let us roll up our sleeves and go to work on crime prevention by biting the bullet now!" To this end, Jackson proposed a "constitutional amendment divesting criminal rights" and advocated the use of the "death penalty for certain crimes." (Iowa had outlawed capital punishment in 1965.) William Peterson from Iowa City also took the paperboy disappearances as a call to action and considered the implementation of citizens' anticrime initiatives to be an existential imperative. Peterson ordered his fellow Iowans to "[j]oin a neighborhood-watch program, or better yet, start one. This has been going on in some neighborhoods as a method of survival in Des Moines for years. Now the whole city needs to watch. We all can and should take more responsibility to protect our children."[37]

Amidst this growing concern for child safety, Iowa governor Branstad convened a conference in November 1984 called "Children in Jeopardy," billed as "the only gathering of its kind in the nation." Many of the state's top policymakers attended the convention, one article indicated, "to defuse some land mines that threaten to explode the notion that Iowa is a safe place for children." By arranging the event, one newspaper story noted, Branstad hoped to demonstrate that "the state might be ready to get tough" on crimes against children. Attendees of the conference pressed for stricter background checks for those who worked with young Iowans, as well as harsher penalties for child molesters. Conference organizers also stressed the importance of developing a "public and a private partnership" between business and government. This "partnership" could be seen in the milk carton campaign spurred by the paperboy incidents and in corporate programs dedicated to "keeping children safe" from abduction, molestation, and general corruption. With President Reagan's support, these kinds of initiatives would flourish nationwide in the mid-1980s, bringing increasing visibility to the stranger danger panic and its attendant imagery of endangered childhood.[38]

While Gannon, Branstad, and other Iowans embraced anger and developed new programs in an attempt to assuage fear, others resigned themselves to the "sick society" that the paperboy disappearances supposedly evidenced. One *Des Moines Register* article published shortly after Martin's disappearance outlined the various steps Iowa parents took to shield their kids from an increasingly dangerous world. "Is there such a thing as being over-protective?" the *Register* story asked before profiling parents who had removed their children from their newspaper routes and others who had begun closely monitoring their children as they played in the neighborhood. "One mother," the article read, "said she doesn't let her pre-teen daughter walk behind her when shopping in a mall," lest an abductor snatch the child behind her back. In a November 1984 poll of 602 Iowa adults, two-thirds of respondents agreed that young Iowans were "less safe today than they were five years ago," before the Gosch and Martin disappearances. Eighty-six percent of parents surveyed said that they were "more strict and cautious in the supervision of their own children as a result of the [Gosch and Martin] kidnappings" and other cases of child exploitation. Another *Des Moines Register* story detected a "climate of fear" enveloping West Des Moines, Johnny Gosch's hometown. "The mood of uneasiness shows itself in several ways," the article explained. "Many children are no longer allowed to walk to school alone. . . . Several neighborhoods have started procedures to 'track' neighborhood children as they play at different homes. . . . Children who were once warned against trusting strangers are now drilled on the subject by parents who stage examples of how strangers might try to get children into a car." For many Iowans, these developments signified a statewide crisis of childhood and parenthood. One mother told the *Register* that her "three young boys . . . are being deprived of their youth," while a letter-writer from Milford called the disappearances "a blight on the state of Iowa . . . a utopia for murderers and kidnappers because it will not impose the death penalty for these crimes." For Karl Schilling of Des Moines, the city's inhabitants should "show the country" that they "are concerned for one another." Roger Corbin of Traer wrote the *Register* "only because of the need I feel to say and/or do something about the shameful problems we have with missing children here in Iowa. I'm sure this problem exists in other areas as well, but it tugs at the heart more here when it hits close to home."[39]

The Martin disappearance hit particularly close to home for Iowa's young paper carriers. A 1984 national television news segment on ABC spotlighted the fears shared among the state's paperboys and girls while portraying their craft as both idealized and endangered. In the field, reporter Karen Burnes praised the newspaper carriers who kept their routes and now delivered papers in pairs. She called them "reliable as always" but explained that the "[f]ear of kidnapping is so deeply etched in this community now that some will not even allow their faces to be photographed." The next shot showed only the back of an adolescent, clad in a ball cap and hooded sweatshirt, in conversation with Burnes. That he opted to remain anonymous suggests that he feared reprisal for speaking out. In the interview, the paperboy tried to grapple with the enormity of the situation: "This has happened twice now, and [it] could happen again, so . . ." He trailed off, seemingly unable to make sense of the threats facing him and his peers. Next, Burnes interviewed an even younger paperboy who agreed to show his face on camera. His bright blond locks and summer tan made him the picture of white Midwestern boyhood innocence, yet he trembled imagining the horrors he might endure as an abductee. "Oh, I don't know what I'd do if somebody kidnapped me because it'd be kinda scary 'cause they might kill me or take me away and then brainwash me or something. I'd never see my family again."[40] For this paperboy, the mysterious circumstances surrounding the Gosch and Martin disappearances aroused dread and confusion, since the threat was simultaneously palpable and abstract.

Still others understood this threat as a sexual (and an implicitly homosexual) one, demonstrative of a national sickness now infecting Iowa's suburbs. "Another child has been snatched from our streets," Irish Cowell from Sioux City exclaimed. "Why? We are obsessed with sex! Nothing pinpoints its vulgarities and sadist pleasure more than the porno material. Our children have become victims of untold horrors for the explicit purpose of bringing joy to those who receive their monthly publication." Cowell echoed Noreen Gosch's hypothesis that pornography precipitated Johnny's abduction. Carolyn Keown from Des Moines blamed not only pornography and perversion but also religious cults for the moral depravity supposedly gripping the country. "As a parent, I raise my 15-year-old to believe that the world is a good and just place. Now it makes you wonder if it is still good and safe," Keown wrote. "You could never have told me when I was 15 years

old that people are like they are now. So many just don't care for one another. There are so many wicked, perverted people. So many religious cults.
So much hatred for each other. So much pornography involving children."
Larry Riley from Perry, Iowa, concurred: "This is one sick country. Our
morals and spiritual values are practically non-existent. When are tougher
laws going to be made for the crime of child molesting?" Even though no
definitive evidence ever emerged linking child pornographers, pimps, or
predators to the Gosch and Martin disappearances, the notion that both
paperboys fell into a seedy underworld of child prostitution remained
plausible to many Iowans. Many observers have seemed unwilling to consider that the boys simply ran away, or that one or more locals stalked,
abducted, and possibly murdered them. To that end, alleged sightings of
both paperboys were reported throughout the United States, particularly
in the South and Southwest. Perhaps by transferring blame onto a face-
less monster like a child prostitution ring or a religious cult operating outside the Midwest, Iowans could absolve their communities, their state, and
their region.[41]

These anxieties traveled all the way to the Oval Office. President Reagan,
himself a Midwesterner who had spent much of his twenties in Iowa,
folded the Gosch and Martin tragedies into his rhetorical appeals to family,
law and order, and a white Midwestern triumphalism. Soon after Eugene
Martin went missing, Reagan phoned *Register* editor James Gannon to
extend his "regrets and sympathies" and assure Gannon that he would
help bring "nationwide attention" to the child safety cause. "Thank God,"
Noreen Gosch rejoiced in response to Reagan's phone call. "Thank God they
recognize that our kids are in danger." At a campaign stop in Cedar Rapids
the following month, Reagan situated the Gosch and Martin cases within
a romanticized rendering of Iowa's past, one that ignored Indian removal,
racial segregation and violence, nativist demagoguery, and other pernicious phenomena. "[T]his was open prairie," Reagan bellowed. "And then
the pioneers began to settle here: Yankees, Germans, Swedes, Norwegians,
and immigrants from many other nations—men and women as hardy as
the land. They ploughed the sod, they planted crops, they dotted the land
with farmhouses and built lovely towns like Cedar Rapids. And soon, Iowa
contained some of the richest farmland in history, feeding tens of millions
in America and around the world." Reagan then tied this reading of Iowa's
history to his vision for 1980s America. "As our economy grows, we'll need
to go forward with the bedrock values that sustained the first Iowa settlers
and that nourish us today. And they're the simple values of faith, family,
neighborhood, and good, hard work. And we're already making a good
start." To foster these values, the president insisted, "We must continue

cracking down on crime. We say with no hesitation, yes, there are such things as right and wrong. And yes, for hardened criminals preying on our society, punishment must be swift and sure."[42] Here Reagan vowed to get "tough on crime" and rejected the culture of permissiveness that had, in his formulation, enabled criminal predation.

This scourge of crime had also gripped Iowa, Reagan explained. "There've been two tragedies in Iowa that have saddened us all," he reminded the crowd. "In 1982, young Johnny Gosch disappeared while delivering newspapers on his morning route in Des Moines. Then, just [six] weeks ago, another newspaper boy, Eugene Martin, also disappeared." The president then reassured his audience:

> Well, I want you to know that I've spoken with Jim Gannon, the editor of the *Des Moines Register*. We've pledged our full support in the search for these two boys. And this past June, we established the National Center for Missing and Exploited Children in Washington [DC] to help locate missing children across America. So far, the Center has received thousands of telephone calls and helped hundreds of parents. Nancy and I join all of you, I'm sure, in praying for the safe return of Johnny and Eugene. And I pledge to you that none of us will rest until

Figure 3.4 President Ronald Reagan addresses his audience during a 1984 campaign stop at the Cedar Rapids airport. In his remarks, Reagan lamented the disappearances of Johnny Gosch and Eugene Martin and vowed to help bring the paperboys home. Courtesy of the Ronald W. Reagan Presidential Library, Simi Valley, California.

the streets in Iowa and throughout this nation are once again safe, particularly for our children.

Reagan juxtaposed Iowa's rich, white-settled farmland with its crime-infested "streets" and extolled the virtues ascribed to the state's pastoral tradition. While he encouraged Americans "to go forward with the bedrock values that sustained the first Iowa settlers," he actually advocated a return to that fictive "open prairie" undergirded by "faith, family, neighborhood, and good, hard work."[43]

This pining for a fictive Midwestern golden age propelled the milk carton campaign. First imprinted with images of and information about Gosch and Martin, milk cartons soon delivered to millions of American households the names, faces, and descriptions of dozens of missing children. In so doing, these cartons not only became a "cultural shorthand" for a seemingly pervasive social problem; they also served as a clarion call for a certain sort of justice and the preservation of childhood innocence. As perhaps the most recognizable example of late twentieth-century endangered child imagery, the "milk carton kid" simultaneously demanded punishment for perverts and the restoration of childhood as it supposedly once existed. In the late twentieth-century crusade to keep kids safe from moral harm, the milk carton project supplied both a logistical blueprint (raising "awareness" about a threat purportedly facing all young Americans) and an affective, effective tool for the circulation of "emotionally resonant child-centered" images. These same strategies would be replicated in state and federal legislation memorializing abducted and/or slain photogenic white children like Jacob Wetterling, Adam Walsh, Megan Kanka, and Polly Klaas. The milk carton campaign, therefore, helped authorize new legal and cultural mechanisms—awash in the imagery of endangered childhood—designed to safeguard young people and to more severely punish those who might hurt them.[44]

MILKING IT

Des Moines' own Anderson Erickson Dairy launched the milk carton campaign soon after Eugene Martin went missing. The dairy took cues from local private sector efforts to publicize news of the paperboy disappearances and to plead for public assistance in bringing the boys home. Such projects included advertisements in the *Register* and the placement of Gosch's and Martin's portraits on the sides of eighteen-wheelers, alongside a reward for information leading to the boys' recovery. (Commercial truckers had disseminated information related to the Gosch case before Martin disappeared.) Anderson Erickson began producing milk cartons with Gosch's and Martin's faces on them in September 1984. The following week Prairie Farms Dairy, also headquartered in Des Moines, started doing the same on the side panels of its milk cartons. In conceptualizing, producing, and distributing these milk cartons, Midwestern dairies gave families a way to discuss the plight of missing youths and to establish guidelines to ensure their children's safety while seated around the kitchen table. The program thereby connected the American home, and the supposedly imperiled child inside it, with the bucolic Midwestern landscape from which the milk inside the cartons had come.[45]

Despite the compelling, regionally specific symbolism embedded in their milk carton programs, Anderson Erickson and Prairie Farms initially garnered little publicity in Iowa or anywhere else. They did, however, set the foundation for similar, more popular milk carton drives overseen by larger dairies and underwritten by national child safety organizations. After coming across a milk carton adorned with pictures of Gosch and Martin in late 1984, Walter Woodbury, the vice president and general manager of Hawthorn Mellody dairy, decided to follow suit. Woodbury approached the Chicago police department with a proposal to implement the milk carton program in the Chicago metropolitan area. The press took notice, likely because Hawthorn Mellody was a sizable milk processor that distributed some two million milk cartons throughout Chicago each month, while also delivering dairy products to markets in Iowa, Wisconsin, Indiana, and other parts of Illinois.[46]

The campaign generated publicity and momentum in late 1984 and 1985 and scored a major victory by helping to reunite a missing California teenager with her family. After running away from her Lancaster, California, home in November 1984, thirteen-year-old Doria Paige Yarbrough was staying with friends about two hundred miles away in Fresno. While watching the television news with her friends, Yarbrough learned that she would be featured on the side panels of milk cartons distributed by Alta Dena, a southern California dairy. With her friends encouraging her to return home, Yarbrough phoned her parents and reunited with them the next day. Not only did Yarbrough's feel-good story probably introduce many Americans to the tactic of placing missing kids' photographs on milk cartons; it also spoke to the supposed efficacy of the campaign. Just days after young Doria returned home, the National Child Safety Council (NCSC) announced that it would standardize the milk carton initiative by supplying milk distributors with twelve side-panel templates, each spotlighting two

Figure 3.5 Photographs of Johnny Gosch and Eugene Martin on the side of a milk carton. Richard R. Kerr, "Processors Unite to Help Children" *Dairy Field* (April 1985): 46–53. Courtesy of *Dairy Field*, BNP Media.

lost children for a total of twenty-four kids. Every month or so, NCSC would draft new templates featuring additional missing children and send them to participating dairies. At the time of NCSC's announcement on January 28, 1985, over one hundred dairies had agreed to take part in the program. The US Department of Justice (DOJ) expressed its support for the NCSC initiative. "From our point of view," the head of the DOJ's missing child project declared in a statement, "one of the benefits of using milk cartons is their short shelf life," which "enables the changing of photos as the children are found and the rotation of the pictures and identity information used."[47]

Yet for all its seeming successes, the milk carton campaign as construed by NCSC perpetuated the mythology of stranger danger. By only featuring children believed to have been "criminally abducted," a term that conjured stranger kidnappings, the NCSC program obscured two key facts: first, runaways comprise the overwhelming majority of missing children; and second, parental and acquaintance kidnappings constitute the clear majority of child abduction cases. Indeed, some of the cartons distributed in schools bore messages that read: "Never go with strangers" and "Report to your parents or a trusted adult at once: Any stranger who tries to lure you away with gifts like money, toys or pets."[48] The milk carton drive thereby distorted the nature of threats to young people.

The mid-1980s represented the apogee of the child safety crusade, a moment in which the news media seemed to legitimate any mechanism that might help recover lost or abducted youths. "[N]ow that the cause of missing children is a national campaign," one February 1985 CBS *Evening News* story detailed, "finding children . . . is no longer being left to chance." In CBS's New York City studios, Dan Rather credited innovative plans like the milk carton initiative with boosting the number of tips received by investigators in missing child cases. "[M]ore than luck," he affirmed, "is involved in the estimated 50 percent increase in reported sightings of missing children around the nation over the past three weeks." That uptick tracked neatly with the nationwide rollout of the milk carton campaign orchestrated by the NCSC. At the time this news story aired, over seven hundred of the nation's 1,800 dairies had agreed to participate in the program.[49]

By 1987, the number of dairies enrolled in the milk carton campaign had dropped considerably, partially due to concerns about frightening kids and partially due to the campaign's inefficacy. Two years after NCSC had formalized the practice of placing missing children's faces on milk cartons, some three to five billion of such cartons had been distributed, but only a handful of young people had been recovered as a result. Moreover, apparently none of these children had been abducted by strangers; they had either fallen victim to parental or familial kidnapping, or they had run away from home. Other publicity tools were actually more effective in bringing missing children home. In early 1987, news reports credited public service announcements, grocery store displays, and other instruments with returning some 109 children over the preceding two-and-a-half years.[50]

But even though it was short-lived, the milk carton initiative, as a cultural product, has proven more durable than any other child safety mechanism. Publicity efforts like ADVO's "Have You Seen Me?" project have enjoyed much longer shelf lives than the milk carton program. Launched in 1985 and still ongoing, "Have You Seen Me?" mails leaflets with missing children's faces on them to over one hundred million American homes weekly.[51] Still, by the time milk distributors had discontinued the practice of putting missing kids' pictures on their milk cartons, the trope had already secured its place in the cultural vernacular. Airing in 1985, the year in which the milk carton program first attained serious national exposure, an episode of the NBC sitcom *Punky Brewster* used a missing child on a milk carton to drive its main storyline.[52] By the early nineties, the milk carton kid had appeared in a variety of popular texts—the 1987 teen vampire film *The Lost Boys*; the 1988 Tom Hanks vehicle *Big*; the 1989 family movie *Honey, I Shrunk the Kids*; a 1993 episode of *The Simpsons*; and Caroline Cooney's young adult novel *The Face on the Milk Carton*, published in 1990.[53]

As the late twentieth-century culture wars blurred the line between the cultural and the political, the milk carton campaign represented a piece of visual culture that directly addressed political concerns. This twinned role was on display in the run-up to the 1988 Iowa Democratic caucuses. At a January debate in Des Moines, Democratic presidential candidate and former Arizona governor Bruce Babbitt invoked the program to comment on Senator Al Gore's (D–Tennessee) two-month absence from the Hawkeye State. "Al, it's good to see you back [in Iowa]," Babbitt remarked. "You know, I thought they might start putting your picture on milk cartons." While the crowd and Babbitt's fellow presidential hopefuls took the joke in stride, the quip "brought protests from the parents of missing children," one ABC *World News Tonight* story reported. Noreen Gosch expressed her disgust. "I think it's in bad taste," she chided. "Why should he make fun of it? To us, it's a big deal." Babbitt apologized to Gosch and called his jab "an inappropriate statement." His disavowal of a seemingly innocuous joke demonstrated the near unassailability of the child safety cause and its associated imagery.[54]

As the trope of the missing child on the milk carton, and more generally the image of endangered childhood, accrued cultural capital throughout the late 1980s and into the 1990s, they helped to formalize a new kind of legal-cultural instrument that would publicize the stranger danger threat. The visibility and allure of milk carton kids—in pop culture, in private sector promotions, and on breakfast tables—provided a foundation for likeminded projects vital to the development of the carceral state. Activists generated new tools to publicize the missing child cause, from the ubiquitous "Have You Seen Me?" leaflets, to the Code Adam campaign and the Justice Department's AMBER Alert initiative.[55] Through their use of children's photographs, these efforts have articulated a potent message about lost childhood innocence and the need to protect American youths from specific moral threats.

"TENUOUS IN A TIME OF CHANGE"

The unsolved Gosch and Martin cases continue to loom large in the minds of many Iowans. As one outside observer indicated, the disappearances belonged within a series of tribulations that left Iowans "tenuous in a time of change." Before the early 1980s, this commentator noted in the pages of the *Des Moines Register*, "Iowans were relaxed in a rural atmosphere where doors could be left open, keys left in the ignition and kids left out to play on the lawn. Problems could be isolated, defined, confronted and solved. Then corporations began to buy out family farms, debts exploded and newspaper boys began to disappear." Because the Gosch and Martin tragedies marked moments of Midwestern misery, on par with a devastating farm crisis, they continue to serve as reliable regional reference points in the twenty-first century. Parties on either side of the death penalty debate in Iowa still leverage the boys' names. Noreen Gosch remains a champion of child protection and a mentor to those who have suffered similar unspeakable losses. After their daughter Elizabeth was kidnapped and murdered in 2012, Iowans Heather and Drew Collins began "crusading for quicker community notification when children disappear" and broadcasting their "concerns over sex offenders who have shirked their registration requirements." Gosch consoled the Collinses in ways that only a bereaved parent could.[56]

Theories regarding Gosch and Martin still abound. In 1991 Noreen Gosch went public with information supplied by a private investigator regarding a "child-sex ring of four men" that had "planned and carried out the abduction of her son." At the time, it was thought that those men might have also been "involved in other abductions, including Martin's and the October 1989 kidnapping of Jacob Wetterling in St. Joseph, Minn." (The Wetterling case was officially solved in 2016; the boy had been abducted, sexually assaulted, and murdered by a local resident.) Conspiracy theories regarding Gosch have flourished online since the 1990s. A quick Internet search turns up myriad websites on which skeptics implicate the government—especially the George H. W. Bush administration—in an organized child prostitution syndicate, based at an Omaha credit union, which had allegedly stolen Johnny.[57]

In one way or another, Gosch and Martin mean something to Iowa's children and adults. Fully 99 percent of Iowans polled in 1984 said they had "read or heard about" Johnny Gosch and Eugene Martin. Decades later, the cases remain tangled up with Iowans' conceptions of crime, security, childhood, and region. For many, 1982 and 1984 brought two separate yet interconnected tragedies through which the state, the region, and its children lost at least a modicum of their innocence. In 2012 Frank Santiago, the main *Register* journalist assigned to the Gosch case, meditated on its significance. "We're talking about the early 1980s," he explained. "Kids were out playing in the dark. Their moms let them go to school unescorted. This was a part of Americana for a long, long time, and it's gone, and it started with those two stories." A Des Moines television reporter provided a similar assessment of Iowa exceptionalism in 2012. "I think people thought, 'I can't believe this could happen here.' I mean, this kind of stuff doesn't happen here."[58]

In the Gosch, Eberle, Walden, and Martin cases, white Midwesterners found evidence of regional, racial, and national decline. In response, they took steps to keep their kids safe and to reclaim the idealized rural and suburban spaces these children inhabited. Developments in Iowa and Nebraska—from laws like the Johnny Gosch Bill, to public fingerprinting programs, to private sector initiatives such as the milk carton campaign, to a growing sense of fear and resentment among parents and children— intersected with processes unfolding nationwide in the early to mid-1980s. Together, these phenomena fed a festering stranger danger panic and formed the contours of a new child safety regime, one that emphasized the moral threats facing American children and privileged heightened vigilance and punishment as the means by which to mitigate those threats.

PART II

———⌇———

"The Battle for Child Safety"

CHAPTER 4

๛

"Great Surface Appeal"

The Department of Justice and the Affective Politics of Child Safety

Less than two months after the gruesome discovery of their son's severed head, John and Revé Walsh testified before the US Senate and laid responsibility for Adam's death at the feet of federal justice officials. "We have been classified in the papers and by many people and [in] interviews with [our] friends as an 'all American family,'" the Walshes' prepared statement read. "I don't know what that means, but I do know that prior to this incident with Adam we were great believers in the United States of America. I have traveled throughout the world and seen the misery that people who live in other countries exist [in] and under the oppression that many of them labor. My beliefs in this [American] system have been shaken to the core." For the Walshes, the fiction that "the FBI comes in immediately . . . when a small child is missing" jarred with the "grim reality." "In most cases the individuals get no support or help whatsoever and return to their homes emotionally and financially devastated," the Walshes explained. "In most cases, the child is either never found alive or dead." In light of these circumstances, John and Revé petitioned for "a centralized system" through which to report missing children and also for swift FBI assistance "whenever possible" in cases of lost or abducted youths. These demands, John and Revé wrote, were "not too much to ask of this 'great society'"—a jab at Lyndon Baines Johnson's ambitious suite of domestic programs.[1]

Criticism of governmental inaction or ineptitude on matters of child safety underpinned the missing child scare. Frequently articulated through a receptive news media, the claims of aggrieved parents like the Walshes, and those of interested politicians and other advocates, pushed Congress to pass the Missing Children and Missing Children's Assistance Acts (MCA and MCAA). But the US Department of Justice (DOJ), and specifically the FBI, at first obstructed child safety advocates and their campaign for the MCA. DOJ and FBI officials expressed particular opposition to the MCA in its Senate form (S. 1701), because it "could inundate the FBI with missing children cases." The DOJ leadership recognized the affective capital of child safety, calling it, among other things, an issue with "great surface appeal." These leaders also understood child disappearances as matters to be handled at the city, county, and state levels, and they considered the MCA, as construed in S. 1701, to be poor and potentially counterproductive policy. DOJ officials most strongly objected to the MCA's proposed "parental access provision," which "would require the FBI to acquire, collect, and classify information concerning a missing person directly from that individual's parent, legal guardian, or next of kin."[2]

DOJ opposition to the MCA played into the hands of child safety activists, who framed federal resistance as evidence of governmental incompetence or callousness. In turn, Justice Department officials sought to temper their position and neutralize the sentimental rhetoric deployed in service of the child protection cause. Ultimately, though, their stance proved untenable, and their front collapsed under political pressure from child safety crusaders, the news media, and the Reagan administration. In October 1982, Congress passed a version of the MCA that was more agreeable to the DOJ, but one that nonetheless forced "FBI field offices to confirm the existence of a missing person record in NCIC [the National Crime Information Center database] when requested by a parent, legal guardian or next of kin." The bill also required the FBI to enter missing children's information into NCIC when "local police refuse to cooperate with a parent or guardian." Passage of the MCA also effectively silenced the DOJ's objections. In the words of US senator Paula Hawkins (R–Florida), one of the most vocal proponents of the missing children movement, the law brought the Justice Department "in line with the priorities" of the Reagan administration: "family, home, neighborhood, peace, and freedom." The DOJ and FBI thus began "taking actions to address and remedy . . . concerns" about their handling of missing child cases.[3]

Accordingly, the DOJ transitioned from a body skeptical of the child safety campaign to the federal department most deeply invested in its success. Since 1982 the Justice Department has worked to define, publicize, and combat issues of child abduction and exploitation. Through these efforts, it has advanced many of the Reagan administration's central themes, principally those of "family values" and "law and order." Just two years after the DOJ's unsuccessful obstruction of the MCA came the passage of the MCAA, which created a national clearinghouse for lost and imperiled children. The National Center for Missing and Exploited Children (NCMEC)—which formally sits outside the aegis of the federal government but is mainly funded by the DOJ—remains a vital instrument through which activists and public officials address issues related to child safety. Under the leadership of US attorney general Edwin Meese III and Office of Juvenile Justice and Delinquency Prevention (OJJDP) administrator Alfred S. Regnery especially, the DOJ endorsed the "traditional" family as an antidote to child abduction and exploitation. Meese railed against the corruptive power of smut, often conflating child pornography with legal, consensual, adult porn. He presided over the US Attorney General's Commission on Pornography and approved its findings, detailed in a 1986 publication colloquially known as the Meese Report.[4]

The DOJ's shift in posture followed the rise of an affective brand of child safety politics on the national stage. As bereaved parents like John Walsh and Noreen Gosch refined a vigilantist rhetorical mode, they reserved special opprobrium for the Justice Department and FBI. These crusaders protested the fact that there was no federal database devoted specifically to "missing children," especially given the existence of FBI databases inventorying lost or stolen items like automobiles or boats. That the FBI maintained both an "unidentified dead persons" and a "missing persons" database mattered little. For these activists, federal justice officials privileged inanimate objects over the most vulnerable Americans and therefore exposed, in the words of John and Revé Walsh, that "the priorities of this great country are in some disorder."[5] By deftly marshaling the image of endangered childhood, child safety activists drew the DOJ and FBI into an indefensible position against the "best interests" of young Americans. Their language reflected the neoliberal economic terms on which the child safety campaign operated, with regular references to the "worth," "value," and "pricelessness" of certain children.

Discounting DOJ objections to the MCA, those petitioning the state on behalf of missing children shaped the national conversation on child safety. Their politicking led not only to the passage of the MCA and MCAA—and the DOJ's "conversion"—but also to the development of a broader legal regime targeting those who kidnap, molest, or otherwise harm American youths. The DOJ has helped to institute and enforce various mechanisms, oftentimes named for child-victims, which concentrate on the "moral threats" ostensibly posed by strangers.[6] Authored and/or authorized by the DOJ, laws memorializing Jacob Wetterling, Megan Kanka, Amber Hagerman, Adam Walsh, and other youths abducted, assaulted, or slain by strangers have worked to preserve childhood "innocence," generally understood as sexual "purity."

The affective politics of child safety rendered the MCA commonsensical and unquestionable, while portraying DOJ and FBI officials as indifferent to the protection of young Americans. Cognizant of the political capital wielded by missing children crusaders, DOJ leaders aimed to communicate their opposition to the MCA while sympathizing with grieving families. Yet the failure of this approach drove the DOJ and FBI to assume positions more receptive and responsive to child safety issues. This shift brought the Justice Department "in line" with the Reagan administration's "family values" and "law and order" politics. In this way, the shift mirrored DOJ action on civil rights; by the early eighties, the Department had begun to pursue the president's antibusing and anti-affirmative-action agendas.[7] The alignment between the Reagan administration and its DOJ on child safety enabled the construction of a legal-cultural regime that has entrusted the Justice Department with safeguarding American youths from moral threats like kidnapping, molestation, exploitation, online predation, and pornography. The affective politics of childhood sanctioned this regime and rendered it virtually uncontestable.

THE PRICELESS CHILD

In the late seventies and eighties, child safety crusaders excoriated the government for its perceived disinterest in what the news media described as "a national epidemic" of youth kidnappings. A common pattern appeared across the personal narratives of aggrieved family members. Stanley and Julie Patz, John and Revé Walsh, John and Noreen Gosch, and others spoke of losing a child, losing faith in an apathetic government, and then engaging in grassroots efforts to recover their child and to raise awareness about missing children. For their part, the Patz family relied on photographs of Etan to generate and sustain interest in their son's case, especially as the investigation into the boy's disappearance floundered. Following his son's abduction and murder in 1981, John Walsh quickly moved to the fore of the burgeoning child safety crusade. Portrayed as a bereaved father with a vigilante streak and nothing to lose, Walsh took aim at the law enforcement shortcomings that, he claimed, had cost his son his life. The sloppy work of Hollywood, Florida, authorities and the FBI's unwillingness to intervene in the investigation served to explain John Walsh's metamorphosis into a self-described "crusader for justice." After the 1982 disappearance of their son Johnny, John and Noreen Gosch laid bare their frustrations with local law enforcement and with federal officials who refused to intervene in Johnny's case. During an appearance on *Donahue*, Phil Donahue's daytime talk show, Noreen Gosch alleged that an FBI agent had told her that the Bureau valued wealthier missing children over others. The FBI denied this accusation. Still, Gosch's account gained enough traction with American audiences—both in *Donahue*'s studio and in living rooms across the country—to spur the FBI's assistant director of congressional and public affairs to write a strongly worded letter to Donahue advising the host to reject "this utter inaccuracy."[8]

In the months preceding the initial congressional hearings on missing children, held in the fall of 1981, an economically minded line of attack—one that might be called the *priceless child argument*—had begun to take hold. As politicians, bereaved parents, and media officials expressed increasing interest in matters of child protection, they seized upon the notion that the DOJ and FBI cared more about lost or stolen personal items and animals than they did about missing youths. After Illinois Democratic congressman Paul Simon introduced the first version of the Missing Children Act on June 3, 1981, he employed the priceless child argument to publicize his efforts on ABC's *World News Tonight* that evening and the following evening. "It's very interesting that we have a bureau and a facility to locate missing cars in this country," Simon noted. "We don't do anything about missing children."[9]

By the time the US Congress convened its first hearings on missing children, child safety advocates had wholly embraced the priceless child argument, and they deployed it in a well-orchestrated assault on existing investigative systems and practices. "When a car, a firearm, a boat, or even a refrigerator is reported stolen in this country," Senator Hawkins declared in a statement opening the October 6, 1981, hearings, "a description of it is circulated nationwide almost immediately. I wish I could say that the same system was as effectively used to locate our children. Do we value these material possessions more than our own children? Must we wait until the tragedy strikes us personally before we act on behalf of these helpless children?" Senator Hawkins hoped to convey both the supposed ubiquity of the missing children problem and the woeful inability of the state to reckon with it.[10]

Figure 4.1 Donning matching bow ties, Senator Paul Simon (D–Illinois) and comedian Al Franken (right) flash "thumbs up" hand signals before a Citizen Action dinner honoring Simon at Washington D.C.'s Mayflower Hotel, June 1991. Photograph by Jamie Howren. Courtesy of the Library of Congress, LC-DIG-ppmsca-35488.

Others followed suit during the October 6 hearings. "We feel we have a definite story to tell," John and Revé Walsh indicated in their statement, "but the general reaction of the public, when we speak with them . . . is one of *complete amazement* that no system exists within this country to look for missing children." The Walshes and the authors of an "action" pamphlet included in the congressional proceedings highlighted the case of Fanfreluche, a prized racehorse worth some $500,000. In their interpretation, the FBI had eagerly joined the search for Fanfreluche after its disappearance from the Claiborne Farm in Paris, Kentucky. The Walshes' statement and the "action" document both took this incident as evidence of the DOJ's skewed priorities. "It seems extremely ludicrous," John and Revé Walsh noted, "that the FBI would enter the case of a $500,000 horse" into its NCIC database when "no ransom note was ever received or proof of it crossing the State line" ever materialized. "I find it very hard to put a price on a child," the Walshes affirmed. Here John and Revé Walsh referenced the 1932 Federal Kidnapping Act, popularly known as the Lindbergh Law after the abduction and slaying of aviator Charles Lindbergh's young son. The Lindbergh Law made the interstate transport of kidnapping victims a federal offense and required federal intervention in such cases. According to the Walshes, the 1932 statute should have precluded any federal response to the Fanfreluche disappearance, even though the Lindbergh Law applied only to human kidnappings. But, the couple conjectured, the horse's hefty price tag had compelled the FBI to act. The "action" pamphlet, likely produced by a cluster of independent child safety agencies and submitted for congressional review, trod similar terrain. "Did you know," it read, "that the FBI would not enter the case of a missing 12 year old Florida girl but did in the case of a missing horse because it was a race horse and had a 'high value'?"[11]

This set of arguments was somewhat misleading. The FBI had operated the NCIC since 1967 and had added to it a "missing persons" database in 1975. Yet because the NCIC lacked a database devoted exclusively to "missing children," child safety activists could (and did) attack the FBI for its presumed indifference toward young people. This semantic sleight of hand performed by missing child crusaders puzzled some legal analysts and policymakers, who questioned the need for legislation to address activists' criticisms. The fixation on the missing children's database also concealed other, more serious logistical problems hindering the search for missing young Americans. Some witnesses testifying before Congress in the early eighties rightly pointed to NCIC's underutilization. Available statistics suggested that authorities only entered about 10 to 14 percent of missing children into the FBI database. However, compared to the priceless child argument—which hinged on emotionally resonant ideas of children's vulnerability and of heartless feds—the charge of underutilization proved a less effective, and less commonly deployed, weapon in child safety activists' arsenal.[12]

While misleading, the priceless child argument caught on in the national conversation, much to the chagrin of the DOJ and FBI officials who opposed the MCA. The Walshes, the Gosches, politicians like Congressman Simon and Senator Hawkins, and others transmitted the priceless child argument through various channels, chiefly public hearings and the television news media. ("I had a car disappear for 24 hours," Simon informed his fellow congresspersons in November 1981. "It is very interesting that when that car disappears, that immediately goes on the Federal records. There is no commensurate movement if I had a 10-year-old child who disappeared.") For her part, Senator Hawkins addressed a symposium organized by the parents of lost, abducted, missing, and slain youths in late 1981. The CBS *Evening News* broadcast footage from Hawkins's speech, which included this clear articulation of the priceless child argument: "We should make it at least as easy for law enforcement officials through[out] the country to acquire information about missing children as it is to locate automobiles." Dan Rather, introducing the news story in the studio, took

LET'S HAVE

ACTION

OUR LOVED ONES HAVE BEEN MISSING TOO LONG!

Figure 4.2 This "action" pamphlet, submitted to Congress in 1981, cited the Fanfreluche case as evidence of federal negligence on matters of child safety. Notice the boy wearing an "I DON'T TALK TO STRANGERS!" T-shirt and struggling to evade a monstrous, "Hulk"-like predator. US Congress, Senate, Committee on Labor and Human Resources, *Missing Children: Hearing before the Subcommittee on Investigations and General Oversight*, Ninety-seventh Congress, first session, October 6, 1981, 93, 104.

the priceless child argument at face value: "Some parents," declared Rather, "now are asking the government to give murdered children the same consideration it gives stolen cars."[13]

The American public absorbed this line of argumentation and incorporated it into their correspondence with elected officials. "We are willing to spend millions on endangered animals," one woman wrote to her congressional representative, Mickey Edwards (R–Oklahoma), "and we have centralized info. centers on missing cars, silver and other valuables, yet our children don't seem as important." Another woman told Edwards, "The Justice Department already has one [national clearinghouse] for automobiles. Surely our children are more important than automobiles." One constituent pleaded for the congressman to "give missing children the *same advantage as missing cars*," while another asked Edwards: "It's wonderful that we are so concerned and take such quick action to save whales and fish but where are our missing children and why have we not done something sooner to help [them]?" Those writing to Edwards struggled to understand why the MCA did not breeze through Congress in 1981 and 1982. These outraged Oklahomans, like others from across the country, expressed their shock through an affective language that elected officials and DOJ leaders alike seemed to take very seriously.[14]

This is not to say that the DOJ and FBI did not mount a significant challenge to the bill. In November 1981, Senator Hawkins succeeded without congressional objection in attaching a version of the MCA to a proposed continuing appropriations bill. But the DOJ mobilized against Hawkins's rider. "[A]fter some effort by DOJ and the FBI," assistant attorney general Robert A. McConnell wrote in an internal DOJ memo, the MCA amendment "was stricken by the Conference Committee." Also, President Reagan ultimately vetoed the appropriations bill on November 23, 1981.[15]

The DOJ and FBI resisted the MCA on account of the bill's presumed cost, impracticality, and inefficacy. In the early 1980s the Reagan administration implemented cuts—or extended austerity measures instituted by President Jimmy Carter—across federal departments and agencies, including the DOJ and FBI. With the MCA under consideration in Congress, justice officials grappled with the projected costs of heightened involvement in missing child cases. "As you know," US attorney general William French Smith wrote to President Reagan, "the FBI's resources decreased substantially during the prior Administration and have not yet increased during this Administration. With the FBI's resources already stretched to the breaking point, greater involvement in missing children cases appears impossible, unless we either curtail a number of other priority matters or increase the FBI's resources." Smith appealed to Reagan's interest in "law and order" by discussing the strain that the MCA might place upon the FBI. According to Smith, charging the Bureau with tracking and recovering missing youths would prevent federal agents from pursuing other, perhaps more pressing, tasks like waging the "war on drugs," rooting out government corruption, thwarting organized and white-collar crime, and engaging in counterintelligence and counterterrorism activities, which together made up the core of the FBI's agenda in the 1980s.[16]

The DOJ objected most strongly to the MCA's so-called parental access provision and its potential costs, pecuniary or otherwise. Underlining the MCA's financial infeasibility, the FBI estimated its expected expenditures under the proposed parental access provision based on "four levels of activity," or four different hypothetical figures of total missing children reported to the NCIC. FBI officials arrived at the projected cost of $2,132,695 for 100,000 missing children ($5.5 million, inflation adjusted); $5,326,857 for 250,000 ($13.9 million, inflation adjusted); $21,298,780 for one million ($56.4 million, inflation adjusted); and $38,335,300 for 1.8 million ($101.2 million, inflation adjusted). "While cost alone should not be determinative," FBI director William H. Webster advised Senator Strom Thurmond (R–South Carolina), "it is worthy of your consideration when viewed in the light of the uncertain benefit and perhaps counterproductivity of the parental access provision." For Webster and other DOJ leaders, the MCA's parental access provision "creates serious [logistical] problems" by requiring the FBI to accept and act upon missing child reports filed by parents, legal guardians, or next of kin. Assistant attorney general McConnell made this case in an internal DOJ memorandum. "From a practical law enforcement perspective," McConnell wrote, "such a provision would be counterproductive in the sense that it might encourage parents of missing children to go directly to the FBI rather than working through the local and state police agency with investigative responsibility."[17]

On a draft of S. 1701, the Senate's version of the MCA, DOJ officials provided a page of notes that demonstrated their wariness of the bill as written. McConnell, who headed the DOJ's Office of Legislative Affairs, forwarded the Department's bill report to the Senate Judiciary Committee and Thurmond, its chairperson, on February 11, 1982. The notes pointed to page three "between lines 4 and 5," before which S. 1701 described the types of missing and deceased persons whose location and identification the US attorney general must oversee. These categories included those "under proven physical or mental disability"; "in the company of another person under circumstances indicating that his physical safety is in danger"; "missing under circumstances indicating that the disappearance was not voluntary"; and legally considered to be "unemancipated." DOJ officials implored lawmakers to insert after this final category the following stipulation: "after such parent, legal guardian or next of kin of such unemancipated person has contacted the appropriate law enforcement agency which has jurisdiction to investigate such matter." The DOJ hoped to ensure that parents and guardians of missing children would abide by an extant chain of command—and that the DOJ or FBI would not be obligated to investigate cases of missing children unnecessarily, especially given the climate of economic austerity. "There are legal relationships," Webster informed Thurmond, "existing between states in the form of interstate compacts on juveniles to which the FBI is not a signatory." By nullifying or ignoring these compacts, the MCA as manifested in S. 1701 "would place the FBI in the untenable position of entering records into the NCIC with no capacity to accomplish the continued detention and return of the missing person." Further, DOJ leaders insisted, the FBI had already "established, on a voluntary basis, certain of the services which the legislation [MCA] would require," including an " 'unidentified dead persons file' and a 'missing persons file' to assist state and local law enforcement authorities in these matters."[18]

According to leading DOJ officials, these logistical snags along with prohibitive costs would render the MCA (especially its Senate version) not just impractical but ineffectual as well. The bill seemed unlikely to prevent abductions or bring kids home, namely because it foisted upon federal officials tasks best suited for investigators at the local and state levels. Ultimately President Reagan, in October 1982, signed into law the House version of the MCA, which lacked the parental access provision but nevertheless ordered the FBI to "acquire, collect, classify, and preserve any information which would assist in the location of any missing person (including an unemancipated person as defined by the laws of the place of residence of such person) and provide confirmation as to any entry for such a person to the parent, legal guardian, or next of kin of that person (and the Attorney General may acquire, collect, classify, and preserve such information from such parent, guardian, or next of kin)." The bill also required the FBI to enter missing children's information into NCIC when "local police refuse to cooperate with a parent or guardian."[19]

Justice officials understood that the DOJ's resistance to the MCA was divisive. "The Department's position is controversial," one internal memorandum read, "and many in Congress would like to see a change." In the spring of 1982, the DOJ struggled to communicate to the public its opposition to the bill while also appearing sympathetic to the plight of missing children and their families. "Time is of the essence!" assistant attorney general McConnell exclaimed in a March 1982 memo to fellow assistant attorney general Rudy Giuliani. "[W]e want to make sure everyone is in agreement and that we are going to stick with [our] position," particularly since the MCA, "whether we like it or not, is going to be passed and passed by a substantial majority in both Houses. Expressing flat out objection to the bill may accomplish nothing and may be [a] very poor legislative strategy." McConnell closed his memorandum, which demonstrated his keen awareness of the political volatility of the issue, by urging DOJ officials to "think long and hard before we line up in straight opposition to this bill."[20]

McConnell and others in the DOJ appeared to be scrambling because of a rumored upcoming meeting between President Reagan and John Walsh in the spring of 1982. US congressman Clay Shaw (R–Florida), "a strong supporter of HR 3871, the House version of the 'Missing Children Act,'" looked to schedule a conference between Reagan and "Jon Walsh [sic], a constituent [of Shaw's] whose young son was missing several years ago [sic] and subsequently found dead."[21] McConnell felt that any such interaction between Walsh and the president could deal a death blow to DOJ attempts to squash the MCA. "If Congressman Shaw is successful in getting an appointment," McConnell told other leading DOJ figures, "the President should be fully briefed on the issues and made aware of the problems this bill would cause the FBI and that it might be counter-productive in terms of locating missing persons." Giuliani concurred: "We should make the White House aware of our position on certain legislation before the President takes any position in a meeting which is to be set up among the President, Congressman Shaw and Shaw's constituent [John Walsh]." Though the DOJ had not confirmed whether Walsh and Reagan were actually scheduled to meet, the Department approved William French Smith's transmission of a preemptive message to the White House, in which Smith noted that "[t]he Walsh case, and others like it, generate a great deal of sympathy." The US attorney general tried to drive a clear wedge between Walsh's emotionally resonant child safety politicking and the DOJ's purportedly more rational approach to child protection. "Proposed legislation dealing with the issue of missing children," Smith wrote to Reagan in early April 1982, "has great surface appeal. However, before you meet with Congressman Shaw, Mr. and Mrs. Walsh or others on this issue, you should know that the Department of Justice, including [FBI director] Bill Webster and I, strongly oppose the legislation." The memo brimmed with the anxious knowledge that no cold, hard logic could persuade Reagan to reject the MCA if he encountered Walsh's variety of activism in person. "We at the Department oppose the legislation," Smith reiterated near the end of his memo. "It is essential that you know our position, and the reasons behind it, before you are asked to take a position on the bill." That Smith stressed the "reasons behind it" implies that he wanted to portray the DOJ's stance as a pragmatic one. By contrast, the attorney general implicitly characterized the positions of child safety activists as irrational, superficial, and governed solely by emotion. But this affective politics, which the DOJ had hoped to neutralize, ultimately proved effective in recruiting the Department into "the battle for child safety."[22]

Senator Hawkins and other MCA supporters singled out the DOJ as particularly cruel for its opposition to the bill, accusing federal officials of being apathetic toward the nation's endangered children. Applying different iterations of the priceless child argument, child safety activists positioned themselves as the "good guys" advocating a commonsensical law that would protect American kids. DOJ officials, then, played the "bad guys" at a moment when the general public might endorse such a negative representation. By 1980 just 26 percent of Americans indicated that they trusted the federal government. While faith in the state rebounded over the course of the decade, President Reagan sowed the seeds of antistatism with calls to "get government off our backs." According to the president, Americans at the dawn of the 1980s were "burdened, stifled and some-times even oppressed by [a] government that has grown too large, too bu-reaucratic, too wasteful, too unresponsive, too uncaring about people and their problems."[23]

Similar themes structured the national discourse on the MCA. For its part, the *Washington Post*'s editorial board championed the bill and deni-grated its detractors. "The widespread support and unobjectionable logic behind this proposal," read a May 1982 *Post* editorial, "make one wonder why such legislation was not enacted long ago. . . . The bureau [FBI] itself objects to a provision that allows citizens to file information on their own, instead of working through local police, but the bill's sponsors believe that problem, if it is one, can be eased." Although the piece acknowledged the DOJ's objections to the MCA, it nonetheless echoed popular sentiment by dismissing these objections and citing the bill's "unobjectionable logic." In closing, the *Post* board members wrote, "Setting up these systems may in-volve technical problems and a bit more work for federal law enforcement officials. But the costs are far outweighed by the benefits of reuniting some parents with their missing children and of ending, however painfully, the distress of other parents who wonder whether their children are alive." The *Washington Post* premised its support for the MCA on the potent inter-woven archetypes of aggrieved parents seeking lost children and of lazy, bumbling bureaucrats. How, the argument went, could anyone deny these families the closure they so justifiably demanded? How could federal justice officials refuse to undertake "a bit more work" on their behalf?[24]

An ABC *World News Tonight* story airing four days before the *Post* published its piece struck a similar chord. Marking the third anniversary of the Patz disappearance, the reporter portrayed child safety advocates as sound and reasonable. "By [a] conservative estimate," journalist Al Dale narrated, "fifty thousand children are abducted each year, not counting parental abductions and custody fights. Most are never found." To remedy this seemingly pervasive problem, Dale reported, "Parents' groups have banded together to press for a nationwide network or clearinghouse to trace missing children. The idea is to use the FBI's computer to find children the way they trace stolen cars, guns, boats, and other items by the millions." Here, Dale repeated the priceless child argument and refused to challenge it. "[U]ntil recently they [the parents' groups] made little progress," Dale indicated. "Now it appears that Congress is about to give the parents of missing children that computerized clearinghouse they sought for so long." In the clip, Senator Paula Hawkins complained that the MCA would already be enshrined in law if not for opposition from the Justice Department and the FBI. According to Hawkins, DOJ officials objected to the notion that Congress could regulate their use of computers and to the presumption that parents should be able to enter information about missing children directly into such a national database. Hawkins contended that neither the DOJ broadly nor the FBI in particular had any conceivable reason to obstruct such a measure.[25]

In a March 1982 letter to President Reagan, Senator Hawkins juxtaposed the emotional toll wrought by the "tragedy of missing children" with the DOJ's supposed indifference on the issue. "Dear Mr. President," she wrote, "I am writing to you about a matter of grave concern to all our citizens—the tragedy of missing children in this country. Official estimates of this national tragedy indicate that as many as 1.8 million children are gone from their homes each year. Our families are being devastated by the loss of their children and the uncertainty of not knowing whether they are safe or in grave danger on the streets—whether they are alive or dead." Hawkins reviewed the finer points of the proposed MCA bill before assuring the president that the "Missing Childrens [sic] Act has attracted widespread bipartisan support and currently has 67 cosponsors." Despite this broad base of support, the senator from Florida noted, "the Department of Justice has formally opposed the enactment of the Missing Childrens [sic] Act. Their objections . . . are not appropriate responses to this problem and are inconsistent with your commitment to the safety and preservation of America's families." Hawkins closed on a hopeful note: "[W]e can bring the Department of Justice in line with the priorities you have set for your administration . . . family, home, neighborhood, peace, and freedom. The families of this nation have placed their trust in your leadership. Under your direction we can address this critical need to locate our missing children."[26]

By putting forth the nebulous yet powerful ideas of "family, home, neighborhood, peace, and freedom," Hawkins situated the MCA and the child

Figure 4.3 President Ronald Reagan meets with Senator Paula Hawkins (R–Florida) in the Oval Office, 1986. Photograph by Carol Highsmith. Courtesy of the Library of Congress, LC-DIG-pplot-13557-00719.

safety cause within the late twentieth-century politics of family values, law and order, taxpaying, and homeownership. In the white, middle-class suburbs of Charlotte, Atlanta, Detroit, and elsewhere, a "colorblind" political vocabulary gained currency in the decades following the Second World War. This language helped obfuscate the state's role in engineering postwar American prosperity and inscribing racial segregation into urban and suburban spaces. In this formulation, white suburban homeowning families enjoyed the status of preferred citizens whose civic-mindedness set them apart from those contributing nothing to the American project. Leveraging their standing "as an 'all American family,'" Hawkins's constituents John and Revé Walsh also fit their activism and the broader child safety crusade within this political framework. As idealized future citizens, vulnerable young Americans like their son Adam deserved protection from criminal predation, they argued. "Granted children don't vote and don't pay taxes," the Walshes affirmed in their October 1981 testimony before the US Senate, "but they are definitely the resources of this country because someday they will be the future lawmakers and the guardians of us in our old age." Adam, the Walshes believed, "would have been a fine citizen." Many of President Reagan's policy positions and rhetorical flourishes flowed from this political reservoir. Senator Hawkins seemed to recognize as much when she exalted the MCA's supporters—including the president and a relatively unified Congress—as the virtuous protectors of American families and children. However, Hawkins alleged that the DOJ fundamentally violated the principles of "family, home, neighborhood, peace, and freedom" by opposing the MCA.[27]

GETTING "IN LINE"

As Hawkins had hoped, the MCA's passage in the fall of 1982 appeared to "bring the Department of Justice in line with the priorities" of the Reagan administration. The concerns that had previously given DOJ officials pause on issues of child safety mostly disappeared from the Department's public pronouncements. While DOJ and FBI leaders continued to insist that local and state agencies should bear primary responsibility for investigating missing children cases, the MCA thrust the Justice Department and FBI into more assertive roles within what one DOJ publication—composed under the auspices of the Office for Victims of Crime, formed under the Reagan administration—called "the battle for child safety." New, moralistic legal measures emerged to protect American children, buttress institutional and parental authority, preserve youthful innocence, and in some cases punish juveniles through the twinned policy tracks of "law and order" and "family values."[28]

Beginning in the 1980s, the DOJ looked to "get tough" on juvenile justice and to shore up the "traditional" American family. Under the leadership of US attorney general Edwin Meese and OJJDP administrator Alfred S. Regnery, the DOJ tried to both safeguard and discipline American children by keeping them in either parental or state custody. In the eighties, nineties, and into the twenty-first century, elected officials also added new tools to the DOJ's toolbox in the name of cracking down on child predators and resolving child exploitation cases. New laws harnessed the affective power of endangered childhood by marshaling the names and faces of missing or murdered (white) child-victims and the idea of child endangerment more generally. The adoption and implementation of these mechanisms illustrated not only the ascent of an affective politics of child safety, but also the federal justice system's reorientation toward missing and exploited children.

Soon after President Reagan signed the MCA, DOJ officials began taking steps to comply with the law. A Senate hearing convened in February 1983 offered more opportunities for bereaved parents and elected officials to criticize the DOJ and FBI. Federal justice officials had already begun to reexamine departmental and agency protocols before this hearing, and FBI representatives had "voluntarily notified" Senator Hawkins's office of the fact "that they are going to be more involved in parental snatching cases." Even so, doubts persisted within the DOJ and FBI. In his testimony, the FBI's assistant director of criminal investigations Oliver B. Revell claimed that "we are an agency of limited jurisdiction." The FBI's "dilemma," Revell maintained, "is that many children, including young children, are not abducted. They wander off, they are lost, they are taken by relatives, or there is some other type of situation that occurs that clearly is not within the statute or the mandate of the Federal kidnaping statute" of 1932. "We do not have the capability or the jurisdiction to search for each missing child." Despite Revell's qualms, the Senate hearing spurred the DOJ to take further action. In a teletype message disseminated to all Bureau field offices just five days after the Senate proceedings, FBI director William H. Webster encouraged agents to respond "accurately and adequately" to missing child cases. "When reports are brought to your attention," he ordered, "without regard for the means of referral, of minors abducted or missing under circumstances indicating a possible abduction, unaccompanied by a ransom demand or evidence of interstate transportation or travel," agents must "immediately" contact FBI headquarters with specific information pertaining to the presumed abduction. "Mere statements that 'local authorities advise no evidence of abduction exists' are not acceptable," Webster warned. The director reiterated "that no ransom demand is required" to treat a missing child as a kidnapping, seemingly invalidating a common explanation for FBI nonintervention in such cases.[29]

Even after the enactment of the MCA, though, the complexities of the missing children problem precluded a unified federal response. Quantitative studies on missing, abducted, runaway, or "thrownaway" young Americans demonstrate the impracticality of FBI involvement in each case. In 1999, for instance, police agencies received nearly 800,000 reports of missing children, 43 percent of which involved "benign explanations" for the juvenile's disappearance. Since researchers estimate that an additional 45 percent of missing children are runaway or thrownaway youths, that only 2 percent fall victim to nonfamily abduction, and that approximately 115 children nationwide are abducted by strangers annually, the FBI's reticence to commit resources to investigate each missing child as a kidnapping victim appears sensible. "Given the large number of youngsters that run away from home each year," assistant attorney general Robert A. McConnell noted, "the routine involvement of the FBI in every reported disappearance would seriously diminish its effectiveness in genuine kidnaping episodes." In spite of these reasonable hesitations and the DOJ's enduring conviction that "the investigation of missing children complaints is primarily the responsibility of local law enforcement agencies," the FBI assumed a more prominent role in investigating presumed child abduction cases following the MCA's passage.[30]

The FBI's mixed record on the Johnny Gosch investigation, compared to its more active participation in the comparable subsequent cases of Danny Joe Eberle, Christopher Paul Walden, and Eugene Wade Martin, provides an instructive example. In her vigilantist rhetoric, honed after her son Johnny's 1982 disappearance, Noreen Gosch targeted the FBI and, in turn, forced its officials to counter charges of ineptitude and cruelty. Conscious of this bad publicity and boosted—or maybe saddled—by the MCA, the FBI seemed to show greater interest in the 1983 disappearances of Eberle and Walden in the greater Omaha area and that of Martin in Des Moines in 1984. Though highly critical of the FBI's work on her son's case, Noreen Gosch acknowledged the Bureau's rapid and more aggressive mobilization following the abductions of Eberle and Walden. John Walsh sensed this transformation, as well. In a televised 1985 town hall appearance in Omaha, Walsh noted the FBI's apparent failure to efficiently and effectively respond to the Gosch disappearance, yet he mentioned a "180-degree" turn since 1982, the year Johnny went missing and also the year in which the MCA became law. Walsh applauded the FBI's "attitude change," which he rooted within a larger policy shift in the child safety arena.[31]

That Hawkins and others registered an uptick in DOJ involvement in child abduction investigations solidified the Justice Department's shift, or at least its imagined shift, on child safety. In a February 1983 letter to Hawkins, William Webster told the senator of his desire "[t]o avoid any further misunderstanding by FBI personnel" on matters of child protection. The FBI director announced that he had "sent all [FBI] field offices a communication clarifying the FBI's jurisdiction and responsibilities in these cases." Moreover, Webster appeared to concede defeat, praising Hawkins and vowing that the FBI would take a more assertive role in battling child abduction and exploitation. "Your work in bringing this problem to my attention is appreciated," he wrote in closing. "I assure you that the FBI is sensitive to the concerns you raised and is taking actions to address and remedy those concerns." After hearing of Webster's teletype message sent to all FBI field offices, Hawkins called it "a tremendous step forward" that "demonstrates a real commitment to the investigation of child kidnappings." As attorney and child safety activist Herbert A. Glieberman put it, "The FBI's response may indicate the Justice Department's long-awaited submission to congressional pressure in this matter." Parents testifying before the Senate in support of the MCAA in 1984 also celebrated the fact that certain "restrictions on the FBI ha[d] been lifted in this past year, in 1983."[32]

Though a variety of jurisdictional and logistical questions continued to hang over the DOJ's missing child policies, the Justice Department had effectively rescinded its objections and started to invest in the child safety campaign in the service of larger policy goals. As policymakers mulled over the MCAA in 1983 and 1984, they focused heavily on juvenile delinquency, in large part because the bill would amend the 1974 Juvenile Justice and Delinquency Prevention (JJDP) Act. The 1974 law followed numerous landmark US Supreme Court rulings in the 1960s and 1970s that had expanded children's rights and liberalized the project of juvenile justice. In 1967, *In re Gault* enunciated the Fourteenth Amendment due process rights of juveniles. *Tinker v. Des Moines*, decided in 1969, applied the First Amendment to public schools and guaranteed the free speech rights of American youngsters. Argued and passed down in 1970, *In re Winship* required juvenile courts to prove every element of a criminal offense, overturning the "preponderance of evidence" standard used previously. The JJDP Act built upon these and other developments by seeking to remove truants, runaway youths, and status offenders from secure adult facilities in a process known as deinstitutionalization. The JJDP Act thus sought to prevent the abuse of youngsters in jails and to affirm children's right to escape familial or household violence without the threat of incarceration. The Reagan DOJ worked mightily to undo these children's rights gains, using the child safety issue to attack deinstitutionalization and to reassert familial and institutional control over young Americans.[33]

The DOJ's conversion on child safety enabled Reagan conservatives to pursue twinned policy objectives vis-à-vis American children—that is, the placement of young people in either parental or state custody. On one hand, Reagan operatives like OJJDP administrator Alfred Regnery hoped to shore up the patriarchal American family in order to protect "innocent" children (coded white and middle-class) from the supposed depravities of the outside world. Regnery and others embraced a familiar style of "pro-family," "law and order" politics that bereaved parents like John Walsh and

Noreen Gosch had employed in debates over missing children. "The most critical point is this," Regnery told the Senate Judiciary Committee during the MCAA hearings. "Any child who has lost his or her home is in significant danger from emotional, physical, sexual, or criminal exploitation." Regnery wielded the sentimentally powerful home and child, both ostensibly imperiled by the "striking mobility of our society." Because "the pornography quickly moves beyond local law enforcement jurisdictions," Regnery held, "[t]here is a definite need for national coordination and dissemination of information concerning missing and exploited children." This view meshed neatly with the stranger danger mythos that depicted home and family as "haven" and the outside world as "heartless." On the other hand, Regnery and his affiliates sought to "get tough" on juvenile delinquents. In an article published in the Heritage Foundation's *Policy Review*, for example, Regnery rejected structural explanations for juvenile crime and explicitly racialized those responsible for such transgressions. According to Regnery, the "typical candidate for juvenile arrest . . . is most likely black, possibly Hispanic, born to an unwed teenaged mother on welfare, living in public housing or a tenement, and has more than five siblings." Perhaps worst of all for conservative *Policy Review* readers, this child's "only way of getting anything of value is either by theft or by going on welfare. This boy will survive, for most of his life, at the taxpayer's expense."[34] For Regnery, such offenders did not deserve the reassuring comforts of home but instead called for swift and sure discipline and placement in state custody.

The pursuit of these dual policy goals reveals the enduring import of the DOJ's shift. In the early 1980s federal justice officials looked askance at proposed child safety legislation driven by emotion rather than reason. But the symbolic capital of a lost, innocent youngster trumped DOJ objections, helping to give rise to a legal regime that has rendered virtually unassailable "apostrophe laws" and "memorial laws" (those commemorating victims), and indeed any measures purported to safeguard certain American children from predation.

ↄᴧɔ

Kids in Custody

Protection and Punishment in the Reagan Era

stablished by the 1984 Missing Children's Assistance Act (MCAA), the US Attorney General's Advisory Board on Missing Children (ABMC) released a report in 1986 titled *America's Missing & Exploited Children: Their Safety and Their Future*. The publication detailed the ABMC's research findings on kidnapped, runaway, and exploited youth. Reinforcing the Reagan administration's thematic emphasis on "family values" and "law and order," the board—which included Etan's mother Julie Patz—stressed the need to reassert institutional and familial control over young Americans. "National recognition of the tragedy of missing and exploited children," the report read, "has been followed quickly by public calls for definitive action." The cases of Adam Walsh, Yusuf Bell, and other Atlanta youths, and scores of runaway children and adolescents nationwide, the ABMC members explained, "have all vividly alerted our Nation to a much larger problem—children who are out of legal, parental custody."[1]

For conservative policymakers like Reagan, US attorney general Edwin Meese, and director of the Office of Juvenile Justice and Delinquency Prevention (OJJDP) Alfred Regnery, any and all crises facing young Americans in the eighties stemmed from the supposed deterioration of legal, institutional, and parental authority. The children's rights gains of the 1960s and 1970s, the logic went, had emancipated young people, undermined the institutions charged with controlling them—the patriarchal, heteronormative family and the juvenile correctional facility chief among them—and unleashed upon American society a host of ills. The presumed epidemic of missing and exploited children represented one such ill, as did an alleged spike in juvenile crime. The 1974 Juvenile Justice and Delinquency Prevention (JJDP) Act, which had created the OJJDP and formalized the increasingly popular strategy of prevention in the area of juvenile justice, proved particularly problematic for Reaganites. By privileging rehabilitation for minors convicted of crimes, as well as the removal of young "status offenders" from correctional control through the process of deinstitutionalization, the JJDP Act empowered American youths to flee abusive domestic situations without fear of incarceration.[2]

For Reagan conservatives, these developments spelled trouble. Because youth liberation threatened to reconfigure age-based power hierarchies in ways that could sow disorder and tear at the social fabric, Reaganites worked to roll back the accomplishments of the children's rights movement and thus to reconsolidate parental, institutional, and adult authority. The president and his acolytes marshaled the 1980s child safety panic in the service of these policy goals. Drawing on public concerns about crime and missing children, Reagan conservatives blurred the boundaries between different classifications of missing youth. By conflating "missing," "runaway," and "exploited" children, they could obscure the divergent factors that contributed to these various phenomena and pursue misguided policy solutions privileging custodial control. As members of the ABMC observed in their 1986 report, "a common thread running through all cases of missing children is the danger of physical and emotional injury and the threat of sexual exploitation to children who are out of lawful and caring custody."[3]

Yet the type of "custody" in which Reagan administration officials sought to place young Americans differed based on the child's perceived level of vulnerability. These designations of vulnerability carried specific racial and class meanings, conferred in part by the image of endangered childhood honed within the child safety scare. Regnant cultural narratives deemed white, photogenic, middle-class youth like Etan Patz and Adam Walsh most susceptible to stranger danger and sexual predation, whether they were willingly "missing" or not. Although (white) "chronic runaways" left home "to challenge authority and seek adventure," the 1986 ABMC publication noted, they were "vulnerable and in constant danger as they try to survive on their own." These young Americans had "a right to family, not independence." Whether they were kidnapping victims or runaways, "[t]he longer children are gone from their homes, the greater the probability that (1) they will *not* be reunited with a family in a stable home environment, and (2) they *will* be victimized on the streets." The report ignored the victimization that a minor might endure at home, situating such threats firmly outside of the glorified family household. By shoring up parental control of vulnerable American children, the ABMC insisted, the presumed epidemics of runaway youth and child kidnapping and exploitation would come to an end.[4]

While these innocent, if at times wayward, young Americans demanded protection through familial custody, other youths required punishment via correctional custody. For Reaganites, youths perceived to be irredeemable—generally, poor young people of color reared by dysfunctional families—deserved to be punished through an increasingly harsh juvenile justice apparatus. These ideas fed off and fed into a larger discourse concerning the urban "underclass." By pathologizing poor and working-class Americans, particularly young black and brown people, conservative and neoliberal thinkers could portray poverty, unemployment, drug use, low educational attainment, and criminality as individual failings rather than products of structural inequality. The "underclass" designation thus worked to dehumanize the dispossessed and to sanction punitive criminal justice and welfare policies focused on these populations.[5]

Alfred S. Regnery was the main exponent of such punitive policies directed at young people during the Reagan years. He served as acting administrator of the OJJDP beginning in 1982 and then as full administrator from 1983 through 1986. The son of conservative publishing magnate Henry Regnery and the grandson of America First Committee cofounder William H. Regnery, Alfred Regnery cut his teeth as college director of Young Americans for Freedom before making his way to law school. During his unsuccessful bid to become the district attorney of Madison, Wisconsin, in 1976, Regnery vowed to get "tough on crime" (juvenile delinquency included), a vow he carried with him to the OJJDP. As administrator, Regnery strove to reorient the OJJDP in order to address new policy goals: punishment for some youths and protection for others. With respect to the former, Regnery argued that the juvenile justice "system must grow some teeth, perhaps even some fangs."[6]

Regnery's interest in the twinned objectives of protection and punishment, and his proposed shift away from preventive mechanisms, crystallized the racial and classist assumptions already embedded within juvenile justice policy. White, suburban youth who committed petty crimes or consumed illicit substances, the thinking went, were simply misguided or possibly corrupted by inner-city drug peddlers "invading" the suburbs. Conversely, urban delinquents ostensibly lacked the discipline or wherewithal to lead productive, virtuous lives. Resting on the work of Daniel Patrick Moynihan, George Gilder, and Charles Murray, this racialized logic of juvenile justice elided the structural conditions—such as poverty, hunger,

educational inequality, deproletarianization, and labor informalization—
that often push dispossessed youth toward extralegal activities outside the
conventional labor market.[7]

In accordance with this racialized logic, Regnery intended to harden juvenile justice through a variety of measures. The Reagan administration
had initially set out to dismantle the OJJDP by decreasing its funding.
When this approach foundered, Reagan mobilized the OJJDP in the service
of his "family values" and "law and order" policies. Detractors saw Reagan's
reconceptualization of the OJJDP, with Regnery manning the helm, as an
ideologically motivated hijacking and a violation of the Office's founding
precepts, which centered on delinquency prevention and judicial fairness
for all young Americans. For these critics, Regnery pursued destructive,
incoherent, or seemingly contradictory policy measures—spending federal
funds "on projects that are of a dubious, even frightening, nature"; seeking
to devolve juvenile justice authority to the states; and subsuming juvenile
delinquency into federal criminal justice policy to make juvenile justice
practically indistinguishable from (adult) criminal justice. When the JJDP
Act came up for renewal in 1984, Regnery and his allies successfully pushed
for amendments that would incarcerate more juveniles for longer periods
of time. The 1984 amendments to the JJDP Act strengthened sentencing
guidelines for juveniles, allowed states to more readily transfer juveniles to
the adult criminal justice system, and initiated a "special emphasis" grant
program that channeled resources toward the punishment of "serious" juvenile offenders.[8]

These amendments also contributed to Reagan's enhanced "war on
drugs" by stressing the importance of drug arrests to crime control. This interest in policing juvenile drug use and abuse reinforced the racial and spatial politics of the larger "war on crime," as drug-related arrests of nonwhite
juveniles increased 259 percent from 1985 to 1989, while drug-related
arrests of white youth decreased by 11 percent over the same four-year period. Not only did OJJDP efforts in the 1980s overlap with highly charged
debates regarding a criminal "underclass"; they also presaged a national discourse, fueled in part by the Clintons, concerning "superpredators" in the
1990s. Both moments, in consecutive decades, revolved around mutually
reinforcing (and highly racialized) images of predatory, "feral, presocial"
juvenile offenders on the one hand and vulnerable missing children and
runaways on the other. In each context, juvenile delinquents represented
not only public safety threats but also welfare-dependent "takers."[9]

In stark contrast to their treatment of these "bad kids," Regnery and
other juvenile justice hardliners accorded to "missing children" (including
runaways) greater compassion and care, for these youths ostensibly

epitomized weakness and innocence. To that end, the OJJDP sought to enact "profamily" child safety policies, sometimes in conjunction with the National Center for Missing and Exploited Children (NCMEC), which the OJJDP oversaw. Specifically, the OJJDP militated against deinstitutional-ization and allocated federal resources toward social conservative (partic-ularly antipornographic) causes. The discourses surrounding such "family values" projects muddled the lines between different "types" of missing children and thereby worked to elicit sympathy for runaway youth, who might otherwise seem incorrigible, if not altogether "bad," since they had voluntarily absconded from home. The complexities and ambiguities of the missing child issue permitted the widely circulated imagery of endangered childhood—anchored by white stranger danger victims like Etan Patz and Adam Walsh—to stand in for all missing children, even runaways.

Indeed, Regnery and other conservatives argued that every missing child faced the same sorts of threats, but this view obscured the distinct causes and scales of various missing child phenomena. Stranger abductions of children, for instance, are exceptionally rare yet demand a more imme-diate police and investigative response. Runaways are far more common and generally preclude such an urgent response. Further, runaways tend to be older teenagers (near the age of majority), not the young children typically seen within the imagery of endangered childhood. Most impor-tantly, perhaps, the most common threat facing runaway youth is physical or sexual abuse inside the home. Drug abuse represents the second most common threat, while prostitution and sexual assault outside the home each occur in just 1 percent (or fewer) of runaway cases. Belying these sta-tistics, the OJJDP and its auxiliaries like the NCMEC and ABMC promoted children's "right to custody with parents or legal guardians" as an antidote to the missing child problem, complemented by "the rights and duties of parents . . . to raise their children according to their own family values." The conflation of different types of missing children empowered Reaganites to pursue such policy solutions—devised and executed in the name of child protection—which served to limit the autonomy of young people.[10]

The protection and punishment planks endorsed by Regnery illus-trated the Reagan administration's investment in controlling American youth. Although Reagan, Regnery, Meese, and other policymakers hoped to impose vastly different forms of control over young "victims" and "victimizers," their proposals for safeguarding the former and disciplining the latter both contributed to a single project of shoring up familial and in-stitutional authority while curbing children's rights. Even though Regnery failed to unmake the OJJDP in toto, his dual vision for juvenile justice and child protection did take hold throughout the country in the 1980s and 1990s, as the law and order politics espoused by Reagan and Regnery emboldened states to embrace more punitive solutions to juvenile and adult crime and more interventionist strategies for protecting young Americans from predation. The overwhelming majority of states modified their laws in the eighties and nineties to enable the transfer of certain accused juvenile offenders into the adult justice system and to make court records more publicly accessible, thus eroding the privilege of confidentiality historically granted to juvenile defendants. Concurrently, juvenile incarceration rates soared, steadily climbing each year from 1983 through 1995. Juvenile detention rose from a rate of 241 youth in confinement per 100,000 in 1975, to 290 per 100,000 in 1983, to 357 per 100,000 in 1987, to a peak of 381 per 100,000 in 1995.[11] At the same time, the "conversion" of the US Department of Justice (DOJ) pushed the Department and its OJJDP into more assertive roles on child safety. This conversion allowed for the creation and maintenance of the NCMEC, as well as the rapid growth of legal and cultural instruments designed to insulate young Americans from particular threats. Reagan-era efforts to diminish children's autonomy, and to reaffirm familial and institutional authority, facilitated the rise of a child safety regime premised on regulating young American bodies in the name of protection—and punishment.

JUSTICE FOR JUVENILES?

Amidst escalating juvenile crime rates in the mid-1970s, the US Congress started to take cues from local police units in the hopes of quelling such delinquency nationwide. Special battalions like the Los Angeles Police Department's CRASH ("Community Resources against Street Hoodlums") offered a compelling model for preventing youth crime, and federal policymakers decided to institute such a program on the national stage via the 1974 JJDP Act. This law, as well as the OJJDP that it established, created two separate tracks through which the federal government could manage juvenile crime. A racial logic guided these two tracks. With the implementation of the JJDP Act, historian Elizabeth Hinton writes, "the social welfare arm of the federal government treated white and middle-income youth" while "the punitive arm handled young people from segregated urban neighborhoods." In spite of their racialized origins, the JJDP Act and the OJJDP seemed to supply modestly progressive solutions for juvenile delinquency. They allocated federal resources to participating states for the deinstitutionalization of status offenders, the separation of minors and adults in institutional settings, programs diverting offenders from the justice system, and "community-based detention" efforts. However, these rehabilitative and non-carceral tools mainly cropped up in suburban and rural areas disproportionately inhabited by white youth, not in the urban centers where young people of color dwelled. By privileging white spaces in its apportionment of non-carceral mechanisms and simultaneously "expand[ing] the formal system of juvenile detention," Hinton notes, the JJDP Act "effectively criminalized black children and teenagers and decriminalized white youth."[12]

Although certain observers consider the OJJDP punitive and regressive from its inception, some of its core objectives reflected the logics of youth liberation and prison reform. Specifically, the JJDP Act mandated the separation of juveniles and adult offenders within detention facilities, and its 1980 amendments included a jail removal provision in an effort to take juveniles out of adult facilities, within which they proved particularly susceptible to sexual abuse and other traumas. While Hinton contends that the JJDP Act "shifted the federal government's approach to delinquency toward punishment and managing the symptoms of urban poverty," the law initially helped to decrease juvenile crime rates and remove youths from adult correctional facilities. In fact, juvenile arrest rates for violent crimes declined for a few years following the JJDP Act's passage. The total number of prisoners incarcerated in juvenile detention facilities also dropped from 74,270 in 1975 to 71,922 in 1979, while annual admissions to juvenile facilities fell from 697,897 in 1975 to 638,309 in 1979.[13]

Only in the 1980s under the leadership of Alfred Regnery did the OJJDP explicitly pursue hardline solutions to "serious juvenile crime" and thereby widen existing racial inequalities in the juvenile justice system. The JJDP Act's criminalization of black juveniles and decriminalization of white youth did not immediately exacerbate racial disparities in the rates of youth confinement. According to DOJ statistics, 68 percent of juveniles incarcerated in 1977 were white; 29 percent were black; and 8 percent were Hispanic. By 1979, incarceration totals had declined, as had the share of black and white youths within those totals: 66 percent of incarcerated youth were white, and 27 percent were black. Only by 1982 and 1983 had the share of incarcerated black and Hispanic juveniles grown: 32 percent of confined juveniles were black, 10 percent were Hispanic, and 63 percent were white. These racial gaps grew just as juvenile incarceration rates began a steady climb from 1983 through the mid-nineties. Though it originated in the 1970s, then, the punitive turn in juvenile justice only rounded the corner in the eighties.[14]

As perhaps the federal government's most vocal proponent of tougher anti-delinquency measures, Regnery helped effect this punitive turn in juvenile justice by shaking the OJJDP from its progressive, reformist moorings, namely the "four Ds": decriminalization, due process, diversion, and deinstitutionalization. Before, during, and after his tenure at the OJJDP, Regnery expressed opposition to what he called the "environmental" and "theoretical" approaches to juvenile justice and to the notion of juvenile rehabilitation. He also seemed to deeply resent the "social theorists" who elaborated such ideas. For Regnery, a holistic and structural understanding of juvenile delinquency—which recognized that crime tracked neatly with poverty and other forms of structural oppression—was "folly." Thus, he largely dismissed the OJJDP's larger mission, enshrined in the Office's name, of preventing juvenile delinquency and unshackling the young people ensnared in the criminal justice system. "Rehabilitation has been the premise of the juvenile court system throughout the 20th century," he wrote in a 1985 article appearing in the Heritage Foundation's *Policy Review*, "but it has failed miserably." Regnery preferred "the deterrent approach, which views punishing the criminal as the best way to prevent future violations, protect the community, and achieve justice."[15]

Yet Regnery's juvenile justice worldview went well beyond deterrence and the alarmist politics of law and order; it also reflected some of the other core principles of Reagan conservatism, chiefly antiwelfarism and family values. In keeping with the ascendant ethos of neoliberalism, Regnery understood juvenile delinquency as an individualized or familial failing. "[T]he criminal justice system, adult as well as juvenile," he proclaimed, "must realize that ultimately crime is a matter of choice." Laws like the JJDP Act

Figure 5.1 Alfred Regnery pictured in 2019 at his home in Rappahannock, Virginia. Photograph by Dennis Brack. Courtesy of the *Rappahannock News*.

were "wishful thinking," in Regnery's telling, the brainchildren of ideal-
istic "social theorists, much of whose work has been a vain search for the
institution which excuses aberrant behavior by young people." According
to Regnery, the "social theorists" supporting the prevailing rehabilitative
model of juvenile justice were naïve. "Despite the beliefs of certain social
theorists," he declared, "juveniles do commit crimes at a rate significantly
higher than the rest of the population. . . . These are criminals who happen
to be young, not children who happen to commit crimes." In his 1985 *Policy
Review* article, Regnery quoted from a DOJ report published under the
Jimmy Carter administration that called for the adoption of "mechanisms
which offer [youths] the communication, coping, and decision-making
skills they need to enter the mainstream of society." For Regnery, such
"buzzwords (and they are little more than that) hardly come to terms with
the reality of juvenile crime," which was very grim indeed. He insisted "that
children commit about 40 percent of the felonies in the United States" and
"that juveniles up to 18 years of age accounted for about 20 percent of all
violent crime arrests, 44 percent of all serious property crime arrests, and
39 percent of all overall serious crime arrests." Regnery also maintained
that the "typical" juvenile offender committed some "75 percent of all serious offenses." Armed with these daunting (and vastly exaggerated) figures, Regnery affirmed "that these youth have to be a major focus of the
office [OJJDP]."[16]

While the numbers Regnery marshaled might have been frightening
enough for some, he also set his depictions of "criminals who happen to
be young" in the political frame of aggrieved whiteness. In Regnery's rendering, virtually all delinquents were nonwhite. And by masking the structural conditions—inordinately present in communities of color—that
foster certain criminal behaviors, Regnery blamed nonwhite juveniles,
their families, and their extended kinship networks for building a culture of dependency and criminality. Unlike the "innocent" white children
whose names and faces animated the 1980s child protection campaign,
these youths were not endangered by moral threats; they *were* the moral
threats. Worse still, miscreants like these purportedly imperiled white
families—not just through their brutish behavior of theft, assault, rape,
and murder, but also through their siphoning of hard-earned tax dollars
from white suburbanites and their disregard for social conservative mores.
Regnery wrote:

> A New York policeman recently profiled for me a typical candidate for juvenile
> arrest. Fourteen years old, the boy has already been arrested a dozen times. He
> dropped out of school years ago and cannot read or write; he has no job skills

nor any hope of getting them. He is most likely black, possibly Hispanic, born to an unwed teenaged mother on welfare, living in public housing or a tenement, and has more than five siblings. A series of men have lived in his mother's house; the boy has not developed a rapport with any, and has tended to be regarded as a nuisance by the adults. He has been physically abused since early childhood, and he has spent a good deal of time living on the street. His only way of getting anything of value is either by theft or by going on welfare. This boy will survive, for most of his life, at the taxpayer's expense.

According to Regnery, this fourteen-year-old hoodlum lived within a "culture of poverty," taking lessons on morality from his promiscuous, welfare-dependent mother and her throng of sexual partners. Blending the problematic findings of the Moynihan Report with those of conservative commentators like George Gilder and Charles Murray, Regnery invented an archetypal juvenile delinquent with no hope for redemption. This subject warranted neither pity nor leniency, and he would likely incense the citizens who would foot the bill for his exploits and those of his siblings, his mother, and his mother's paramours.[17]

Regnery gave two more examples of flesh-and-blood juvenile delinquents, albeit with altered names, to make his case. (Whether these individuals actually existed is unknown.) "Consider, for example," Regnery submitted, "two typical juvenile cases which appeared recently in Miami's juvenile courts." It is unclear what made these cases "typical" in Regnery's mind, given the severity of the crimes allegedly committed by these juveniles. But Regnery's discussion of race and class in these vignettes may have served to substantiate the prevailing racial and class assumptions of the conservative *Policy Review* readership. "The first involves 'Lester,' a 15-year-old recently 'adjudicated' by the court for burglary. Lester is black and has been arrested 12 times. His mother abandoned him at an early age, and he grew up in the streets of Miami, with occasional stops for a hot meal at a grandmother's house. . . . He commonly breaks into homes, steals cars, and hustles, then robs, homosexuals." Another case, also in Miami, "involves a Hispanic male, 15 years old, recently convicted of armed robbery. Call him Marco. He has been arrested 12 times, is a member of a housing project gang, and is actively involved in drugs, burglary, and robbery. . . . His mother is on welfare, and has seven children. Marco, who is slight for his age, cries whenever he is first locked up, but soon starts to thrive within the training school. As soon as he is released, he goes on a drug binge." The horror stories expertly woven by Regnery—replete with homosexuality, drug abuse, and welfare dependency—demanded a forceful response. During his 1983 confirmation hearings, Regnery explained "that the juvenile justice system of today is different than it was ten or even five years ago . . . if we are to be a truly effective organization, we are going to have to take those bold steps necessary to meet our changing times." Noting the disproportionate rates at which "juveniles aged 10 to 17" committed serious and violent crime, Regnery affirmed, "We will put our resources where they are needed."[18] By this, Regnery surely meant that OJJDP resources ought to be funneled toward the incarceration of certain young people.

Not only had Regnery long petitioned for a more punitive juvenile justice system, but he had also long displayed a fixation with what he called "profiles in carnage," which justified the strict policing of nonwhite bodies. While running for district attorney of Madison, Wisconsin, in 1976, he had suggested "maybe sending a juvenile to Wales"—an adult detention facility in Wisconsin—"for a week as sort of a shock treatment, to show him what it's like." During the same electoral campaign, Regnery's wife Christina had contacted the police multiple times to complain that she had received inappropriate, threatening phone calls. She then alleged that, while eight months pregnant, she had endured a brutal assault. Two men, Christina Regnery claimed, had stabbed her over seventy times with an embroidery knife and forced her to perform oral sex on them. Yet police determined that she had concocted the entire story. The Regnerys' neighbors had not seen or heard anything suspicious during the alleged attack, and not one of the seventy-three slash marks on Christina Regnery's body "required a stitch or a Band-Aid." The police report stemming from the fabricated assault indicated "that Mr. Regnery would not disclose any of the circumstances surrounding the incident." But he did just that, informing a journalist in the hospital "that his wife had been raped by a white male and a black male and had been stabbed." Even though Madison law enforcement had debunked the Regnerys' charges, the local paper validated them, running a story with a headline that read: "Two attack wife of DA candidate."[19] This affair illuminated Alfred Regnery's interlocking obsessions with violence, race, and hardline approaches to criminal justice. He continued to toe this punitive line into the 1980s, when Reagan tapped him to head the OJJDP.

From the outset of his first presidential term, Reagan had plans for the OJJDP. He had intended to "move the OJJDP's individual agency grant money into an executive-branch wide social services block grant," thereby furthering his administration's "effort to return management of health and social service programs to States and localities." Through such block grants, the federal government would allocate a fixed sum to each state, which could use those funds as they saw fit. The president had also allegedly placed the OJJDP on a mysterious "hit list" that generated great speculation and consternation in the popular press and in congressional hearings.

(Regnery did not deny the existence of such a list but claimed to have no knowledge of its contents, telling the Senate that he had "never seen that hit list.") When this approach floundered in the face of congressional resistance, the Reagan administration deployed Regnery to lead the OJJDP and to detach it from its foundation. Regnery, as the *New Republic* put it, "faithfully followed the president's policy of seeking to abolish the office." Though Reagan conservatives tried, during Regnery's tenure and beyond, to defund or otherwise demolish the OJJDP, their failures pushed them to employ the policy strategies of conversion, the "active reinterpretation of existing formal rules to serve new ends," and layering, "the grafting of new elements onto an otherwise stable institutional framework" to "alter the overall trajectory of an institution's development."[20] Regnery set out, first, to deemphasize deinstitutionalization and the separation of juveniles from adult offenders, two cornerstones of the 1974 JJDP Act; second, to undermine prevention while privileging the punishment of the "serious juvenile offender"; and third, to emphasize the protection of children against moral threats.

Regnery hoped to move the OJJDP away from rehabilitation and prevention by arguing that the goals of deinstitutionalization, the separation of youth and adult offenders, and the removal of juveniles from adult jails had all been adequately achieved. "Deinstitutionalization of status offenders," Regnery testified before a March 1984 Senate hearing, during which he urged Congress not to reauthorize the OJJDP, "has largely been accomplished as a result of the JJDP Act, at least to the extent that juvenile status offenders are now only rarely held in secure detention facilities." He concluded that the OJJDP should ease up on its enforcement of the deinstitutionalization statute and leave compliance to the states. "We believe that the states which now participate in the [JJDP] program will continue to deinstitutionalize [status offenders] without the federal government's money," Regnery contended, "and will be able to do so more successfully without the unyielding and strict requirements of federal law."[21]

Nevertheless, available data indicated that status offenders still wound up in secure facilities with some regularity in the 1980s, and the number of juveniles in adult jails stayed mostly consistent across the late seventies and throughout the eighties. Because some thirty-five thousand juveniles remained "in inappropriate detention," per the DOJ's own statistics in the mid-1980s, US senator Arlen Specter (R–Pennsylvania) explained that he was "very concerned about [Regnery's] conclusions on the lack of need for reauthorization of OJJDP." Specter also challenged Regnery's "assumption that States now meeting the requirements of the [JJDP] Act would continue to do so if the funding now available under the Act were eliminated."

The rapid growth of "privately operated detention and shelter facilities" in the eighties further undermined Regnery's claim that "the job" of deinstitutionalization was "very close to being completed" in the mid-1980s. The numbers of juveniles incarcerated in private facilities had largely offset the gains of the late 1970s and early 1980s deinstitutionalization movement.[22]

As OJJDP administrator, Regnery also publicly doubted the efficacy and reigning definition of "prevention" and set out to alter its meanings. He portrayed punishment as a kind of prevention, dismissed as naïve existing understandings of prevention, and channeled OJJDP funds toward more punitive ends. US senator Strom Thurmond (R–South Carolina), chairman of the Senate Judiciary Committee, asked the OJJDP head in 1983, "Mr. Regnery, your critics also report that you have decided to use [OJJDP] funds for the apprehension and prosecution of juvenile criminals, rather than for juvenile delinquency prevention. Is that correct, and will you please tell the committee where you feel your office should place its emphasis?" Regnery responded in the affirmative, albeit circuitously. "Delinquency prevention is a difficult area to get a handle on," he replied. "There really is not any definition, I guess, of what delinquency prevention means. . . . We have spent a great deal of money on things that we call delinquency prevention over the years. The statute has a good many things in it besides prevention, including the mandate that we try to do something about serious and violent crime. We are putting together some new programs which will be prosecutorial in nature to deal with serious juvenile crime." Although Regnery held that "it is not accurate to say that we have abandoned prevention," he confessed that "we are trying to redirect our efforts to adjust the system because I think we have the expertise to be able to do that, being in the Justice Department."[23] This statement implied that Regnery saw his office as one devoted to punishment.

In casting the OJJDP as a punitive, juridical institution rather than "a social agency," Regnery hoped to shepherd the Office toward punishment and away from rehabilitation or prevention. Under his leadership, Regnery claimed, the agency would "be more Justice Department-oriented and less Health and Human Services-oriented." Indicative of Regnery's antiwelfarism, such statements denigrated the "social engineering" of the New Deal and Great Society, deeming the government ineffectual and the OJJDP project of prevention (and juvenile justice more broadly) "folly." While Regnery maintained that "[p]revention is still very much alive and well in our office," denying media reports "that we have 'scrapped' prevention," he also lamented the durability of prevention as an OJJDP strategy. "We have spent, over the years, tens of millions of dollars on delinquency prevention," and "[t]he result has been, unfortunately, less than successful . . . evaluations of those prevention activities have been almost universally pessimistic." For Regnery, such failed "prevention activities" spoke to the ineptitude of the federal government and the naiveté of the "social theorists" who shaped policy. "Some advocates of rehabilitation," he wrote flippantly in *Policy Review* in 1985, wish "to build a society so devoid of evil that young people would not be inclined to do wrong. If crimes are committed because of societal forces beyond the control of the individual offender, the logic runs, then remove those forces and change society. What better way to do so than to use the power, and the money, of the federal government?"[24] Underlining the OJJDP's perceived inefficacy and misuse of tax dollars on "rehabilitation" and "prevention activities," Regnery ensured *Policy Review* readers that their tax dollars would be more wisely spent on the incarceration and incapacitation of particular juveniles.

Concealing the successes of the OJJDP, its holistic scope, and the structural factors that drive juvenile delinquency, Regnery set his office's sights on the "serious" or "chronic offender," the forerunner to the 1990s "superpredator." Regnery leveraged this racialized archetype of the irredeemable young, urban offender to undermine the notion that juvenile justice should operate differently than the adult criminal justice system. Accordingly, as Congress deliberated the OJJDP's reauthorization in 1984, Regnery called for the Office's elimination and the transferal of its primary duties to the Office of Justice Assistance (OJA) and other federal bodies. "We believe in dealing with this problem of serious juvenile crime," Regnery declared before the House Subcommittee on Human Resources in 1984, "that the law enforcement and the criminal justice system need to coordinate better. We believe that will be done more easily through the programs that would be funded by the Office of Justice Assistance than through two separate offices" (the OJA and the OJJDP). "We believe that we can do that by bringing law enforcement, courts, recordkeeping agencies, corrections, and others . . . together to work more closely with a program that is on a continuum—that is, the fact that the serious, more chronic offenders are the same people who go on to be the clients of the criminal justice system later on. By dealing with those offenders in a more cohesive way than we now do, we may be able to better address the problem." Regnery went on, "We believe that [the] emphasis on serious juvenile crime must be primarily in the chronic offender, since he is the one who commits most of the juvenile crime and the one that is predictably the person who is going to go on to continue to commit most of the crime. We believe this focus can best be done by the Office of Justice Assistance."[25] Regnery presented as a policy solution the long-term incarceration of "chronic" juvenile offenders, who in his own rendering were disproportionately nonwhite.

In stoking fears about a supposedly new, more virulent strand of juvenile offender, Regnery misrepresented the scope, severity, and nature of
juvenile delinquency in the late twentieth century. He argued that juvenile crime had reached epidemic proportions and an unprecedented level
of "violence and intensity" in the 1980s. Such crime did not constitute
"trivial indiscretions committed by misguided youth" but instead signaled
the emergence of a more vicious young offender. Regnery used fallacious
quantitative data to corroborate his claims. "Juvenile crime rates since the
1950s have tripled," he asserted. "There are currently about 15 million
Americans between [the ages of] 14 and 17, or about seven percent of
the entire US population; but about 30 percent of all people arrested for
serious crimes are juveniles—a total of some 1.5 million arrests per year."
Experts determined that Regnery had inflated the number of juveniles
arrested for serious offenses by over 150 percent and exaggerated by over
75 percent the number of murders committed by youths. The "serious
crime" designation also included property crimes, meaning a juvenile who
stole a nemesis's bike could qualify as a "serious" offender, in Regnery's
framework. As one might assume, youth offenders were far more likely to
commit burglary or theft than murder or rape. Furthermore, the existing
evidence contradicted Regnery's larger point about the worsening of juvenile delinquency across time. As one scholar wrote in direct response to
Regnery's remarks, "the rates of serious juvenile crime rose significantly
during the late 1960s and early 1970s. The rates stabilized during the
mid- to late 1970s, declined between 1979 and 1984, and increased for the
first time in six years in 1985," the year in which *Policy Review* published
Regnery's article.[26]

Some critics took the "hardening" of juvenile justice as a plan to
"disciplin[e] the poor" and the nonwhite. Criminologists Stephen J. Brodt
and J. Steven Smith identified the "obvious racial and class biases which
would seem to underlie [Regnery's] analysis and conclusions." These
scholars, in dialogue with Regnery in a 1987 *Criminal Justice Policy Review*
forum, compared 1980s juvenile justice efforts with President Richard
Nixon's law and order politics. According to Brodt and Smith, Nixon had
"set in motion an aggressive refocusing of the criminal justice system on
apprehending and punishing street crime and poor criminals." In spite of
this broad-based attack on certain offenses, crime rates "remained essen-
tially unchanged" in the 1970s. And yet, Brodt and Smith charged, Regnery
and other anticrime stalwarts proposed similar policies in the 1980s—not
because they are effective but because "[i]n practice, getting tough means
'let's get tough' with the following groups: (1) blacks; (2) Chicanos; (3) the
poor; (4) the uneducated; (5) youth from single parent families; (6) the

unemployed; (7) illegitimate youth; (8) welfare families; and (9) abused children."[27]

In his reply, Regnery articulated a familiar line of "colorblind" argumentation refined by conservatives and neoliberals following the classical phase of the African American freedom struggle. "Smith and Brodt seem to think that criminal justice policy should not focus on the offenders, whoever they are," Regnery wrote, "if to do so would offend the groups to which the offenders belong. Instead they apparently believe that we should judge certain people, namely the poor, minorities, the uneducated and illiterate, etc., by a different standard than that by which everybody else is judged. I cannot subscribe to that." Regnery conceded that structural factors may foster juvenile delinquency but added, "Whether public policy (or perhaps more accurately government programs) has contributed to this state of affairs is, for [the] purposes of this paper, irrelevant." Yet, citing the work of Charles Murray, Regnery did indeed blame the state for "having created" the conditions necessary for juvenile delinquency to flourish. "But what *is* relevant," Regnery continued, "is the fact that the state will not, and cannot, fix the situation," even though he advocated for the incarceration of "chronic offenders" in public (and private) facilities, which obviously required the deployment of government resources.[28]

While bipartisan congressional oversight thwarted Reagan and Regnery's plans to shutter the OJJDP, Regnery's efforts to "get tough" on juvenile crime—and thus to exercise greater institutional control over certain American minors—ultimately proved successful. With the 1984 reauthorization of the JJDP Act, the OJJDP toughened sentencing guidelines for juveniles, enabled states to more easily insert juveniles into the adult criminal justice system, and launched a "special emphasis" grant program that channeled more resources toward caging and disciplining young people. In the same moment, from the 1980s through the end of the century, state governments adopted punitive measures that allowed for the incarceration of more juveniles. The overhaul of transferal provisions meant that juveniles could be more readily reassigned to adult courts. Moreover, the expansion of sentencing options and the elimination of confidentiality practices in juvenile courts smoothed over the historical distinctions between the juvenile and adult criminal justice systems. Because of these developments, the juvenile incarceration rate rose sharply in the early to mid-eighties and continued to increase through the mid-nineties. Black juveniles, as the racial or ethnic group most likely to face detention at some point in the adjudication of their cases, suffered most acutely. Conversely, white juveniles were the least likely to be incarcerated. Regnery and his conservative allies had a different type of "custody" in mind for white, middle-class minors. Concentrating on the moral threats facing these vulnerable young Americans, the NCMEC, the ABMC, Regnery, and others called for the placement of some American children in the "lawful, caring custody" of a patriarchal, heteronormative, two-parent family.[29]

PROTECTIVE CUSTODY

The criminalization of "serious juvenile offenders"—coded as poor and nonwhite—stood in stark contrast to the treatment of vulnerable, innocent young Americans, portrayed in media dispatches as white, middle-class, and photogenic. As the OJJDP took steps in the 1980s to punish certain young people, it also looked to protect other youths deemed susceptible to the perils lurking outside the family home. These vulnerable youths included runaways, by far the largest category of missing children. But despite minimal attempts to parse out the various "types" of missing children—"nonfamily abduction," "family abduction," "runaway children," and "throwaway children," in the ABMC's formulation—Regnery, the ABMC, and others seemed to offer similar policy solutions across these different categories.[30]

The 1980s child safety scare, and the imagery of endangered childhood cultivated therein, bred these sorts of reductive policy proposals. While runaways have always tended to be older adolescents either forced or drawn out of their homes, the visibility of young stranger danger victims like Etan Patz and Adam Walsh repainted this complex portrait in a perceived moment of national and familial decline, rendering home and family as "haven" and the outside world as "heartless." "When we group the four categories of missing children," child safety activist Ken Wooden lamented in congressional testimony in 1985, "we only serve to muddle the public's mind and diffuse law enforcement priorities." The seemingly unassailable goal of "bring[ing] these children home" papered over the unpleasant domestic circumstances that frequently encourage young people to run away and situated the moral threats facing American youth outside of the idealized household. By obscuring the structural conditions that often drive young people to leave their families—including poverty, joblessness, domestic violence, and substance abuse—reformers could tout the idealized American family as the antidote to all "categories of missing children." Reagan, Regnery, and their compatriots thereby strove to restore the authority of the dual-parent, pronatal American family while undercutting the autonomy of the child. As Reagan put it in 1983, "More children with permanent homes mean fewer children with permanent problems."[31]

Under Regnery's leadership, the OJJDP approached child protection in three main ways. First, the Office oversaw the launch and ensured the sustained operation of the NCMEC, established by the 1984 MCAA. Second, in a maneuver that dovetailed with his hardline approach to juvenile justice (and criminal justice, more generally), Regnery contended that the JJDP Act's deinstitutionalization provision endangered American youth, destabilized the family unit, and encouraged young people to run away from home. Regnery, along with the ABMC, hoped to repeal the JJDP Act's deinstitutionalization provision, to reconsolidate familial authority, and to more harshly punish those who might hurt young Americans. Finally, Regnery—alongside US attorney general Edwin Meese—redirected OJJDP and DOJ resources toward socially conservative, "profamily" causes, all in the name of protecting select young Americans. Together, these undertakings reflected the Reagan-era project of reasserting familial, patriarchal, and institutional power—to discipline some youths and protect others, but ultimately to exert control over all young Americans.

The NCMEC emerged out of the MCAA as a "national clearinghouse" for lost, abducted, missing, and vulnerable youth. In press and political accounts, its formation signified a victory for the child safety cause, even

Figure 5.2 President Ronald Reagan speaks at the opening ceremony for the National Center for Missing and Exploited Children on June 13, 1984, flanked by US attorney general William French Smith, John and Revé Walsh, the Walshes' young daughter Meghan, and US senator Paula Hawkins (R–Florida). Courtesy of the Ronald W. Reagan Presidential Library and Museum, Simi Valley, California.

though the Center's mission and methods seemed poorly defined, if not altogether unintelligible. As perhaps its primary function, the NCMEC maintained a telephone hotline through which individuals could share or obtain information about missing and exploited children. Reporting on the Center's opening in 1984, CBS's Dan Rather diagnosed a presumably pervasive peril: "Between half a million and two million children are reported missing in this nation each year." But, Rather rejoiced, "today the first federally funded nationwide service to take tips on missing children opened operations." The newscaster provided viewers with detailed information about the hotline and the NCMEC, more broadly, as footage from inside the call room appeared onscreen. Though billed as an independent agency beyond the purview of the federal government, the NCMEC received most of its funding through OJJDP grants. (The rest came through donations.) The NCMEC relied upon $2 million to $4 million awards distributed annually via the OJJDP; these awards constituted the OJJDP's "largest single grant."[32] That Reagan, Regnery, and other conservatives championed the NCMEC—despite its unclear purpose and the government's very modest investment in the Center—conveyed the administration's concern with safeguarding "good" white kids, or at least giving the appearance of safeguarding them.

The NCMEC seemed to do very little apart from advancing the stranger danger myth and, in turn, justifying its own existence. Critics lambasted the NCMEC for its supposed aimlessness. "What is the mission of the National Center?" William Treanor of the American Youth Work Center asked congressional representatives in 1986. To answer his own rhetorical question, Treanor quoted NCMEC director Jay Howell, who sounded unsure about the Center's basic functions. "The National Center is not a location center," Howell had told the House Subcommittee on Human Resources in 1985. "It is not an investigative agency. It is not a legal services provider. Instead it is a clearinghouse of information and technical assistance. Does that mean we locate . . . children? No, we don't locate missing children." Nonetheless, since its founding in 1984, the NCMEC has publicized its role in helping to recover lost, abducted, and runaway youth.[33]

Treanor and other children's rights activists criticized the embellished statistics and skewed media narratives that buoyed the missing child panic and gave rise to the NCMEC. For Treanor, the NCMEC had helped perpetrate "one of the most outrageous scare campaigns in modern American history" by exaggerating exponentially the number of children who fell victim to stranger abductions each year and by obfuscating the fact that runaways comprise the overwhelming majority of missing youths. According to Treanor, Regnery and the NCMEC leadership deliberately

suppressed any data that might puncture the inflated missing child statistics floated in media reports and congressional proceedings. Howell, for
his part, proclaimed on national television that 1.3 to 1.8 million young
Americans went missing annually, even as journalists and social scientists
debunked such astronomically high figures. Media coverage also generally
overlooked runaways, as an abiding news media focus on stranger danger
created a slippage between "stranger kidnappings" and "missing children."
Cases like Etan Patz's and Adam Walsh's came to stand in for all missing
children. As one CBS *Evening News* reporter declared in March 1985, Patz's
"photograph has come to symbolize *all* missing children," even though
such stranger abductions of young kids represented just a tiny fraction of
missing child cases.[34]

When the NCMEC and its federal support system did pay attention to
runaway youth, it was primarily to undermine the deinstitutionalization
movement. Established, as the NCMEC was, by the 1984 MCAA, the ABMC
concentrated on the family as the principal basis of order in American society. Its 1986 report, *America's Missing & Exploited Children: Their Safety
and Their Future*, identified the placement of runaway youth in "secure
facilities" as a way for "parents or authorities to make arrangements to
return [runaways] home safely or provide a caring environment." To this
end, Regnery and the ABMC both argued "that in many cases the deinstitutionalization part of the Juvenile Justice and Delinquency Prevention
Act went too far in absolutely prohibiting the use of secure facilities for
runaways." In this rendering, "home" and "family" offered young people
safety and care, while the outside world could only endanger them. For the
ABMC members, deinstitutionalization had destabilized the family and
limited the capacity of state governments, law enforcement agencies, and
the courts to safeguard vulnerable children. The ABMC decried "the breakdown of the family in our society" and enunciated children's "right to custody with parents or legal guardians who provide care, support, discipline,
and love." The 1986 report also made clear that children "do not have a
right to freedom from custody," with the board members objecting to "the
attitude that has been common among some professional child-advocates
that parents and legal guardians should not interfere with a child's decision
to leave home in search of an individual identity." This view had formed the
contours of "legislation and public policy and unintentionally created a situation that endangers our children." Here the ABMC members were refer-
ring to the 1974 JJDP Act, which emerged as a corrective to the abuses and
indignities often visited upon young runaways jailed "in detention homes
or other secure facilities." According to the ABMC, the JJDP Act grew from
"dramatic accounts of the ill treatment of runaway children in detention

homes and adult jails" in the 1960s and early 1970s. These "dramatic accounts" presented to the US Congress, the ABMC implied, did not necessarily reflect the experiences of most institutionalized runaways. Ironically,
to buttress their arguments about the need to control young Americans,
the ABMC members used "dramatic accounts" of stranger danger cases,
which most certainly did not accurately represent the broader problems of
child kidnapping, runaway youth, and child exploitation. "The abduction
and murder of Adam Walsh," the report indicated, and "the series of child
murders in Atlanta" had "alerted our Nation to a much larger problem—
children who are out of legal, parental custody. Our Nation now sees its
runaway, abandoned, and abducted children in a new perspective."[35]

For the ABMC, the "new perspective" provided by the missing child scare
had delegitimized the efforts of "some professional child-advocates" to
upend firmly entrenched hierarchies of age. In the wake of the liberationist
sixties, the ABMC report detailed, "Some professionals concluded that the
juvenile justice system's exercise of control and authority over children was
counter-productive," and these "[s]elf-proclaimed 'child advocates' argued
that the only way to change the juvenile justice system was to curtail the
authority of law enforcement agencies to arrest runaway children, and juvenile courts to detain them." The resulting JJDP Act became law in 1974.
Thereafter, "runaway children, school truants, alcohol users, and incorrigible children" fell under the heading of "status offenders," and the JJDP
Act "required them to be 'deinstitutionalized,' not controlled, treated, or
protected." With the enactment of this law, "the historic notion that children have a right to be in the custody of their parents or legal guardians
was rejected, and the premise that children have a right to freedom from
custody was adopted." The removal of young Americans from custody and
control had purportedly unleashed upon civil society "a series of unin-
tended consequences, similar to the consequences of deinstitutionalizing
the mentally ill." While "the vast majority of children opted for control, discipline, care, support, love, and attention from their families," the ABMC
publication explained, "thousands did not, and they were set adrift" by
experts who "had relegated these children to the status of 'little adults.'"
By blaming "professional[s]" and "[s]elf-proclaimed 'child advocates'"
for the perceived crisis in child safety, the ABMC tapped into an intensifying national resentment of civic institutions and expertise, even as the
board members (themselves federally supported experts) proffered policy
solutions for the putative "national epidemic" of missing and exploited
children.[36]

The ABMC members also took aim at the federal government.
They claimed that, by embracing the professional consensus on

deinstitutionalization, elected officials and other government operatives had weakened the family and exacerbated the problems of stranger abduction and runaway youth. The JJDP Act, the board members admitted, had produced some "community services" that had proven "helpful," but "where resources are scarce and a commitment to keeping families intact is lacking, children and families may never be able to resolve fundamental problems that cause repeated family disruptions." In order to receive federal funding, halfway houses, youth shelters, and other sites "designed to deal with runaway and throwaway children" could not physically restrain their occupants. The ABMC bemoaned this fact. "By mandating nondetention and nonsecure holding intervention by police and juvenile courts," the JJDP Act had "fostered and encouraged the very result it sought to avoid— the tragedy of more and more children who are out of parental control." Board members accordingly called for the full repeal of the JJDP Act's deinstitutionalization provision.[37]

Regnery endorsed the ABMC report and similarly blamed the JJDP Act and the federal government for the issues of missing and exploited children. In correspondence with William Bradford Reynolds, assistant attorney general and head of the DOJ's civil rights division, Regnery expressed dismay over the ABMC's findings. "Much of what the Board has to say is alarming," he wrote. "Many of our Nation's children are being exploited and sexually abused by pimps, pornographic filmmakers, and drug pushers. Their childhoods are filled with pain, abandonment, and the dehumanizing horrors of life on urban streets." Regnery saw federal policymakers as the principal architects of this crisis. Though he acknowledged the misplaced emphasis on stranger kidnappings, Regnery camouflaged the fact that parental and familial abductions make up the overwhelming majority of child kidnappings. "While abduction by nonfamily members is a visible and dramatic chapter in the missing children's story [sic], it is only part of the tale," he told Reynolds. "America's forgotten missing children are the runaways who are vulnerable and in constant danger as they struggle to survive on the streets, at least partially because of Federal law." Runaways were and remain a serious social problem, to be sure, but so are parental and familial abductions, phenomena that Regnery ignored altogether. He likely avoided any mention of "family danger" because it might have undermined the Reagan administration's appeals to "family values," as well as his own hope "that the juvenile justice system can guarantee every child's right to supervision and protection."[38]

The ABMC report did note that many American youths faced threats from their own family members and discussed the disproportionate attention garnered by stranger kidnapping cases; nonetheless, the board members stated that the family unit held the keys to keeping children safe and maintaining social order. A purported late twentieth-century spike in parental or other familial abductions, the ABMC members wrote, had resulted from broader shifts in family forms and other lamentable structural transformations. "As divorce, separation of parents, and single parenting in a mobile society increase," read the report, "the problems of family abduction also increase." Only by fortifying the two-parent American family and mitigating the issues of divorce, separation, and single parenting would the issue of familial kidnapping subside. While the young "victims of family abduction may be properly cared for," the ABMC members concluded, "they are deprived of contact with those left behind and often suffer enormous feelings of guilt and isolation." By contrast, the report indicated that young Americans who fell victim to "nonfamily abduction are statistically the smallest group of missing children," yet "this category is the most highly publicized and certainly the one families fear most." By foregrounding "nonfamily abduction" as perhaps the most troubling type of child disappearance for "families," the ABMC seemed to absolve parents and other family members, who commit the overwhelming majority of child kidnappings. Further, the ABMC report neglected to discuss child sexual abuse perpetrated by parents or relatives, insinuating that strangers and acquaintances alone were responsible for such attacks upon young people. The Advisory Board thus took parental and familial kidnappings as somehow less worrisome than those perpetrated by nonfamily members, even though the latter were (and remain) far more common, and family members commit a sizable proportion of sexual assaults against minors.[39]

Fittingly, *America's Missing & Exploited Children: Their Safety and Their Future* suggested that familial stability—and the placement of certain children in parental custody—could remedy what ailed young Americans. In the introduction to their report, the board members identified "certain steps [that] must be taken to reduce the heartbreaking problem of abducted, abandoned, and runaway children," the first of which hinged upon "family values" and the reconsolidation of the American family. "We believe the first step is to bolster "family values" and to stop the continued disintegration of the family," the report read. "Caring parents or legal guardians who give children love, discipline, and support can be powerful influences. We have outlined special roles for the family and government in an effort to prevent children from being out of their homes unlawfully." To that end, one section of the ABMC publication bore the title, "What Can Families and the Government Do?" At the beginning of this section appeared a photograph of a small white child happily perched upon his father's shoulders, his mother gazing on approvingly. Families like this one, whose outward appearance pointed to "a cohesive home life," were paramount "in preventing the terror and hazard of missing children." As the board members wrote, "The family holds our greatest hope of bringing stability to children's maturation processes. To resolve the many problems of missing children, we must recognize and commit ourselves to every child's right to family nurturing, protection, discipline, and family structure." For the ABMC, the government's role in resolving the child safety issue "should be limited," and state and federal laws ought to ensure "the maintenance or reunification of families without undue government interference."[40]

At first blush, the ABMC's policy recommendations seemed to comport with the antistatist politics of the Reagan era, through which conservatives purportedly sought to implement deregulatory policies and to devolve power to the states, private entities, and families. Many of the same impulses animated the US Attorney General's Commission on Pornography, commonly known as the Meese Commission after Attorney General Edwin Meese III. Released just two months after *America's Missing & Exploited Children*, the Commission's 1986 report advocated "the regulation of sexuality" through "increasingly privatized and less democratic forms of governance," historian Gillian Frank observes. The Meese Commission thereby empowered private actors, oftentimes religious conservatives, to dictate the terms on which pornography circulated throughout the country. The ABMC pursued similar outcomes, with the board's 1986 report calling for the formation of "[p]ublic awareness programs" and the federal provision of "[t]raining incentives and assistance" to "child-serving professionals and personnel in local criminal and juvenile justice systems." At the same time, of course, the ABMC maligned the "inconsistent and counterproductive" federal policies that had supposedly harmed the "endangered American family."[41]

This devolutionist logic informed the third prong of the Reagan DOJ's child protection efforts, through which Regnery and other DOJ operatives funneled federal resources toward "profamily" initiatives in the private sector or within "less democratic forms of governance." In addition to the grants awarded to the NCMEC, an agency that aroused the suspicions of child welfare advocates, Regnery and other Reagan conservatives used OJJDP grants to promote "family values" projects devised to shield young Americans from the moral threats of smut and exploitation. Edwin Meese picked Regnery to informally administer the Reagan administration's antiporn efforts, and the OJJDP under Regnery's leadership issued a $125,000 grant to the President's Commission on Pornography. The Meese Commission's eleven-member board—which included James Dobson, founder of the conservative evangelical organization Focus on the Family— distorted the findings of social science studies and conflated the "child-porn black market" and "violent pornography" with "consensual adult pornography to cast a shadow over the entire field of adult entertainment." The controversial Meese Report focused disproportionate attention on child pornography, exaggerating the size of this "black market" without adequate supporting evidence and creating "the illusion of a monolithic porn industry that preyed on children." Some forty-five of the Commission's ninety-two policy recommendations dealt with child pornography.[42]

In much the same vein, Regnery extended dubious OJJDP grants to researchers examining complex social issues from a moralistic vantage. He allotted $734,371 for a study exploring how *Playboy*, *Hustler*, and *Penthouse* magazines depicted children through cartoons and photographs. The grant proposal for the study lamented that "millions" of American children participated in a commercial sex enterprise fueled, in part, by pornographic images displaying "[a]n adult attacking a child sexually." Senator Arlen Specter once again questioned Regnery's decision making in light of this research plan. "I have read those magazines myself," Specter remarked during a 1985 Senate hearing. "We have had them at these hearings, and I have never seen a picture of a child being the victim of a crime actually appearing in the magazine." Specter pressed on in his questioning. "After you had the detailed analysis" of such images, "what good does that do you? . . . I do not see the value of this study if its content analysis stops short of the cause and effect to child molestation. It gives you a body of information for $734,000 which stops short of the only question involved, and that is, does this material cause sexual molestation[?]" Senator Strom Thurmond too doubted the need for such an analysis in a time of economic austerity. Still, Regnery insisted the project could pave the way for subsequent research on child molestation and exploitation. Other OJJDP grants authorized on Regnery's watch also raised eyebrows, including a $186,710 award to help a Liberty University dean design a high school course on the US Constitution and a noncompetitive $4.25 million grant to assist Meese's friend and associate in founding the National School Safety Center at Pepperdine University.[43]

Nevertheless, efforts by the Reagan DOJ to keep kids safe, even those that devolved power to private agencies and to the states, cannot be understood exclusively within the framework of antistatism, especially considering the carceral buildup that complemented such projects. As historians like Julilly Kohler-Hausmann, Brent Cebul, Lily Geismer, and Mason Williams have shown, the reductive dichotomy of "big government" and "small government" fails to capture the continuities between the penal and welfare systems administered (to a large extent) through the federal government. The expanding carceral apparatus of the late twentieth century did not supplant the welfare state. Rather, the functions of the penal and welfare systems became increasingly punitive and increasingly intertwined over this period. The "state transformations" underwriting the rise of mass incarceration and the reconfiguration of the welfare state turned less on questions of growing or constraining government power and more on "struggles over *how* to direct (while also obscuring) state intervention."[44]

On that score, the private sector action endorsed by Regnery, the ABMC, and the Reagan DOJ coincided with the emergence of more punitive federal solutions to child protection in the late 1980s and early 1990s. Attempts to place particular children in the "lawful, caring custody" of the family and to raise awareness about the problems of missing and exploited children through private sector programs like the milk carton initiative corresponded with a growing federal reliance on imprisoning and monitoring those who harmed young Americans. The ABMC's 1986 report took a hardline stance on locking up "the adult offender," alleging that "the primary focus of prevention activities has been to alert parents and children to the possibility of victimization." The criminal justice system should concentrate instead on prosecuting and punishing "[t]he adult offender who abuses children, leads them into prostitution, victimizes them by pedophilic conduct or pornography, or pushes them into street crime." The board members also called for harsher prison sentences and for deeper consideration of "victims' rights," in accordance with the themes guiding Reagan-era anticrime efforts.[45]

This proposed restructuring of the criminal justice system required the application of more federal resources to enforce new, punitive child protection laws and to formalize the connection between "missing" and "exploited" children. In the 1970s and 1980s, Americans increasingly petitioned for more punitive solutions to an array of social problems—from drug abuse and drunk driving, to domestic battery and sex crimes; from the "nuisance" offenses of which transients were disproportionately accused, to minor property crimes committed by juveniles. The same impulse undergirded government responses to matters of child protection in the late twentieth century. With the passage of the 1978 Protection of Children Against Sexual Exploitation Act, the federal government began, in earnest, to regulate child pornography. The law made the production and distribution of child porn a federal offense and established mandatory-minimum sentences for all convicted traffickers, including first-time offenders. The 1984 Child Protection Act built on the 1978 legislation by escalating penalties for the production and distribution of child pornography.[46]

On the heels of the 1986 Meese Report, the US Congress passed the Child Sexual Abuse and Pornography Act, as well as the Child Abuse Victims'

Rights Act, both in 1986. The former made gender-neutral the 1910 Mann Act, which had imposed federal restrictions on the interstate transportation of women and girls "for the purpose of prostitution or debauchery, or for any other immoral purpose." The Child Abuse Victims' Rights Act created new civil mechanisms through which victims of child abuse or exploitation could seek restitution. The Child Protection and Obscenity Enforcement Act, tucked into the 1988 Anti-Drug Abuse Act, declared the dissemination via computer of illicit material involving children to be a federal offense. The 1988 law also enumerated recordkeeping requirements for the manufacture and distribution of pornographic materials. It demanded those producing any "visual depiction of actual sexually explicit conduct" to "ascertain, by examination of an identification document containing such information, the performer's name and date of birth." The Child Protection Restoration and Penalties Enhancement Act, part of the 1990 Crime Control Act, made it a federal offense to possess child pornography and ordered the US Sentencing Commission to impose "more substantial penalties" on those convicted of sex crimes against children. These developments expanded federal authority in the realm of child protection and augmented the DOJ's role in "patrolling the frontiers of innocence," just as the Internet revolutionized the ways in which moral threats like pornography, kidnapping, and exploitation took shape. The growing federal emphasis on shielding young people from these moral threats, while punishing those who embodied such threats, curbed the children's rights gains of the 1960s and 1970s and paved the way for the enhanced policing and punishment of child exploitation in the digital age.[47]

These punitive child protection projects intersected with efforts to "get tough" on juvenile delinquency. As construed by the DOJ, OJJDP, NCMEC, and Reagan administration officials, these policy tracks focused on two categories of children, each of which assumed particular racial and class associations. The main proponent of these policy pursuits, Alfred S. Regnery, had fallen short in his attempts to close the OJJDP. But he had, upon resigning as OJJDP administrator in May 1986, succeeded in moving the Office into a more hardline position on juvenile justice.[48] In so doing, Regnery contributed to a carceral boom—orchestrated by federal, state, and local actors—that was felt most heavily among youth of color. On the other policy track, Regnery had helped the DOJ transition into the federal body most deeply invested in child safety. He also took steps to buttress familial and institutional authority in the name of protecting American youths. Even as journalists and social scientists in 1985 and 1986 chipped away at the embellished statistics and sensationalized reporting that had propelled the missing child campaign, Regnery toed the administration line.

"I don't think there's any epidemic of fear at all," he opined on a national news broadcast in December 1985. For Regnery, the child safety crusade "certainly has raised, in the consciousness of parents and of the American society generally, that the world is a dangerous place for unescorted children, for children not in the custody of an adult." Regnery's Manichean formulation, pitting the "dangerous" world against the reassuring "custody of an adult," hinged upon a romantic imagining of the American family and a nightmarish view of the world beyond the two-parent household.[49]

When stitched together, these complex (and, at times, seemingly contradictory) policy threads promoted private and public sector tools through which to control American youth—and to punish those who might do them harm. Regnery and other Reagan conservatives used the stranger danger scare and concerns about juvenile delinquency to call for the placement of young Americans in various types of custody. They implored the business and nonprofit sectors to formulate new child safety solutions and championed the heteronormative dual-parent family as a panacea for the problems confronting children and adolescents nationwide. Regnery and other Reagan acolytes sought to weaken the OJJDP and its dictates on deinstitutionalization and to empower state and local agencies to place young Americans in "custody"—whether in the form of the two-parent household, a secure juvenile detention facility, or an adult jail. Beyond these proposed solutions to the youth-oriented issues of stranger danger and juvenile delinquency—interlocking concerns ostensibly engendered by youth liberation—Reagan's DOJ became more invested in matters of youth abduction and exploitation, increasingly targeting the adults who supposedly threatened childhood innocence.

Spurred to action by the affective politics of child safety and the imagery of endangered childhood, the DOJ under Ronald Reagan cracked down on child pornography and endangerment with greater swiftness and certainty beginning in the mid- to late 1980s. Under Reagan, the DOJ transformed into the federal entity most involved in combating moral threats against children, a posture the Department maintained through the administrations of George H. W. Bush and Bill Clinton. As fears about crime and child endangerment proliferated in the 1980s and 1990s, so too did DOJ efforts to punish "predators." These DOJ instruments became key fixtures of a metastasizing child safety regime, whose growth depended on the diminishing autonomy of young people, a steadfast belief in the transformative power of "family values," and a punitive, carceral streak in policy-making at all levels of governance.

CHAPTER 6

ᴄⱴꙄ

"The Business of Missing Children"

Child Protection in Public and Private

Upon announcing the establishment of the President's Citation Program for Private Sector Initiatives in 1984, President Ronald Reagan shared an anecdote intended to illustrate both the efficacy of the business sector and the inefficacy of the federal government. Jim Kerrigan, a representative from Trailways, had contacted Reagan to ascertain how the bus company could help address the missing children problem. Soon thereafter Trailways launched its Operation Home Free program, which allowed runaway youths to return home on its buses free of charge. "Perhaps you're wondering how much time passed between Jim's phone call and the first child's ride on a Trailways bus," Reagan told an audience gathered at the White House. "It was 10 days. You know, I can't help thinking how long it would have taken and how many millions of taxpayers' dollars would have been spent if the program had been put together by a Federal agency." The crowd laughed approvingly.[1]

The private sector first addressed the issue of missing children in the late 1970s and early 1980s, a moment in which the victims' rights movement achieved tremendous visibility and success.[2] Nonprofit organizations— some, like Child Find, Inc., founded by parents of lost, abducted, or murdered youths and funded through public contributions—led the charge to raise awareness about child kidnapping and to lobby the government for assistance. The Missing Children and Missing Children's Assistance Acts (MCA and MCAA) and the rhetoric marshaled behind them celebrated not just the efforts of private nonprofits and the bereaved parents who often spearheaded them, but also the activities of for-profit companies. In this context, the veneration of the private sector served at once to promote voluntarism, a central tenet of the Reagan presidency, and to criticize government ineptitude—all while touting the administration's accomplishments in the realms of child safety, "law and order," and "family values."

At the urging of the Reagan administration, private nonprofit and for-profit bodies formulated new child safety programs. These took three main forms: (1) in-kind benefits and services, such as free bus rides home for missing kids; (2) publicity tools, such as the milk carton initiative, designed to raise awareness about missing and exploited children; and (3) prevention programs and products like fingerprinting drives, insurance plans, and restraint devices. This explosion of private sector activity worked to obscure any distinction between public and private in the arena of child safety and therefore suggested a concerted national interest in preventing the commission of certain transgressions against young Americans. By cutting across boundaries of public and private, the burgeoning child safety regime found strength from a variety of sources.

To this end, such private sector solutions enlisted the American public in the increasingly punitive, pervasive, and invasive project of child safety. Liberally deploying the image of endangered childhood, private sector programs and products surrounded Americans with evidence of stranger danger and called on them to police and prevent predatory behavior against the nation's children. For instance, the Code Adam system, named for John Walsh's slain son Adam, supplies step-by-step directions for bystanders to follow in the wake of a child abduction perpetrated in public. First implemented in Walmart stores in the early 1990s and then adopted for use in other spaces nationwide, Code Adam scripts public behavior by dictating the appropriate response to an exceptionally rare event. The AMBER Alert program, unveiled in Texas shortly after the 1996 kidnapping and murder of nine-year-old Amber Hagerman and subsequently incorporated into federal law, has functioned in a similar manner, recruiting motorists, shoppers, bystanders, and others to participate in the search for missing kids. The same goes for the "Have You Seen Me?" program, founded in 1985, which continues to distribute missing children's photographs to over one hundred million American households weekly.[3]

Through these and other programs, the private sector enterprise of child safety also established a feedback loop. Private sector initiatives, visible in public and private settings alike, seemed to illustrate the sheer scope and severity of the missing child "epidemic." The proliferation of endangered child imagery in spaces of consumption, recreation, governance, family, and beyond signaled to Americans that the problems of child kidnapping and exploitation were widespread and worsening. From the milk carton campaign to Code Adam, a spate of new instruments rooted in the 1980s child kidnapping panic cropped up nationwide. By inundating Americans with the names and faces of missing kids, these instruments justified, through their very existence, the need for more and more tools to keep kids safe from predators. The enterprise of child safety, then, proved central to the development of the child safety regime in the late twentieth and early twenty-first centuries. Just as the Reagan administration championed the family, rather than the government, as the key instrument by which to mitigate the problems of missing, run-away, and exploited youth, it also lauded the role of the private sector, and specifically the for-profit sector, in resolving such issues. Further, just as the principles of child and family protection legitimated the expansion of the carceral state, so too did the propagation of private sector child safety instruments contribute to the growing project of monitoring young people and surveilling child predators. Thus, the family, the non-profit sector, and the business sector joined with the state in the late twentieth century to keep kids safe and punish the strangers who ostensibly threatened them.

MARKETING CHILD SAFETY

The child safety enterprise emerged in the early 1980s amidst diminishing public faith in government and in civic life more generally. The Vietnam quagmire, Watergate, a series of economic convulsions, and a succession of ineffectual presidents had corroded American confidence in the state. Further, the rights revolutions of the 1960s and 1970s had destabilized various sociocultural norms and previously sacrosanct institutions. Though these liberation campaigns, in the main, petitioned the state on behalf of progressive or radical causes, they also stressed the importance of identity, expression, and choice. Business and political elites coopted these floating signifiers. Lobbyists, public relations experts, and intellectuals—within and alongside organizations like the US Chamber of Commerce, National Association of Manufacturers, Business Roundtable, and even the Heritage Foundation—trafficked in the language of positive rights and identified consumer-citizenship and market capitalism as the vehicles through which to vanquish extant inequalities. They also imbued "business" with connotations of efficiency and efficacy while simultaneously denigrating the state. For these architects of the emergent neoliberal order, the "natural" free market would deliver in ways that a bloated and belea-guered bureaucratic state could not.[4]

As the stranger danger panic took hold in the late 1970s and early 1980s, private citizens and nonprofit groups lamented the federal government's seeming disinterest in tackling the problems of missing and exploited children. They situated such appeals within a burgeoning free-market funda-mentalism and a concomitant mistrust of government. As some of the first bodies to mobilize on matters of child safety in the seventies and eighties, private nonprofits demanded greater federal involvement in their cause. Founded by bereaved parents in 1980 and 1981, organizations such as Child Find Inc., the Vanished Children's Alliance, and the Adam Walsh Outreach Center wielded tremendous affective capital, building on a broader victims' rights movement and sensibility. The Reagan administration allied with these nonprofits by passing child protection legislation and encouraging the private sector, namely for-profit entities, to address public concerns about child protection. The outpouring of private and public sector activity sanctified voluntarism, underscored the severity of threats confronting young Americans, and produced new mechanisms by which to "publicize the plight of missing children."[5]

Bereaved parents and other child safety crusaders in the private sector conceived of their activism as a corrective to governmental inaction, and the news media buttressed this view. Nightly news broadcasts shared the grievances of anguished parents—some of whom "complain[ed] that there is no national network for information on missing children" while others, frustrated by "police dawdling," opened "private storefront operations" to find lost youths. A 1981 story on ABC's *World News Tonight* documented the work of the Clinkscales family in Georgia. A student at Auburn University in Alabama, Kyle Clinkscales had disappeared in 1976. By 1981, his family had invested $15,000 in "their personal search to find Kyle" and "started an organization called 'Find Me,' one of a growing number of groups of missing person's families." The Clinkscales had waged their campaign without the help of the government. As ABC journalist Al Dale explained, "in a day of high crime and with the Reagan administration pushing hard for budget cuts and less, not more, federal involvement in our lives, help for the parents" of missing children "may not come soon," despite their pleas for government assistance.[6]

Through the priceless child argument and other means, child safety activists chided the government for its perceived indifference to the issue of missing and exploited youth. During the congressional hearings on the proposed Missing Children Act in October 1981, John and Revé Walsh delivered a searing statement denouncing the state's putative disinterest in their campaign. Accompanied by a cover page from their Adam Walsh Outreach Center for Missing Children, on which appeared a widely circulated photograph of their late son holding a baseball bat, the Walshes' printed remarks placed the government's "disorder[ed]" priorities within the context of Reagan-era austerity and credited the private sector for picking up the slack. The couple noted "President Reagan's call for budget cuts in every area," which did not bode well for the development of a "centralized reporting system for missing children." Accordingly, the Walshes insisted, "We have to approach this [problem] from a business standpoint." The creation of a national database dedicated exclusively to storing the names and identification data of missing children, the couple contended, would prove cost-effective. Adam's disappearance and slaying "devastated us financially," they argued. "It cost every bit of savings we had as well as whatever money we could borrow. . . . The amount of time lost at work, the need for emotional counseling, the lost tax dollars, and the emotional wrecks of surviving parents that are cast on the welfare system of our society [are] enormous." The Walshes thereby portrayed their cause as financially sensible and consistent with neoliberal strategies for reconfiguring the welfare state. They also stressed the massive individual, familial, and national damage wrought by the missing children issue, which was only exacerbated by the seemingly cruel or indifferent orientation of the Reagan administration. "It is almost inconceivable," the couple indicated, "in this great country with its resources, that this problem exists and continues to exist." John Walsh offered a similar assessment on the CBS *Evening News* in 1981. Concerning the establishment of a missing child database, reporter Ned Potter paraphrased Walsh, "'Surely we can come up with the money,' says John Walsh. I can't imagine what could be more important than the children." The nationally broadcast CBS story ended with a close-up of the iconic photograph of Adam clutching a baseball bat, smiling gleefully (despite his missing front teeth), strands of his shaggy brown hair poking out from under his ballcap.[7]

Other Americans, even those who had not lost children, echoed the Walshes' claims. Mitch McConnell, a Jefferson County, Kentucky, judge, acknowledged the harmful effects of federal cutbacks in the sphere of child protection. In a November 1981 congressional hearing, McConnell explained, "The national reduction of resources for social services and local assistance at this particular time complicates the follow up" in cases of missing and exploited children, meaning the "[g]overnment must increasingly enlist private-sector assistance and involvement." McConnell alleged "that a chief cause of child tragedies is the inability of government to recognize a problem and to respond." Kristin Cole Brown, the information director for Child Find Inc., chastised federal officials for dragging their feet but commended other institutions like hers for effectively addressing the missing child problem. "I think that most Americans have a healthy respect, and an even healthier skepticism, for our government," Brown affirmed. Yet, she lamented, "There is no national Missing Persons' Bureau . . . no publicly funded clearinghouse assigned exclusively to missing children's names . . . [and] no publicly funded national program which helps searching parents find their missing children." Thankfully, Brown explained, "Child Find was created to help fill in this gap," and more generally, "the private sector has stepped into the void left by the government" on matters of child safety.[8]

In both rhetoric and action, the Reagan administration harnessed these emotionally resonant criticisms to paint the federal government as caring and well-intentioned yet flawed and to press for more private sector involvement on child protection. While Reagan had certainly gestured to the missing child issue before, he began to address it more explicitly with the June 1984 establishment of the National Center for Missing and Exploited Children (NCMEC). In this moment, the Reagan administration also assembled a public–private coalition on child safety, which enlisted for-profit entities as altruistic partners in the campaign to safeguard young Americans. At a ceremony marking the NCMEC's opening, Reagan announced the launch of "a public–private partnership" that would "take advantage of every opportunity available . . . to protect our children and keep them safe." The president discussed his recent appeals to the private sector and took heart in the robust response from businesses. "America is responding," he beamed. To this end, Reagan mentioned the development by Trailways—in coordination with the International Association of Chiefs of Police—of the Operation Home Free program and applauded television stations for their regular dissemination of missing children's photographs.[9]

As the president took a more vocal stance on child safety following the passage of the MCAA and the launch of the NCMEC, he continued his push for private sector involvement and his glorification of the "traditional" American family. In a radio address broadcast during the week of the NCMEC's opening, the president invited the family, the state, and the market to collaborate on the project of child protection. Reagan stressed his administration's efforts to assist the American family, as well as the ways in which his approach diverged from that of "big government" and "Big Brother" liberals, in his words. The president vowed, "we can and should preserve family values—values of faith, honesty, responsibility, tolerance, kindness, and love." Unlike the New Deal statists who "urged huge government subsidies, paying parents for expenses they used to handle themselves . . . pushing parents aside, [and] interfering with one parental responsibility after another," Reagan offered new ways to shore up the American family. "We came to Washington with a better idea," the president asserted, to "help working parents to better provide for themselves and their children by enabling them to keep more of their earnings and help them by making government do its job so the terrifying specter of runaway price increases never returns." Reagan then looked beyond fiscal policy. "We're trying hard to help fathers and mothers in other ways, too," he told listeners. "Many innocent children are exploited by those who traffic in the gutter of drugs, child pornography and prostitution . . . [a]nd this past week, we opened a National Center for Missing and Exploited Children to help educate parents and authorities on how to protect their loved ones." Reagan's "family values" platform, then, blended tax policies favorable to certain families with a concentrated private and public sector campaign to shield the American home from "moral threats" such as stranger danger, drugs, and "the smut merchants."[10]

The federal endorsement of private sector child safety efforts reflected Reagan's approach to voluntarism and business. From his establishment of the White House Office of Private Sector Initiatives in 1981 and the President's Advisory Council on Private Sector Initiatives in 1983, to the institution in 1984 of the President's Citation Program for Private Sector Initiatives, Reagan made voluntary, individual, and nonstate action central to his presidency. Nowhere was such action more apparent than in the sphere of child protection. To be sure, for-profit and nonprofit private sector entities regularly boasted of their community service accomplishments in all arenas. But with rhetorical and material reinforcement from the White House, programs centering on the safety of young Americans received considerable attention. This emphasis can be attributed to the public's significant interest, drummed up by news media coverage, in missing children and child safety; the seemingly pervasive notion that the state had failed to adequately protect American youths from stranger danger; and the nation's larger fears of criminal depravity and familial decline and dissolution.[11]

"KEEPING CHILDREN SAFE IS GOOD BUSINESS"

Out of this terrain grew an extensive collection of for-profit and nonprofit private sector programs intended to address the problem of missing and exploited children. The Reagan White House touted such projects (and the ways in which they supposedly benefited the American family) throughout the mid-eighties. In addition to creating the NCMEC, the

1984 MCAA formed the US Attorney General's Advisory Board on Missing Children, which supplied proposals for public and private sector action on child safety. In April 1985, the president issued Executive Order 12511 establishing the President's Child Safety Partnership (PCSP). Charged with "examin[ing] issues and mak[ing] recommendations to the President on preventing the victimization and promoting the safety of children," the PCSP would also "encourage the development of public/private sector initiatives to prevent and respond to the victimization of children." On that score, one US Department of Justice memo read, "The government needs to be a 'guiding light'" for such child safety programs, "but the impetus must come from the private sector. There is a need for more corporate involvement, and the corporations that do get involved need recognition from such high level officials as the President and the Attorney General periodically." Accordingly, the PCSP envisaged the private sector, and especially for-profit entities, as vital pieces in the "Circle of Safety for Our Children," which also included families and the government. "To be credible," another Justice Department memorandum read, the PCSP "must include private (corporate and private non-profit) sector representatives who have made contributions in this area [of child protection], as well as representatives of state and local government." The PCSP asked businesses to "provide support for child safety programs" and to "increase child safety awareness among the public and the business community," assuring companies that "[k]eeping children safe is good business."[12]

In his remarks upon signing the April 1985 PCSP executive order, President Reagan fit the PCSP within a larger "challenge" he had issued the previous year when he asked the private sector to assist "in combating the problem of missing children." Speaking before a display spotlighting child safety ventures undertaken by American businesses, the president cited a slew of programs overseen by well-known companies like Woolworth, K-Mart, Ringling Brothers & Barnum and Bailey Circus, and Safeway. Taking Reagan's cue, the PCSP championed programs such as Mobil's "year-long public awareness and education campaign focused on missing children," which gave the appearance of improving young people's lives but actually amounted to little more than public relations maneuvers. Still, without presenting any evidence, the PCSP insisted that child safety programs underwritten by businesses "help reduce crime" and "are critical investments for safeguarding America's future workforce and maintaining healthier communities." Such initiatives "offer an opportunity for business to demonstrate its concern for customers and employees' children, which readily translates into enhanced business image and improved employee morale." Indeed, "some companies visibly involved in child safety efforts

Figure 6.1 Established to encourage collaboration between the public and private sectors on the issue of missing and exploited children, the President's Child Safety Partnership (PCSP) employed this graphic in its 1987 report to the president. "By joining hands," this report read, "we will encircle one child, then another and another, until together we have created a circle of safety to surround and protect every child in America." The PCSP envisioned the business sector as a vital player in this "circle of safety." President's Child Safety Partnership and the Office for Victims of Crime, *A Report to the President*, 11, in Richard B. Abell to Edwin Meese III, September 25, 1987, box 269, Edwin Meese files, subject files of the Attorney General (1975–93), RG 60, National Archives and Records Administration, College Park, Maryland.

have experienced welcome but unexpected increases in business." Not only did these private sector endeavors supplement government efforts, then; they were also designed to capture market share for "responsible," family-oriented, child-friendly businesses. "[A]ll of these companies," Reagan reminded listeners during his speech inaugurating the PCSP, "are just part of a larger effort" of "organizations coming up with creative programs using their resources." Almost as an afterthought, he added, "It's important to note here that the Federal Government, too, is involved."[13]

Though evident before Reagan issued his "challenge," this "larger effort" of private sector activity flourished in 1984 and 1985 and took three principal forms: (1) in-kind benefits and services, (2) awareness and publicity programs, and (3) prevention programs and products. The extent of these private sector measures, specifically those executed by for-profit companies, suggests that businesses adequately met Reagan's challenge. The range of participating institutions also demonstrated the sheer reach of the problems of missing and exploited children—and pointed to the many spaces inhabited by the imagery of endangered childhood. By surrounding Americans with proof of stranger danger, these initiatives justified their very existence. Furthermore, by promoting the companies that engineered them and the families that supposedly reaped their benefits, such efforts advanced some of the Reagan administration's core thematic objectives vis-à-vis social and economic policy: glorifying families and businesses, restoring "law and order" and moral "commonsense," and impugning the federal government.[14]

First, for-profit companies extended in-kind benefits and services to missing youths, their families, and child safety organizations. American Airlines, through the NCMEC, transported parents and guardians free of charge to recover missing, abducted, and runaway children. Jack Rabbit Lines, a bus line serving the "Mountain Plains states," ferried runaway children and adolescents to homes within its service area or to a location where a transfer could be made onto a Trailways bus. Each Quality Inn hotel functioned as "a 'safe harbor' for any child in danger of abduction or exploitation," and the chain also housed parents traveling to meet their lost, kidnapped, or otherwise missing kids. Moreover, every Quality Inn hotel lobby provided "a direct access line to the National Center for Missing and Exploited Children" and showcased pictures of missing children.[15]

Media outlets set aside airtime and print space for the delivery of endangered child narratives and imagery. Television and newspaper coverage also allowed elected officials to communicate their ideas about child safety to the public. At a 1985 White House meeting of the National Newspaper Association, a private trade association, Reagan called on members of the print media to join the child protection campaign. In a wide-ranging speech that touched on various facets of his second term agenda, the president decried "national edicts and mandates that are issued from Washington" and lauded "the toil and creativity of [American] people working at the local level through their own private institutions and associations" as "the real source of America's economic and social progress." He impressed upon the audience the importance of limiting federal expenditures and summoning the "great power for public service that [newspapers] possess." Reminding those gathered that "a President can only do so much," Reagan identified "the problem of missing children" as "one especially tragic area where your newspapers can do a great deal of good." By following the lead of NBC in its production and dissemination of *Adam*, Reagan submitted, local papers "could publish, as a regular feature, pictures and descriptions of children missing in or near your circulation areas."[16]

Other elected officials too used the power of the national media to disseminate statements about child protection, voluntarism, and private sector involvement. On several occasions in 1984 and 1985, US congressman Mickey Edwards (R–Oklahoma)—working in tandem with the

NCMEC—directed televised events in which congresspersons spotlighted missing children from their districts. Through speeches on the House floor that were broadcast via C-SPAN, representatives "provide[d] information about children who have been abducted by strangers in their congressional districts." Edwards conceded that "publicity about specific cases has been helpful," but "there is no current effort to focus television coverage on specific individuals, with the exception of occasional local, regional, or national news stories." His initiative therefore leveraged the power of the relatively new (and publicly owned) C-SPAN network and the ascendant medium of cable television to raise awareness about missing children and specifically stranger danger.[17]

Edwards also reached out to for-profit television outlets to secure their assistance in the child safety crusade. He proposed a joint resolution in May 1985 to "express the sense of the Congress that the television broadcasting stations of the Nation should provide television coverage concerning missing children." Later that year, Edwards wrote to Terri Rabel, the government relations manager at the National Association of Broadcasters—another private trade association—to request information about televised "public affairs programming" related to missing children. In her response, Rabel compiled relevant newspaper clippings that revealed the impressive extent of media industry involvement. From short public service announcements starring Bill Cosby, who appeared at the FBI's behest, to the NBC television special *Missing . . . Have You Seen This Person?*, media outlets, according to one 1985 news story, had "join[ed] the ranks of corporations and other organizations helping in the campaign to find missing children."[18]

Companies outside the media realm also transmitted the message of endangered childhood in the mid-1980s. Safeway, Winn-Dixie, and other supermarket chains placed missing children's photographs on their grocery bags. Nestle Food Inc. sent to over 5,500 stores displays featuring pictures of missing youths. K-Mart enclosed in "customers' photo-finishing envelopes" some 135 million images of missing children annually. The NCMEC teamed up with toy manufacturer Worlds of Wonder to designate plush animal Teddy Ruxpin the "official Spokesbear of the National Center." Ruxpin also provided therapeutic comfort to "child victims testifying against their abusers." The rental car company Avis put missing children's photographs in the rental agreement folders of at least eight million customers each year. NASCAR partnered with the National Crime Prevention Council (NCPC), which had developed McGruff the Crime Dog, to circulate child safety materials to 250,000 people. The convenience store chain 7-Eleven also collaborated with the NCPC and McGruff, "delivering child safety tips" through some 1,500 "McGruff houses" located in 7-Eleven shops.[19]

In 1985 ADVO Inc., introduced its "Have You Seen Me?" (or "America's Looking for its Missing Children") program in coordination with the NCMEC and the US Postal Service. The campaign distributed direct-mail leaflets featuring missing children's photographs and descriptive information, as well as coupons and advertisements for various retailers and service providers. Perhaps more than any other program, "Have You Seen Me?" reflected the commodification of childhood that characterized the child safety enterprise. As literary theorist Marilyn Ivy has detailed, the name "ADVO" refers both to "*advertising*" and "*advocacy*," suggesting that

Figure 6.2 McGruff the Crime Dog hugs a child at Woodmen Hills Elementary School in Peyton, Colorado, during "Crime Prevention Month," October 2012. Photograph by Duncan Wood. Courtesy of the United States Air Force. https://www.peterson.af.mil/News/Article/326553/scruff-mcgruff-takes-a-bite-out-of-crime-prevention-month/.

the "Have You Seen Me" initiative cultivates in its audience both "the desire to recover the missing child" and "the desire to find the missing commodity thing," whether it be hot wings or an oil change. The US Senate adopted a similar initiative, also in 1985, authorizing the dissemination of missing children's photographs on official government mail.[20]

Beyond such awareness and publicity programs, segments of the child safety enterprise fixated on the prevention of child abduction, sometimes in overzealous ways. Fingerprinting drives (often conducted at police stations) and do-it-yourself fingerprinting kits proliferated in the early 1980s. Some credited police sergeant Richard T. Ruffino of Bergen County, New Jersey, with popularizing the idea of fingerprinting at a November 1981 conference on missing children in Louisville, Kentucky, but others like the Patzes had endorsed the practice earlier. In 1983, New York City mayor Ed Koch initiated a voluntary program through which a projected four hundred thousand area schoolchildren would be fingerprinted. That same year, *Time* magazine declared that a "Frenzy of Fingerprinting" had swept the country. The corporate world helped facilitate this frenzy. In conjunction with Pepsi-Cola, Safeway, and an organization called Find the Children, NBC spearheaded an identification project that fingerprinted an estimated twenty-four thousand youngsters in the Los Angeles area. Media coverage of such efforts generally stressed the severity of the missing child problem and underscored the wisdom of having youngsters fingerprinted.[21]

But others viewed fingerprinting and other child identification initiatives as invasions of privacy, manifestations of the police and surveillance states. Some representatives from the American Civil Liberties Union (ACLU) vehemently opposed such programs. One Connecticut ACLU leader opined that fingerprinting "smacks of big brotherism" and that these records "could be misused at some point and involve children in criminal investigations." Civil-libertarian skeptics wondered who would maintain physical control of fingerprints and other identification records. In some cases, parents or guardians kept the only copies of fingerprint sheets, while in others law enforcement agencies retained copies for their records. The national ACLU officially endorsed, or at least tolerated, the practice of fingerprinting youngsters, though it opposed the retention of these records by government bodies. For his part, the publisher of *Search* magazine, a quarterly publication distributed to law enforcement agencies and hospitals to help locate missing persons, objected to child fingerprinting because of its supposed inefficacy and invasiveness. He called it a "10-cent solution to a $100 problem" and lamented, "[i]f the police start keeping children's fingerprints, then 1984 is here for sure," alluding to the dystopian George Orwell novel. Popular pediatrician Benjamin Spock likewise spoke out against fingerprinting, comparing it to the Cold War atomic bomb drills that, he argued, did little more than fuel fears of nuclear holocaust. Fingerprinting children, Spock held, "gives parents a false sense of security and does nothing to prevent kidnapping."[22]

Private entities began selling child identification kits, drawing the ire of those who felt fingerprinting and other comparable services should only be performed by law enforcement officials. In Los Angeles, private firms contacted local schools offering to fingerprint children at a cost of $2 to $12 per person. Child Find Inc., an independent organization founded in New Paltz, New York, came under scrutiny in 1980 for its questionable fundraising tactics and allocation of resources. Although it purported to be a nonprofit organization, Child Find allegedly pocketed a staggering percentage of the donations received in exchange for its fingerprinting and identification kits, as well as its investigative and publicity services, which, some parents alleged, the group had failed to provide. Authorities from the New York state attorney's office investigated Child Find and discovered that the organization, which reported $461,367 in donations in 1983–1984, "didn't deliver promised services." Further, the state attorney's investigators concluded, Child Find "had misled people into thinking the group located missing children," when in fact it only served as a repository or registry for the lost.[23]

Launched in 1985 as a part of Reverend Jerry Falwell's conservative evangelical group the Moral Majority, the Child Protection Task Force (CPTF) also aroused suspicion for its fingerprinting and broader child protection efforts. The CPTF's promotional materials, awash in sensationalist rhetoric, deemed missing children "the slaves of perverted molesters." Falwell's words and image appeared in some CPTF advertisements, while others featured a photograph of President Reagan, accompanied by his quotation designating American children as "our most precious resource . . . the bond that binds our past with the future." These ads solicited donations from the public to cover the costs of generating and delivering Child Protection Safety Kits. Law enforcement officials and others questioned the utility of such do-it-yourself kits, advising that only professionals should record and archive children's fingerprints and that Americans could assemble such supplies free of charge with the assistance of local authorities. A Moral Majority letter to potential donors stated that the task force needed "to raise $200,000 just in the next three weeks" in order to fulfill requests for the safety kits, which contained identification cards and other educational materials. Though these kits lacked value, the CPTF hauled in about $100,000 in donations to support the distribution of such kits before the organization folded.[24]

Some enterprising businesses provided even more invasive products and services through which parents could monitor their children or obtain vital information for use in the event of a kidnapping. Parents flocked to Circuit City retail stores in New York City and other major urban centers to professionally videotape their children. Should any of these kids fall victim to a kidnapping, their tapes could serve as documentary evidence of the young person's appearance and mannerisms. The Missouri-based Ident Corporation of America produced a microchip that could be attached to a child's tooth and used to track their movements. For his part, Massachusetts dentist David Tesini developed a program called Toothprints after hearing John Walsh discuss the role of pediatric dentists in positively identifying his son's body. Drawing inspiration from the Walsh case, Tesini decided to supply parents with their children's unique dental information. Employing "a patented, arch-shaped thermoplastic dental impression wafer," Toothprints recorded "a young patient's unique tooth characteristics by showing the size and shape of the teeth, tooth position within the arch, and maxillomandibular (jaws) relation, all of which can serve as important identifiers." Dentists across the country, sometimes in coordination with private organizations like Child Find, sponsored child safety drives through which they compiled dental charts to place alongside other items in a child identification pack. Other dental professionals even affixed onto children's teeth "microdots," tiny implants that worked as a kind of barcode that could be read by doctors, law enforcement officials, or virtually anyone with a microscope. Journalist Bill Geist, reporting on Circuit City's child videotaping program, encountered a concerned mother who told another parent "considering identifying tatoos [sic] for his son and daughter" that "dental implants were better because they were flame retardant."[25]

In addition to promoting child tracking technologies like Toothprints, private nonprofit and for-profit entities also offered instruments designed to physically restrict the movements of young Americans. Retailing for $129.95, an electronic device called Kiddie Alert sounded an alarm if a child wandered too far from their parent. "You would certainly pay $129.95 to help protect your child's life," read an advertisement for the gadget, and its product packaging called the device "A Breakthrough in CHILD SAFETY." In a television spot, an older spokesman introduced Kiddie Alert as a "new electronic monitoring system that can keep your child out of the headlines," a reference to the high-profile cases that gave rise to the stranger danger panic. Another product, dubbed Kid-Kuffs, used nylon straps to connect a child's wrist to the waist of a parent or guardian. The president of Zelex Inc., the manufacturer of Kid-Kuffs, discussed the utility of his company's product: "Where the adult goes, the child goes. He doesn't get stolen, run over or in trouble. And when the children are grown, you can use [Kid-Kuffs] as a dog leash." Companies produced leashes made especially for children as well. Founded in 1984, Safety 1st pioneered the "Baby on Board" logo and slogan, with which it marketed child leashes and other products. Mommy's Helper opened its doors in 1986 and manufactured the Kid Keeper, a harness that fastened to a child's torso.[26] All these products no doubt benefited from Reagan's endorsement of private sector responses to the child safety scare.

"A SAFE POLITICAL ISSUE"

Benjamin Spock and the ACLU were not the only ones dismayed about the child safety enterprise. Journalists, child welfare advocates, and others criticized businesses for preying on parents' anxieties to "mak[e] dollars and cents off this issue, off this national tragedy," in the words of one Kentucky state official. "Profiteers are cashing in nationwide," *Chicago Tribune* reporters Hanke Gratteau and Ray Gibson wrote in 1985, "on the millions of dollars generated in a growing public concern over the problem of missing children." Gratteau and Gibson exposed a slew of businesses "hawking products and services" that were either "useless" or redundant— that is, "available free of charge" elsewhere. The *Tribune* story also highlighted ethically suspect startups like the for-profit Missing Children Information Services Inc., based in Lexington, Kentucky. In its promotional materials, the company included "photographs of a half-naked girl shackled to a bed frame, one eye appearing bruised and blackened." But a company partner, a former professor in the Department of Psychiatry at the University of Kentucky's medical school, confessed to staging these photos using his seven-year-old daughter. The *Chicago Tribune* article was part of a larger news media effort to challenge the bases of the child safety panic, namely the inflated statistics undergirding it.[27]

Various medical professionals and child welfare advocates chastised those responsible for barraging Americans young and old with "horror stories about missing children," "photos on grocery bags, billboards, and milk cartons," and "advertisements for products and services to protect children from strangers." Testifying before the House Subcommittee on Human Resources in 1985, Kenneth Wooden, himself a child safety hawk, raged against the "army of child-saving charlatans." These hucksters, Wooden claimed, were "marching over the newly-turned soil of parental fears with an array of unlimited quick and easy solutions" to the stranger danger threat.

As the founder of Child Lures Prevention, a group established in 1983 to protect kids from sexual and other forms of abuse, Wooden had made a career
out of alerting children and their families to the perils of sexual predation.
Yet he objected to the "national paranoia" that had spawned an industry
of "disgracefully ineffective" child protection mechanisms. "Identification
kits are selling at $30 to $35 each," he informed Congress. "Bite prints [like
Toothprints] are coming on strong. Insurance companies are selling abduction policies, and a company offers custom made extended handcuffs that
link the child to the parent as they shop in the local supermarket." Such
"entrepreneurism," Wooden maintained, "reflect[ed] an increasing climate of fear in this country." Curiously, though, Wooden pinned this "climate of fear" on the government's supposed inability to prioritize what he
called "the criminally abducted child"—that is, a young person kidnapped
by a stranger. While Wooden insisted he was "not minimizing the trauma
inflicted in parental snatchings," he viewed such incidents as mostly benign
and "seriously question[ed] why these missing children [taken by parents in
custody disputes] are given the same, if not more, national attention than
the children abducted by strangers." Wooden's interpretation jarred with
the fact that most, if not all, of the prominent missing child cases featured
in news media and pop culture accounts involved stranger kidnappings,
which were and remain extremely rare.[28]

Others linked the child safety enterprise to the disproportionate media
and political emphasis on stranger danger. Doak Bloss, a Michigan social justice activist committed to issues of runaway and "thrownaway"
youth, condemned the twinned business and political manipulation of
stranger danger fears. "Business[es] are interested because it's a safe political issue," Bloss argued in an interview with Toledo Blade reporter Laurie
Krauth. "It improves their image." To that end, Krauth indicated, companies "have hopped on the 'stranger danger' bandwagon with goodwill and
profit-making projects. They have put reproductions of the faces of missing
children on signs, products, junk mail, and utility bills without concrete
information that these methods help locate children." Because "parents
are so alarmed" about the issue of stranger danger, Bloss insisted, "they
become vulnerable to businesses offering products that offer more symbolic than helpful [assistance]." Such private sector pursuits, said Bloss,
mirrored political responses to the stranger danger problem. "There are
some real dangers to the hotness of the 'stranger abduction' issue, with
businesses and state agencies pushing projects that aren't well thought
out," Bloss explained. Paraphrasing Bloss, Krauth wrote, "Politicians are
guaranteed praise from constituents for pushing missing-children legislation, regardless of its proven value."[29]

Writing in the influential journal *Pediatrics* in 1986, pediatrician Abraham Bergman conveyed a similar sense of outrage over what he termed "The Business of Missing Children." "No pediatric issue has so captured the attention of the American public during the past year as that of missing children," he noted. "It is impossible to escape the haunting faces who peer out at us from television screens, milk cartons, breakfast cereal boxes, grocery sacks, bus posters, and business envelopes. Corporations vie with each other over sponsorship of public service campaigns to 'publicize the plight of missing children,' while television stations compete with a whole variety of specials." But, for Bergman, this "whole new industry" formed in the wake of the missing child scare "is a fraud" that "needs to be exposed." Many of the entrepreneurs "involved are misguided, and some are plain greedy," he continued. "Children and parents are being victimized by the campaign itself. . . . [I]t seems unfortunate to constantly confront children with the specter of being hoisted off by a wicked stranger, when, in fact, that danger is about as likely as being struck by lightning."[30]

These sorts of responses put a slight damper on the child safety cause and the private sector enterprise built in response to it. In its 1988 report, the US Attorney General's Advisory Board on Missing Children lamented this apparent ebb in the stranger danger panic. For the newly reconstituted ABMC—which now included Focus on the Family founder James Dobson and Missouri governor John Ashcroft—the problem of missing and exploited children was "at a crossroad . . . no longer accompanied by television movies, cover stories in major national magazines or other signs of a newly discovered issue that captures public attention and demands an effective response." Contrary to the ABMC's account, though, stranger danger remained a pervasive concern in the late eighties and into the final decade of the twentieth century. Just as President Reagan had issued a "challenge" to the private sector in 1984 and 1985, the ABMC proclaimed in 1988 that "the challenge continues." For both Reagan and the ABMC, the "challenge" referred to private sector efforts to rectify the child safety issue. "Today," the 1988 ABMC report read, "the challenge of continuing to enlist the energies of the private sector is straightforward: to convey to the American public that while progress has been made, the tragedy of missing and exploited children is not some trendy issue whose time in the spotlight has passed, but rather a serious and disturbing social problem that requires—and deserves—a sustained commitment by America's business community and not-for-profit organizations."[31]

The private sector's child safety programming persisted into the 1990s and 2000s, when such initiatives intersected with emergent legal mechanisms to expand the child safety regime. By the second decade of the twenty-first century, an American commuter might pass a highway billboard—donated by Lamar advertising, CBS Outdoor, or Clear Channel Communications—flashing an AMBER Alert with information regarding a missing child. This commuter might receive the same emergency notice on her smart phone and on the evening news upon returning home. The next day, while at the post office or a Walmart store, she might walk past a bulletin board filled with missing children's photographs. Her local police department and sheriff's office might dedicate portions of their websites to child safety tips or missing child notices. While listening to National Public Radio or conservative talk radio programs during her morning commute, she might hear conversations about "free range" kids or news regarding an accused sex offender. And through the US Justice Department's Dru Sjodin National Sex Offender Public Website, formalized through the 2006 Adam Walsh Child Protection and Safety Act, she can determine if any registered sex offenders live in her neighborhood.

These ubiquitous child safety mechanisms, which cross and collapse the porous boundary between public and private, originated in the stranger danger scare of the 1980s. Bolstered by the names, faces, and stories of lost children, these instruments continue to populate spaces both public and private and to enlist the law-abiding public in the project of shielding select kids from select perils. Since its inception in the eighties, this enterprise has served to confront Americans young and old with the moral threats that ostensibly face young people. In so doing, it has justified the increasing surveillance of young Americans—and those who might do them harm. The child safety enterprise, publicized through pop culture, news media, and political channels, stoked the panic gripping the American public in the eighties and enabled the explosion of similarly conceived (yet increasingly punitive) private and public mechanisms in the 1990s and into the twenty-first century.

CHAPTER 7

ↀ

Circling the Wagon

Child Safety and the Punitive State in the Clinton Years

The Wetterlings had enjoyed their Sunday. It was October 22, 1989, and the kids had the day off from school the following day. The weather was unseasonably warm, with temperatures reaching the seventies, a good ten to fifteen degrees warmer than the average October high for central Minnesota. That morning, Jerry Wetterling had gone fishing with his son Jacob, an effervescent, handsome, and bright eleven-year-old. Jerry and Jacob then returned to their home in St. Joseph, a fifteen- to twenty-minute drive from the city of St. Cloud. They joined the rest of the family, wife and mother Patty and the three other Wetterling children—thirteen-year-old Amy, ten-year-old Trevor, and eight-year-old Carmen—to watch the Minnesota Vikings defeat the Detroit Lions, twenty to seven, at the Silverdome. After the game, the Wetterlings visited an indoor ice skating rink, and that evening, Jerry and Patty left for a dinner party some twenty miles from St. Joseph. Their eldest child Amy was visiting a friend's house, while the other Wetterling kids stayed home, along with Jacob's best friend Aaron Larson, also eleven years old. Jacob, Trevor, and Aaron eventually decided to ride their bikes and scooter (Aaron's preferred mode of transportation) to the Tom Thumb grocery store, about a mile and a half from the Wetterling residence, to rent a VHS copy of the 1988 slapstick comedy *The Naked Gun: From the Files of Police Squad!* Trevor called his mother Patty to ask if he, Jacob, and Aaron could go to the Tom Thumb, but she turned him down, insisting it was too dark outside. After some prodding, however, Jerry assented. Jacob arranged for a babysitter to look after his sister Carmen, and he left for the store with his brother and best friend.[1]

The boys made their way to the Tom Thumb at a leisurely pace, at times riding their bikes and scooter, and at other times walking. The Wetterling house, on Kiwi Court, sat at the southern edge of St. Joseph. A two-way, north-to-south road flanked by cornfields, trees, and a smattering of homes connected the Wetterling residence to downtown St. Joseph. Jacob, Trevor, and Aaron traveled along this road toward the Tom Thumb, arriving at the store around nine o'clock. After successfully renting *The Naked Gun*, the boys began the trek back to Kiwi Court to watch the movie.

Well into their return trip—close to the Wetterling home, yet far from the lights of the St. Joseph retail district—they were accosted by a masked assailant, later identified as twenty-six-year-old Danny James Heinrich. Claiming he had a gun, Heinrich asked the boys their ages. After learning Trevor's age, the masked man ordered the ten-year-old to run into the woods, lest he be shot. Aaron then told Heinrich that he was eleven, after which the armed man groped him. Finally, it was Jacob's turn. After learning Jacob's age, Heinrich instructed Aaron to run away without looking back. The assailant then took Jacob, handcuffed him behind his back, and drove him out of St. Joseph, listening to the police scanner to ensure that he could make a safe getaway. "What did I do wrong?" Jacob asked Heinrich as he transported the boy to Paynesville, about forty minutes from St. Joseph. Once there, Heinrich stopped in a field by a grove. He uncuffed Jacob and molested him, after which the boy asked if he would be returned home. Heinrich told Jacob, "I can't take you all the way home," causing the eleven-year-old to cry. Soon thereafter, a police cruiser, sirens blaring and lights flashing, flew down an adjacent road. Panic-stricken, Heinrich instructed Jacob to turn around; he loaded his revolver, pressed it to the back of Jacob's head, and shot him twice, killing him. The Wetterlings would not learn their son's fate until 2016, when Heinrich confessed.[2]

By the time of Wetterling's abduction and murder in October 1989, the missing child panic had already sparked a significant public, legislative, and business sector response and prompted a minor backlash against scaring children with "stranger danger" narratives. Despite attempts by some journalists and child welfare activists to debunk the exaggerated statistics animating the child protection scare, the logic of stranger danger remained firmly entrenched in 1989 and persisted into the nineties and the twenty-first century. Child safety mechanisms implemented during the presidential administration of Bill Clinton hinged upon this logic and the image of

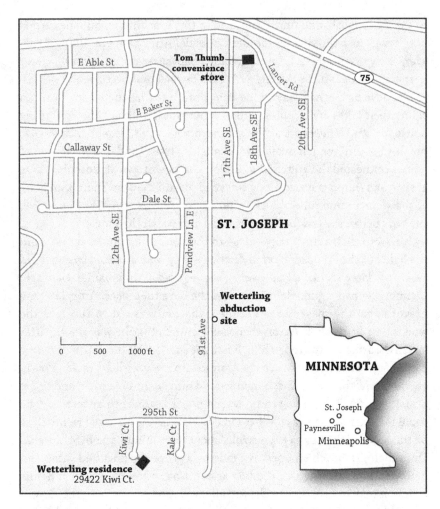

Figure 7.1 Map of St. Joseph, Minnesota, spotlighting the Wetterling home, the Tom Thumb grocery store, and the site at which Jacob was abducted. Map by Erin Greb Cartography.

endangered childhood at its heart. Often inscribed with the names of photogenic (white) child-victims, these legal instruments (commonly known as "memorial laws") flowed from a growing federal emphasis on protecting young Americans while punishing those who wished them harm. Among others, these federal instruments included the Jacob Wetterling Crimes against Children and Sexually Violent Offender Registration Act and the "three strikes, and you're out" provision—both contained in the controversial 1994 crime bill—and the 1996 amendments to the Wetterling Act, known as Megan's Law. Such laws spotlighted the moral threats ostensibly facing young Americans and identified incarceration, surveillance, control, and shame as the proper means by which to mitigate these threats. The Wetterling Act, three strikes, and Megan's Law bolstered federal support for the mythology of stranger danger while expanding a carceral net that served to disproportionately ensnare LGBTQ Americans and people of color. Building on the developments of the 1980s, these mechanisms shored up the child safety regime and its increasingly punitive cast, enabling its continued expansion in the twenty-first century.[3]

REGISTERING DANGER

In the late eighties and early nineties, American fears of crime matched or exceeded previous highs seen in the early eighties. A majority of Americans responding to Gallup surveys conducted in 1989, 1990, and 1992 had identified a spike in criminal activity in their neighborhoods over the previous year, and over 84 percent of those polled by Gallup in 1989, 1990, 1992, and 1993 agreed that there was "more crime in the US than there was a year ago." In this climate of intense anticrime sentiment, Bill Clinton set out to demonstrate his "law and order" bona fides, both in Arkansas (where he served as governor from 1979 to 1981 and again from 1983 through December 1992) and on the national political stage as he sought, and eventually occupied, the Oval Office. As a so-called New Democrat, Clinton worked to shed the image of "softness" that had dogged the Democratic party. Ahead of the all-important Iowa caucuses on February 10, 1992, Clinton left the campaign trail, returning to Arkansas to oversee the execution of Ricky Ray Rector, an African American man who had sustained severe brain damage following a gunshot to the head. Citing Rector's level of impairment, a range of voices—from Jesse Jackson to Jeff Rosenzweig, one of Rector's attorneys and an old friend of Clinton's—urged the Arkansas governor and presidential candidate to stay the execution and commute Rector's sentence. But Governor Clinton refused, and Rector was killed by lethal injection at ten o'clock, the night of January 24—less than three weeks before the Iowa caucuses.[4]

Once in the White House, President Clinton continued his punitive streak, allowing "the largest increase in federal and state prison inmates of any president in American history" and working mightily to "end welfare as we know it." Though criminal justice policy and social policy may seem like discrete pursuits, the logic of "disciplining the poor" increasingly defined both in the late twentieth century. Poverty governance grew more punitive beginning in the late sixties, as incarceration and supervision joined other instruments of "neoliberal paternalism" in the service of cultivating a pliant, precarious low-wage workforce. Accordingly, Clinton's crowning achievement in the criminal justice realm—the Violent Crime Control and Law Enforcement Act (VCCLEA), commonly known as the 1994 crime bill—dovetailed neatly with his key social policy accomplishment, the 1996 Personal Responsibility and Work Opportunity Reconciliation Act (PRWORA). In their own ways, both laws stressed the need to discipline and surveil suspect populations. Together, the laws offered a clear federal response to the crime, drug use, fraud, and depravity believed to be localized in "deviant" communities—namely, urban communities of color and fringe organizations like the Aryan Nations and Branch Davidians.[5]

The VCCLEA authorized the hiring of 100,000 new police officers across the country, expanded the use of the death penalty at the federal level, instituted a federal assault weapons ban, and created new federal offenses for which individuals could be charged, convicted, and punished. The PRWORA eliminated Aid to Families with Dependent Children and replaced it with Temporary Assistance to Needy Families (TANF), which incorporated "sanctions" in order "to punish recipients for noncompliance with regulations" or with "work and reporting requirements." Just as the VCCLEA functioned as a federal index of, and response to, widespread anticrime sentiment, the PRWORA seized upon pervasive public suspicion

Figure 7.2 Flanked by vice president Al Gore and Marc Klaas, President Bill Clinton signs the Violent Crime Control and Law Enforcement Act, September 13, 1994. Photograph by Ralph Alswang. Courtesy of the William Jefferson Clinton Presidential Library and Museum, Little Rock, Arkansas.

of welfare recipients, especially the so-called welfare queen. To this end, TANF not only established "work requirements and lifetime limits on aid"; it also ordered "that every state implement an anti-fraud program" to prevent abuse by those seeking aid. As legal scholar Kaaryn Gustafson notes, this new set of policies and practices "equated welfare receipt with criminality; policed the everyday lives of poor families; and wove the criminal justice system into the welfare system, often entangling poor families in the process."[6]

Though seldom discussed in this context, the politics of stranger danger and child protection figured prominently in Clinton's efforts to "get tough." Three stranger danger cases—those of Wetterling, Polly Klaas, and Megan Kanka—provided the affective and political capital necessary to implement punitive new child safety laws during the 1990s. The VCCLEA included the Wetterling Act, as well as the federal three strikes provision instituted in response to the 1993 kidnapping, molestation, and murder of twelve-year-old Polly Klaas in Petaluma, California. The Wetterling Act established state guidelines for the registration, for a ten-year period, of those "convicted of a criminal offense against a victim who is a minor" or those "convicted of a sexually violent offense." This subsection, like the rest of the crime bill, also articulated compliance requirements. States that failed to implement the Wetterling Act's registration protocols before 1997 would face a 10-percent garnishment of federal funds "that would otherwise be allocated . . . under section 506 of the Omnibus Crime Control and Safe Streets Act of 1968." In coordinating the nationwide adoption of sex offender registries (SORs) and securing their position in the US carceral machinery, the Wetterling Act "formed the basis of federal sex offender laws" on which subsequent amendments and additional legislation, like the federal Megan's Law of 1996, built. Antecedents to the Wetterling Act's registration protocols had appeared on the state level in California, Arizona, Nevada, and Alabama in the 1950s and 1960s. Numerous states—Illinois (1986); Arkansas (1987); Oklahoma (1989); Washington (1990); Colorado and Maine (1991); Louisiana, Minnesota, and Rhode Island (1992); Idaho and West Virginia (1993)—had also created their own registration systems in the eighties and early nineties, before the 1994 Wetterling Act mandated the adoption by all states of such registries. (New Jersey and Delaware implemented such protocols later in 1994, after the passage of the VCCLEA.) While the Wetterling Act only required specific offenders to register with law enforcement agencies, and permitted but did not mandate the public dissemination of registration information, the law laid the foundation for the pervasive and systematic public shaming of those deemed morally and sexually threatening, especially to children.[7]

The Wetterling Act foregrounded child sex abuse as a principal site of concern, one inexorably bound up with child kidnappings, specifically those perpetrated by strangers. In its earliest iterations, the act targeted only those convicted of "crimes against children." The House version of the 1991 VCCLEA, an unsuccessful precursor to the 1994 crime bill, included the proposed Jacob Wetterling Crimes against Children Registration Act. After this iteration of the Wetterling bill floundered, along with the omnibus crime legislation in which it sat, another version appeared as a standalone House bill, introduced in January 1993 by Republican Minnesota congressman Jim Ramstad. This proposed bill, also called the Jacob Wetterling Crimes against Children Registration Act, focused exclusively on the registration of those convicted of particular offenses against minors. Though this bill, independent of a larger anticrime package, did not become law, it did find its way into the 1994 VCCLEA, albeit with an expanded scope. The Clinton communications team went so far as to identify the Wetterling Act as "a key element of the 1994 Crime Bill." The Jacob Wetterling Crimes against Children and Sexually Violent Offender Registration Act, as constituted in the VCCLEA, addressed "criminal offense[s] against a victim who is a minor" as well as "sexually violent offense[s]" committed against minors and adults alike. The Wetterling Act explicated the sexual offenses for which subjects would be forced to register, which included "criminal sexual conduct toward a minor," "solicitation of a minor to engage in sexual conduct," and "use of a minor in a sexual performance." But the law also enumerated nonsexual offenses for which individuals could be required to register, including "kidnapping of a minor, except by a parent" and "false imprisonment of a minor, except by a parent."[8]

With this language, the final version of the Wetterling Act reinforced the problematic logic of stranger danger, indelibly branding the ascendant technology of SORs as a deterrent to "molesters" residing outside the family home. Because the law did not require parents convicted of abducting or falsely imprisoning their offspring to register, it singled out "strangers," or anybody whose identity and location ostensibly demanded regular policing, as the chief threats to young Americans. As formulated in the Wetterling Act, the practice of registration served a disciplinary function, first and foremost, by forcing "deviants" to identify as such and to submit to constant surveillance and scrutiny. Offender registration also had the discrete yet related purpose of aiding investigations into incidents of sexual abuse or child kidnapping. By registering and monitoring offenders, the reasoning went, law enforcement officials could more effectively protect communities from the predators lurking within them. Yet such a system ignored, both explicitly and implicitly, the threats of abduction and abuse which loomed inside the idealized American household. To wit, the Wetterling Act expressly excluded from registration parents convicted of kidnapping or falsely imprisoning their child. Further, the law implied that locating and figuratively containing the individuals presumed most likely to perpetrate acts of violence would mitigate the risk of such behaviors. Yet this spatial logic was not applied to the family home. Rather, the Wetterling Act sought to constrain dangerous offenders within their own registered domestic spheres under the assumption that unregistered subjects did not and could not pose threats to innocents with whom they shared a dwelling.

The Wetterling Act also reflected the common slippage between "stranger kidnapping" and "molestation." The notion that strangers abducted young Americans with the deliberate purpose of sexually assaulting them had grown more popular with the onset of the missing child scare and with frequent media-induced child sex abuse panics, such as the one involving the McMartin preschool in Manhattan Beach, California. Even though the Wetterling Act as enshrined in the 1994 VCCLEA had adopted language that concentrated not only on "crimes against children" but also "sexually violent offender[s]" more generally, it remained symbolically fixed upon the former, as evinced by its young namesake and by the terms on which policymakers conceived of the legislation. Indeed, in the Clinton administration's written recommendations "concerning the reconciliation of the final House and Senate versions of HR 3355, the Violent Crime Control and Law Enforcement Act of 1994," US attorney general Janet Reno specified that "the 'Jacob Wetterling' proposal . . . is designed to promote the establishment by states of registration systems for convicted child molesters." The report did convey White House support for "the establishment of registration systems for violent sex offenders who prey on adult victims." But administration officials encouraged the development of "more definite criteria . . . concerning the class of covered offenders and the duration of registration requirements" and sought "to combine this proposal with the Jacob Wetterling proposal for child molester registration." Into the twenty-first century, official White House narratives continued to frame the Wetterling Act as a law targeting "child molesters and other sexually violent offenders," even though registration requirements also extended to certain nonsexual offenses committed by nonparents.[9]

Narrowly construed, first and foremost, as a law to inventory and monitor "child molesters," the Wetterling Act helped to create a national system of sex offender registration. Because such a broad, totalizing technology did not exist before the 1990s, the very concept of monitoring convicted sex offenders in such a systematized manner ensued directly from the 1980s missing child panic and helped expand the child safety regime.

"MAKE AMERICA SAFE FOR CHILDREN"

Another component of the 1994 federal crime bill, the "three strikes, and you're out" provision mirrored in spirit and practice a 1994 California state statute motivated, in part, by the 1993 Klaas abduction and slaying in Petaluma. Twelve-year-old Polly Klaas had been kidnapped from her own home during a slumber party, sexually assaulted, and strangled to death. Repeat felon Richard Allen Davis directed officials to Klaas's remains in early December 1993, two months after her disappearance. Employing Polly's name and image to bolster their cause—some media outlets and politicians called her "America's Child"—California legislators passed in March 1994, and the electorate affirmed via a November 1994 referendum, the so-called three strikes law, which mandated "a minimum sentence of 25 years to life for three-time repeat offenders with multiple prior serious or violent felony convictions."[10]

In late 1993 and much of 1994, Polly's father Marc Klaas had simultaneously petitioned for the passage of three strikes laws in California and on the federal level. Klaas met with President Clinton and White House staffers on December 20, 1993, just weeks after the recovery of his daughter's body, to discuss the crime bill and share his vision for the Polly Klaas Foundation established in the wake of Polly's abduction. The president assured Marc Klaas that he endorsed a federal three strikes law, much to the satisfaction of the still-grieving parent. "We are heartened to know," Klaas wrote in a thank-you note sent a few days after his meeting with Clinton, "that you support [the Foundation's] mission statement to 'make America safe for children.'"[11]

Clinton invoked Polly's name and gruesome demise as he lobbied for tougher anticrime provisions. "But while Americans are more secure from threats abroad," Clinton explained in his 1994 State of the Union address, citing the close of the Cold War and the passage of the North American Free Trade Agreement, "we all know that in many ways we are less secure from threats here at home. Every day the national peace is shattered by crime. In Petaluma, California, an innocent slumber party gives way to agonizing tragedy for the family of Polly Klaas." After marshaling Klaas's murder as proof of a national scourge, Clinton laid out a plan to end that scourge. "[T]hose who commit repeated violent crimes," he declared in his State of the Union, "should be told, 'When you commit a third violent crime, you will be put away, and put away for good [. . .] three strikes and you are out.'" Marc Klaas adored Clinton's speech. "This is the first time in recent memory," he wrote the president a week after the address, "that a State of the Union message has addressed the needs and desires of the common citizen. There were no references to tax credits to major corporations, no promises of tax cuts to the rich and no proposals to spend huge amounts of money on esoteric science projects. It is refreshing to realize that at last there is a President that is an advocate of real people with real problems, hopes and fears." With this note, Klaas touched on many of the "victims' rights" themes that animated the activism of the Walshes, the Gosches, and other bereaved parents of lost children. But he also elaborated left-populist, anticorporate sentiments that clashed with the economic platforms of both major political parties in the 1990s. Klaas's politics, then, defied easy categorization.[12]

Cognizant of the broad appeal of "tough on crime" politics and eager to wrest the issue of crime control away from Republicans, the White House played tug-of-war with some "law and order" conservatives over the Klaas saga and, more broadly, over matters of crime and punishment. In the months following the discovery of Polly's body, Senator Orrin Hatch (R–Utah) and conservative firebrand Don Feder both highlighted the young girl's abduction and slaying to criticize Clinton's "soft-on-crime policies," in Hatch's formulation. "The nation was rightly outraged by the recent kidnap-murder of 13-year-old [sic] Polly Klaas," the Utah senator wrote in the conservative Washington Times on January 25, 1994, the day of Clinton's State of the Union address. "Yet, most were not surprised to learn that the man charged with her murder, Richard Allen Davis, had a long criminal record and was out of prison on parole." Hatch implicitly pinned the blame for Klaas's killing on the Clinton administration and its Department of Justice. According to Hatch, Clinton privileged "violent, ca-reer criminals" like Davis over the embattled "American people." Embracing "the soft-headed approaches of the 1960s and 1970s," Clinton and his fellow New Democrats had "effectively thwarted truth-in-sentencing at the federal level by ordering its prosecutors to engage in more plea bargaining and by encouraging lower sentences." Hatch rejected outright Clinton's "tough on crime" posturing, claiming that the president had "adopted soft-on-crime policies that will exacerbate rather than diminish the crisis of vio-lent crime." If Clinton's "dangerous see-no-evil policy" continued unabated, Hatch warned in closing, "tragedies like Polly Klaas's death—which the president mourns so eloquently—will occur again and again." The senior US senator from Utah pilloried the president for his "eloquent" odes to young Polly and his "tough" rhetoric which, Hatch contended, belied his "decision to go easy on criminals."[13]

Don Feder denigrated the Clinton administration in much the same way. "See Bill fight crime," his February 2 Washington Times editorial began. "See his administration foster crime." Feder saw Clinton's State of the Union address, and his entire "law and order" platform, as hypocritical. "[W]hile Mr. Clinton postures," wrote Feder, "those he appoints to Cabinet posts and judgeships—slaves of '60s social dogma—labor to undo his ostensible agenda." According to Feder, tongue firmly in cheek, Clinton's attorney general Janet Reno had developed a "finely tuned moral antenna" by imbibing this "social dogma." Reno "is a root causer," Feder argued, "as in, the root causes of crime are poverty, discrimination and the lack of a federal teddy bear program." Her opposition to expanding the death penalty because of the "moral dilemmas" it might present also irked Feder. "Would the parents of Polly Klaas, the 12-year-old abducted and murdered in California, agonize over the execution of their daughter's killer?" Feder asked.[14]

White House officials too deployed the Klaas tragedy for political purposes, actively seeking Marc Klaas's endorsement for the federal crime bill under deliberation in late 1993 and early 1994. From December 1993 through the 1996 reelection campaign, Clinton mentioned the Klaas case in at least sixteen separate public speeches. (He and his aides had also planned to discuss Polly Klaas in a February 1994 address to a group of law enforcement officials in London, Ohio, but deleted the reference from the final draft of the speech.) As one 1996 White House communications memo indicated, "Marc Klaas joined the President on many occasions during his campaign for the Crime Bill, and the bill was subsequently dedicated in Polly Klaas' name." The president, the memorandum continued, "frequently invokes the Klaas story when he talks about the type of crime his efforts aim to prevent in the future." White House officials considered Marc Klaas a key ally in Clinton's anticrime politicking. "Klaas's support for the Administration's anti-crime efforts is invaluable to us," policy advisor Bruce Reed stated in a February 1994 memo, "not just in the coming weeks as we push to pass the crime bill, but over the long haul as we seek to prove that Democrats are not soft on crime." To this end, Reed sought to "underscore that [Marc Klaas] supports our version of three-strikes—so long as he's for it, we can't be criticized for being soft." Reed called Klaas "the country's leading proponent of the three-strikes-and-out idea" and, as such, hoped to solidify the linkage (however symbolic) between Klaas and "the Administration's anti-crime efforts."[15]

Likewise, Marc Klaas looked to cultivate a relationship with the Clinton administration. In a shrewd maneuver, Klaas simultaneously advocated for the passage of three strikes laws in California and on the federal level. By doing so, he leveraged his growing visibility in California politics and his influence within the White House to consolidate support for three strikes legislation nationwide. "Your support of 'Three Strikes And You're Out Legislation' is important and meaningful," Klaas's note to President

Clinton read. "It will increase the steamroller of support the initiative has picked up in California and make it virtually unstoppable." Klaas considered California to be "the first big domino in three strikes legislation": once California adopted its three strikes law, other states and the US government would follow. "It is important that the citizens have a law that spells out exactly what punishments and penalties are in store for those that chose a life of violent crime," Klaas's letter to Clinton continued. "The American people want protection[,] not rhetoric."[16] The efforts of Klaas, Clinton, and other child protection hardliners culminated in the passage of three strikes laws in California and on the federal level in 1994. Though the state of Washington had implemented such a law in 1993, before California did, the sheer scale of California's criminal justice system ensured that developments there would bear heavily on national debates concerning sentencing guidelines. Accordingly, the next few years saw the passage of three strikes bills in dozens of other states, and by 1997 half of all states had adopted such measures.[17]

Scholars and journalists dispute the degree to which three strikes laws at the state and federal levels exacerbated mass incarceration. Wherever they were instituted, three strikes statutes provided a new mechanism through which to prosecute repeat felons. As a 1995 memo from Assistant Attorney General Jo Ann Harris to all US Attorneys explained, "Under the Violent Crime Control and Law Enforcement Act of 1994, we have a powerful new federal tool . . . to help us deal with violent repeat offenders. This provision should play a key role in every district's anti-violent crime strategy." Incarceration rates increased in the 1990s, but this spike fit within a long-term trend. Local, state, and federal imprisonment rates had risen steadily since the late 1970s, well before the adoption of three strikes in the early to mid-1990s. Furthermore, only in certain states did three strikes laws lead to substantial growth in prison populations in the mid-nineties. In the decade after implementing three strikes, California sentenced some eighty thousand "two strikers" and 7,500 "three strikers" to state prison. (Under the state's "two strikes" provision, any individual previously convicted of a serious or violent crime who received a second felony conviction, regardless of the severity or nature of that offense, would be sentenced to a prison term twice as long as that required under the state's criminal sentencing guidelines.) Despite certain absurd applications of three strikes and other sentence enhancement statutes in states other than California—such as the Texas man sentenced to life in prison for stealing a sandwich from Whole Foods Market—there is little evidence to suggest that such statutes significantly expanded prison populations beyond the Golden State. Indeed, Washington state's three strikes statute yielded 121 convictions between 1993 and 1998, while Florida's provision, passed in 1995, had generated just 116 convictions by the same date. Most of the other states that adopted three strikes laws in the mid-nineties employed these provisions even more sparingly. Through August 1998, Wisconsin, Colorado, New Mexico, North Carolina, Pennsylvania, and Tennessee had each sentenced fewer than five offenders under their respective three strikes provisions.[18]

Likewise, the three strikes statute included in the VCCLEA did not dramatically expand the federal prison population. Federal prosecutors have seldom invoked the three strikes provision since its adoption in 1994. In the four years after the VCCLEA became law, only thirty-five offenders were convicted under the bill's three strikes clause. Moreover, local and state jails and prisons house the overwhelming majority of the country's incarcerated population. Less than 10 percent of inmates held in American correctional institutions sit within federal prisons.[19] But even though local and state criminal justice policies were the primary engines of mass incarceration, the explosion of the federal prison population in the late twentieth century—and the VCCLEA's role in this development—cannot be discounted. While state prisons accounted for 87 percent of the growth in the incarcerated population during Clinton's time in the White House, the number of inmates held in federal prisons grew from 56,909 in 1990 to 131,739 in 2000, President Clinton's final full year in office. This figure reached an all-time high of 186,545 in 2010 before dipping slightly in 2015. The rapid expansion of the federal prison population certainly predated the VCCLEA, but the 1994 crime bill did nothing to arrest its growth. On the contrary, the controversial law created new federal offenses—particularly related to drug trafficking, "immigration-related crimes," and the manufacture and possession of "military-style assault weapons"—that brought thousands more Americans into federal prisons.[20] In its application, the VCCLEA's three strikes provision may not have been directly responsible for this surge in the federal prison population. Still, the inclusion of Klass's three strikes statute (and the Wetterling Act) within the crime bill itself reflected the logic of child protection that inhered in the late twentieth-century push for "law and order."

The image of endangered childhood proved vital in this environment of intense anticrime sentiment. The tragedies that had befallen Polly Klaas and Jacob Wetterling served to justify the creation of new, draconian tools designed to protect young Americans from stranger danger. As two photogenic, white, middle-class children abducted and harmed by subjects previously unknown to them, Wetterling and Klaas provided the raisons d'être for new legal mechanisms intended to secure the future for similarly vulnerable children. According to Marc Klaas, he and his associates had disseminated "approximately two billion images of Polly . . . world-wide" in the first few months following her kidnapping. These pictures initially served as aids in the search for the young girl, building on the visual architecture established by the milk carton campaign and other initiatives. Once Polly's pictures entered the cultural lexicon, however, they no doubt worked to gin up support for the federal crime bill, California's three strikes statute, the Klaas Foundation, and the cause of child safety more broadly. "The world froze on the evening of December 4, 1993," Marc Klaas wrote in 1996, "when Polly Klaas, the beautiful girl shown smiling in home videos for millions of TV viewers, was found dead in Cloverdale, California." As "America's Child," Klaas went on, Polly epitomized "love and lost innocence," and her death "symbolized much that [is] wrong with our society." Such imagery took certain young Americans as precious, threatened commodities who required increased protection through a fortified carceral state.[21]

VIGILANCE AND VULNERABILITY

In July 1994, just months before the passage of the VCCLEA, Megan Kanka was brutally murdered. Unbeknownst to the Kanka family and many of their neighbors, three convicted sex offenders had moved into a house across the street from the Kankas' Hamilton Township, New Jersey, residence. Thirty-three-year-old Jesse Timmendequas was one of these sex offenders. Richard and Maureen Kanka, parents of seven-year-old Megan, nine-year-old Jeremy, and eleven-year-old Jessica, seldom interacted with Timmendequas. While the Kankas considered Timmendequas somewhat peculiar, they had no idea that he had twice been convicted of sex offenses against minors. In 1981, Timmendequas had received a suspended prison sentence for luring a five-year-old into the woods and pulling down her pants. The following year, he was convicted of attempted sexual assault after choking a seven-year-old girl unconscious. For this offense, Timmendequas was sentenced to ten years in the Adult Diagnostic and Treatment Center, a prison for adult sex offenders in Avenel, New Jersey, but was released after serving six years. Timmendequas then moved into the Kankas' quiet suburban neighborhood with two other sex offenders he had met in prison.[22]

According to witnesses, Megan Kanka had stopped to speak with Timmendequas on the evening of July 29, 1994. She had been out playing in the neighborhood when she stumbled upon Timmendequas washing a boat in his driveway. The two chatted and frolicked in the driveway before he coaxed the seven-year-old into his home with the promise of seeing his new puppy. In so doing, Timmendequas preyed upon an "[u]nsuspecting, trusting" child, a prosecutor asserted during Timmendequas's trial in 1997. He then brought her into his cramped bedroom, where he bludgeoned, strangled, and raped her before stuffing her body into a toy chest and disposing of it in a park some two miles away. By the time Timmendequas returned home, the Kankas had determined their daughter was missing and launched a search to find her. Playing the part of the conscientious citizen, Timmendequas joined his neighbors in the search. But by the next day, he had confessed to kidnapping, raping, and killing young Megan.[23]

Megan's abduction, sexual assault, and slaying shocked Hamilton Township and spurred New Jersey's lawmakers into action. Within days of the vicious attack, Richard and Maureen Kanka, along with many of their neighbors, had started advocating for "Megan's Law," which "would require authorities to notify communities when a child-sex offender comes to live among them." Some 1,500 locals signed a petition imploring New Jersey's Republican governor Christine Todd Whitman to take additional steps to shield the state's children from stranger danger. News of their efforts soon appeared in the pages of the *New York Times*, and within a week of Megan's kidnapping and murder, Governor Whitman had joined an impressive coalition of parents, lawmakers, and media officials calling for new registration and notification laws in and beyond the Garden State. Eschewing the customary committee hearings, the New Jersey General Assembly hastily approved a set of bills "aimed at cracking down on sexual offenders" exactly one month after Megan's death. The New Jersey Senate moved with similar urgency, amending the legislative package known collectively as Megan's Law on October 3, 1994. The General Assembly agreed to the Senate's amendments on October 20 and forwarded the legislation to Governor Whitman, who signed the package into law on November 1. The law went into full effect on January 1, 1995.[24]

New Jersey's knee-jerk Megan's Law raised serious constitutional questions and, as some critics predicted it would, activated a legal backlash. While the Wetterling Act allowed for the initiation of community notification procedures when certain offenders moved into certain communities, it deemed sex offender information "private data" and did not mandate the release of such information to the public. Megan's Law, as implemented in New Jersey in 1994, did. It "require[d] the police to notify a neighborhood, nearby schools and other institutions when a convicted sex offender intends to move in." The American Civil Liberties Union (ACLU) spearheaded challenges to such laws implemented in New Jersey and elsewhere, arguing that alarmist policies like these supplied overly simplistic and overly harsh solutions to complex social problems. ACLU lawyers and other legal experts also quibbled with the "retroactive nature of the registry" created by New Jersey's Megan's Law, which penalized offenders convicted before the enactment of such registration and notification protocols. "My primary class of clients," one West Trenton, New Jersey, attorney explained, "are guys who pleaded guilty many years ago, went to jail, sought and received treatment and were released and have had no other contact with the system. That class of citizen should not have to register under the new law."[25]

Not only did constitutional concerns loom over the Megan's Law provisions passed in New Jersey; so too did questions of efficacy. If New Jersey's state lawmakers sincerely wished to curtail child sex abuse, critics charged, they would equip the state's correctional and mental health facilities with the resources needed to treat and rehabilitate offenders. Simply tagging and stigmatizing these individuals would do little to protect the state's vulnerable populations from sexual predation. "Sex offenders' particular kind of personality disorder can often be controlled, if not necessarily 'cured,'" read a *New York Times* editorial published days after the passage of Megan's Law in New Jersey. "Yet while several therapies have been shown to lower recidivism rates, most jailed sex offenders get no treatment." New Jersey's incarcerated sex criminals received "very little" treatment, the *Times* editorial continued, "even at the state-run Adult Diagnostic and Treatment Center at Avenel, which is devoted to treating adult sex offenders." A third of the inmates there "refused treatment," as Jesse Timmendequas did when he was lodged at the facility in the 1980s. In addition, the editorial pointed out that New Jersey's Megan's Law wrongly focused on stranger danger by promoting the surveillance of itinerant, unattached subjects. "Children are more apt to be sexually abused in the home than outside it," the editorial correctly noted. Yet its author or authors still seemed to identify with the spirit of Megan's Law. "Even so, the threat posed by an unknown predator terrifies American families the most. That is the reason for the community-notification provision that is now part of Federal law—and for the New Jersey bills that inspired it."[26]

The stigma surrounding sex offenders put registration and notification opponents at a competitive disadvantage in debates over such measures. Proponents of Megan's Law in New Jersey could draw upon the image of endangered childhood and the potent discourse of victims' rights to position themselves as foils to child molesters and their civil libertarian apologists. As such, proponents of registration and notification statutes—including bereaved parents like the Kankas—honed an effective (and affective) line of attack by intimating that the law's opponents privileged the rights of convicted sex offenders over those of victims and vulnerable children. The editorial board of the conservative *Washington Times*, for example, derided the judges, attorneys, and other legal experts wary of the social death wrought by Megan's Law. "To us non-legal types," a January 6, 1995, editorial in the *Washington Times* read, "it might seem that stigma and ostracism are the least of what is coming to a kidnapper and rapist; it might seem to us that men who rape and murder small children . . . may not themselves deserve to be alive—let alone 'enjoying' a decent 'quality of life'; and it may seem to us that our right to protect our children from monsters ought to take precedence over anything else—particularly when we live in a society that insists on returning those monsters to us."[27]

Despite the emotionally resonant appeals elaborated by Megan's Law proponents, several courts sided with those questioning the constitutionality of registration and notification provisions. The January 6 *Washington Times* editorial came in response to a federal court ruling in favor of convicted rapist Carlos Diaz. Nearing release after an eleven-year prison sentence, the forty-six-year-old Diaz had submitted a petition seeking exemption from New Jersey's Megan's Law. Federal judge John W. Bissell granted Diaz the exemption, citing the "punitive impact" of the law and its *ex post facto* design. The following month, a state judge in Burlington County, New Jersey, deemed unconstitutional the Megan's Law provision granting "county prosecutors sole authority to classify a released offender as someone at low, moderate or high risk of committing another sexual crime." Later in February, less than two months after Megan's Law went into effect in New Jersey, Nicholas H. Politan of the federal district court in New Jersey determined its community notification protocols to be a violation of constitutional *ex post facto* restrictions. Politan's ruling, rendered in response to a lawsuit filed by the forty-nine-year-old sex offender Alexander Artway, upheld the registration requirements embedded within New Jersey's Megan Law but invalidated its notification mandate.[28]

The Kankas and their allies objected to Politan's reasoning and methods. The judge had provocatively suggested that community notification protocols resembled the placement by Nazis of Stars of David on Jewish peoples. "Some parallel," columnist Suzanne Fields wrote derisively in the *Washington Times*. Yet, in the same editorial, Fields seemed to reify Politan's critique. She gleefully advocated for Jesse Timmendequas's indefinite detention, or "[s]hort of that, he could have had an X engraved on his forehead, like Cain, or an R for Rapist, or SOB for Sex Offender, Beware." By Fields's own admission, then, registration and community notification served to label certain social outcasts even after they had served their prison sentences. In a letter to the editor published in *USA Today*, Maureen and Richard Kanka also had scathing words for Politan. "How inappropriate," the Kankas declared, "to make a remark that identifies as a Nazi every person in our state who supported 'Megan's Law.' We are outraged that a federal judge would compare a law that will protect our children to all the horrendous acts done by the Nazi's [sic] to the Jewish people." To undercut Politan's ruling, and his salacious comparison of community notification statutes to Nazi tactics, the Kankas employed their symbolic capital as grieving parents seeking "to take our streets back for . . . families" like theirs. In doing so, they pitted the rights of "pedophiles" (with "their perverted pleasures") against the rights of victims and imperiled children. "Our children have the right to grow without the scars of sexual abuse by a pedophile. We had the right to watch our child, Megan, grow and prosper under our roof and lead a productive life. Where were Megan's rights when she was raped and murdered?" the couple asked. "Where were all the children's constitutional rights when they lost their childhood due to the compulsive nature of a pedophile as they were raped and molested?"[29]

The demonization of sex offenders and the endorsement of vigilantism implicit in Megan's Law and the discourses around it also disturbed the law's critics. Soon after Bissell had exempted Carlos Diaz from Megan's Law, members of the Guardian Angels—a nonprofit, public safety organization founded in New York City in 1979—descended upon the Passaic, New Jersey, neighborhood that Diaz would likely call home upon his release from custody. Mobilized by Bissell's ruling, the group members took it upon themselves to notify residents of Diaz's impending move into their community. Days later, a father and son broke into the Phillipsburg, New Jersey, house in which a recently paroled sex offender, Michael Groff, was temporarily staying. The pair had identified the residence, primarily occupied by Groff's aunt and uncle, through the community notification provision of Megan's Law. One of the intruders, donning a black ski mask, accosted another resident and asked if he was Groff. The man, named Thomas Vicari, demurred. "Who wants to know?" Convinced that he had found "the child molester," the intruder began pummeling Vicari, mistaking him for Groff. Another resident quickly phoned the police, and the father and son were soon apprehended and booked on charges of "second-degree burglary and misdemeanor counts of assault, harassment, malicious damage and conspiracy." While no one, not even Vicari, sustained serious injury during the assault, the incident appeared to validate fears about the threat of vigilantism in the wake of New Jersey's Megan's Law and similar measures. "This is exactly the concern that we had when the law was being considered for passage," lamented the legal director for ACLU's New Jersey branch, "that it would be used to enable vigilantism rather than for any legitimate community interest."[30]

Despite uncertainties about the constitutionality of New Jersey's Megan's Law and about its potential to provoke vigilante action, the Clinton administration sided with the Kankas and the state government in courtroom battles over the law. Administration officials sought to guarantee the constitutionality of Megan's Law, presumably in the hope that a version of the law could be adopted on the federal level. In February 1995, shortly after a New Jersey state judge had ruled against the Megan's Law provision that permitted county officials alone to determine the classification risks of released sex offenders, the Clinton Department of Justice (DOJ) announced that it would assist New Jersey in defending its recently enacted law. "The federal government has a major interest in seeing to it that the constitutionality of such efforts is sustained in the courts," US attorney general Janet Reno explained. "We feel strongly that the states must have the flexibility to enact laws they believe will provide immediate and necessary protection, as New Jersey has done in this case." Reno also rejected the notion that registration and notification statutes would incite vigilante violence against convicted offenders. "I think any time people take the law into their own hands," she affirmed, "government has got to respond. But I think that's part of the balance." Even though Reno failed to fully engage with the substance of criticisms levied against the law in New Jersey, she nonetheless conveyed in unequivocal terms the DOJ's support for the state government in this matter.[31]

This federal declaration of support came near the beginning of a prolonged period of legal limbo for New Jersey's Megan's Law, one that would last over eighteen months. The New Jersey Supreme Court heard oral arguments regarding Megan's Law in May 1995. The court would need to determine whether community notification represented a viable safety measure to safeguard "the most vulnerable members of society," in the words of the state's attorney general, or an overly punitive practice designed principally to shame certain offenders. In its July 1995 ruling, the New Jersey Supreme Court upheld the constitutionality of Megan's Law yet also reinforced the right of each registrant to challenge their classification as either a low-, moderate-, or high-risk offender. The justices of the court rewrote parts of the law "from the bench," according to the *New York Times*, "inserting safeguards that a panicky New Jersey State Legislature [had] failed to include last year." After incorporating these protections for offenders, the state reactivated Megan's Law in September 1995. The next month, an appeal of Judge Politan's February 1995 ruling—which had declared the community notification prong of Megan's Law to be a violation of the *ex post facto* clause—found its way to the US Court of Appeals for the Third Circuit Court, located in Philadelphia.[32]

As New Jersey lawmakers, the Clinton DOJ, and other interested parties awaited a decision from the Third Circuit into the spring of 1996, news broke of mounting challenges to Megan's Law by convicted sex offenders. Overwhelmed by petitions from forty-four individuals seeking exemption from New Jersey's community notification provision, federal district court Judge Bissell blocked any further implementation of the community notification statute in the state, at least until the Third Circuit could issue its decision in the Politan appeal. The federal appeals court delivered its ruling the following month, affirming the constitutionality of the registration component of Megan's Law. Though the three-judge panel unanimously agreed that Politan had acted hastily in ruling against community notification protocols, the justices refused to rule on the constitutionality of the practice, plunging Megan's Law into further legal uncertainty. Bissell provided some clarity in the summer of 1996, however, when he deemed community notification constitutional, a reversal of the decision he had handed down in January 1995. The Bissell ruling put New Jersey's Megan's Law on surer footing, although it continued to face minor, ill-fated legal challenges into 1997.[33]

Even as Megan's Law fate in New Jersey remained unclear, the Clinton administration looked to pass a similar bill on the federal level. In July 1995, two days after the New Jersey Supreme Court had upheld Megan's Law, Congressman Dick Zimmer (R–New Jersey) introduced a version of the legislation in the US House of Representatives (HR 2137). Subcommittee hearings took place in March 1996, by which point the Clinton DOJ had already intervened in three separate legal challenges to Megan's Law in New Jersey, all "to protect the federal interest in promoting state sex offender registration laws." Once HR 2137 made it out of the House Judiciary Committee, the House approved it unanimously, 418–0, and the Senate passed the bill without amendment by unanimous consent. President Clinton signed the bill into law on May 17, 1996, before Bissell had issued his decision in New Jersey. Modeled on New Jersey's law, the federal version of Megan's Law amended the Wetterling Act (and thus the VCCLEA) and commanded states to "release relevant information that is necessary to protect the public concerning a specific person required to register under this section."[34]

The federal Megan's Law hinged on the image of endangered childhood constructed by Megan Kanka, Polly Klaas, Jacob Wetterling, Adam Walsh, and the white, middle-class vulnerable "everychildren" for whom they stood. Without the passage of Megan's Law on the federal level, Dick Zimmer cautioned, "sexual predators will begin to move from State to State, settling in jurisdictions where they are able to ensure their anonymity. . . . As a result, critical information will not necessarily get into the hands of those who need it the most, parents, in order to take commonsense steps to protect their children." Upon signing the bill into law, President Clinton—flanked by Maureen Kanka, son Jeremy, Congressman Zimmer, John Walsh, and Marc Klaas—instrumentalized Megan's name and face. "To understand what this law really means," the president declared, "never forget its name—the name of a seven-year-old girl taken wrongly in the beginning of her life. The law that bears a name of one child is now for every child, for every parent and every family. It is for Polly [Klaas] and Jacob [Wetterling] and Adam [Walsh], and, above all, for Megan." By joining these four children into a single assemblage of young white victimhood, Clinton drew a direct line from the child kidnapping panic of the late 1970s and 1980s through the "tough on crime" fervor of the early to mid-nineties. Echoing the "rights talk" of Marc Klaas, the Kankas, the Walshes, and other bereaved parents, Clinton avowed, "We respect people's rights, but today America proclaims there is no greater right than a parent's right to raise a child in safety and love. Today, America warns: If you dare to prey on our children, the law will follow you wherever you go, state to state, town to town." The president went on: "Today, America circles the wagon around our children. Megan's Law will protect tens of millions of families from the dread of what they do not know."[35]

Before HR 2137 had even passed the US House of Representatives, White House officials were already thinking about how to expand on it—namely, with the creation of a nationwide sex offender registry. In a March 4, 1996, memorandum (marked "URGENT") addressed to senior Clinton advisor Rahm Emanuel and domestic policy director Bruce Reed, deputy director of the DOJ's Office of Policy Development Grace Mastalli laid out several paths that the Clinton administration might take on the proposed Zimmer bill. Mastalli also shared with Emanuel and Reed news of Senator Phil Gramm's (R–Texas) proposal "to create a nationwide computer identification and tracking system to keep a close eye on the transitory population of sexual offenders." Consistent with the evolution of similar proposals, Gramm had developed his plan following the January 1996 abduction and murder of nine-year-old Amber Hagerman in the senator's home state. Hagerman's kidnapping and slaying had encouraged Gramm to take action, although he insisted that he had "always believed there should be a national database of convicted pedophiles, available to local and federal law enforcement officers." In her memo to Reed and Emanuel, Mastalli expressed her concerns about the timing and potential political ramifications of Gramm's proposal. She endorsed the idea but hoped to guarantee that Clinton, not Gramm, would receive primary credit for the initiative. "Note," she wrote by hand, "we hope to add announcement of [a] new initiative to preempt this Gramm proposal." While the Clinton administration failed to preempt Gramm, who formally introduced his bill in the Senate on April 16, 1996, the president nonetheless took a leading role in the establishment of such a national database.[36]

As Clinton's reelection campaign kicked into high gear, administration officials touted the proposed national sex offender registry as an outgrowth of the president's aggressive "tough on crime" and child safety policymaking. Clinton operatives portrayed the database as "the next logical step" following the passage of the 1994 crime bill, the Wetterling Act, three strikes, and Megan's Law. In June 1996, Clinton ordered US attorney general Janet Reno to develop a plan to guarantee the smooth implementation and seamless use of such a database by law enforcement agencies across the country. "The Clinton Administration has a longstanding commitment to ensuring the safety of families and protecting them from child molesters and sexually violent offenders," read the memorandum to Reno. This directive also argued that "[t]he 1994 Clinton Crime Bill, which included the Wetterling Act[,] laid the groundwork to develop a national system," which "is the next logical step." A radio address airing days after the president issued his directive touched on familiar themes. The president highlighted his administration's efforts to protect American children from particular moral threats. "Nothing is more important than keeping our children safe," he asserted. "We have taken decisive steps to help families protect their children, especially from sex offenders, people who, according to study after study, are likely to commit their crimes again and again." (On the contrary, recidivism rates for convicted child molesters are quite low, although critics attribute these numbers to the similarly low rates at which sexual assault survivors report their attacks.) Clinton continued to make his case for the database, contending that "[t]he crime bill laid the foundation for this national registry," while "Megan's Law makes sure parents get [the necessary] information so they can take steps to watch out for their children." According to the president, "Too many children and their families have paid a terrible price because parents didn't know about the dangers hidden in their own neighborhood," thereby reinforcing the stranger danger myth and deploying it in the service of the proposed national sex offender database.[37]

The bill introduced by Gramm easily passed the US Senate and the House of Representatives, and President Clinton signed the Pam Lychner Sexual Offender Tracking and Identification Act into law on October 3, 1996. Named for a white, blonde, thirty-seven-year-old sexual assault survivor who died in a plane crash while the bill was under consideration in the Senate, the Lychner Act ordered the US attorney general to "establish a national database at the Federal Bureau of Investigation [FBI] to track the whereabouts and movement[s] of—(1) each person who has been convicted of a criminal offense against a victim who is a minor; (2) each person who has been convicted of a sexually violent offense; and (3) each person who is a sexually violent predator." The Lychner Act expanded upon the Wetterling Act and the federal version of Megan's Law by buttressing the law enforcement resources available to track and discipline those deemed sexually dangerous, particularly to American children.[38]

CAUGHT IN THE WEB

Bill Clinton's "law and order" policies alone may not have significantly exacerbated mass incarceration. Yet, as Clinton himself indicated while advocating for a national sex offender registry, the Wetterling Act and Megan's Law extended the reach of the child safety regime and set the stage for the expansive sex offender tracking systems of the twenty-first century. In keeping with his approach to other issues, President Clinton pursued a punitive politics of child safety, endorsing carceral solutions to the problem of stranger danger. He readily trafficked in the imagery of endangered childhood and employed the names of slain children to pass draconian laws that have drastically increased the number of Americans under some form of correctional control or supervision. Building on the 1980s stranger danger panic and acting on pervasive public fears related to crime, Clinton-era child safety developments contributed to the explosion of SORs in the late twentieth and early twenty-first centuries. Bearing the names of young American victims, these SORs formalized the increasingly common conflation of "child kidnapping" and "child molestation." Charged with the seemingly unassailable task of tracking and shaming sex offenders (and particularly child molesters), SORs worked to expand the carceral state.

SORs were a relatively novel and small-scale technology when Clinton, alongside other "law and order" Democrats and Republicans, began to mandate their use nationwide. In response to the stranger danger scare, various state governments had instituted sex offender registration systems in the late 1980s and early 1990s. But the number of individuals listed within such databases rose dramatically with the passage of the 1994 Wetterling Act. Indeed, only since the late twentieth century have convicted sex criminals been forced to register as such in a broad-based manner, meaning that the number of listed offenders has risen from a few thousand (at most) in the early 1990s to over half a million by 2005. Even since the National Center for Missing and Exploited Children started compiling statistics on sex offender registrants in the mid-2000s, the rolls have grown considerably. In 2005, some 551,987 were registered nationally (and in US territories that keep statistics); by 2018, there were over 900,000.[39]

As Americans spent more and more of their time in cyberspace in the nineties, President Clinton and his DOJ also took steps to protect American children and punish American "perverts" in the digital realm. In 1995, the FBI launched the Innocent Images National Initiative, "an intelligence driven, proactive, multi-agency investigative operation to combat the proliferation of child pornography/child sexual exploitation . . . facilitated by an online computer." Moreover, the Office of Juvenile Justice and Delinquency Prevention established the Internet Crimes Against Children task force in 1998.[40]

The foundation set during the Clinton era enabled systems of registration, notification, and punishment for sex offenders to flourish in the twenty-first century, but it did not have to be this way. Clinton and his counterparts on both sides of the aisle might have more seriously considered the civil libertarian case against registration and notification protocols. The prospect of branding American citizens, even those as widely reviled as convicted sex offenders, on a national scale ought to trouble even the most hawkish of "law and order" types. Leaving aside the ethical and constitutional troubles of SORs and community notification practices, their flawed design and general ineffectiveness and impracticality could have dissuaded President Clinton and others from supporting such mechanisms. By the time Washington lawmakers were deliberating and rolling out such measures on the federal level in the mid-1990s, violent crime rates had already been in decline for a number of years, and the stranger danger myth had been thoroughly debunked.

Still, this powerful myth won out. The 2003 PROTECT (Prosecutorial Remedies and Other Tools to End the Exploitation of Children Today) Act and the Adam Walsh Child Protection and Safety Act of 2006, among other tools created in the George W. Bush era, built upon the Wetterling Act and Megan's Law. The PROTECT Act federalized, and implemented nationally, the AMBER Alert system; toughened sentencing guidelines for convicted sex offenders; and broadened the definition of, and strengthened penalties for possessing, child pornography, including computer-generated images devoid of "flesh-and-blood children." The Walsh Act, named for John Walsh's slain son, "intensified federal penalties for failure to register as a sex offender . . . widened the range of offenses for which adults could be forced to register to include possession of child pornography; and standardized the information to be obtained from offenders for publication and dissemination" within SORs online. The Walsh Act also formalized the Dru Sjodin National Sex Offender Public Website, named for a twenty-two-year-old white, blonde college student who was abducted and murdered by a registered sex offender in 2003. Through this nationally administered website—or through individual sites operated by states, territories, and Indian reservations—anyone with an Internet connection can see the convicted sex offenders who live around them, or who live anywhere in the country.[41]

As the child safety regime grew in the twenty-first century, its excesses became more readily apparent. Though it purported to expose and combat the grisly crimes of child abduction and exploitation, in its most bloated form this regime has embodied some of the most pernicious human impulses. In the drive to shame, surveil, ostracize, cage, terrorize, and perhaps even exterminate other humans, Americans have constructed and found solace in the child safety regime. By formally delimiting the movements of young people and all but banishing those who might do them harm, this regime—with its many laws, customs, practices, and informal expectations—has shaped the lives of millions of Americans. Whether it will remain firmly entrenched, whether it will continue to prey on the public, depends upon whether Americans can identify this predator. If the seductive, interlocking myths of stranger danger and endangered childhood can maintain their stranglehold, there is little hope. But if Americans can recognize the perils of shielding young people from the outside world, of obscuring the realities of child sexual abuse, of decentering child hunger and poverty, and of governing through crime, the predator might very well be caught.[42]

Conclusion

To Catch a Predator

On July 27, 2006, exactly twenty-five years after six-year-old Adam Walsh's abduction, President George W. Bush signed into law a sweeping bill in the boy's honor. The Adam Walsh Child Protection and Safety Act bolstered the child safety regime by imposing new and enhanced penalties for crimes committed against American children. Among its many provisions, the Walsh Act expanded the national network of sex offender registries (SORs) formed, in earnest, under Bill Clinton; established a three-tiered classification system for convicted sex offenders; and increased the number of offenses for which individuals could be forced to register. Perhaps the most draconian component of the Walsh Act was its civil commitment statute, which authorized the indefinite incarceration of certain "sexually dangerous persons" after the completion of their prison or jail terms. Even though no evidence existed to indicate that Adam Walsh had been sexually abused following his kidnapping, the 2006 law used the boy's name and image to intensify the punishments levied against convicted sex offenders.[1]

John and Revé Walsh joined George W. Bush in the Rose Garden for the Walsh Act signing ceremony. So too did a cast of political heavyweights including Senate majority leader Bill Frist (R–Tennessee), Senator Joe Biden (D–Delaware), and US attorney general Alberto Gonzales, in addition to several celebrity-victims such as Elizabeth Smart, who had risen to national prominence after her 2002 abduction and dramatic return home the following year. The president attributed the strong turnout to John Walsh, the resilient father and tough television personality. "John, as you can see," Bush told the longtime *America's Most Wanted* host, "you've attracted quite a crowd here." Without missing a beat, Walsh called those gathered a "SWAT [special weapons and tactics] team for kids." President Bush smiled and concurred. "Yes, it is, SWAT team for kids." The Walshes, and especially John, had worked tirelessly since 1981 to assemble such a "SWAT team for kids"—enlisting politicians, law enforcement authorities, corporations, and TV audiences in "the battle for child safety." The 2006 law bearing Adam's name represented a crowning achievement in the Walshes' long campaign.[2]

If the Walsh Act marked a triumph for young Adam's parents, it also demonstrated the steady ascendance of the child safety regime since the late 1970s and early 1980s, when the disappearances of Etan Patz, Adam Walsh, and dozens of Atlanta youths alerted Americans to the problem of missing and exploited children. An ensuing moral panic had given rise to various legal and cultural mechanisms designed to safeguard young people from the moral threats of stranger kidnapping and molestation. These mechanisms proliferated into the 1990s and 2000s. With the enactment of the Walsh Act, the 2003 PROTECT (Prosecutorial Remedies and Other Tools to End the Exploitation of Children Today) Act, and other child protection laws, the child safety regime reached its zenith in the George W. Bush years. As the self-styled masculinist protector of the republic, President Bush looked to shield young Americans from a range of perversions, perils, and predators lurking within and beyond the republic.

In the fall of 2002, for example, as a neo-Taliban insurgency gained strength in Afghanistan and the US Congress authorized the use of military force in Iraq, Bush sought to "root out the enemy within" by targeting child predators at home. Responding to a putative "wave of horrible violence" that had swept up four girls over the previous half year, the president affirmed his commitment "to help our children feel safer by fighting terror" and by cracking down on "twisted criminals in our own communities." To that end, he convened the first-ever White House Conference on Missing and Exploited Children. Held in early October 2002, the conference brought together an impressive array of panelists including US attorney general John Ashcroft, Federal Bureau of Investigation (FBI) director Robert Mueller, and US secretary of state Colin Powell, as well as business leaders like Walmart president and CEO Tom Coughlin and bereaved parents Patty Wetterling and John Walsh. Later that same month, in a speech concerning children's online safety, the president explicitly

Figure C.1 John Walsh delivers remarks at the White House Conference on Missing, Exploited, and Runaway Children, October 2, 2002. Courtesy of the George W. Bush Presidential Library and Museum, Southern Methodist University, Dallas, Texas.

paralleled the FBI's Innocent Images initiative, launched in 1995, with the so-called war on terror. "Just like we're hunting the terrorists down one at a time," Bush asserted, "we're hunting these predators down one at a time too."[3]

Consistent with Bush's discursive and policy emphasis on rescuing innocents from sexual and terroristic threats, Americans fixated on tales of lost and/or slain girls and young women in the 2000s. Media scholars diagnosed this collective fascination, manifested most vividly in discrete cycles of anxious press coverage, as "missing white woman syndrome." Stoked by the growing popularity of twenty-four-hour cable and Internet news in the post-9/11 era, missing white woman syndrome brought harrowing stories of "innocent girls, inexplicable violence, and villainy" to the forefront of the popular consciousness. Newspapers and TV news programs, from *Nancy Grace* to *America's Most Wanted*, obsessed over cases such as those of Danielle van Dam, Elizabeth Smart, Laci Peterson, Pvt. Jessica Lynch, Carlie Brucia, Lori Hacking, Jennifer Wilbanks, and Natalee Holloway. Media narratives often worked to infantilize these victims (even adults like Laci Peterson) and thus to heighten their innocence and victimhood. Occasionally, victims turned out not to be victims at all, as in the cases of "runaway bride" Wilbanks or Jessica Lynch, whose "rescue" was a highly choreographed media-military-industrial affair intended to drum up public support for the Iraq war. Such renderings legitimated efforts to safeguard those Americans deemed worthy of protection.[4]

The Peterson case helped spawn the 2004 Unborn Victims of Violence Act (UVVA), which endeavored "to protect unborn children from assault and murder." To justify passage of the UVVA, Bush marshaled the names of Laci Peterson and her unborn son Conner. In consonance with "pro-life" and "victims' rights" logics, the president endowed Conner with personhood and specifically the privilege of vulnerable childhood. By doing so, Bush laid claim to the mantle of masculine protection, stepping in for the disgraced Scott Peterson, murderer of his wife and unborn child. For Bush, the passage of the UVVA meant not only that "[t]he moral concern of humanity extends to those unborn children who are harmed or killed in crimes against their mothers," but that "the protection of federal law [now] extends to those children, as well." The UVVA "widen[ed] the circle of compassion and inclusion in our society," Bush insisted, proving "that the United States of America is building a culture of life." The president expanded the child safety regime, then, by bringing the unborn under its aegis.[5]

Bush also extended the child safety regime overseas in new and daunting ways. Beyond federalizing domestic programs like AMBER Alert and escalating penalties for offenses against children—including the possession of child pornography—the 2003 PROTECT Act targeted international child sex trafficking and tourism. Following the post-9/11 restructuring of the US national security apparatus, the PROTECT Act tapped Immigration and Customs Enforcement (ICE), part of the newly formed Department of Homeland Security, to execute Operation Predator, which targets "foreign pedophiles and human traffickers and sex tourists and Internet pornographers who prey on our children." Empowered by the PROTECT Act, ICE special agents can investigate potential instances of child sex trafficking and tourism across the world; prosecutors can more easily bring charges against an alleged offender; and US citizens convicted of international sex tourism are more likely to serve time in an American correctional facility. To publicize these efforts, ICE launched a global promotional campaign in conjunction with the evangelical Christian humanitarian organization World Vision and the US State Department. Billboard ads in Phnom Pehn, Cambodia; San José, Costa Rica, and other popular sex tourism destinations, as well as televised commercials broadcast in thirty-nine major US airports, warned potential global sex tourists of the consequences they might face. "I am not a tourist attraction," a child declared in a TV voiceover. "Abuse a child in this country" or "Sexually exploit a child in this country," billboards read, "go to jail in yours." On

CNN's *Anderson Cooper 360* in 2010, John Walsh applauded federal efforts to imprison American sex tourists in the United States yet relished in the punishment meted out to those nabbed in Cambodia. There, law enforcement authorities crammed "fourteen guys in a cell" that was "hot as hell" and served the accused offenders "bad, terrible food." "Good idea," Walsh beamed. "You know, that's the punishment I would like to see, as the father of a murdered child." Under Bush, then, the US carceral state, already bloated in the name of keeping American kids safe, grew to encompass the illicit and informal sex economies of Thailand, Cambodia, and other countries in the global south.[6]

Beyond the sensationalized news media accounts of missing girls and women in the Bush era, the broader popular culture reflected a public obsession with policing, punishing, and perhaps even eliminating "the enemy within," especially the insidiously cunning and "monstrous" child sex predator. Hollywood films like the violent neo-noir *Sin City* (2005) and the unsettling low-budget thriller *Hard Candy* (2005) fulfilled viewer fantasies by torturing and executing characters deemed sexually threatening to young innocents. On the small screen, NBC's *Dateline: To Catch a Predator* made a spectacle of the tech-savvy "child-saving" operations of law enforcement agencies and private vigilante group Perverted Justice. Airing from 2004 to 2007, *To Catch a Predator* featured carefully choreographed sting operations undertaken by NBC investigative journalists, Perverted Justice, and local authorities. Posing as minors in chat rooms, members of Perverted Justice persuaded adults to meet at the "minor's" residence for a possible sexual encounter. An adult decoy resembling a juvenile would greet the perp at the home before disappearing from view. Host Chris Hansen would then accost the suspect and ask him—all the accused solicitors were men—to sit. Hansen chastised the perp, sometimes recited portions of his chat transcript with the decoy, and informed him that he was free to leave. But once the suspect exited the residence, police would descend upon him, weapons drawn, and arrest him. These stings, which NBC directed, subsidized, filmed, edited, and broadcast, led to over two hundred convictions under varying statutes. Just like the child safety regime within which it belonged, though, *To Catch a Predator* largely absolved family members and acquaintances, who perpetrate most acts of child sexual abuse. It also presented an overly simplistic morality tale by suggesting that "predators" can be easily identified, captured, and neutralized. *To Catch a Predator* neatly resolved the sorts of cases that are usually wrought with ambiguity and confusion. How many sexual assaults of children go unreported? How might gendered, economic, and age-based power asymmetries within the family promote sexual violence against women and children? How do romantic conceptualizations of the heteronormative family and the tightly knit community discourage young Americans from reporting sexual abuse committed by kin or close acquaintances? The Manichaeism of the Bush years, most obvious in the war on terroristic "evildoers," precluded consideration of such complexities.[7]

Bush's fortification of the child safety regime, and the decades of stranger danger politicking that preceded it, did touch off a backlash led by "free range" parents. Troubled by the increasingly sedentary, anxious, and ostensibly socially inept twenty-first century American child, some parents sought a return to the romanticized childhoods of yore. Parents interviewed in a 2012 study recalled "childhoods of nearly unlimited freedom, when they could ride bicycles and wander through woods, streets, and parks, unmonitored by parents." Many remembered "being instructed to 'come home when the street lights go on.'" Whether or not these accounts accurately reflected the experiences of Americans raised before the rise of the child safety regime, ample evidence shows that children reared since the 1980s have spent less and less free time outside, alone (without parental supervision), or socializing with their peers.[8]

The free range movement began in earnest with an April 2008 *New York Sun* editorial penned by mother and *Sun* columnist Lenore Skenazy. After permitting her nine-year-old son to peruse the racks of Bloomingdale's Upper East Side flagship store, before taking the subway and bus home, all by himself, Skenazy explained her rationale. "Half the people I've told this episode to now want to turn me in for child abuse," she wrote. "As if keeping kids under lock and key and helmet and cell phone and nanny and surveillance is the right way to rear kids. It's not. It's debilitating— for us and for them." Tellingly, some of Skenazy's opponents deployed the image of endangered childhood, and specifically the names and faces of young stranger danger victims, in their criticisms. If her child had never made it back from Bloomingdale's, Skenazy insisted, "It would just be one more awful but extremely rare example of random violence" perpetrated against kids in the United States, "the kind that hyper parents cite as proof that every day in every way our children are more and more vulnerable." In conversation with Skenazy, Katharine Francis—founder and CEO of SafetyNet4Kids, a now-defunct company that produced software to help recover missing children—wielded the horrifying tale of eleven-year-old Carlie Brucia. "I don't know if you're familiar with that case or not," Francis told Skenazy, "but . . . she was abducted by a guy who violated her several times, killed her, and left her behind a church." Francis, Skenazy informed readers, "runs a company that makes wallet-sized copies of a child's photo and fingerprints, just in case," and thus seizes upon and perpetuates parents' anxieties about stranger danger. "Well of course I know the story of Carlie Brucia," Skenazy bristled. "That's the problem. We all know that story—and the one about the Mormon girl in Utah and the one about the little girl in Spain—and because we do, we all run those tapes in our heads when we think of leaving our kids on their own. We even run a tape of how we'd look on Larry King." Parents, Skenazy lamented, bear the brunt of the blame when their child falls victim to kidnapping or is slain. Nevertheless, Skenazy noted, quoting a representative of the statistical research foundation Sense about Science, trying to protect children from such exceptionally rare tragedies "would be like trying to create a shield against being struck by lightning."[9]

After stirring passions on both sides of the free range debate and earning national news coverage from the likes of National Public Radio, Fox News, and NBC's *Today Show*, Skenazy parlayed her column into a blog called Free-Range Kids (freerangekids.com). Since its inception just days after the publication of her editorial, Skenazy's blog has proven remarkably successful, attracting millions of visitors and, in turn, cultivating a robust online community of likeminded parents. The blog spawned a 2009 book, and Skenazy landed a gig hosting the short-lived Discovery Life television program *World's Worst Mom*. As the leader of the free range movement, Skenazy continues to appear with some regularity on television news programs, and her efforts to challenge the wisdom of "helicopter parenting" remain the subject of pieces in the *New Yorker*, Germany's *Der Spiegel*, and scores of other periodicals.[10]

But the free range campaign, and responses to it, have centered on relatively narrow questions concerning the autonomy of the cared-for, middle-class American child. Both the "commonsense," nostalgic appeal of free range parenting and the searing critiques levied against it by more cagey parents focus on the sensational, uncommon moral threats confronting young Americans once they step outside the idealized two-parent household. Both sides of the free range debate obscure the moral threats facing children within their own homes, as well as the material threats that disproportionately impact young people in neoliberal economies. In the George W. Bush era, for instance, as wars abroad and a burgeoning homeland security and surveillance apparatus cost US taxpayers $3 trillion, per some estimates, American child poverty rates spiked. From 2000 to 2010, the rate of young Americans in poverty increased by 36 percent. Extreme poverty rates for children in the United States climbed as well. These troubling developments can partially be attributed to the 2007–2009 economic collapse, yet President Bush's dogged, intertwined pursuit of terrorists and child predators, in lieu of more generous material support for American families (with or without children), also deserves scrutiny. Such material threats hardly appear on the pages of Skenazy's blog, where the designated "Hot Topics" include "Censorship," "Crazy Parents," "Eek! A Male! (and Stranger Danger)," "Helicopter Effect on Kids," and "Sex Offender Issues."[11]

At the outset of the so-called Great Recession, Skenazy even penned a post welcoming a coming era of austerity that might force children to lose their snazzy videogame consoles, leave the stultifying comforts of their homes, and go outside to play with their peers. "Not that I want this to be a Great Depression," Skenazy mused. "I hope it's not. But if it is . . . I see kids dropping out of travel soccer, when their parents can't afford gas. I see kids figuring out how to retool their bikes and skates and maybe even their MP3 players when their parents can't immediately buy them the newest, niftiest models." Skenazy admitted, "I know I have a tendency to romanticize the past—not to mention poverty," but she nonetheless argued "that affluence has been really miserable for our kids." That Skenazy rendered plenty, not privation, as perilous reveals the myopic focus of the free range movement.[12]

For all the merits of the free range campaign, its limitations suggest the need for more capacious understandings of child protection and, indeed, childhood. While the free range gospel certainly helps to undermine the stranger danger myth, this parenting style seems tailored for white, middle-class, dual-parent, suburban households, in which the labor of childrearing generally falls to a single caretaker, perhaps with the assistance of a financially compensated domestic. Indeed, single-family homes in suburban and rural environments tend to be surrounded by more land, which encourages spatial and social separation between neighbors. Further, the material comforts more frequently seen in such communities diminish the need for extrafamilial networks of support and care. By contrast, nonwhite, poor, working-class, or single-parent households often make use of alternative kinship networks—friends, extended family, neighbors, fictive kin, and congregational acquaintances—in the practice of childrearing. The former group, then, partakes in a more individualized, atomized parenting experience that nurtures anxieties about catastrophic threats like stranger danger. This strand of fretful parenting also villainizes the parents, especially the mothers, of the (few) children who fall victim to such threats. "I do not want to be the one on TV explaining my daughter's disappearance," one father told Skenazy in 2008. "These days, when a kid dies," Skenazy explained, "the world—i.e., cable TV—blames the parents." But it is a privilege for these parents to worry about the extraordinarily rare phenomena of stranger abduction, exploitation, and murder—rather than the less salacious yet far more common problems of hunger, poverty, sickness, intrafamilial abuse, or even car accidents.[13]

While the free range campaign has done much to dislodge the stranger danger myth, the movement has proven less successful in articulating a compelling, countervailing vision that looks beyond the individual choices of parents. On that score, those contesting the stranger danger myth cannot simply address its illogic. They must also grapple with its immense costs: the creation and growth of carceral tools, the immeasurable anxiety induced in young people and parents since the late 1970s, and the obsessive concern over moral threats. Most importantly, the child safety regime forged in the last forty years has done little to actually improve the lives of American children. The poverty rates of young Americans in 2011 matched or exceeded those recorded in 1976. While "sav[ing] our children" became politically expedient in the 1970s and 1980s, when terms like *child safety* and *child protection* gained currency, nothing suggests that today's young people are any safer from material or moral threats.[14] The child safety regime does not adequately respond to the most pressing needs of the nation's young people. It lifts the relatively minor threats of stranger abduction, molestation, and exploitation to epidemic status and masks those that make bad copy.

And yet it is a regime that even the ostensibly progressive Barack Obama refused to challenge. In 2010, for instance, President Obama invited John Walsh to the White House for an interview, segments of which subsequently aired on *America's Most Wanted*. During the course of their conversation, the president affirmed his support for the Adam Walsh Act and touted his success in securing "an additional hundred US marshals to focus on this issue." "Now," Obama told Walsh, "that represents a 25 percent increase in enforcement capability. The problem, as you well know, is you've got 150,000 sex offenders out there that these US marshals have to chase down. And so it's very important for us to continue to build up the US marshals' capacity." Beyond enhancing the "enforcement capability" of federal authorities targeting "bad guys" (in Obama's formulation), Walsh and the president also agreed on the need for a "national registry" of DNA samples taken from arrestees during the booking process. "[I]f this country could put a man on the moon," Walsh proclaimed, "we could have a national DNA database." Obama concurred: "Absolutely." This proposed expansion of state surveillance powers in the name of public safety—particularly the safety of young Americans—echoed calls for a national missing child database in the 1980s and for a national sex offender registry in the 1990s and 2000s. That Obama welcomed Walsh to the White House reveals a stunning continuity between his administration and those of his predecessors.

As Obama's press team noted—no doubt in an attempt to underscore the president's bipartisan bona fides—"Walsh has been honored five times by four presidents: Ronald Reagan (twice), George H. W. Bush, Bill Clinton, and George W. Bush."[15]

As George W. Bush had, Obama furthered the global reach of the child safety regime. Signed into law on February 8, 2016, the International Megan's Law to Prevent Child Exploitation and Other Sexual Crimes through Advance Notification of Traveling Sex Offenders built on the state and federal versions of Megan's Law passed during the Clinton years, as well as post-9/11 efforts to combat global child sex tourism. The International Megan's Law required convicted American sex offenders traveling internationally to notify foreign governments of their sex offender status. The legislation also permitted the US Secretary of State to regulate or limit the travel of convicted American sex offenders. Even as Obama petitioned for criminal justice reform and helped to mitigate the stark racial disparities in cocaine sentencing guidelines, he shored up the child safety regime. If a seemingly transformative leader committed to "hope" and "change" could not and would not confront existing norms of child protection, the chances of unmaking the regime may seem bleak.[16]

Those seeking to topple the child safety regime and the broader carceral state of which it is part might take solace in the push for criminal justice reform undertaken not just by liberals and leftists but also by some movement conservatives. Ironically, many of the key architects of late twentieth-century mass incarceration and the child safety regime have expressed support for the Right on Crime initiative, which sees the American prison-industrial complex as anathema to the professed conservative precepts of limited government and limited taxation. Signatories to Right on Crime's "Statement of Principles," published in 2010, included Edwin Meese III, US attorney general under Ronald Reagan and notorious antiporn crusader; John DiIulio Jr., progenitor of the "superpredator" appellation and the larger Clinton-era panic over "feral, presocial" young criminals; and Alfred S. Regnery, administrator of the Office of Juvenile Justice and Delinquency Prevention in the 1980s. Given Donald Trump's obsession with "law and order," it is unclear whether Right on Crime signals a concerted rightwing realignment on criminal justice concerns or simply proves the existence of a conservative constituency (however slight) amenable to prison reform. Either way, Right on Crime's drive to exempt juveniles from sex offender registration and notification protocols deserves some commendation.[17]

In the past fifteen or twenty years, furthermore, some popular cultural representations of sex offenders have opted for empathy over demonization—and thus contributed to a broader project of rethinking

SORs, the child safety regime, and the carceral state. (As Judith Levine and Erica Meiners astutely observe, though, there are limits to empathy and humanization. "Asking whether the sex offender is human only legitimizes the question and reinforces the doubt it arises from," they trenchantly write.) Tom Perrotta's 2004 novel *Little Children* and its 2006 film adaptation feature a tormented sex offender who cannot shake his sexual attraction to underage girls. Readers and viewers come to sympathize with him and to detest the vigilantes who seek to surveil, harass, and perhaps even exterminate him. Sufjan Stevens's haunting 2005 song about the serial rapist and murderer John Wayne Gacy Jr. invites listeners to consider Gacy's troubled upbringing. At the end of the song, Stevens interrogates his own demons and transgressions, boldly equating them with Gacy's atrocities. "And in my best behavior, I am really just like him," Stevens divulges. "Look beneath the floorboards for the secrets I have hid," alluding to the crawlspace in which Gacy stored some of his thirty-three victims. Finally, the critically acclaimed 2014 documentary *Pervert Park* details the social marginality and general precarity in which some of Florida's convicted sex offenders live. Encumbered by legal restrictions that prevent them from living in virtually any established community, the individuals featured in the documentary inhabit a St. Petersburg trailer park occupied solely by sex offenders. While many of the crimes committed by the film's principal subjects will no doubt repulse even the most open-minded viewers, *Pervert Park* nonetheless forces its audience to question whether physically removing certain individuals from civil society and subjecting them to constant harassment and crushing shame is effective or desirable. That residents of this St. Petersburg community must only spend their evenings there and can otherwise roam beyond the confines of their trailer park undermines the very logic of segregating such individuals from the general population.[18]

Efforts to dismantle SORs, the child safety regime, and other products of the late twentieth-century stranger danger scare remain marginal. Few, if any, officials on the national political stage seem willing to take up the cause, presumably for fear of being smeared as "anti-child" or "propedophile." Even well-intentioned causes like Florida's Amendment Four—which, upon voter approval in November 2018, presumably restored the voting rights of millions of formerly incarcerated Floridians—have explicitly excluded those convicted of sex crimes. Data confirm the popularity of SORs and other instruments within the child safety regime. In one 2010 study, fully 79 percent of Americans surveyed expressed confidence in the effectiveness of SORs and notification statutes in lowering the recidivism rates of sex offenders. A 2005 Gallup poll found that 94 percent of Americans support "laws requiring registration of people convicted of child molestation." Given the low recidivism rates of sex offenders, however, these daunting mechanisms and the culture of fear that enables them demand reevaluation.[19]

If American adults wish to "save our children," they will recognize the dangers of stranger danger. They will acknowledge that young Americans *do* face exploitation and abuse from those they do not know, but they will also understand that family members and acquaintances are responsible for the overwhelming majority of kidnappings, physical assaults, sexual assaults, and other acts of abuse committed against children. They will take steps to ameliorate the conditions that increase the risk of familial and acquaintance abuse. They will endorse robust, universal social programs that assist children and adolescents, as well as those who raise them. They will resolve to teach young people the value of safe and healthy sexual relations, rather than relying upon ineffectual and unrealistic sex education programs that privilege abstinence and stigmatize desire. They will instruct children and adolescents not to fear strangers but to maintain a healthy skepticism of those they do not know—and those they do. They will care about young people as much when they are nonwhite as when they are white; as much when they are homely as when they are adorable; as much when they are born as when they are unborn; as much when they are found as when they are missing. If American adults, within the course of a few decades, supplanted a more balanced set of policies and practices with a draconian child safety regime, they can undo this regime in the coming years. Until then, the regime will remain intact, preying on Americans young and old.

ACKNOWLEDGMENTS

While my name alone appears on the cover of this book, this is a project that bears many fingerprints. I have incurred many debts in my academic career and in the making of this book, and I will do my best to acknowledge them all here. For all those who helped along the way, I express my deepest gratitude.

This book began as a dissertation at the University of Iowa (UI). There, I benefitted from the generosity, warmth, and intellectual prowess of those in the Department of History, the Department of American Studies, and beyond. My advisor Landon Storrs always believed in this project. Her insights concerning social policy, gender/sexuality, and the historian's craft proved invaluable as I wrote and revised the dissertation and eventually transformed it into a book. Colin Gordon challenged me to approach my project in different ways and to foreground the carceral state. His sharp feedback shaped the contours of this book. If Landon and Colin pushed me to grapple with policy history and material reality, Doug Baynton and Tom Oates helped me consider the interplay between policy and culture. I owe them all so much.

I was extremely lucky to learn from Linda Kerber and Shel Stromquist just as they were retiring from their positions at UI. Their kindness and wisdom gave me comfort and confidence. Mariola Espinosa, Cathy Komisaruk, Lisa Heineman, Omar Valerío-Jiménez, and Elke Stockreiter urged me to think through the transnational dimensions of my work. Through their knowledge of critical theory and historiography, Michel Gobat and Glenn Penny broadened the terrain on which I understood my scholarship. Jacki Rand, Michaela Hoenicke-Moore, and Stephen Warren expanded my conceptualization of place, space, and nation. Pat Goodwin, Sheri Sojka, Heather Roth, Janalyn Moss, Emmanuel Enekwechi, and Paul Natvig equipped me with the tools needed to make it through graduate school. Keisha Blain offered assistance as I navigated the academic job market for the first time.

My colleagues at the University of Iowa challenged me, supported me, and enriched my graduate school experience. I found magnificent friends and comrades in Allison Wells, Eric Zimmer, Kelsey Potdevin, Colleen Davis, John Kelly, and the entire "AmericanHists" writing group. The brilliant and incredibly generous Caroline Radesky discussed queer futurity with me and invited everybody over to her home for potluck dinners. The similarly brilliant and generous Christina Jensen hosted us at her family's lake house during the summers. Chris McFadin and I regularly played basketball together—albeit very poorly. Mary Wise, Noaquia Callahan, Scott Sulzener, Brianna Smith, Sylvea Hollis, Danielle Hoskins, Aldrin Magaya, Ally Gorga, Youlia Tzenova, Tyler Dryg, Pam Stek, Katrina Rose, Faye Bertram, Janet Weaver, and Jake Altman made me laugh and made me think. Other friends in Iowa City put me at ease as I worked on my dissertation: Brian Ruden, Nathan Jochum, Samantha Zimmer, Bri Sulzener, Ashley Fahey, and Mike Bedinger.

I am indebted to those who made the research for this project possible. Specifically, I must thank the archivists at the National Archives (I and II) in Washington, DC, and College Park, Maryland; Emory University's Stuart Rose Manuscript, Archives, and Rare Book Library (MARBL); Rice University's Benjamin Woodson Research Center; the State Historical Society of Iowa (SHSI); the Archives Research Center at Atlanta University Center; the presidential libraries of Ronald Reagan, Bill Clinton, and George W. Bush; the William Paley Center for Media; the Archives of Iowa Broadcasting at Wartburg College; the Carl Albert Center (CAC) at the University of Oklahoma; and the Television News Archive at Vanderbilt University. Kainien Chuang Morel and Aidan Swanson conducted research on my behalf at the University of Georgia's Hargrett Rare Book and Manuscript Library and the New York Public Library, respectively.

This book and the research on which it rests were supported through grants and fellowships from the American Historical Association, MARBL, CAC, the Graduate College at the University of Iowa, the UI Department of History, the UI Graduate Student Senate, the UI Graduate and Professional Student Government, SHSI, and the Center for Presidential History (CPH) at Southern Methodist University (SMU).

My two-year postdoctoral fellowship at SMU enabled me to retool and refine the book manuscript. I am incredibly grateful for that opportunity and for the wonderful intellectual community to which I belonged. In the CPH, Jeff Engel, Brian Franklin, Tom Knock, and Ronna Spitz made me feel at home—even as a Houstonian living in our rival city of Dallas. My fellow fellows—Sarah Ross Coleman, Evan McCormick, Aaron Crawford, Lindsay Chervinsky, and Blake Earle—offered feedback and friendship and accompanied me on excursions to Velvet Taco, Torchy's Tacos, Digg's Taco Shop, and other taco destinations. Others in the William P. Clements Department of History, the Clements Center for Southwest Studies, and the broader SMU community provided encouragement, sustenance, and camaraderie. Kate Carté always expressed interest in my work; her guidance and reassurance meant so much to me. I sincerely appreciated Andy Graybill's compassion and humor, David Doyle's zest for teaching, and the invigorating scholarship of Crista DeLuzio, Aimee Villarreal, and Uzma Quarishi. Bruce Levy and Beth Newman always put a smile on my face.

After my time at SMU, I was very fortunate to land in the Department of History at Florida State University (FSU), where I have found a dynamic and welcoming community. I am surrounded by terrific scholars and terrific people—Katherine Mooney, Suzy Sinke, Jen Koslow, Andrew Frank, Maxine Jones, Anasa Hicks, Lauren Scholz, Max Scholz, Nilay Özok-Gündogan, Robinson Herrera, Pam Robbins, Laurie Wood, Claudia Liebeskind, Rafe Blaufarb, Cathy McClive, Ben Dodds, George Williamson, Nathan Stoltzfus, Kurt Piehler, Chuck Upchurch, Michael Creswell, Kristine Harper, Ron Doel, Richard Soash, Diane Dittgen, Anne Kozar, John Netter, Julie Register, Ashley Sadler, Mary Beth Thompson, and others. I have enjoyed heady, fruitful discussions about politics and academia with Joe Gabriel and Will Hanley. Our fearless leader Ed Gray shares my love of Patagonia vests. Carrie Pettus-Davis and Stephen Tripodi have kindly welcomed me into their community of criminal justice researchers and activists. I am lucky to call all these folks my friends and colleagues.

Allyson Gates, Sara Lane Mischler, Megan Groninger, John Cable, Kent Peacock, and Zach Reddick, among many others, reflect the ingenuity and dedication of the graduate students in our department and at our university. The undergraduates in SMU's University Honors Program and at UI and FSU have helped color my thinking about mass incarceration, gender/ sexuality, and the American past and present. Their energy and enthusiasm have brought me great joy and reinforced my sense of purpose.

Beyond Iowa City, Dallas, and Tallahassee, scholars read drafts, provided criticism, or otherwise offered assistance as I undertook this project. Sara Fieldston and Susan Eckelmann Berghel are fantastic scholars and collaborators. Elaine Tyler May graciously agreed to serve on my dissertation committee and to write letters of recommendation on my behalf. Matt Lassiter is a phenomenal historian and human being. His work has long inspired and galvanized me, and he has spent a significant amount of time reading my manuscripts, composing recommendation letters on my behalf, and discussing history and politics with me. Warm thanks also go to Natalia Mehlman Petrzela, Ben Waterhouse, Tamara Myers, Anita

Casavantes Bradford, Scott De Orio, Michael Stauch, Erica Meiners, Emily
Horowitz, Gillian Harkins, Bethany Moreton, Ted Miller, Paula Fass, Brent
M. S. Campney, Crystal Moten, Jason Morgan Ward, Marilyn Ivy, Bernard
Headley, Peter Coclanis, Anthony Mora, Marc Rodriguez, Meg Jacobs,
Kevin Kruse, Reiko Hillyer, Martyn Bone, and Danny LaChance.

Friends, old and new, both within and beyond the academy, lent sup-
port as I wrote, revised, reconfigured, reframed, and resubmitted the man-
uscript: Byrd McDaniel, Clara Schwager, Marco Villegas, Amy Westfall,
Matt Green, Chris Sullivan, Matt Stanley, Emily Woodruff Stanley, Scott
Huffard, Shawn Balthazar, Jasmine Martin, Andreas Jozwiak, Tim Fritz,
Chris Ruehlen, Clayton Garner Turcotte, Laura Ewen, Christopher Walker,
Rob Puglisi, Chase Clayton, Taylor Clayton, Ben Thomas, Drew Johnson,
Jacob Lee, Christina Snyder, Doug Kiel, Brandon Jett, Chris Williams,
Yasmine Alotaibi Williams, Matthew McDaniel, Roy Howard Baskin IV,
Brittanie Knowles Baskin, Bob Hutton, Angela Diaz, Scott De Orio, Kevin
Kokomoor, Zach Garrison, Matt Hulbert, Carlos Reyes, Russ Hayes, Ian
Alexander Schuster, and Cody Farrill.

Because I wrote much of this book on college campuses, I am especially
thankful for the groundskeepers, custodians, and other workers who keep
all universities running. The baristas and bussers at Prairie Lights and
Java House in Iowa City; Open Eye and Looking Glass in Carrboro, North
Carolina; Caffè Driade in Chapel Hill; Houndstooth in Dallas; and Lucky
Goat in Tallahassee (especially comrade Gabby Maynard) supplied coffee
and ambiance. Adrianne Lenker, Ezra Koenig ("So keep that list of who
to thank in mind"), Terrence LeVarr Thornton, Solange Knowles, Michael
Render, Matt Berninger, Emekwanem Ogugua Biosah Jr., Justin Vernon,
and Sufjan Stevens helped me decompress during my evening jogs. Daniel
Denvir, Mehdi Hasan, Katie Halper, and Jeremy Scahill kept me informed.

Before my book landed at Oxford University Press (OUP), I had the
pleasure of meeting and interacting with some amazing editors at other
publishing houses, especially Brandon Proia, Gisela Fosado, Tim Mennel,
Clara Platter, and Thomas LeBien. My conversations with these and other
folks helped me better understand my project and the acquisitions and
publishing processes.

The folks at OUP have been spectacular. Susan Ferber is one of the best
in the game, and it is such an honor to work with her. She has handled
my book with tremendous care at every stage and patiently responded
to my (many) questions. Nick Syrett, Joel Best, and another anonymous
reader supplied superb reports that helped me sharpen my argumentation,
analysis, and prose. Jeremy Toynbee with Newgen facilitated the production process, which was smooth and utterly painless. Erin Greb created

gorgeous maps for this book. Many thanks to Brent Campney for the recommendation.

Cambridge University Press, the Business History Conference, the Center for the Study of the American South at the University of North Carolina at Chapel Hill, the University of Georgia Press, and SHSI granted permission to republish portions of the book that previously appeared elsewhere. Thanks also go to those who helped with illustrations, especially Stanley Patz, the Southern Christian Leadership Conference, Jill DeVries from BNP Media, Dennis Brack from Rappahannock Media, Enrico Natali, and David Rattray from the *East Hampton Star*.

Several folks deserve special praise. Byrd McDaniel is my wicked smart, trustworthy, hilarious best friend. He's one of my favorite interlocutors, and collaborating with him is such a pleasure. He has a fantastically promising career ahead of him, and I hope we can wind up at the same institution again.

Blake Barton Renfro has loved and encouraged me amidst the tumult and uncertainty of the academic job market. We have had a lot of fun together—riding electric scooters around the University of Tennessee campus, mountain biking in Chiang Mai, hiking around Montserrat, lounging on St. George Island—and we will continue to do so.

My mother and father are rocks. I love them dearly and cannot thank them enough for all they have done for me. This book is dedicated, in part, to them.

I also dedicate this book to the lost, missing, exploited, and dispossessed.

NOTES

INTRODUCTION

1. Ronnie Greene, "6-Year-Old's Murder Still Haunts Nation," *Seattle Times* (WA), March 17, 1996, community.seattletimes.nwsource.com/archive/?date=19960317&slug=2319536; Dan Harris and Claire Pedersen, "Adam Walsh Murder: John and Revé Walsh Re-Live the Investigation," ABC News, March 2, 2011, https://abcnews.go.com/US/adam-walsh-murder-john-reve-walsh-live-investigation/story?id=13037931; US Congress, Senate, Committee on the Judiciary, *Exploited and Missing Children: Hearing before the Subcommittee on Juvenile Justice*, Ninety-seventh Congress, second session, April 1, 1982, 63; NBC, *Nightly News*, October 22, 1983, record no. 527060, Television News Archive, Vanderbilt University, Nashville (hereafter VTNA).

2. John Walsh with Susan Schindehette, *Tears of Rage: From Grieving Father to Crusader for Justice—The Untold Story of the Adam Walsh Case* (New York: Simon and Schuster, 1998), 139–41; NBC, *Nightly News*, October 22, 1983, VTNA.

3. Walsh, *Tears of Rage*, 141; NBC, *Nightly News*, August 15, 1981, record no. 518523, VTNA (emphasis added).

4. Carrie A. Rentschler, *Second Wounds: Victims' Rights and the Media in the US* (Durham, NC: Duke University Press, 2011), 43.

5. Adam Walsh Child Protection and Safety Act of 2006, PL 109–248, July 27, 2006, 120 STAT. 587; Laura Rogers, "Sex Offender Registry Laws: From Jacob Wetterling to Adam Walsh," Sex Offender Sentencing, Monitoring, Apprehension, Registration, and Tracking Office, Office of Justice Programs, US Department of Justice, July 2007, https://ojp.gov/smart/pdfs/so_registry_laws.pdf; "President Signs HR 4472, the Adam Walsh Child Protection and Safety Act of 2006," White House, Office of the Press Secretary, July 27, 2006, https://georgewbush-whitehouse.archives.gov/news/releases/2006/07/20060727-6.html.

6. Andrea J. Sedlak, David Finkelhor, Heather Hammer, and Dana J. Schultz, "National Estimates of Missing Children: An Overview," National Incidence Studies of Missing, Abducted, Runaway, and Thrownaway Children (NISMART), Office of Juvenile Justice and Delinquency Prevention, Office of Justice Programs, US Department of Justice, October 2002, https://www.ncjrs.gov/pdffiles1/ojjdp/196465.pdf; Janis Wolak, David Finkelhor, and Andrea J. Sedlak, "Child Victims of Stereotypical Kidnappings Known to Law Enforcement in 2011," *OJJDP Juvenile Justice Bulletin*, June 2016, Office of Juvenile Justice and Delinquency Prevention, Office of Justice Programs, US Department of Justice, https://www.ojjdp.gov/pubs/249249.pdf; Howard N. Snyder, "Sexual Assault of Young Children

as Reported to Law Enforcement: Victim, Incident, and Offender Characteristics," Bureau of Justice Statistics, Office of Justice Programs, US Department of Justice, July 2000, https://bjs.gov/content/pub/pdf/saycrle.pdf, especially 10.

7. ABC, *World News Tonight*, June 4, 1981, record no. 72458, VTNA.

8. For "emotionally resonant child-centered" images, see Anita Casavantes Bradford, *The Revolution is for the Children: The Politics of Childhood in Havana and Miami, 1959–1962* (Chapel Hill: University of North Carolina Press, 2014), 90.

9. NBC, *Nightly News*, December 6, 1985, record no. 541637, VTNA; Lawrence Feinberg, "Poll of Schoolchildren Reflects Satisfaction, Positive Attitudes," *Washington Post*, March 11, 1987, A12; James H. Price and Sharon M. Desmond, "The Missing Children Issue: A Preliminary Examination of Fifth-Grade Students' Perceptions," *American Journal of Diseases of Children* 141, no. 7 (1987): 811–15; Gunnar B. Stickler, Margery Salter, Daniel D. Broughton, and Anthony Alario, "Parents' Worries about Children Compared to Actual Risks," *Clinical Pediatrics* 30, no. 9 (September 1991): 522–28; Richard Laliberte, "Missing Children," *Redbook* (February 1998), quoted in Tonya L. Brito, "Paranoid Parents, Phantom Menaces, and the Culture of Fear," *Wisconsin Law Review* 2000, no. 3 (May–June 2000): 524n23; Barbara Kantrowitz, "Off to a Good Start: Why the First Three Years Are So Crucial to a Child's Development," *Newsweek* (Spring–Summer 1997): 6–9. See also Ernest E. Allen, "Keeping Children Safe: Rhetoric and Reality," *Juvenile Justice* 5, no. 1 (May 1998): 16–23. Material concerns like hunger, poverty, racism, or education seemed ancillary in such surveys, perhaps attesting to the "predominantly white middle-class" status of parents responding to these questionnaires. For "predominantly white middle-class," see Stickler et al., "Parents' Worries about Children Compared to Actual Risks," 523.

10. ABC, *World News Tonight*, June 3, 1981, record no. 72411, VTNA; Joel Best, "Rhetoric in Claims-Making: Constructing the Missing Children Problem," *Social Problems* 34, no. 2 (April 1987): 103.

11. The concept of moral panic is most commonly traced back to the work of Jock Young and Stanley Cohen, both of whom studied at the London School of Economics. Their scholarship influenced Stuart Hall and others affiliated with the Centre for Contemporary Studies at the University of Birmingham. In their 1978 book *Policing the Crisis*, Hall and his Birmingham School colleagues drew on Young and Cohen to analyze Britons' racialized fears over "mugging," or violent street crime, in the early seventies. They found that Brits understood "crime in general, and 'mugging' in particular, as an index of the disintegration of the social order, as a sign that the 'British way of life' [was] coming apart at the seams." In the eighties and nineties, theorists of gender and sexuality repurposed the moral panic frame engineered by Young, Cohen, Hall, and others, thereby giving birth to the complementary theory of sex panic. See Jock Young, *The Drugtakers: The Social Meaning of Drug Use* (London: MacGibbon and Kee, 1971); Stanley Cohen, *Folk Devils and Moral Panics: The Creation of the Mods and Rockers* (New York: Routledge Classics, 2011 [1972]); Stuart Hall, Chas Critcher, Tony Jefferson, John Clarke, and Brian Roberts, *Policing the Crisis: Mugging, State, and Law and Order* (London: MacMillan Press, 1978), vii; Gayle S. Rubin, "Thinking Sex: Notes for a Radical Theory of the Politics of Sexuality," in *Pleasure and Danger: Exploring Female Sexuality*, ed. Carole S. Vance (New York: Routledge, 1984), 267–319. Carole Vance is credited with coining the term "sex panic" in 1984.

12. Janice M. Irvine, "Transient Feelings: Sex Panics and the Politics of Emotions," *GLQ: A Journal of Lesbian and Gay Studies* 14, no. 1 (2008): 6; Kenneth Thompson,

Moral Panics (New York: Routledge, 1998), 2, 3; Susan Christine Chimonas, "Moral Panics: Towards a New Model" (PhD diss., University of Michigan, 2000), x; Cohen, *Folk Devils and Moral Panics*.

13. Sedlak, Finkelhor, Hammer, and Schultz, "National Estimates of Missing Children: An Overview." See also Heather Hammer, David Finkelhor, and Andrea Sedlak, "Runaway/Thrownaway Children: National Estimates and Characteristics," NISMART, Office of Juvenile Justice and Delinquency Prevention, Office of Justice Programs, US Department of Justice, October 2002, https://ncjrs.gov/pdffiles1/ojjdp/196469.pdf.

14. ABC, *World News Tonight*, June 3, 1981, VTNA; ABC, *World News Tonight*, June 4, 1981, VTNA; Rentschler, *Second Wounds*.

15. Shawn Michelle Smith, *At the Edge of Sight: Photography and the Unseen* (Durham, NC: Duke University Press, 2013).

16. Diana Griego and Louis Kilzer, "Truth about Missing Kids: Exaggerated Statistics Stir National Paranoia," *Denver Post*, May 12, 1985, 1A.

17. Roger N. Lancaster, *Sex Panic and the Punitive State* (Berkeley: University of California Press, 2011), 96; Gillian Frank, "Save Our Children: The Sexual Politics of Child Protection in the United States, 1965–1990" (PhD diss., Brown University, 2009), 271.

18. For the enmeshment of the welfare state and the carceral state, see Joe Soss, Richard C. Fording, and Sanford F. Schram, *Disciplining the Poor: Neoliberal Paternalism and the Persistent Power of Race* (Chicago: University of Chicago Press, 2011). For panopticism and other theories regarding security and social control, see Michel Foucault, *Discipline and Punish: The Birth of the Prison*, trans. Alan Sheridan (New York: Pantheon Books, 1977); Simone Browne, *Dark Matters: On the Surveillance of Blackness* (Durham, NC: Duke University Press, 2015). And for social death, see Orlando Patterson, *Slavery and Social Death: A Comparative Study* (Cambridge, MA: Harvard University Press, 1982). The 2006 Adam Walsh Act initiated a federal civil commitment program.

19. Robert O. Self, *All in the Family: The Realignment of American Democracy since the 1960s* (New York: Hill and Wang, 2012).

20. In the 1980s and 1990s media landscape, "[d]istinctions between news, opinion, entertainment, and celebrity gossip became vanishingly thin," historian Philip Jenkins argues, "as tabloid values and ethos became commonplace." Jenkins, *Rethinking a Nation: The United States in the Twenty-First Century* (New York: Red Globe Press, 2019), 25.

21. Max Felker-Kantor, *Policing Los Angeles: Race, Resistance, and the Rise of the LAPD* (Chapel Hill: University of North Carolina Press, 2018), 211–12. See also Rentschler, *Second Wounds*; Frank, "Save Our Children"; Whitney Strub, *Perversion for Profit: The Politics of Pornography and the Rise of the New Right* (New York: Columbia University Press, 2010); Timothy Cole, "'Old Enough to Live': Age, Alcohol, and Adulthood in the United States, 1970–1984," in *Age in America: The Colonial Era to the Present*, ed. Corinne T. Field and Nicholas T. Syrett (New York: New York University Press, 2015), 237–58.

22. Connie Ellison to Mickey Edwards, no. 5637, November 18, 1981, box 12, folder 14, Mickey Edwards Collection, Carl Albert Center Congressional Archives, University of Oklahoma, Norman; Tom Witosky, "Bill requiring faster responses to missing children reports passes," *Des Moines Register* (IA), March 1, 1984, 2A; Juvenile Justice, Runaway Youth, and Missing Children's Act Amendments of 1984, PL 98-473, 98 STAT. 2127 and 2129, October 12, 1984.

23. US Attorney General's Advisory Board on Missing Children, *America's Missing & Exploited Children: Their Safety and Their Future* (Washington, DC: Office of Juvenile Justice and Delinquency Prevention, US Department of Justice, March 1986), 2, 5; Alfred S. Regnery to William Bradford Reynolds, May 15, 1986, Juvenile Justice: Report on Missing and Exploited Children, box 379, Jennifer Boeke files, subject files of the special assistants to the assistant attorney general (compiled 1974–2000), record group (RG) 60: General Records of the US Department of Justice, National Archives and Records Administration, College Park, MD; Melissa Sickmund and Charles Puzzanchera, eds., *Juvenile Offenders and Victims: 2014 National Report* (Pittsburgh, PA: National Center for Juvenile Justice, 2014), 86.

24. Laura Kavesh, "Sunday Tempo: Fingerprints ease fears of parents—just in case," *Chicago Tribune*, February 20, 1983, J1; ABC, *World News Tonight*, May 25, 1985, record no. 96299, VTNA; US Congress, House of Representatives, Committee on Education and Labor, *Oversight Hearing on the Missing Children's Assistance Act: Hearing before the Subcommittee on Human Resources*, Ninety-ninth Congress, first session, May 21, 1985, 58; "Daily Diary of President Ronald Reagan," April 1, 1985, Ronald W. Reagan Presidential Library, Simi Valley, CA, 5, https://www.reaganlibrary.gov/digitallibrary/dailydiary/1985-04.pdf; United Press International, "Roll Call of Missing Children: Reagan Appeals for Viewers' Help in Search," *Washington Post*, April 30, 1985, PC-3.

25. Benjamin Gray, "Deviance and Discourse: Child Molesters in the United States" (MA thesis, University of Kansas, 2011), 27. Antecedents to the Wetterling Act's registration protocols had appeared on the state level in California, Arizona, Nevada, and Alabama in the 1950s and 1960s. Several states (Illinois [1986]; Arkansas [1987]; Oklahoma [1989]; Washington State [1990]; Colorado and Maine [1991]; Louisiana, Minnesota, and Rhode Island [1992]; Idaho and West Virginia [1993]; and New Jersey and Delaware [1994]) also created their own registration systems in the eighties and early nineties, before the 1994 Wetterling Act mandated the adoption by all states of sex offender registries.

    While scholars and journalists debate the extent to which three strikes laws at the state and federal levels exacerbated mass incarceration, the cultural and political significance of such laws—and comparable measures buttressed by the image of endangered childhood—cannot be overstated. See "A Primer: Three Strikes—The Impact After More than a Decade," California Legislative Analyst's Office, October 2005, lao.ca.gov/2005/3_strikes/3_strikes_102005.htm; Mike Males and Dan Macallair, "Striking Out: The Failure of California's 'Three Strikes and You're Out' Law," *Stanford Law and Policy Review* 11, no. 1 (Winter 1999): 65–72; " 'Three Strikes' Laws," n.d., Prison Policy Initiative, prisonpolicy.org/scans/sp/3strikes.pdf.

26. Violent Crime Control and Law Enforcement Act of 1994, PL 103-322, 108 STAT. 1816, September 13, 1994.

27. "Proposed Guidelines for Megan's Law and the Jacob Wetterling Crimes against Children and Sexually Violent Offender Registration Act," Office of the Attorney General, US Department of Justice, AG order no. 2073-97, *Federal Register* 62, no. 65 (April 4, 1997), https://www.govinfo.gov/content/pkg/FR-1997-04-04/html/97-8702.htm; Lawrence A. Greenfeld, *Sex Offenses and Offenders: An Analysis of Data on Rape and Sexual Assault*, Bureau of Justice Statistics, Office of Justice Programs, US Department of Justice, February 1997, https://bjs.gov/content/pub/pdf/soo.pdf; Jeremy Travis, Bruce Western, and Steve Redburn, eds.,

The Growth of Incarceration in the United States: Exploring Causes and Consequences (Washington, DC: National Academies Press, 2014), 49; Alfred Blumstein and Allen J. Beck, "Population Growth in US Prisons, 1980–1996," *Crime and Justice* 26 (1999): 21.

28. For "flesh-and-blood children," see Casavantes Bradford, *The Revolution is for the Children*, 2. Robin Bernstein troubles the dichotomy between "flesh-and-blood" and "symbolic" children, contending that the latter shapes performances of the former. See Robin Bernstein, "Childhood as Performance," in *The Children's Table: Childhood Studies and the Humanities*, ed. Anna Mae Duane (Athens: University of Georgia Press, 2013), 203–12.

29. *Ashcroft v. Free Speech Coalition*, 535 US 256 (2002); Strub, *Perversion for Profit*, 293. See also *US v. Whorley*, no. 06-4288, Fourth Circuit Court of Appeals (2008); *New York v. Ferber*, 458 US 747 (1982); *US v. Handley*, no. 1:07-cr-00030-JEG, order, US District Court, Southeastern Iowa, July 2, 2008. The PROTECT Act also federalized the Code Adam and AMBER Alert programs. See "OJJDP Activities to Combat Child Abduction," box 45, folder 16, Jay Lefkowitz Subject Files, Hollinger ID no. 63551, Domestic Policy Council, White House Staff Member Office Files, George W. Bush Presidential Library and Museum, Southern Methodist University, Dallas.

30. Steven Yoder, "Why Sex Offender Registries Keep Growing Even as Sexual Violence Rates Fall," *The Appeal*, July 3, 2018, https://theappeal.org/why-sex-offender-registries-keep-growing-even-as-sexual-violence-rates-fall/; Gallup, "Sex Offenders," June 9, 2005, found in Lancaster, *Sex Panic and the Punitive State*, 88; Judith Levine and Erica R. Meiners, "Are Sex Offenders Human?" *The Baffler*, November 15, 2016, https://thebaffler.com/latest/sex-offenders-human-levine-meiners.

31. For more on the crime press, see Carol A. Stabile, *White Victims, Black Villains: Gender, Race, and Crime News in US Culture* (New York: Routledge, 2006). For Indian captivity narratives as an ideologically motivated form, see Paula S. Fass, *Kidnapped: Child Abduction in America* (Berkeley: University of California Press, 1997). For more on the construction of whiteness and the "Othering" of Natives, see Peter Silver, *Our Savage Neighbors: How Indian War Transformed Early America* (New York: W. W. Norton & Co., 2007); Jill Lepore, *The Name of War: King Philip's War and the Origins of American Identity* (New York: Knopf, 1998).

32. Fass, *Kidnapped*; Viviana A. Zelizer, *Pricing the Priceless Child: The Changing Social Value of Children* (Princeton, NJ: Princeton University Press, 1985); Susan J. Pearson, *The Rights of the Defenseless: Protecting Animals and Children in Gilded Age America* (Chicago: University of Chicago Press, 2011); Michael Grossberg, "Liberation and Caretaking: Fighting over Children's Rights in Postwar America," in *Reinventing Childhood after World War II*, edited by Paula S. Fass and Michael Grossberg (Philadelphia: University of Pennsylvania Press, 2011), 19–37.

33. Jessica Pliley, *Policing Sexuality: The Mann Act and the Making of the FBI* (Cambridge, MA: Harvard University Press, 2014); Regina Kunzel, "Sex Panic, Psychiatry, and the Expansion of the Carceral State," in *The War on Sex*, ed. David M. Halperin and Trevor Hoppe (Durham, NC: Duke University Press, 2017), 231. See also Regina Kunzel, *Criminal Intimacy: Prison and the Uneven History of American Sexuality* (Chicago: University of Chicago Press, 2008); Estelle B. Freedman, "'Uncontrolled Desires': The Response to the Sexual Psychopath," *Journal of American History* 74, no. 1 (June 1987): 83–106; George Chauncey, "The Postwar Sex Crime Panic," in *True Stories from the American Past*, ed. William Graebner (New York: McGraw-Hill, 1993), 160–78.

34. Lancaster, *Sex Panic and the Punitive State*, 25. See also Jean Baudrillard, "Simulacra and Simulations," in *Jean Baudrillard: Selected Writings*, ed. Mark Poster (Stanford, CA: Stanford University Press, 1988), 166–84.

35. Natasha Zaretsky, *No Direction Home: The American Family and the Fear of National Decline* (Chapel Hill: University of North Carolina Press, 2007); Daniel T. Rodgers, *Age of Fracture* (Cambridge, MA: Belknap Press of Harvard University Press, 2012); "Public Trust in Government, 1958–2014," Pew Research Center, November 13, 2014, https://www.people-press.org/2014/11/13/public-trust-in-government; Kim Phillips-Fein, "Our Political Narratives," *Modern American History* 1, no. 1 (March 2018): 86. For "breadwinner liberalism," see Self, *All in the Family*. See also Melinda Cooper, *Family Values: Between Neoliberalism and the New Social Conservatism* (Cambridge: Zone Books/Massachusetts Institute of Technology Press, 2017); Nancy Fraser and Linda Gordon, "A Genealogy of Dependency: Tracing a Keyword of the US Welfare State," *Signs: Journal of Women in Culture and Society* 19, no. 2 (Winter 1994): 309–36.

36. As Whitney Strub notes, conservatives deployed the term "permissive society" with some regularity in the wake of the midcentury social revolutions. Strub, *Perversion for Profit*, 146. See also Boris Sokoloff, *The Permissive Society* (New York: Arlington House, 1971); Self, *All in the Family*, especially part III. Gallup, "In Depth: Topics A to Z—Crime," https://news.gallup.com/poll/1603/crime.aspx; Elaine Tyler May, "Security against Democracy: The Legacy of the Cold War at Home," *Journal of American History* 97, no. 4 (March 2011): 941.

37. Barry C. Feld, *The Evolution of the Juvenile Court: Race, Politics, and the Criminalizing of the Juvenile Court* (New York: New York University Press, 2017), 66; *In re Gault et al.*, 387 US 1 (1967); *In the Matter of Samuel Winship, Appellant*, 397 US 358 (1970).

38. *Tinker v. Des Moines Independent Community School District*, 393 US 503 (1969); Rebecca de Schweinitz, "'The Proper Age for Suffrage': Vote 18 and the Politics of Age from World War II to the Age of Aquarius," in *Age in America*, ed. Field and Syrett, 209–36; Cole, "'Old Enough to Live'."

39. Christopher Lasch, *Haven in a Heartless World: The Family Besieged*, revised edition (New York: W. W. Norton & Company, 1995 [1978]), 4; Jan Dizard, "Haven in a Heartless World," *Radical History Review* 19 (Winter 1978–79): 182. For "disciplinary matrix," see J. Jack Halberstam, *The Queer Art of Failure* (Durham, NC: Duke University Press, 2011), 72. Halberstam here draws on work by Judith Butler and David Eng while also nodding to the "alternative kinship" bonds celebrated by queer anthropologists like Kath Weston and Gayle Rubin.

40. Lancaster, *Sex Panic and the Punitive State*, 42. See also A. Nicholas Groth and H. J. Birnbaum, "Adult Sexual Orientation and Attraction to Underage Persons," *Archives of Sexual Behavior* 7, no. 3 (May 1978): 175–81; Carole Jenny, Thomas A. Roesler, and Kimberly L. Poyer, "Are Children at Risk for Sexual Abuse by Homosexuals?" *Pediatrics* 94, no. 1 (July 1994): 41–44; Wolak, Finkelhor, and Sedlak, "Child Victims of Stereotypical Kidnappings Known to Law Enforcement in 2011."

41. See Yvonne Tasker and Diane Negra, eds., *Interrogating Postfeminism: Gender and the Politics of Popular Culture* (Durham, NC: Duke University Press, 2007); Elizabeth Bernstein, "Carceral Politics as Gender Justice? The 'Traffic in Women' and Neoliberal Circuits of Crime, Sex, and Rights," *Theory and Society* 41, no. 3 (May 2012): 233–59. For "child-victims," see Joel Best, *Threatened Children: Rhetoric and Concern about Child-Victims* (Berkeley: University of California Press, 1990).

42. Paul M. Renfro, "'Hunting These Predators': The Gender Politics of Child Protection in the Post-9/11 Era," *Feminist Studies* 44, no. 3 (Fall 2018): 567–99; Eugene Robinson, "(White) Women We Love," *Washington Post*, June 10, 2005, A23.

43. For histories that interrogate the politics of American childhood, see (among others) Rebecca de Schweinitz, *If We Could Change the World: Young People and America's Long Struggle for Racial Equality* (Chapel Hill: University of North Carolina Press, 2009); Margaret Peacock, *Innocent Weapons: The Soviet and American Politics of Childhood in the Cold War* (Chapel Hill: University of North Carolina Press, 2014); Marcia Chatelain, *South Side Girls: Growing Up in the Great Migration* (Durham, NC: Duke University Press, 2015); Susan Eckelmann Berghel, Sara Fieldston, and Paul M. Renfro, eds., *Growing Up America: Youth and Politics since 1945* (Athens: University of Georgia Press, 2019). For the "war on sex," see Halperin and Hoppe, eds., *The War on Sex.*

44. For historiographical challenges to the "conservative ascendency" narrative, see Brent Cebul, Lily Geismer, and Mason B. Williams, *Shaped by the State: Toward a New Political History of the Twentieth Century* (Chicago: University of Chicago Press, 2019); Julian E. Zelizer, "Reflections: Rethinking the History of American Conservatism," *Reviews in American History* 38, no. 2 (June 2010): 367–92; Lily Geismer, *Don't Blame Us: Suburban Liberals and the Transformation of the Democratic Party* (Princeton, NJ: Princeton University Press, 2015); Matthew D. Lassiter, "Political History beyond the Red–Blue Divide," *Journal of American History* 98, no. 3 (December 2011): 760–64.

45. For an overview of the burgeoning literature on HIV/AIDS, see "Interchange: HIV/ AIDS and US History," *Journal of American History* 104, no. 2 (September 2017): 431–60.

46. Lassiter, "Political History beyond the Red–Blue Divide"; Brent Cebul, Lily Geismer, and Mason B. Williams, "Introduction—Beyond Red and Blue: Crisis and Continuity in Twentieth-Century US Political History," in *Shaped by the State*, ed. Cebul, Geismer, and Williams, 3–23.

47. Elizabeth Hinton, *From the War on Poverty to the War on Crime: The Making of Mass Incarceration in America* (Cambridge, MA: Harvard University Press, 2016).

48. Ilan H. Meyer, Andrew R. Flores, Lara Stemple, Adam P. Romero, Bianca D. M. Wilson, and Jody L. Herman, "Incarceration Rates and Traits of Sexual Minorities in the United States: National Inmate Survey," *American Journal of Public Health* 107, no. 2 (February 2017): 234–40, williamsinstitute.law.ucla.edu/wp-content/ uploads/Meyer_Final_Proofs.LGB_.In_.pdf.

CHAPTER 1

1. *CNN Tonight*, June 19, 2001, transcript, http://www.cnn.com/TRANSCRIPTS/ 0106/19/tonight.02.html; Joanne Wasserman, "Etan is Declared Dead," *New York Daily News*, June 20, 2001, https://www.nydailynews.com/archives/news/etan-declared-dead-article-1.910768; Rick Rojas, "38 Years, 2 Trials and Conviction in Boy's Killing," *New York Times*, February 15, 2017, A1.

2. Peter Kihss, "Boy Missing from SoHo was on Own First Time," *New York Times*, May 30, 1979, B3; Rojas, "38 Years, 2 Trials and Conviction in Boy's Killing"; George Goodman, "Volunteers Take Major Role in Search for Missing 6-Year-Old SoHo Boy," *New York Times*, May 28, 1979, B1.

3. Rojas, "38 Years, 2 Trials and Conviction in Boy's Killing": Rick Rojas and Kate Pastor, "In Patz Trial, Focus Turns to Words of Suspect," *New York Times*, November 2, 2016, A19.

4. Kihss, "Boy Missing from SoHo was on Own First Time"; CBS, *Evening News*, December 20, 1982, record no. 281733, Television News Archive, Vanderbilt University, Nashville (hereafter VTNA).

5. Natasha Zaretsky, *No Direction Home: The American Family and the Fear of National Decline, 1968–1980* (Chapel Hill: University of North Carolina Press, 2007); Melinda Cooper, *Family Values: Between Neoliberalism and the New Social Conservatism* (Cambridge: Zone Books/Massachusetts Institute of Technology Press, 2017).

6. Kim Phillips-Fein, *Fear City: New York's Fiscal Crisis and the Rise of Austerity Politics* (New York: Picador, 2017).

7. Barbara Kantrowitz, "Etan Patz is Still Missing, But His Parents Have Hope," *Philadelphia Inquirer* (PA), January 3, 1983, A02; Larry Goldsmith, "NAMBLA Disproves Kidnapping Allegations," *Gay Community News* 10, no. 25, January 8, 1983, 1; Daniel T. Rodgers, *Age of Fracture* (Cambridge, MA: Belknap Press of Harvard University Press, 2011).

8. Paula S. Fass, *Kidnapped: Child Abduction in America* (Berkeley: University of California Press, 1997), 260; Bryce Nelson, "Etan Patz Case Puts New Focus on a Sexual Disorder, Pedophilia," *New York Times*, January 4, 1983, C1; Richard Beck, *We Believe the Children: A Moral Panic in the 1980s* (New York: PublicAffairs, 2015). Roger Lancaster excavates the deep history of intergenerational relationships within the gay community. He argues that such couplings have emerged almost by necessity in contexts of intense homophobia, as adolescents and young men disowned by their parents and other family members have sought refuge in the arms of older gay men and within their broader kinship networks. Lancaster, *Sex Panic and the Punitive State* (Berkeley: University of California Press, 2011), especially 110–13.

9. Anne Higonnet, *Pictures of Innocence: The History and Crisis of Ideal Childhood* (New York: Thames and Hudson, 1998), 7; David Finkelhor and Lisa Jones, "Why Have Child Maltreatment and Child Victimization Declined?" *Journal of Social Issues* 62, no. 4 (2006): 692. One study published in *Pediatrics* compared data on child sex abuse from the 1970s and 1980s with figures from the 1940s; researchers found no discernible increase in the actual incidence of child sexual abuse. See William Feldman, Eva Feldman, John T. Goodman, Patrick J. McGrath, Robert P. Pless, Linda Corsini, and Susan Bennett, "Is Childhood Sexual Abuse Really Increasing in Prevalence? An Analysis of the Evidence," *Pediatrics* 88, no. 1 (July 1991): 29–33.

10. Viviana A. Zelizer, *Pricing the Priceless Child: The Changing Social Value of Children* (Princeton, NJ: Princeton University Press, 1985), 3; Jill Lepore, "Annals of Children's Welfare: Baby Doe," *New Yorker*, February 1, 2016; Margaret Peacock, *Innocent Weapons: The Soviet and American Politics of Childhood* (Chapel Hill: University of North Carolina Press, 2014), 2–3; Laura Briggs, *Somebody's Children: The Politics of Transracial and Transnational Adoption* (Durham, NC: Duke University Press, 2012), 131, 133–34.

11. Peacock, *Innocent Weapons*, 2–3; Robert B. Westbrook, "Fighting for the American Family: Private Interests and Political Obligation in World War II," in *The Power of Culture: Critical Essays in American History*, ed. Richard Wightman Fox and T. J. Jackson Lears (Chicago: University of Chicago Press, 1993), 194–221; Briggs, *Somebody's Children*, 131–37, 143.

12. Nina J. Easton, "The Crime Doctor is In," *Los Angeles Times*, May 2, 1995, https://www.latimes.com/archives/la-xpm-1995-05-02-ls-61478-story.html. See also Mary Dudziak, *Cold War Civil Rights: Race and the Image of American Democracy*

(Princeton, NJ: Princeton University Press, 2000); Joe Soss, Richard C. Fording, and Sanford F. Schram, *Disciplining the Poor: Neoliberal Paternalism and the Persistent Power of Race* (Chicago: University of Chicago Press, 2011); Loïc Wacquant, *Punishing the Poor: The Neoliberal Government of Social Insecurity* (Durham, NC: Duke University Press, 2009); "Day of Reckoning," *New Republic*, August 12, 1996.

13. Michael W. Flamm, *Law and Order: Street Crime, Civil Unrest, and the Crisis of Liberalism in the 1960s* (New York: Columbia University Press, 2005); Steve Macek, *Urban Nightmares: The Media, the Right, and the Moral Panic over the City* (Minneapolis: University of Minnesota Press, 2006); Phillips-Fein, *Fear City*.

14. "In Depth: Topics A to Z—Crime," Gallup, https://news.gallup.com/poll/ 1603/crime.aspx; Kevin Baker, "'Welcome to Fear City': The Inside Story of New York's Civil War, 40 Years On," *Guardian*, May 18, 2015, https://www. theguardian.com/cities/2015/may/18/welcome-to-fear-city-the-inside-story-of- new-yorks-civil-war-40-years-on.

15. Ralph Blumenthal, "Recalling New York at the Brink of Bankruptcy," *New York Times*, December 5, 2002, https://www.nytimes.com/2002/12/05/nyregion/ recalling-new-york-at-the-brink-of-bankruptcy.html; Samuel M. Ehrenhalt, "Economic and Demographic Change: The Case of New York City," *Monthly Labor Review* (February 1993): 41, 43.

16. Claire Jean Kim, *Bitter Fruit: The Politics of Black–Korean Conflict in New York City* (New Haven, CT: Yale University Press, 2000), 28; Jonathan Soffer, *Ed Koch and the Rebuilding of New York City* (New York: Columbia University Press, 2010), 107, 343–44; David F. Weiman and Christopher Weiss, "The Origins of Mass Incarceration in New York State: The Rockefeller Drug Laws and the Local War on Drugs," in *Do Prisons Make Us Safer? The Benefits and Costs of the Prison Boom*, ed. Steven Raphael and Michael A. Stoll (New York: Russell Sage Foundation, 2009), 92. See also Julilly Kohler-Hausmann, "'The Attila the Hun Law': New York's Rockefeller Drug Laws and the Making of a Punitive State," *Journal of Social History* 44, no. 1 (Fall 2010): 71–95.

    Commentators anointed Goetz the "*Death Wish* vigilante," an allusion to the 1974 film starring Charles Bronson as the timid liberal Paul Kersey. *Death Wish* charts Kersey's radicalization. After Latino burglars break into his home, murder his wife, and rape his daughter, Kersey transforms into an anticrime vigilante. In one of the film's most memorable scenes, Kersey shoots two muggers in a subway car, an act that Goetz would replicate (in real life) exactly ten years later. *Death Wish*, dir. Michael Winner (1974); Soffer, *Ed Koch and the Rebuilding of New York*, 343.

17. "Mayor Bloomberg and Police Commissioner [Raymond] Kelly Announce 2012 Sets All-Time Record for Fewest Murders and Fewest Shootings in New York City History," New York Police Department press release, December 28, 2012, www. nyc.gov/html/nypd/html/pr/pr_2012_all_time_records_lows_for_murders_ and_shootings.shtml; Michael Oreskes, "Fiscal Crisis Still Haunts the Police," *New York Times*, July 6, 1985, https://www.nytimes.com/1985/07/06/nyregion/ fiscal-crisis-still-haunts-the-police.html?pagewanted=all; Leonard Buder, "1980 Called Worst Year of Crime in City History," *New York Times*, February 25, 1981, https://www.nytimes.com/1981/02/25/nyregion/1980-called-worst-year-of- crime-in-city-history.html.

18. Mark K. Levitan and Susan S. Wieler, "Poverty in New York City, 1969–99: The Influence of Demographic Change, Income Growth, and Income Inequality," *Economic Policy Review* 14, no. 1 (July 2008): 14–15; Phillips-Fein, *Fear City*; Oreskes, "Fiscal Crisis Still Haunts the Police"; Alan Finder, "Financial Control

Board Loses Most of It's [*sic*] Control," *New York Times*, June 30, 1986, https://www.nytimes.com/1986/06/30/nyregion/financial-control-board-loses-most-of-it-s-control.html; Nicholas Freudenberg, Marianne Fahs, Sandro Galea, and Andrew Greenberg, "The Impact of New York City's 1975 Fiscal Crisis on the Tuberculosis, HIV, and Homicide Syndemic," *American Journal of Public Health* 93, no. 3 (March 2006): 424–34. For deproletarianization and labor informalization, see Ananya Roy, "Urban Informality: The Production of Space and Practice of Planning," in *The Oxford Handbook of Urban Planning*, ed. Randall Crane and Rachel Weber (New York: Oxford University Press, 2011), 692.

19. For "crime epidemic," see Sydney H. Schanberg, "Windows Are Breaking," *New York Times*, March 9, 1982, A23.

20. Soffer, *Ed Koch and the Rebuilding of New York City*, 343, 345; "Ford to City: Drop Dead," *New York Daily News*, October 30, 1975; Joe Austin, *Taking the Train: How Graffiti Art Became an Urban Crisis in New York City* (New York: Columbia University Press, 2002).

21. Oreskes, "Fiscal Crisis Still Haunts the Police"; Andy Cush, "Fear City: The Insane Pamphlet the NYPD Used to Terrorize 1970s New York," *Gawker*, January 8, 2015, https://gawker.com/fear-city-the-insane-pamphlet-the-nypd-used-to-terrori-1678292956.

22. Council for Public Safety, *Welcome to Fear City: A Survival Guide for Visitors to the City of New York* (1975); Baker, "'Welcome to Fear City.'"

23. Aaron Shkuda, *The Lofts of SoHo: Gentrification, Art, and Industry in New York, 1950–1980* (Chicago: University of Chicago Press, 2016), 44.

24. Mary Cantwell, "The Long Year of the Patz Family," *New York Times*, June 8, 1980, SM9, 112; *CNN Tonight*, June 19, 2001; Goodman, "Volunteers Take Major Role in Search for Missing 6-Year-Old SoHo Boy"; CBS, *Evening News*, April 19, 2012, record no. 1021197, VTNA. See also Lisa R. Cohen, *After Etan: The Missing Child Case that Held America Captive* (New York: Grand Central Publishing, 2009).

25. Anna Quindlen, "Etan Patz Case: Anguish and Mystery," *New York Times*, May 2, 1980, B1; *Vanished: Missing Children*, HBO, 1983, catalog ID: B:43332, Paley Center for Media, New York City; NBC, *Nightly News*, July 29, 1979, record no. 505494, VTNA.

26. US Congress, Senate, Committee on Labor and Human Resources, *Missing Children: Hearing before the Subcommittee on Investigations and General Oversight*, Ninety-seventh Congress, first session, October 6, 1981, 14; "Etan Patz News Resurrects Parents' Nightmares," *Talk of the Nation*, National Public Radio, May 24, 2012; "Israel Reports No Proof Etan Patz Went There," *New York Times*, January 19, 1986, https://www.nytimes.com/1986/01/19/nyregion/israel-reports-no-proof-etan-patz-went-there.html. Peyser switched his party affiliation from Republican to Democratic in 1977.

27. ABC, *World News Tonight*, June 3, 1981, record no. 72411, VTNA; Senate, Committee on Labor and Human Resources, *Missing Children*, October 6, 1981, 14.

28. ABC, *World News Tonight*, May 24, 1982, record no. 78290, VTNA. For "everychild," see Anita Casavantes Bradford, *The Revolution is for the Children: The Politics of Childhood in Havana and Miami, 1959–1962* (Chapel Hill: University of North Carolina Press, 2014).

29. CBS, *Evening News*, December 20, 1982, VTNA; CBS, *Evening News*, March 27, 1985, record no. 302658, VTNA (emphasis added); ABC, *World News Tonight*, June 19, 2001, record no. 197601, VTNA; ABC, *World News*, April 19, 2012, record no. 1019927, VTNA.

30. Kathryn Bond Stockton, *The Queer Child, or Growing Sideways in the Twentieth Century* (Durham, NC: Duke University Press, 2009), 30; "After Murder Suspect's Arrest, a Look at the Legacy of Etan Patz," PBS *Newshour*, May 25, 2012, https://www.pbs.org/newshour/bb/law-jan-june12-etanpatz_05-25.

31. Edward Klein, "The Long Search for Etan Patz," *Vanity Fair* 54, no. 6 (June 1991): 141; Stanley Patz, letter to the editor, *New York Times*, December 7, 1980, E22.

32. CBS, *Evening News*, December 20, 1982, VTNA.

33. Timothy Stewart-Winter, "Queer Law and Order: Sex, Criminality, and Policing in the Late Twentieth-Century United States," *Journal of American History* 102, no. 1 (June 2015): 70.

34. Stewart-Winter, "Queer Law and Order"; Kevin Ehrman-Solberg, "The Battle of the Bookstores and Gay Sexual Liberation in Minneapolis," *Middle West Review* 3, no. 1 (Fall 2016): 1–24.

35. Stewart-Winter, "Queer Law and Order"; Scott De Orio, "The Invention of Bad Gay Sex: Texas and the Creation of a Criminal Underclass of Gay People," *Journal of the History of Sexuality* 26, no. 1 (January 2017): 53–87.

    Political theorist Cathy Cohen uses the term "secondary marginalization" to describe the ways in which historically subjugated groups shed their most "deviant" elements in a bid for "respectability" and broad-based acceptance. Cathy Cohen, *The Boundaries of Blackness: AIDS and the Breakdown of Black Politics* (Chicago: University of Chicago Press, 1999), 9. See also Christina B. Hanhardt, *Safe Space: Gay Neighborhood History and the Politics of Violence* (Durham, NC: Duke University Press, 2013); Christina B. Hanhardt, "Broken Windows at Blue's: A Queer History of Gentrification and Policing," in *Policing the Planet: Why the Policing Crisis Led to Black Lives Matter*, ed. Jordan T. Camp and Christina Heatherton (New York: Verso Books, 2016), 41–61.

    For "carceral" feminists' tenuous alliances with social and religious conservatives, see Carolyn Bronstein, *Battling Pornography: The American Feminist Anti-Pornography Movement, 1976–1986* (New York: Cambridge University Press, 2011); Whitney Strub, *Perversion for Profit: The Politics of Pornography and the Rise of the New Right* (New York: Columbia University Press, 2010); Gillian Frank, "Save Our Children: The Sexual Politics of Child Protection in the United States, 1965–1990" (PhD diss., Brown University, 2009).

36. Quindlen, "Etan Patz Case."

37. Associated Press, "Boston Herald American Sold to Rupert Murdoch," *Eugene Register-Guard* (OR), December 4, 1982, 9A; FBI memorandum, Albany teletype to Bureau, "NORTH AMERICAN MAN/BOY LOVE ASSOCIATION (NAMBLA) ITOM [interstate transportation of obscene materials?]–SEXUAL EXPLOITATION OF CHILDREN," Newark 145B–1511, January 4, 1983, 5; Geoffrey Rowan, "Sex ring recruited with gifts," *Boston Herald American* (MA), December 7, 1982, 5; "Gay group has chapters world-wide," *Boston Herald American* (MA), December 7, 1982, 5; Geoffrey Rowan, "Literature defends homosexuality," *Boston Herald American* (MA) December 7, 1982, 5; "SEX CLUB CLUE IN HUNT FOR SOHO BOY," *New York Post*, December 20, 1982, 1, box 6, folder 19, Harold Pickett Papers, MSS Col. 2423, New York Public Library (hereafter HP).

38. Kevin P. Murphy, Jason Ruiz, and David Serlin, "Editors' Introduction," *Radical History Review* 100 (Winter 2008): 4. See also Margot Canaday, *The Straight State: Sexuality and Citizenship in Twentieth-Century America* (Princeton, NJ: Princeton University Press, 2009); Heather Murray, *Not in This Family: Gays*

and the Meaning of Kinship in Postwar North America (Philadelphia: University of Pennsylvania Press, 2010).

39. David Thorstad, "A Statement to the Gay Liberation Movement on the Issue of Man/Boy Love," *Gay Community News* 6, no. 23, January 6, 1979, 5; "man/boy love and the march on albany [sic]," *Gay Community News* 7, no. 44, May 31, 1980, box 4, folder 14, HP; David Thorstad, "Man/Boy Love and the American Gay Movement," *Journal of Homosexuality* 20, nos. 1–2 (1991): 251–74; Philip Shehadi, "Conflict over Speaker Splits March on Albany," *Gay Community News* 7, no. 39, April 26, 1980, 3; Harold Pickett, "Gay News," *Michael's Thing* 10, no. 18, May 5–11, 1980, box 4, folder 14, HP.

40. A. Damien Martin, "The Case against NAMBLA: Why Are We Ignoring the Obvious?" *New York City News*, March 9, 1983, box 6, folder 20, HP; Mitchell Halberstadt, "No Easy Answers," *New York City News*, January 26, 1983, box 6, folder 20, HP.

41. Halberstadt, "No Easy Answers" (emphasis in original); Harold Pickett, "MEDIA SMEAR!" *New York City News*, December 28, 1982, box 6, folder 20, HP; David Rothenberg, "Another Voice," *New York City News*, January 26, 1983, box 6, folder 20, HP.

42. Pickett, "MEDIA SMEAR!"; Rothenberg, "Another Voice." For the construction of this standard ("consenting adults in private"), see De Orio, "The Invention of Bad Gay Sex." See also Gayle S. Rubin, "Thinking Sex: Notes for a Radical Theory of the Politics of Sexuality," in *Pleasure and Danger: Exploring Female Sexuality*, ed. Carole S. Vance (New York: Routledge, 1984), 267–319.

43. "Conservative Forum," *Human Events* 43, no. 2, January 8, 1983, 14.

44. Sydney H. Schanberg, "Not Getting Involved," *New York Times*, December 28, 1982, A23.

45. CBS, *Evening News*, December 22, 1982, record no. 281777, VTNA; *New York v. Ferber*, 458 US 747 (1982).

46. Casavantes Bradford, *The Revolution is for the Children*.

47. *NAMBLA News*, no. 5, n.d., reprinted in Rowan, "Sex ring recruited with gifts," 5; Brian Eric Quinby, "Speaking Out; Victims," *Gay Community News* 10, no. 25, January 8, 1983, 5; David Thorstad, NAMBLA news conference statement, December 28, 1982, box 6, folder 19, HP; Thorstad, NAMBLA press release, December 24, 1982, box 6, folder 19, HP.

48. Thorstad, NAMBLA news conference statement, December 28, 1982, HP.

49. Thorstad, NAMBLA news conference statement, December 28, 1982, HP.

50. Gallup, July 21–24, 1978, Roper Center for Public Opinion Research, Cornell University, Ithaca (hereafter Roper); CBS News Exit Poll, November 7, 1978, Roper; Virginia Slims, "American Women's Poll," October 6–20, 1979, Roper; Connecticut Mutual Life Insurance, "American Values in the '80s" poll, September 1–November 15, 1980, Roper.

   Several polls conducted in the late seventies and early eighties found that a majority or plurality of Americans supported fair housing and employment laws for gays and lesbians. A General Mills survey from October 1978 also showed that 52 percent of Americans "welcome . . . the more open talk about . . . homosexuality" in the press and in daily conversation. See General Mills, "Family Health in an Era of Stress" poll, conducted by Yankelovich, Skelly, and White Inc., October 1978, Roper; NBC News/Associated Press poll, June 27–28, 1978, Roper; NBC News/Associated Press poll, October 16–17, 1978; NBC News/Associated Press poll, November 13–14, 1978, Roper; NBC News/Associated Press poll, May 18–19, 1981, Roper.

51. Rogers Worthington, "Gay World's Sound and Fury over 'Cruising,'" *Chicago Tribune*, February 18, 1980, A1; "The *Window*: A Look Inside," *Off Our Backs: A Women's Newsjournal* 10, no. 3 (March 31, 1980): 16.

52. Glenn Collins, "The Patzes: When Fiction Imitates Life," *New York Times*, July 26, 1982, A13; Higonnet, *Pictures of Innocence*; Gutcheon, *Still Missing*, 123–24.

53. Gutcheon, *Still Missing*, 140, 143.

54. David Finkel, "The Legacy of Adam Walsh: Son's Death Transforms a Father's Life," *Chicago Tribune*, September 17, 1984, F1.

55. Gutcheon, *Still Missing*, 254, 255, 256.

56. Gutcheon, *Still Missing*, 253–59, 262, 275, 271. Lucienne exemplifies the narrative trope, bordering on cliché, of the tragic or ill-fated queer. Literary and media critics (as well as fans) have used the term "bury your gays" to describe how authors, screenwriters, and other artists tend to kill off fictional LGBTQ characters. The discourse surrounding the "bury your gays" trope follows a long line of queer theoretical inquiry pertaining to LGBTQ mortality, tragedy, and futurity. See, for instance, Stockton, *The Queer Child, or Growing Sideways in the Twentieth Century*; Lee Edelman, *No Future: Queer Theory and the Death Drive* (Durham, NC: Duke University Press, 2004); José Esteban Muñoz, "Cruising the Toilet: LeRoi Jones/Amiri Baraka, Radical Black Traditions, and Queer Futurity," *GLQ: A Journal of Lesbian and Gay Studies* 13, nos. 2–3 (June 2007); Leo Bersani, "Is the Rectum a Grave?" *October* 43 (Winter 1987): 197–222.

57. Gutcheon, *Still Missing*, 282, 299, 311.

58. *Without a Trace*, dir. Stanley Jaffe (1983).

59. Frank, "Save Our Children," 4.

60. CBS, *Evening News*, December 20, 1982, VTNA; Ronald Reagan, "Proclamation 5064: Missing Children Day," May 25, 1983, Public Papers of Ronald W. Reagan, Ronald W. Reagan Presidential Library, Simi Valley, CA, https://www.reaganlibrary.gov/research/speeches/52583b; Michael Coakley, "Parents of Missing Boy Demand Reform," *Chicago Tribune*, June 21, 1981, B1; *Vanished*, Paley Center for Media, New York City.

CHAPTER 2

1. While this rally took place on the second anniversary of Etan Patz's disappearance, a day memorialized as Missing Children Day ever since 1983, there is no evidence to suggest that the event planners chose this date to commemorate Patz's abduction.

2. News release, Committee to Stop Children's Murders, April 16, 1981, box 120, folder 3, Atlanta Child Murders subseries, mayoral administrative records, series B: first and second term mayoral records, Maynard Jackson Papers, Archives Research Center, Robert W. Woodruff Library, Atlanta University Center (hereafter MJP); Wendell Rawls Jr., "Washington Rally Marks Atlanta Murders," *New York Times*, May 26, 1981, A14.

3. The precise number of missing and murdered in Atlanta has been the subject of much controversy ever since investigators developed a "list" of victims. Some object to the very existence of a list, while others consider it arbitrary, contending that city officials had omitted some black youths who had disappeared or lost their lives under similarly suspicious circumstances over the same timeframe (1979–1981) or soon thereafter. For more on these discussions, see Chet Dettlinger with Jeff Prugh, *The List* (Atlanta: Strode Communications, 1984); Maurice J. Hobson, *The Legend of the Black Mecca: Politics and Class in the Making of Modern Atlanta* (Chapel Hill: University of North Carolina Press, 2017), chapter 3.

Though some refer to these incidents as the "Atlanta child murders," the term "Atlanta youth murders" seems more appropriate given the ages of those included on "the list." Indeed, while most of the victims on the list of missing and murdered Atlantans were under the age of sixteen, five were over the age of twenty, and the oldest was twenty-seven. See "Disappearances and Murders of Atlanta Children," November 21, 1980, box 134, folder 135, series III: speeches (1966–2007), MS 509, Lee P. Brown Papers, Benjamin N. Woodson Research Center, Walter W. Fondren Library, Rice University, Houston (hereafter LPB). The Lee P. Brown Papers have recently been reprocessed, and thus the precise locations of the materials cited here may have changed.

4. Memorandum, STOP, n.d., box 228, folder 4, Missing and Murdered Children records (1980–81), subseries 4.5, Albert E. Love files (1973–92), Office of the Executive Director and National Administrator records, MSS 1083, Southern Christian Leadership Conference records, Stuart A. Rose Manuscript, Archives, and Rare Book Library, Robert W. Woodruff Library, Emory University, Atlanta (hereafter SCLC); "Chronology of Activities," April 2, 1981, box 135, folder 295, series III, LPB; Mike Christensen, "Movie Omits or Alters Key Facts in Williams Case," *Atlanta Journal-Constitution*, February 10, 1985, n.p.

5. Art Harris, "Atlanta's Doubts: Some Unconvinced of Williams' Guilt Despite Verdict," *Washington Post*, March 1, 1982, A1; Associated Press, "Williams Linked to 26 Killings," *Gainesville Sun* (FL), March 1, 1982, 1A; ABC, *Nightline*, March 1, 1982, audio tape recording, box 90, series VII: videos and audiocassettes, LPB; Monica Reeves, "Atlantan chosen as Houston chief," *Dallas Morning News* (TX), March 10, 1982, 1A, box 180, series I: office files (1960–2004), LPB.

6. Harris, "Atlanta's Doubts"; Reginald Stuart, "Atlantans' Feelings Mixed on Verdict," *New York Times*, March 1, 1982, A12; ABC, *Nightline*, March 1, 1982, LPB.

7. "State of the city" address, delivered by Maynard Jackson, February 2, 1981, box 26, series I, LPB; "Atlanta's Missing and Murdered Children" panel, National Medical Association, Atlanta, July 1981, tape recording, box 90, series VII, LPB. For an analysis of the white power movement during this period, see Kathleen Belew, *Bring the War Home: The White Power Movement and Paramilitary America* (Cambridge, MA: Harvard University Press, 2018). For early critiques of elite "image-preservation and damage-control" (in Bernard Headley's formulation) during the Atlanta youth murders, see Adolph Reed Jr., "Narcissistic Politics in Atlanta," *Telos* (Summer 1981): 98–105; Bernard Headley, "The Atlanta Establishment and the Atlanta Tragedy," *Phylon* 46, no. 4 (1985): 333–40.

8. CBS, *The Agony of Atlanta* news special, March 5, 1981, record no. 870623, Television News Archive, Vanderbilt University, Nashville (hereafter VTNA). See also Ahmed Shawki and Retha Hill, "The Atlanta Story," *Socialist Worker* (July 1981): 8–9.

9. "All grown up, 'a hustler from the word go,'" *Atlanta Journal-Constitution*, June 28, 1981, 5C; Ken Willis and David Johnston, "Baltazar: A 'Hustler' with Street Sense," *Atlanta Journal-Constitution*, February 13, 1981, 1A.

10. ABC, *World News Tonight*, April 9, 1981, record no. 71506, VTNA; Stanley Crouch, "Atlanta Reconstructed," *Village Voice* 26, no. 18 (April 29–May 5, 1981), 22–23.

11. Art Harris, "Atlanta's Child Victims: All Poor and Black, and All Dead or Missing," *Washington Post*, May 3, 1981, A1; "'Arrest parents,' FBI challenged," *Chicago Tribune*, April 17, 1981, 6.

12. Camille Bell, "Save the Children," *Washington Post*, May 10, 1981, B7.

13. Matthew D. Lassiter, *The Silent Majority: Suburban Politics in the Sunbelt South* (Princeton, NJ: Princeton University Press, 2005), 115–16.
14. ABC, *World News Tonight*, August 20, 1979, record no. 61247, VTNA; CBS, *Evening News*, August 13, 1979, record no. 265602, VTNA; NBC, *Nightly News*, August 18, 1979, record no. 505838, VTNA; Susan Harrigan, "Fading Image: Crime Wave in Atlanta Threatens Bid to Lure Business, Conventions," *Wall Street Journal*, August 8, 1979, 1.

    It should be noted that "crime waves," and other phenomena related to the quantification and broader experience of crime, are in large measure socially constructed. Historian Elizabeth Hinton considers the conflict of interest inherent in the FBI's tabulation of crime statistics. That an agency, particularly one as expansive and powerful as the FBI, could be tasked both with stymying crime and with "collecting and disseminating crime data" is, at the very least, problematic. Moreover, that the field of "crime statistics"—as "a new technology of knowledge production"—developed hand-in-glove with "early federal law enforcement measures" in the 1960s "meant that rising crime rates . . . correlated directly to rising crime reporting, a fact that skewed perceptions of violence." Elizabeth Hinton, *From the War on Poverty to the War on Crime: The Making of Mass Incarceration in America* (Cambridge, MA: Harvard University Press, 2016), 6, 7. Special thanks to Matt Lassiter for his assistance on this point.
15. "Chronology of Activities," LPB.
16. Harris, "Atlanta's Child Victims"; "Rites Today for Yusef [*sic*] Bell," *Atlanta Daily World*, November 13, 1979, 1; M. A. Farmer, "Investigators Feel Many Killers, Separately, Slew Atlanta Children," *New York Times*, March 15, 1981, 1.
17. Harris, "Atlanta's Child Victims"; Reba M. Harrington to Maynard Jackson, February 20, 1981, box 120, folder 16, Atlanta Child Murders subseries, mayoral administrative records, series B, MJP; Martin King and Don Singleton, "Blacks in poll rap Atlanta police on slayings of 28," *New York Daily News*, June 16, 1981, box 180, series I, LPB; NBC, *Nightly News*, February 15, 1981, record no. 515103, VTNA.
18. Mildred Glover to William Bradford Reynolds, August 19, 1982, FBI Report on the Atlanta Child Murders, file no. 7-18251 (section 19), 76; Chet Fuller and Orville Gaines, "Several Agencies Joining to Probe Friedman Blast," *Atlanta Journal-Constitution*, August 19, 1982, n.p., enclosed with Glover to Reynolds, FBI Report on the Atlanta Child Murders, 84; Chet Fuller and Orville Gaines, "FBI Enters Probe of Car Explosion," *Atlanta Journal-Constitution*, August 20, 1982, n.p., enclosed with Glover to Reynolds, FBI Report on the Atlanta Child Murders, 84.
19. "State of the city" address, LPB.
20. Hobson, *The Legend of the Black Mecca*, 110.
21. Cecil A. Alexander to Alvin Sugarman, February 25, 1981, box 121, folder 3, Atlanta Child Murders subseries, mayoral administrative records, series B, MJP; "Action request," Maynard Jackson to Community Relations Commission/Douglass [Jewish Federation of Atlanta], March 20, 1981, box 121, folder 3, Atlanta Child Murders subseries, mayoral administrative records, series B, MJP.
22. "State of the city" address, LPB (emphasis added); ABC, *World News Tonight*, February 23, 1981, record no. 70223, VTNA; CBS, *The Agony of Atlanta*, March 5, 1981, VTNA; Richard Harris, "Atlanta's Solidarity in Time of Sudden Crisis," *Atlanta Voice*, October 25–31, 1980, n.p., box 180, series I, LPB; Emily F. Rubin, "City's Grace under Stress Laid to Black Power Base," *Atlanta Constitution*, July 15, 1981, 1-C, box 180, series I, LPB; Robert M. Press, "Atlanta 'coming together'

to quell violence against black children," *Christian Science Monitor*, November 17, 1980, 5, box 48, series II: newsclips/publicity (bulk 1980s–1990s), LPB.

23. T. L. Wells and Linda Field, "Techwood Patrol Chiefs Cite Slow Police Response," *Atlanta Constitution*, March 18, 1981, 1-A; Hobson, *The Legend of the Black Mecca*, 118; "Group Meets Here on Racial Tension," *Atlanta Daily World*, November 4, 1980, 1. These efforts drew from the deep well of African American self-defense. See Charles E. Cobb Jr., *This Nonviolent Stuff'll Get You Killed: How Guns Made the Civil Rights Movement Possible* (New York: Basic Books, 2014); Akinyele Omowale Umoja, *We Will Shoot Back: Armed Resistance in the Mississippi Freedom Movement* (New York: New York University Press, 2013).

24. Harris, "Atlanta's Child Victims."

25. Harris, "Atlanta's Child Victims." Photographs of the missing and murdered youths appeared occasionally in the *Atlanta Journal-Constitution*, but very rarely in national newspaper or television coverage. Aside from the May 1981 *Washington Post* story by Art Harris, *LIFE* magazine supplied perhaps the only other national print piece that prominently displayed the pictures of multiple Atlanta victims. Doris Betts, "Atlanta Weeps for its Children," *LIFE* (April 1981): 66–78, box 177, series I, LPB.

26. Harris, "Atlanta's Child Victims."

27. ABC, *World News Tonight*, August 13, 1984, record no. 91195, VTNA; Willis and Johnston, "Baltazar" ; "All grown up, 'a hustler from the word go'"; "Dumping ground for cars . . . and bodies," *Atlanta Journal-Constitution*, June 28, 1981, 5C; Gail Epstein, "Victim Lived a Nightmare, Died in One," *Atlanta Journal-Constitution*, May 1, 1981, 1-A; "Living his own life," *Atlanta Journal-Constitution*, June 28, 1981, 5C; CBS, *Evening News*, February 21, 1981, record no. 275551, VTNA.

28. At the time he authored the report, Moynihan was serving as assistant secretary of labor under Lyndon Baines Johnson. Daniel Patrick Moynihan, *The Negro Family: The Case for National Action* (Washington, DC: US Department of Labor, Government Printing Office, 1965); Laura Briggs, *Somebody's Children: The Politics of Transnational and Transracial Adoption* (Durham, NC: Duke University Press, 2012), 44; Susan D. Greenbaum, *Blaming the Poor: The Long Shadow of the Moynihan Report on Cruel Images about Poverty* (New Brunswick, NJ: Rutgers University Press, 2015); Michael B. Katz, *The Undeserving Poor: America's Enduring Confrontation with Poverty*, second edition (New York: Oxford University Press, 2013), 21.

29. Harris, "Atlanta's Child Victims"; ABC, *World News Tonight*, February 25, 1981, record no. 70268, VTNA; CBS, *The Agony of Atlanta*, March 5, 1981, VTNA; David Real, "Street Kids," *San Antonio Express News* (TX), n.d., n.p., box 76, folder 9, mayoral administrative records, series B, MJP; US Congress, Senate, Committee on Labor and Human Resources, *Missing Children: Hearing before the Subcommittee on Investigations and General Oversight*, Ninety-seventh Congress, first session, October 6, 1981, 40.

30. Chester A. Higgins Sr., "Atlanta Holds Its Breath!" *Crisis*, August–September 1981, 352–63, box 177, series I, LPB; Renelda Higgins, "Trauma of Death Acted Out by Atlanta Children," *Crisis*, August–September 1981, 358–59, box 177, series I, LPB; interview with Charlayne Hunter-Gault by James M. Blount, *about . . . time* magazine 9, no. 3 (March 1981), 9–10, box 177, series I, LPB; CBS, *The Agony of Atlanta*, March 5, 1981, VTNA. See Robin Bernstein, *Racial Innocence: Performing American Childhood from Slavery to Civil Rights* (New York: New York University

Press, 2011); Robin Bernstein, "Let Black Kids Just Be Kids," *New York Times*, July 26, 2017.

31. "'Arrest parents,' FBI challenged"; Brenda Mooney, "Slain Youths' Mothers Discussing Suing FBI," *Atlanta Journal-Constitution*, May 5, 1981, 23; Wendell Rawls Jr., "FBI Agent's Remarks on Murders Strain Bureau's Ties with Atlanta," *New York Times*, April 16, 1981, A24; STOP to William Webster, n.d. (likely April or May 1981), box 120, folder 3, Atlanta Child Murders subseries, mayoral administrative records, series B, MJP.

32. Joseph Lowery to LaBaron Taylor, May 26, 1981, box 215, folder 5, Love files, SCLC; press release, Carrie Allison, Hartford section, National Council of Negro Women, February 1981, box 120, folder 16, Atlanta Child Murders subseries, mayoral administrative records, series B, MJP.

33. Senate, Committee on Labor and Human Resources, *Missing Children*, October 6, 1981, 39; interview with Maynard Jackson, box 4, folder 2, Gary M. Pomerantz Papers, MSS 890, Stuart A. Rose Manuscript, Archives, and Rare Book Library, Robert W. Woodruff Library, Emory University, Atlanta (hereafter GMP); CBS, *Evening News*, October 13, 1980, record no. 267248, VTNA; "Explosion rips day care center," *Wilmington Morning Star* (NC), October 14, 1980, 1; Evelyn L. Newman, "Furnace, Not Bomb, Blew Up Nursery," *Atlanta Daily World*, October 16, 1980, 1; ABC, *World News Tonight*, October 13, 1980, record no. 62640, VTNA; ABC, *World News Tonight*, October 14, 1980, record no. 62657, VTNA.

34. Tommy Battle to Maynard Jackson, February 26, 1981, box 120, folder 16, Atlanta Child Murders subseries, mayoral administrative records, series B, MJP; Barbara Anita Nunn to Maynard Jackson, February 28, 1981, box 120, folder 17, Atlanta Child Murders subseries, mayoral administrative records, series B, MJP; Toni Cade Bambara, *Those Bones Are Not My Child* (New York: Pantheon Books, 1999), 288.

35. Newman, "Furnace, Not Bomb, Blew Up Nursery"; interview with Maynard Jackson, box 4, folder 2, GMP. For more on the Klan in twentieth-century Atlanta, see Tomiko Brown-Nagin, *Courage to Dissent: Atlanta and the Long History of the Civil Rights Movement* (New York: Oxford University Press, 2011), especially 33–38.

36. William Luther Pierce (under the pseudonym "Andrew Macdonald"), *The Turner Diaries* (Hillsboro, WV: National Vanguard Books, 1978); Steve Johnson, "14 Men Hear Charges; 5th Victim Dies in NC," *Atlanta Constitution*, November 6, 1979, 1A; "Klan Saw the Permit for Parade by its Foes 2 Days before Killings," *New York Times*, November 8, 1979, A17; "Report on Riots," *Washington Post*, September 15, 1980, A20; Belew, *Bring the War Home*. Special thanks to Jason Morgan Ward for his guidance on this point.

37. Bernard Headley, *The Atlanta Youth Murders and the Politics of Race* (Carbondale: Southern Illinois University Press, 1998), 69–71.

38. NBC, *Nightly News*, October 23, 1980, record no. 507520, VTNA; Edward Walsh, "Black Ministers Stage 'Revival' at White House," *Washington Post*, October 24, 1980, A5; Don Irwin, "Carter Vows to 'Root Out' Killers of Blacks," *Los Angeles Times*, October 24, 1980, B14; "Klan Opponents Urge March in Washington on Inauguration Day," *New York Times*, December 7, 1980, 29. For more on Reagan's use of "states' rights" rhetoric, particularly at the Neshoba County Fair, see Joseph Crespino, *In Search of Another Country: Mississippi and the Conservative Counterrevolution* (Princeton, NJ: Princeton University Press, 2007), especially 1–5, 110–16; David Brooks, "History and Calumny," *New York Times*,

November 9, 2007, https://www.nytimes.com/2007/11/09/opinion/09brooks. html; Joseph Crespino, "Did David Brooks Tell the Full Story about Reagan's Neshoba County Fair Visit?" *History News Network*, November 12, 2007, https:// historynewsnetwork.org/article/44535.

39. Carole Ashkinaze and Bean Cutts, "Busbee Promises More Kids-Case Help," *Atlanta Constitution*, February 13, 1981, 23A; "Inside Story," WPBA, May 7, 1981, audio recording, box 90, series VII, LPB (emphasis added); Adam Clymer, "Bush Visits Families of Murdered Children in Atlanta," *New York Times*, March 15, 1981, 31.

40. Marcella Alsan and Marianne Wanamaker, "Tuskegee and the Health of Black Men," National Bureau of Economic Research, working paper 22323 (June 2016), https://www.nber.org/papers/w22323; Vann R. Newkirk, "A Generation of Bad Blood," *Atlantic Monthly* (June 17, 2016), https://www.theatlantic.com/politics/ archive/2016/06/tuskegee-study-medical-distrust-research/487439/; Paul A. Lombardo and Gregory M. Dorr, "Eugenics, Medical Education, and the Public Health Service: Another Perspective on the Tuskegee Syphilis Experiment," *Bulletin of the History of Medicine* 80, no. 2 (Summer 2006): 291–316; James H. Jones, *Bad Blood: The Tuskegee Syphilis Experiment*, revised edition (New York: Free Press, 1993), 222.

41. Patricia Turner, "The Atlanta Child Murders: A Case Study of Folklore in the Black Community," in *Creative Ethnicity: Symbols and Strategies of Contemporary Ethnic Life*, ed. Stephen Stern and John Allan Cicala (Logan: Utah State University Press, 1991), 78; Nick Brown, "Gregory Gives Theory on Atlanta Murders," *Los Angeles Sentinel*, May 21, 1981, A1.

42. Allison, February 1981, MJP; Mrs. L. B. Whittico and Vivian Hairston to Maynard Jackson, March 14, 1981, box 121, folder 9, Atlanta Child Murders subseries, mayoral administrative records, series B, MJP; Ozell Sutton to Joseph E. Lowery, October 23, 1980, box 93, folder 5, subseries 2.3, Joseph E. Lowery files (1968–97), Office of the President records, MSS 1083, SCLC; flyer, Lehman D. Bates, "United for Survival," First Baptist Church of Marshall Heights, Washington, DC, February 7, 1981, box 152, folder 8, Lowery files, SCLC (emphasis in original; "legal" is underlined in the original document, but it appears in italics here).

43. Arthur A. Mauge to Maynard Jackson, March 17, 1981, box 121, folder 3, Atlanta Child Murders subseries, mayoral administrative records, series B, MJP; Gladys L. Harper to Maynard Jackson, March 17, 1981, box 121, folder 2, Atlanta Child Murders subseries, mayoral administrative records, series B, MJP; Dennis McCluster, "Rash of Killings and Abductions Terrorize Atlantans," unpublished newspaper article, n.d. (likely 1981), box 348, folder 13, subseries 6.2, Department of Communications office files (1960–2004), MSS 1083, SCLC.

44. Albert E. Love to Joseph Lowery, "re: Proposal for SCLC Involvement in Atlanta Black Boys Murders," September 11, 1980, box 228, folder 4, Love files, SCLC (emphasis in original). "Saving Our Black Youth" and "Tomorrow's Leaders" are underlined (in pen) in the original document; they appear in italics here.

45. ABC, *World News Tonight*, April 9, 1981, VTNA; CBS, *Evening News*, April 23, 1981, record no. 276679, VTNA; Brenda Mooney, "Computers Trace Gays Near Kids," *Atlanta Constitution*, February 13, 1981, 1-C.

46. Crouch, "Atlanta Reconstructed," 22–23; Senate, Committee on Labor and Human Resources, *Missing Children*, October 6, 1981, 39. For the FBI's discussion of homosexuality in the Atlanta cases, see: Teletype, Atlanta FBI branch (7A-1835)

to FBI director, March 18, 1981, FBI Report on the Atlanta Child Murders, file no. 7-18251 (section 5), 35; teletype, Atlanta FBI branch (7A-1835), April 1981, FBI Report on the Atlanta Child Murders, file no. 7-18251 (section 5), 83; teletype, Philadelphia FBI branch, April 23, 1981, FBI Report on the Atlanta Child Murders, file no. 7-18251 (section 8), 29.

47. Chris Roberts, "Green ribbons memorialize Atlanta's murdered children," *Vistas* (Sunday feature), *Kingman Daily Miner* (AZ), March 22, 1981, 3; Tom Callahan, "From Georgetown, ribbons for 16 children," *Miami News* (FL), February 24, 1981, 3C; Allison, February 1981, MJP.

48. Jen Baker, "'Stranger Danger': The Public Service Film and the Protection of Child Sexuality," *Notches* blog, May 15, 2014, notchesblog.com/2014/05/15/stranger-danger-the-public-service-film-and-the-protection-of-child-sexuality;   Gillian Frank, "Stranger Danger and the Sexual Revolution," *Notches* blog, June 12, 2014, notchesblog.com/2014/06/12/stranger-danger-and-the-sexual-revolution.   This is not to say that all such slogans have an antigay subtext. Take, for instance, the Save the Children fund, established in the United Kingdom in 1919. Yet given the visibility and success of Bryant's "Save Our Children" campaign (founded in 1977), the fact that Atlantans adopted the same phrase just three years later does not seem coincidental.

49. Michelle Cliff, "Travel Notes," *Iowa Review* 12, nos. 2/3 (Spring–Summer 1981): 34; David Thorstad, "Homosexuality and the State: What the Atlanta Murders Reveal," *Philadelphia Gay News* (PA), April 1–7, 1983.

50. Thorstad, "Homosexuality and the State"; "Here's Part of What Wayne Williams Told Jury," *Atlanta Constitution*, February 23, 1982, 10A; Art Harris, "Williams Sticks to His Version of Events on the Chattahoochee," *Washington Post*, February 24, 1982, A6. The assistant Fulton County prosecutor asked Williams if a "Twinkie" was "a gay who is under 18 years old," to which Williams responded that he did not know. The term "twink" generally refers to younger, "boyish," or more "effeminate" gay men. Harris, "Williams Sticks to His Version of Events on the Chattahoochee"; Ken Willis and Gail Epstein, "Williams Dislikes Gays, Say Witnesses," *Atlanta Constitution*, February 18, 1982, 1A; "Williams: Guilty as Charged," *Newsweek*, March 8, 1982, box 180, series I, LPB.

51. Schedule of events, "I Love My Family Week: A Call for Family Unity," April 19–25, 1981, box 337, folder 15, Department of Communications office files, SCLC; news release, STOP, April 16, 1981; Lee P. Brown, remarks, I Love My Family Day forum, "A Strong Family Life: Its Impact on Public Safety," Martin Luther King Jr. Middle School, April 25, 1981, box 134, folder 146, series III, LPB; news release, STOP, April 16, 1981, MJP; interview with Lee P. Brown, April 27, 1981, LPB; Renelda Higgins, "Trauma of Death Acted Out by Atlanta Children," *Crisis*, August–September 1981, 358–59, box 177, series I, LPB.

52. Natasha Zaretsky, *No Direction Home: The American Family and the Fear of National Decline, 1968–1980* (Chapel Hill: University of North Carolina Press, 2007), 11, 13–14.

53. Senate, Committee on Labor and Human Resources, *Missing Children*, October 6, 1981; Bell, "Save the Children," *Washington Post*.

54. John J. DiIulio Jr., "Stop Crime Where It Starts," *New York Times*, July 31, 1996, A15; Clyde Haberman, "When Youth Violence Spurred 'Superpredator' Fear," *New York Times*, April 6, 2014; Hinton, *From the War on Poverty to the War on Crime*; Matthew D. Lassiter, "Impossible Criminals: The Suburban Imperatives of America's War on Drugs," *Journal of American History* 102, no. 1 (June

2015): 126–40; Bradford Smith, "Children in Custody: 20-Year Trends in Juvenile Detention, Correctional, and Shelter Facilities," *Crime and Delinquency* 44, no. 4 (October 1998): 535.

55. Steve Macek, *Urban Nightmares: The Media, the Right, and the Moral Panic over the City* (Minneapolis: University of Minnesota Press, 2006).

CHAPTER 3

1. James P. Gannon, "Commentary: The dark threat of terror now stalking D.M. should make us all 'mad as hell,'" *Des Moines Register* (hereafter *DMR*), August 15, 1984, 1A.
2. Gannon, "Commentary"; Paul Jackson, letter to the editor, *DMR*, September 5, 1984, 11A; Scott B. Neff, letter to the editor, *DMR*, August 29, 1984, 13A; Jan Tonasket, letter to the editor, *DMR*, August 29, 1984, 13A; Carolyn Keown, letter to the editor, *DMR*, September 2, 1984, 6C.
3. See, for example, Arnold Hirsch, *Making the Second Ghetto: Race and Housing in Chicago, 1940–1960*, revised edition (Chicago: University of Chicago Press, 1998 [1978]); Thomas J. Sugrue, *The Origins of the Urban Crisis: Race and Inequality in Postwar Detroit* (Princeton, NJ: Princeton University Press, 1996); David M. P. Freund, *Colored Property: State Policy and White Racial Politics in Suburban America* (Chicago: University of Chicago Press, 2007); Kevin Mumford, *Newark: A History of Race, Rights, and Riots in America* (New York: New York University Press, 2008); Lilia Fernández, *Brown in the Windy City: Mexicans and Puerto Ricans in Postwar Chicago* (Chicago: University of Chicago Press, 2012). For the white Midwestern politics of resentment, see Katherine J. Cramer, *The Politics of Resentment: Rural Consciousness in Wisconsin and the Rise of Scott Walker* (Chicago: University of Chicago Press, 2016).
4. "Racial and Ethnic Minority Group Percentage of the Population, Historical," Iowa Community Indicators Program, Iowa State University (based on the US Census Bureau's Decennial Census), https://www.icip.iastate.edu/tables/population/minority; R. Douglas Hurt, "Midwestern Distinctiveness," in *The American Midwest: Essays on Regional History*, ed. Andrew R. L. Cayton and Susan E. Gray (Bloomington: Indiana University Press, 2001), 173; Doug Kiel, "Untaming the Mild Frontier: In Search of New Midwestern Histories," *Middle West Review* 1, no. 1 (Fall 2014): 20.
5. For studies of Iowa that cast the state as moderate and lacking in extremes, see Joseph Frazier Wall, *Iowa: A Bicentennial History* (New York: W. W. Norton & Co., 1978); Dorothy Schweider, "Iowa: The Middle Land," in *Heartland: Comparative Histories of the Midwestern States*, ed. James H. Madison (Bloomington: Indiana University Press, 1988), 276–96. For the Midwest as a site of violence and disorder, see Michael J. Pfeifer, "At the Hands of Parties Unknown? The State of the Field of Lynching Scholarship," *Journal of American History* 101, no. 3 (December 2014): 832–46.
6. See, for instance, Kathryn Bond Stockton, *The Queer Child, or Growing Sideways in the Twentieth Century* (Durham, NC: Duke University Press, 2009).
7. KCCI-TV, CBS affiliate, Des Moines (hereafter KCCI), September 5, 1982; Carol Pitts, "Police hunt for missing WDM boy," *DMR*, September 6, 1982, 1A; Noreen N. Gosch, *Why Johnny Can't Come Home* (West Des Moines, IA: Johnny Gosch Foundation, 2000), 3; Frank Santiago, "Massive search for car seen when boy vanished," *DMR*, October 1, 1982, 1; DCI Special Bulletin, Gerald W. Shanahan to Terry Branstad, October 26, 1982, box 7, folder 21, 532/5/7, departmental and subject files, Robert D. Ray Papers, State Historical Society of Iowa, Des Moines; *Missing Johnny*, MSNBC documentary, originally aired December 23, 2012.

8. Pitts, "Police hunt for missing WDM boy"; KCCI, September 5, 1982; Carol Pitts, "1,000 volunteers search for missing WDM boy," *DMR*, September 7, 1982, 1A; KCCI, September 6, 1982; KCCI, September 7, 1982; Santiago, "Massive search for car seen when boy vanished," *DMR*.

9. KCCI, October 7, 1982; "While You Were Out," written message transcribed by an assistant, Noreen Gosch for Robert D. Ray, n.d., folder 21, 532/5/7, 1982, box 7, departmental and subject files, Robert D. Ray Papers, State Historical Society of Iowa, Des Moines; personal notes, Robert D. Ray, n.d., box 7, folder 21, 532/5/7, departmental and subject files, Robert D. Ray Papers, State Historical Society of Iowa, Des Moines; Frank Santiago, "Gosches refuse lie-detector tests," *DMR*, October 8, 1982, 1M.

10. KCCI, September 9, 1982; KCCI, September 12, 1982.

11. Associated Press (hereafter AP), "Gosch case is just one of 150,000," *DMR*, November 21, 1982, 1B; Gosch, *Why Johnny Can't Come Home*, 14; KCCI, February 4, 1983; KGAN-TV (hereafter KGAN), May 18–22, 1984, clip no. 238, Archives of Iowa Broadcasting, Wartburg College, Waverly, Iowa (hereafter AIB); Lindsey Moon and Charity Nebbe, interview with Noreen Gosch, "New Documentary Asks: Who Took Johnny Gosch?" Iowa Public Radio, April 16, 2015, https://www.iowapublicradio.org/post/new-documentary-asks-who-took-johnny-gosch; Frank Santiago, "After 2 years, Gosches continue their struggle," *DMR*, August 19, 1984, 1A.

12. Viviana Zelizer, *Pricing the Priceless Child: The Changing Social Value of Children* (Princeton, NJ: Princeton University Press, 1985); KCCI, November 7, 1982; Missing Children's Assistance Act, PL 98–473, 42 USC 5574, Title IV: amendment to the Juvenile Justice and Delinquency Prevention Act, October 12, 1984; Moon and Nebbe, interview with Gosch.

13. AP, "Gosch case is just one of 150,000"; Willis David Hoover, "Kids' fingerprinting makes mark," *DMR*, February 20, 1983, 1B; Iowa Data Center, total population for Iowa's incorporated places: 1850–2000, https://www.iowadatacenter.org/datatables/PlacesAll/plpopulation18502000.pdf; KGAN, March 23–29, 1983, clip no. 249, AIB; Tom Alex, "DM students are first to get fingerprinted," *DMR*, April 6, 1983, 4M; "News carrier program is set," *DMR*, May 17, 1983, 4M. The "safe space" prong of the HOPE program resembled earlier efforts in Atlanta as the city struggled to address the 1979–1981 abductions and murders discussed in chapter 2, as well as in Chicago, Oakland, and other urban centers grappling with crime and unrest in the "law and order" sixties and seventies. See Jaci M. Vickers to Lee P. Brown, June 1, 1981, box 177, MS 509, series I: office files (1960–2004), Lee P. Brown Papers, Benjamin N. Woodson Research Center, Walter W. Fondren Library, Rice University, Houston; "'Block Parents' to Aid Hyde Park Children," *Chicago Tribune*, February 4, 1968, SCL2; "Hand Symbol to Aid Young in Distress," *Chicago Tribune*, November 20, 1966, O1; "Children Get Help from Block Parents," *Oakland Post* (CA), February 19, 1970, 1.

14. KCCI, n.d., 1983 (emphasis added); KGAN, May 2–5, 1983, clip no. 312, AIB; KCCI, May 5, 1983; Frank Santiago, "Walk, dog add $4,700-plus to Gosch fund," *DMR*, May 18, 1983, 4M.

15. Mark Horstmeyer, "What worries our kids: Family ills, the future," *DMR*, May 26, 1983, 1A.

16. Chapter 1084, Investigations of Missing Persons, SF 517, also known as the Johnny Gosch Bill, Acts and Joint Resolutions passed at the 1984 Regular Session of the Seventieth General Assembly of the State of Iowa, approved April 13, 1984,

117–18; Tom Witosky, "Bill requiring faster responses to missing children reports passes," *DMR*, March 1, 1984, 2A.

17. Stern, "Mrs. Gosch: Iowa Errors Helped in Sarpy"; Frank Santiago, "Anger flares as Gosch hunt drags," *DMR*, January 2, 1983, 1B; West Des Moines city council proceedings, tape 143, side A, 000 to 729, January 3, 1983, in author's possession; KCCI, January 3, 1983; John and Noreen Gosch to Virgil E. Corey, December 22, 1983, "Missing Children" folder, N41/8/3, box 8, departmental and subject files, Terry Branstad Papers, State Historical Society of Iowa, Des Moines (hereafter TB); Gosch, *Why Johnny Can't Come Home*, 5.

18. According to the 1980 Census, Story City had a population of 2,762. Carolyn M. Schultze to Terry Branstad, May 18, 1984, constituent correspondence (McK–Z), box 2, Almo Hawkins files (1983–84), TB; Iowa Data Center, total population for Iowa's incorporated places: 1850–2000; Shirley Frette to Terry Branstad, February 1984, constituent correspondence (McK–Z), box 1, Almo Hawkins files (1983–84), TB; Carolyn Heuser to Terry Branstad, May 5, 1983, constituent correspondence (A–McK), box 1, Almo Hawkins files (1983–84), TB.

19. Stockton, *The Queer Child*, 30; Eileen Ogintz, "' . . . If you're not safe in W. Des Moines . . .'" *Chicago Tribune*, June 20, 1983, 1.

20. Gabriella Stern, "Mrs. Gosch: Iowa Errors Helped in Sarpy," *Omaha World-Herald*, March 4, 1984, n.p.; Frank Santiago, "Hideous picture of killer emerging," *DMR*, December 11, 1983, 1A; "Omaha carrier disappears," *DMR*, September 19, 1983, 3A; Frank Santiago, "'Several leads' in case of missing paper carrier," *DMR*, September 21, 1983, 4M; Frank Santiago, "No suspects in massive search for Nebraska newsboy's killer," *DMR*, September 23, 1983, 1M.

21. Santiago, "Hideous picture of killer emerging"; Frank Santiago, "Airman charged in Omaha-area slayings," *DMR*, January 13, 1984, 1M; Frank Santiago, "Gosch, slayings not related," *DMR*, January 18, 1984, 6M; Joy Powell, "The Prayers of a Killer: Joubert Seeks an End to His Dark Thoughts," *Omaha World-Herald*, June 16, 1996, 1A.

22. Charlene Zatloukel, letter to the editor, *DMR*, October 19, 1983, 15A; Alice Noble, "Missing paperboys prompt carrier protection programs," United Press International, September 25, 1983, n.p.; James Ivey, "Slayings Bring Nightmares, Sleeplessness," *Omaha World-Herald*, December 19, 1983, n.p.; Gary Newman, "Carter Lake Takes Steps to Prevent Child Abductions," *Omaha World-Herald*, December 8, 1983, n.p.

23. KGAN, October 19, 1983, clip no. 163, AIB.

24. Stern, "Mrs. Gosch: Iowa Errors Helped in Sarpy"; AP, "Mrs. Gosch takes credit for fast police action," *Oelwein Daily Register* (IA), March 5, 1984, 2.

25. Stern, "Mrs. Gosch: Iowa Errors Helped in Sarpy."

26. Frank Santiago, "Gosch talk with 'weird' man told," *DMR*, November 25, 1982, 1M; Frank Santiago, "Officials clear Gosch 'mystery man,'" *DMR*, January 5, 1983, 1M; KCCI, September 29, 1982; Frank Santiago, "Leader of The Way: We didn't kidnap John Gosch," *DMR*, October 9, 1982, 3A. For further discussion of potential cult involvement in Gosch's disappearance, see Charles Bullard, "Mother fears missing son abducted by religious cult," *DMR*, September 22, 1982, 1A; AP, "News in brief: Missing boy," *Oelwein Daily Register* (IA), September 22, 1982, 1; United Press International, "2nd boy's disappearance fuels Gosch hunt," *Chicago Daily Herald*, September 3, 1984, section 1-6.

27. Frank Santiago, "Noreen Gosch denies assault," *DMR*, August 28, 1984, 4M; US Congress, Senate, Committee on the Judiciary, *Effect of Pornography on Women*

and Children: Hearings before the Subcommittee on Juvenile Justice, Ninety-eighth Congress, second session, August 8, September 12 and 25, October 18 and 30, 1984, 67; ABC, *World News Tonight*, August 8, 1984, Television News Archive, Vanderbilt University, Nashville (hereafter VTNA); "JOHN GOSCH—PHONE HOME!" NAMBLA *Bulletin* 4, no. 5 (June 1983): 3, in Senate, Committee on the Judiciary, *Effect of Pornography on Women and Children*, 80; editorial, NAMBLA *Bulletin* 4, no. 5 (June 1983): 2, enclosed in Senate, Committee on the Judiciary, *Effect of Pornography on Women and Children*, 79 (emphasis in original; "any" is underlined in the original document but appears in italics here). While NAMBLA has been a lightning rod for controversy since its inception in 1978, there is no definitive evidence to suggest that the organization has ever endorsed or facilitated the abduction of minors.

28. Senate, Committee on the Judiciary, *Effect of Pornography on Women and Children*, 70–71, 68.

29. Rainbow Rowell, "Another summer of fear for kids," *Omaha World-Herald*, September 4, 2002, 1B.

30. Tom Alex, "Missing paper carrier is believed kidnapped," *DMR*, August 13, 1984, 1A; Frank Santiago, "Martin case is a photocopy of disappearance of Gosch," *DMR*, August 16, 1984, 1A; Frank Santiago, "'Mystery man' continues to elude police," *DMR*, September 6, 1984, 2M; ABC, *World News Tonight*, August 13, 1984, VTNA (emphasis added).

31. Gannon, "Commentary"; Stockton, *The Queer Child*, 30; Rebecca Wanzo, "The Era of Lost (White) Girls: On Body and Event," *differences: A Journal of Feminist Cultural Studies* 19, no. 2 (Summer 2008): 101.

32. "Newark: The Predictable Insurrection," *LIFE* magazine 63, no. 4 (July 28, 1967); Steve Macek, *Urban Nightmares: The Media, the Right, and the Moral Panic over the City* (Minneapolis: University of Minnesota Press, 2006); Mumford, *Newark*; Mark Krasovic, *The Newark Frontier: Community Action in the Great Society* (Chicago: University of Chicago Press, 2016); Sugrue, *The Origins of the Urban Crisis*, especially 259–71.

33. Gannon, "Commentary." Gannon reappropriated the "mad as hell" line from the film *Network*, which had become a touchstone for politically disaffected Americans in the mid- to late seventies. See *Network*, dir. Sidney Lumet (1976). For a popular history of the 1970s that deploys "mad as hell" as an analytical device, see Dominic Sandbrook, *Mad as Hell: The Crisis of the 1970s and the Rise of the Populist Right* (New York: Alfred A. Knopf, 2011).

34. Neil Miller, *Sex-Crime Panic: A Journey to the Heart of the Paranoid 1950s* (New York: Alyson Books, 2002); Samuel M. Fahr, "Iowa's New Sexual Psychopath Law: An Experiment Noble in Purpose?" *Iowa Law Review* 41 (1955–56): 523–57.

35. *Brewer v. Williams*, no. 74-1263, 430 US 387, 97 S. Ct. 1232, March 23, 1977; Robert M. Regoli and John D. Hewitt, *Exploring Criminal Justice: The Essentials* (Burlington, MA: Jones & Bartlett Learning, 2010), 134; Mara Bovsun, "Bury her for Christmas: How the murder of Pamela Powers, 10, reached the Supreme Court," *New York Daily News*, December 16, 2012, https://www.nydailynews.com/news/justice-story/bury-christmas-article-1.1219790; Mark Brown, "Fugitive from Mental Hospital Charged in Murder of Iowa Girl, 10," *Gettysburg Times* (PA), December 27, 1968, 8.

36. For a list of missing persons in Iowa, administered by the state's Department of Public Safety (DPS) and beginning with Guy Heckle, see the Missing Person Information Clearinghouse, Iowa DPS, www.iowaonline.state.ia.us/mpic/

Controller.aspx. For more on Heckle, see Jeff Burnham, "Murdered. Missing. Unsolved.: 2 Iowa boys gone but not forgotten," *Gazette* (Cedar Rapids-Iowa City), March 20, 1992, n.p.; Cindy Hadish, "'Not knowing is hard,'" *Gazette*, July 24, 1995, n.p.; Steve Gravelle, "How did Guy die? 29 years after an 11-year-old boy vanished, his mother still hopes to find out what happened," *Gazette*, February 3, 2002, n.p.; AP, "Gosch case is just one of 150,000."

37. Letters to the editor, *DMR*, August 29, 1984, 13A (emphasis added); letters to the editor, *DMR*, September 5, 1984, 11A.

38. Paul Mokrzycki Renfro, "Keeping Children Safe is Good Business: The Enterprise of Child Safety in the Age of Reagan," *Enterprise & Society* 17, no. 1 (March 2016): 151–87; Frank Santiago, "Leaders meet to tackle issues of child safety," *DMR*, November 25, 1984, 1A.

39. Melinda Voss, "Recent tragedies take toll on parents trying to protect children," *DMR*, August 19, 1984, 3B; David Elbert, "Poll finds fear for safety of children on rise in Iowa," *DMR*, November 25, 1984, 1A; Anne Carothers-Kay, "Climate of fear in WDM," *DMR*, October 31, 1984, 1N-WS; letters to the editor, *DMR*, September 11, 1984, 9A.

40. ABC, *World News Tonight*, August 14, 1984, record no. 91206, VTNA.

41. Letters to the editor, *DMR*, September 2, 1984, 6C. For examples of these sightings, see Frank Santiago, "Family reports nine sightings of Gosch youth," *DMR*, June 25, 1983, 3A; Steve Kline, "Newspaper Carrier Cases Eerily Similar," AP, September 25, 1983, n.p.; Mark Horstmeyer, "FBI Checks Out Texas Sighting of John Gosch," *DMR*, March 31, 1983, 5M; AP, "Report: Child Kidnapped in 1982 Sighted," January 30, 1984, n.p.; Mark Mittelstadt, "Johnny Gosch's Mother Says Her Son Seen in South," AP, February 23, 1984, n.p.; Margaret Stafford, "Parents Keep Working to Find Missing Son," AP, March 3, 1984, n.p.; United Press International, "2nd boy's disappearance fuels Gosch hunt"; Frank Santiago, "Martin look-alike is reported hitchhiking in Washington state," *DMR*, September 19, 1984, 3M; Frank Santiago, "Possible Martin sighting likely another mistake," *DMR*, October 31, 1984, 3M; Frank Santiago, "Noreen Gosch: I saw Johnny," *DMR*, February 7, 1999, B1; Frank Santiago, "Johnny Gosch's dad questions that his ex-wife saw their son in 1997," *DMR*, February 8, 1999, M1; *Who Took Johnny*, dirs. David Beilinson, Michael Galinski, and Suki Hawley (2014).

42. Frank Santiago and Tom Alex, "Reagan calls to offer aid on missing boys," *DMR*, August 17, 1984, 1A; James P. Gannon, "*Register* editor's account of call from the president," *DMR*, August 17, 1984, 1A; Ronald Reagan, "Remarks at a Reagan-Bush Rally in Cedar Rapids, Iowa," September 20, 1984, Ronald W. Reagan Presidential Library and Museum, Simi Valley, CA, https://www.reaganlibrary.gov/research/speeches/92084b.

43. Reagan, "Remarks at a Reagan-Bush Rally in Cedar Rapids, Iowa."

44. Annie Brown and Roman Mars, "Milk Carton Kids," *99 Percent Invisible*, September 15, 2015, https://99percentinvisible.org/episode/milk-carton-kids. For "emotionally resonant child-centered images," see Anita Casavantes Bradford, *The Revolution is for the Children: The Politics of Childhood in Havana and Miami, 1959–1962* (Chapel Hill: University of North Carolina Press, 2014), 90.

45. KGAN, May 7–9, 1984, clip no. 480, AIB; "Truckers to aid Gosch search," *DMR*, May 8, 1984, 3M; Frank Santiago, "Volunteers, police keep hunting boy," *DMR*, August 25, 1984, 3A; "Cross-country eye-catcher," *DMR*, September 15, 1984, 1A; Richard R. Kerr, "Processors Unite to Help Children," *Dairy Field*, April 1985, 47.

46. Kendra Smith-Howard, *Pure and Modern Milk: An Environmental History since 1900* (New York: Oxford University Press, 2013); Leo Marx, *The Machine in the Garden: Technology and the Pastoral Ideal* (New York: Oxford University Press, 1964); Kerr, "Processors Unite to Help Children."

47. AP, "Missing Girl Sees Picture on TV, Comes Home," January 23, 1985; AP, "Teen-Ager Reunited with Mother after Milk Carton-Photo Campaign Publicized," January 24, 1985; Kiley Armstrong, "Missing Kids' Pictures Enter America's Kitchens," AP, January 28, 1985.

48. "Knudsen Participates in 'Abducted Children Milk Carton Side Panel Program,'" *Business Wire*, February 4, 1985; "Milk Cartons: New Role," *New York Times*, February 13, 1985, C14.

49. CBS, *Evening News*, February 13, 1985, record no. 301791, VTNA; Fred Bayles, "Images of Missing Children on Pizza Boxes, Toll Tickets," AP, March 3, 1985.

50. Peter Brewer, "Millions of Milk Carton Photographs Yield Only a Few Missing Children," AP, February 14, 1987; Eleanor Blau, "Follow-Up on the News; Pictures of Children," *New York Times*, October 5, 1986.

51. "Valassis' Have You Seen Me? Program Marks 30th Anniversary," Valassis Communications, Inc. [previously ADVO], May 26, 2015, https://www.valassis.com/about-us/newsroom/item/150526/30th-anniversary-have-you-seen-me-program; Marilyn Ivy, "Have You Seen Me? Recovering the Inner Child in Late Twentieth-Century America," *Social Text*, no. 37 (Winter 1993): 227–52; Eric Freedman, *Transient Images: Personal Media in Public Frameworks* (Philadelphia: Temple University Press, 2011), 48–52.

52. "Milk Does a Body Good," *Punky Brewster*, season two, episode twelve (1985).

53. *The Lost Boys*, dir. Joel Schumacher (1987); *Big*, dir. Penny Marshall (1988); *Honey, I Shrunk the Kids*, dir. Joe Johnston (1989); "Rosebud," *The Simpsons*, season five, episode four (1993); Caroline B. Cooney, *The Face on the Milk Carton* (New York: Bantam Doubleday Dell Publishing Group, Inc., 1990).

54. Daniel T. Rodgers, *Age of Fracture* (Cambridge, MA: Belknap Press of Harvard University Press, 2011); ABC, *World News Tonight*, January 16, 1988, record no. 111859, VTNA; Marcia Dunn, "Babbitt Blames 'Spontaneity' for Inappropriate Joke," AP, January 17, 1988.

55. See also Ivy, "Have You Seen Me?"; Freedman, *Transient Images*; Perry Howell, "Got worry? Missing children notices on milk cartons in the United States," *Interactions: Studies in Communication & Culture* 2, no. 1 (May 2010): 35–46; Renfro, "Keeping Children Safe is Good Business."

56. Mitch Gelman, "On the road to the future, but where does it lead?" *DMR*, November 4, 1984, 1C; Rod Boshart, "Petitioners back capital punishment," *Gazette* (Cedar Rapids-Iowa City), September 7, 1994, 1A; Rod Boshart, "Death-penalty foes speak," *Gazette*, February 27, 1997, 10A; MacKenzie Elmer, "Lawmaker seeks death penalty bill," *Telegraph Herald* (Dubuque, IA), January 26, 2013, 6C; Jeff Reinitz, "1 year later: Collins family remains active after disappearance of Elizabeth, Lyric," *Waterloo-Cedar Falls Courier* (IA), July 12, 2013, https://wcfcourier.com/news/evansdale_search/year-later-collins-family-remains-active-after-disappearance-of-elizabeth/article_64d051f8-ea75-11e2-b216-0019bb2963f4.html; *Who Took Johnny*; "The Farm Crisis and the Midwest," special issue, guest edited by Jenny Barker Devine and David D. Vail, *Middle West Review* 2, no. 1 (Fall 2015).

57. AP, "Johnny Gosch: Family, investigators disagree on evidence," *Daily Iowan* (University of Iowa, Iowa City), July 22, 1991, 3; *In the Dark* podcast, American

Public Media Reports (2016); Erin Crawford, "Is he Johnny Gosch?" *DMR*, April 5, 2005, E1.

58. Elbert, "Poll finds fear for safety of children on rise in Iowa"; *Missing Johnny*, MSNBC.

CHAPTER 4

1. US Congress, Senate, Committee on Labor and Human Resources, *Missing Children: Hearing before the Subcommittee on Investigations and General Oversight*, Ninety-seventh Congress, first session, October 6, 1981, 28, 29, 30. For rightwing opposition to the Great Society, see Annelise Orleck, "Conclusion: The War on the War on Poverty and American Politics since the 1960s," in *The War on Poverty: A New Grassroots History, 1964–1980*, ed. Annelise Orleck and Lisa Gayle Hazirjian (Athens: University of Georgia Press, 2011), 437–61.

2. William French Smith to Ronald Reagan, April 1, 1982, Missing Children's Act, box 20, Ken Caruso and Robert Bucknam files, subject files of the assistants to the associate attorney general, January 1981–June 1983, Record Group (RG) 60: General Records of the US Department of Justice, National Archives and Records Administration, College Park, MD (hereafter NARA II); William H. Webster to Strom Thurmond, September 29, 1982, box 20, Caruso and Bucknam files, RG 60, NARA II.

   This chapter nods to the academic subfield of affect studies, which theorizes and intellectualizes emotion and sentiment in the human experience. Scholars of affect take actorhood, performativity, and bodily responses as key features of human sociality. See Patricia Ticineto Clough and Jean Halley, eds., *The Affective Turn: Theorizing the Social* (Durham, NC: Duke University Press, 2007); Eve Kosofsky Sedgwick, *Touching Feeling: Affect, Pedagogy, Performativity* (Durham, NC: Duke University Press, 2003); Eve Kosofsky Sedgwick and Adam Frank, eds., *Shame and Its Sisters: A Silvan Tompkins Reader* (Durham, NC: Duke University Press, 1995).

3. William H. Webster to all FBI field offices, February 7, 1983, box 20, Caruso and Bucknam files, RG 60, NARA II; Paula Hawkins to Ronald Reagan, March 24, 1982, box 20, Caruso and Bucknam files, RG 60, NARA II; William H. Webster to Paula Hawkins, February 18, 1983, box 20, Caruso and Bucknam files, RG 60, NARA II.

4. Whitney Strub, *Perversion for Profit: The Politics of Pornography and the Rise of the New Right* (New York: Columbia University Press, 2010), especially chapter 6.

5. Senate, Committee on Labor and Human Resources, *Missing Children*, October 6, 1981, 25.

6. For "moral threats," see Robert O. Self, *All in the Family: The Realignment of American Democracy since the 1960s* (New York: Hill and Wang, 2012).

7. For more on the Reagan DOJ and civil rights, see George Derek Musgrove, *Rumor, Repression, and Racial Politics: How the Harassment of Black Elected Officials Shaped Post-Civil Rights America* (Athens: University of Georgia Press, 2012), especially chapter 5.

8. John Walsh with Susan Schindehette, *Tears of Rage: From Grieving Father to Crusader for Justice—The Untold Story of the Adam Walsh Case* (New York: Simon & Schuster, 1997); William M. Baker to Phil Donahue, March 23, 1984, box 1, constituent correspondence (1983–84), A–McK, Almo Hawkins files, Terry Branstad Papers, State Historical Society of Iowa–Des Moines. For "a national epidemic," see ABC, *World News Tonight*, June 4, 1981, record no. 72458, Television News Archive, Vanderbilt University (hereafter VTNA).

9. ABC, *World News Tonight*, June 3, 1981, record no. 72411, VTNA; ABC, *World News Tonight*, June 4, 1981, VTNA.

10. Viviana A. Zelizer, *Pricing the Priceless Child: The Changing Social Value of Children* (Princeton, NJ: Princeton University Press, 1985); Senate, Committee on Labor and Human Resources, *Missing Children*, October 6, 1981, 2.

11. Senate, Committee on Labor and Human Resources, *Missing Children*, October 6, 1981, 29, 55, 104 (emphasis in original). The phrase "complete amazement" is underlined in the original document; it appears in italics here. See also Federal Kidnapping Act, 18 USC § 1201 (1932).

12. United Press International, "FBI Deploys Potent Weapon against Crime," *Los Angeles Times*, January 28, 1967, B3; news release, "Missing Children Bill Clears Committee," Office of Congressman Peter W. Rodino, August 19, 1982, box 61, HR 6825–HR 6993, House Judiciary files, Records of the US House of Representatives, RG 233, National Archives and Records Administration, Washington, DC; Karen Ann Joe, "Milk Carton Madness: The Heart of the Missing Children's Crisis" (PhD diss., University of California, Davis, 1991), 123.

13. US Congress, House, Committee on the Judiciary, *Missing Children's Act: Hearings before the Subcommittee on Civil and Constitutional Rights*, Ninety-seventh Congress, first session, November 18 and 30, 1981, 11; CBS, *Evening News*, December 1, 1981, record no. 274755, VTNA.

14. Sarah McNamara to Mickey Edwards, no. 9865, August 17, 1982, box 17, folder 19, Mickey Edwards Collection, Carl Albert Center Congressional Archives, University of Oklahoma, Norman (hereafter MEC); Janet A. LaMotte to Mickey Edwards, no. 5114, October 11, 1981, box 12, folder 14, MEC; Mrs. Fred Ragland to Mickey Edwards, no. 5106, October 23, 1981, box 12, folder 14, MEC (emphasis in original; the phrase "same advantage as missing cars" is underlined in the original document, but it appears in italics here); Mrs. W. Allen Sparks to Mickey Edwards, no. 5108, October 22, 1981, box 12, folder 14, MEC; S.UP.AMDT. 661 to H.J.RES. 357, Missing Children Act, introduced November 10, 1981, Ninety-seventh Congress, first session.

15. Robert A. McConnell to William French Smith, Edward Schmults, Rudolph W. Giuliani, William H. Webster, and D. Lowell Jensen, March 1, 1982, box 20, Caruso and Bucknam files, RG 60, NARA II.

16. Smith to Reagan, April 1, 1982, box 20, Caruso and Bucknam files, RG 60, NARA II. For more on the FBI's priorities in the 1980s, see Jeffrey B. Bumgarner, *Federal Agents: The Growth of Federal Law Enforcement in America* (Santa Barbara, CA: Greenwood Publishing Group, 2006), especially chapter 4. See also Gerald M. Caplan, "War on Drugs Could Backfire: Law-Enforcement Crackdown Might Make Things Worse," *Los Angeles Times*, June 10, 1981, D7.

17. Webster to Thurmond, September 29, 1982, box 20, Caruso and Bucknam files, RG 60, NARA II. The sheer size of these projected numbers also speaks to the perceived extent of the missing child "epidemic" at the time. Incidence studies of missing children cases do consistently yield large figures. For example, the DOJ found that 800,000 juveniles were reported missing in 1999. Upon closer inspection, though, a large chunk of these incidents can be dismissed through "benign explanations"—a child wandering off, for instance, or failing to communicate their whereabouts to a caretaker. Some 115 of these children fell victim to what experts call "stereotypical" kidnappings—"the particular type of nonfamily abduction that receives the most media attention and involves a stranger or slight acquaintance who detains the child overnight, transports the child at least 50

miles, holds the child for ransom, abducts the child with intent to keep the child
permanently, or kills the child." See Andrea J. Sedlak, David Finkelhor, Heather
Hammer, and Dana J. Schultz, National Incidence Studies of Missing, Abducted,
Runaway, and Thrownaway Children, "National Estimates of Missing Children: An
Overview," Office of Juvenile Justice and Delinquency Prevention, Office of
Justice Programs, US Department of Justice, October 2002, ncjrs.gov/pdffiles1/
ojjdp/196465.pdf. McConnell to Smith, Schmults, Giuliani, Webster, and Jensen,
March 1, 1982, box 20, Caruso and Bucknam files, RG 60, NARA II.

18. Webster to Thurmond, September 29, 1982, box 20, Caruso and Bucknam files,
RG 60, NARA II; McConnell to Smith, Schmults, Giuliani, Webster, and Jensen,
March 1, 1982, box 20, Caruso and Bucknam files, RG 60, NARA II; DOJ notes,
S. 1701 draft, Ninety-seventh Congress, first session, October 5 (legislative day
September 9), 1981, box 20, Caruso and Bucknam files, RG 60, NARA II; Smith
to Reagan, April 1, 1982, box 20, Caruso and Bucknam files, RG 60, NARA II.
"Unemancipated" generally refers to a minor who remains legally under the au-
thority of another individual, typically a parent or guardian.

19. Missing Children Act, PL 97–292, Ninety-seventh Congress, second session,
October 12, 1982; Webster to FBI field offices, February 7, 1983, box 20, Caruso
and Bucknam files, RG 60, NARA II.

20. McConnell to Smith, Schmults, Giuliani, Webster, and Jensen, March 1, 1982,
box 20, Caruso and Bucknam files, RG 60, NARA II; Robert A. McConnell to
Rudolph W. Giuliani, March 10, 1982, box 20, Caruso and Bucknam files, RG 60,
NARA II.

21. Adam Walsh had been kidnapped and killed the previous year (1981), not "several
years ago."

22. McConnell to Smith, Schmults, Giuliani, Webster, and Jensen, March 1, 1982,
box 20, Caruso and Bucknam files, RG 60, NARA II; Rudolph W. Giuliani to
William French Smith, March 18, 1982, box 20, Caruso and Bucknam files, RG
60, NARA II; Smith to Reagan, April 1, 1982, box 20, Caruso and Bucknam files,
RG 60, NARA II. Reagan's cabinet secretary Craig Fuller, in response to Smith's
memorandum, claimed that the White House had "not yet" received "a request
for a meeting with Mr. and Mrs. Walsh." See Craig L. Fuller to William French
Smith, April 7, 1982, box 20, Caruso and Bucknam files, RG 60, NARA II. For "the
battle for child safety," see President's Child Safety Partnership and the Office
for Victims of Crime, *A Report to the President*, 16, in Richard B. Abell to Edwin
Meese III, September 25, 1987, Edwin Meese: Children—Partnerships in Child
Safety (1987), box 269, entry 1092, subject files of the attorney general (compiled
1975–93), RG 60, NARA II.

23. "Public Trust in Government, 1958–2014," Pew Research Center, November 13,
2014, https://www.people-press.org/2014/11/13/public-trust-in-government;
Ronald Reagan, "Election Eve Address: 'A Vision for America,'" November 3, 1980,
American Presidency Project, University of California, Santa Barbara, https://
www.presidency.ucsb.edu/documents/election-eve-address-vision-for-america.

24. "Finding Missing Children," *Washington Post*, May 28, 1982, A30.

25. ABC, *World News Tonight*, May 24, 1982, record no. 78290, VTNA.

26. Hawkins to Reagan, March 24, 1982, box 20, Caruso and Bucknam files, RG 60,
NARA II.

27. Senate, Committee on Labor and Human Resources, *Missing Children*, October
6, 1981, 28, 30. See Matthew D. Lassiter, *The Silent Majority: Suburban Politics in
the Sunbelt South* (Princeton, NJ: Princeton University Press, 2005); Kevin M.

Kruse, *White Flight: Atlanta and the Making of Modern Conservatism* (Princeton, NJ: Princeton University Press, 2005).

28. President's Child Safety Partnership and the Office for Victims of Crime, *A Report to the President*, 16, in Richard B. Abell to Edwin Meese III, September 25, 1987, Edwin Meese: Children—Partnerships in Child Safety (1987), box 269, entry 1092, subject files of the attorney general (compiled 1975–93), RG 60, NARA II.

29. US Congress, Senate, Committee on the Judiciary, *Child Kidnapping: Hearing before the Subcommittee on Juvenile Justice*, Ninety-eighth Congress, first session, February 2, 1983, 35, 66, 67; Webster to FBI field offices, February 7, 1983, box 20, Caruso and Bucknam files, RG 60, NARA II.

30. Sedlak et al., "National Estimates of Missing Children"; Robert A. McConnell to Arlen Specter, June 15, 1982, enclosed in Robert A. McConnell to Oliver B. Revell, February 16, 1983, box 20, Caruso and Bucknam files, RG 60, NARA II. McConnell offered this explanation before the MCA's passage, but he continued to support this reasoning after the law's implementation.

31. Gabriella Stern, "Mrs. Gosch: Iowa Errors Helped in Sarpy," *Omaha World-Herald*, March 4, 1984; Frank Santiago, "'Mystery man' continues to elude police," *Des Moines Register*, September 6, 1984, 2M; *Town Hall: Missing Children*, KMTV (Omaha, NE), April 29, 1985, catalog ID: T87:0218, Paley Center for Media, New York City.

32. Webster to Hawkins, February 18, 1983, box 20, Caruso and Bucknam files, RG 60, NARA II; Herbert A. Glieberman, "A Child is Missing," *Barrister* 10, no. 4 (Fall 1983): 20; US Congress, Senate, Committee on the Judiciary, *Missing Children's Assistance Act: Hearings before the Subcommittee on Juvenile Justice*, Ninety-eighth Congress, second session, February 7 and 21; March 8, 13, and 21, 1984, 58.

33. *In re Gault* et al., 387 US 1 (1967); *Tinker v. Des Moines Independent Community School District*, 393 US 503 (1969); *In the Matter of Samuel Winship, Appellant*, 397 US 358 (1970); US Congress, Senate, Committee on the Judiciary, *Juvenile Justice and Delinquency Prevention Act of 1974*, report no. 93–1103, Ninety-third Congress, second session, August 16, 1974. "Status offenders" are those whose actions are criminal purely by virtue of their age. Examples of status offenses include running away, skipping school, or consuming alcohol. The Reagan administration's opposition to deinstitutionalization paralleled efforts to raise the minimum drinking age, wage a "war on drugs," police pornography and counternormative sexual behavior, and censor explicit media content. See, for one, Timothy Cole, "'Old Enough to Live': Age, Alcohol, and Adulthood in the United States, 1970–1984," in *Age in America: The Colonial Era to the Present*, ed. Corinne T. Field and Nicholas T. Syrett (New York: New York University Press, 2015), 237–58.

34. Senate, Committee on the Judiciary, *Missing Children's Assistance Act*, 238; Christopher Lasch, *Haven in a Heartless World: The Family Besieged* (New York: Basic Books, 1977); Alfred S. Regnery, "Getting Away with Murder: Why the Juvenile Justice System Needs an Overhaul," *Policy Review*, no. 34 (Fall 1985): 66.

CHAPTER 5

1. US Attorney General's Advisory Board on Missing Children, *America's Missing & Exploited Children: Their Safety and Their Future* (Washington, DC: Office of Juvenile Justice and Delinquency Prevention, US Department of Justice, March 1986), 1, 3.

2. *In re Gault* et al., 387 US 1 (1967); *In the Matter of Samuel Winship, Appellant*, 397 US 358 (1970).

3. Advisory Board on Missing Children, *Their Safety and Their Future*, 5. For the gender and racial conservatism of the Reagan years, see Nancy MacLean, *Freedom is Not Enough: The Opening of the American Workplace* (Cambridge, MA: Harvard University Press, 2006), especially chapter 9; Charles Noble, *Welfare as We Knew It: A Political History of the American Welfare State* (New York: Oxford University Press, 1997).

4. Advisory Board on Missing Children, *Their Safety and Their Future*, 6, 5, 3 (emphasis in original).

5. Michael B. Katz, ed., *The "Underclass" Debate: Views from History* (Princeton, NJ: Princeton University Press, 1993).

6. US Congress, Senate, Committee on the Judiciary, *Abolishing the Office of Juvenile Justice and Delinquency Prevention: Hearing before the Subcommittee on Juvenile Justice*, Ninety-ninth Congress, second session, March 5, 1986, 99.

7. Elizabeth Hinton, *From the War on Poverty to the War on Crime: The Making of Mass Incarceration* (Cambridge, MA: Harvard University Press, 2016); Matthew D. Lassiter, "Impossible Criminals: The Suburban Imperatives of America's War on Drugs," *Journal of American History* 102, no. 1 (June 2015): 126–40; Ananya Roy, "Urban Informality: The Production of Space and Practice of Planning," in *The Oxford Handbook of Urban Planning*, ed. Randall Crane and Rachel Weber (New York: Oxford University Press, 2011), 692; Thomas J. Sugrue, *The Origins of the Urban Crisis: Race and Inequality in Postwar Detroit* (Princeton, NJ: Princeton University Press, 1996), 5.

8. Wendy Ginsberg, "Responses to Reagan: An Analysis of Congressional Reactions to Administration Attempts to Eliminate Federal Agencies" (PhD diss., University of Pennsylvania, 2011), 87; US Congress, Senate, Committee on the Judiciary, *Missing Children's Assistance Act: Hearings before the Subcommittee on Juvenile Justice*, Ninety-eighth Congress, second session, March 13, 1984, 223; Justice Assistance Act of 1984, PL 98-473, 98 STAT. 2082, Ninety-eighth Congress, second session, October 12, 1984; Juvenile Justice, Runaway Youth, and Missing Children's Act Amendments of 1984, PL 98-473, 98 STAT. 2114, October 12, 1984.

9. John J. Wilson and James C. Howell, *A Comprehensive Strategy for Serious, Violent, and Chronic Juvenile Offenders* (Washington, DC: Office of Juvenile Justice and Delinquency Prevention, US Department of Justice, 1993), 4; John J. DiIulio Jr., "Stop Crime Where It Starts," *New York Times*, July 31, 1996, A15; Peter Schweizer, *Makers and Takers: How Conservatives Do All the Work While Liberals Whine and Complain* (New York: Doubleday, 2008).

10. Heather Hammer, David Finkelhor, and Andrea J. Sedlack, National Incidence Studies of Missing, Abducted, Runaway, and Thrownaway Children, "Runaway/Thrownaway Children: National Estimates and Characteristics," October 2002, Office of Juvenile Justice and Delinquency Prevention, Office of Justice Programs, US Department of Justice, https://www.ncjrs.gov/html/ojjdp/nismart/04/ns4.html; Advisory Board on Missing Children, *Their Safety and Their Future*, 1.

11. Melissa Sickmund and Charles Puzzanchera, eds., *Juvenile Offenders and Victims: 2014 National Report* (Pittsburgh, PA: National Center for Juvenile Justice), 86; Bradford Smith, "Children in Custody: 20-Year Trends in Juvenile Detention, Correctional, and Shelter Facilities," *Crime & Delinquency* 44, no. 4 (October 1998): 535.

12. Hinton, *From the War on Poverty to the War on Crime*, 222.

13. Hinton, *From the War on Poverty to the War on Crime*, 227; Lassiter, "Impossible Criminals," 127; Smith, "Children in Custody," 533. For "serious juvenile crime," see National Advisory Committee for Juvenile Justice and Delinquency Prevention, *Serious Juvenile Crime: A Redirected Federal Effort* (Washington, DC: Office of Juvenile Justice and Delinquency Prevention, US Department of Justice, 1984); US Congress, Senate, Committee on the Judiciary, *Oversight: Office of Juvenile Justice and Delinquency Prevention—Hearing before the Subcommittee on Juvenile Justice*, Ninety-eighth Congress, second session, August 1, 1984, 6.

14. *Historical Corrections Statistics in the United States, 1850–1984*, compiled by Margaret Werner Cahalan with the assistance of Lee Anne Parsons, Bureau of Justice Statistics, US Department of Justice, December 1986, table 5-31, 137. The term "Hispanic" is used in this collection of statistics.

15. Edmund F. McGarrell, *Juvenile Correctional Reform: Two Decades of Policy and Procedural Change* (Albany: State University of New York Press, 1988), 14; Alfred S. Regnery, "Getting Away with Murder," *Policy Review*, no. 34 (Fall 1985): 67.

16. Regnery, "Getting Away with Murder," 66, 67; US Senate, Committee on the Judiciary, *Confirmation Hearings on Federal Appointments: Hearings before the Committee on the Judiciary*, Ninety-eighth Congress, first session, April 6, 1983, 49, 117. As Tera Eva Agyepong notes, "whether the juvenile justice system was ever actually rehabilitative in practice is debatable." Tera Eva Agyepong, *The Criminalization of Black Children: Race, Gender, and Delinquency in Chicago's Juvenile Justice System, 1899–1945* (Chapel Hill: University of North Carolina Press, 2018), 3.

17. Regnery, "Getting Away with Murder," 66; Daniel Patrick Moynihan, *The Negro Family: The Case for National Action* (Washington, DC: Office of Policy Planning and Research, US Department of Labor, 1965); George F. Gilder, *Wealth and Poverty* (New York: Basic Books, 1981); Charles A. Murray, *Losing Ground: American Social Policy, 1950–1980* (New York: Basic Books, 1984). For more on the gender and sexual dimensions of US social policy, see Gwendolyn Mink, *The Wages of Motherhood: Inequality in the Welfare State, 1917–1942* (Ithaca, NY: Cornell University Press, 1995); Linda Gordon, *Pitied but Not Entitled: Single Mothers and the History of Welfare* (Cambridge, MA: Harvard University Press, 1994); Margot Canaday, *The Straight State: Sexuality and Citizenship in Twentieth-Century America* (Princeton, NJ: Princeton University Press, 2009); Alice Kessler-Harris, *In Pursuit of Equity: Women, Men, and the Quest for Economic Citizenship in 20th-Century America* (New York: Oxford University Press, 2001).

18. Regnery, "Getting Away with Murder," 66; Senate, Committee on the Judiciary, *Confirmation Hearings on Federal Appointments*, 117. Charles Murray also frequently used anecdotal evidence to make his arguments. See Murray, *Losing Ground*; Richard J. Herrnstein and Charles Murray, *The Bell Curve: Intelligence and Class Structure in American Life* (New York: Free Press, 1994).

19. Anita Clark, "Candidates for DA's Office Vow Changes," *Wisconsin State Journal* (Madison), October 26, 1976, enclosed in US Congress, House of Representatives, Committee on Education and Labor, *Oversight Hearing on the Administration of the Office of Juvenile Justice and Delinquency Prevention: Hearing before the Subcommittee on Human Resources*, Ninety-seventh Congress, second session, December 16, 1982, 6; Regnery, "Getting Away with Murder," 66; "Al Regnery's

Secret Life," *New Republic*, June 23, 1986, newrepublic.com/article/64596/al-regnerys-secret-life; "Two attack wife of DA candidate," *Wisconsin State Journal*, November 1, 1976.

20. Ginsberg, "Responses to Reagan," 87; Senate, Committee on the Judiciary, *Confirmation Hearings on Federal Appointments*, 34; Mary Thornton, "Juvenile Office Nominee Quizzed on Inexperience," *Washington Post*, April 7, 1983, A6; "Al Regnery's Secret Life." Regnery worked to convert the OJJDP in the service of punishing certain juveniles and protecting others in the wake of the child safety panic—and also to layer the OJJDP with "new elements," from the NCMEC to controversial grants promoting antiporn and "profamily" causes. See Jacob S. Hacker, Paul Pierson, and Kathleen Thelen, "Drift and Conversion: Hidden Faces of Institutional Change," in *Advances in Comparative-Historical Analysis*, ed. James Mahoney and Kathleen Thelen (New York: Cambridge University Press, 2015), 185; Kathleen Thelen, *How Institutions Evolve: The Political Economy of Skills in Germany, Britain, the United States, and Japan* (New York: Cambridge University Press, 2004), 35, quoted in Daniel Béland, "Ideas and Institutional Change in Social Security: Conversion, Layering, and Policy Drift," *Social Science Quarterly* 88, no. 1 (March 2007): 22.

21. Senate, Committee on the Judiciary, *Missing Children's Assistance Act*, 251.

22. Senate, Committee on the Judiciary, *Missing Children's Assistance Act*, 243; US Congress, House of Representatives, Committee on Education and Labor, *Oversight Hearing on the Juvenile Justice and Delinquency Prevention Act*, Ninety-ninth Congress, first session, May 7, 1985, 135; Ira M. Schwartz, Martha Wade Steketee, and Jeffrey A. Butts, "Business as Usual: Juvenile Justice during the 1980s," *Notre Dame Journal of Law, Ethics, and Public Policy* 5, no. 2 (1991): 377–96; US Congress, House of Representatives, Committee on Education and Labor, *Oversight Hearing on the Administration of the Office of Juvenile Justice and Delinquency Prevention: Hearing before the Subcommittee on Human Resources*, Ninety-seventh Congress, second session, December 16, 1982, 10; House of Representatives, Committee on Education and Labor, *Oversight Hearing on the Juvenile Justice and Delinquency Prevention Act*, 35, 16.

23. Senate, Committee on the Judiciary, *Confirmation Hearings on Federal Appointments*, 31–32.

24. Thornton, "Juvenile Office Nominee Quizzed on Inexperience"; Mary Thornton, "Critics See Juvenile-Justice Nominee Emphasizing Punishment," *Washington Post*, April 3, 1983, A5. For criticism of Regnery's view "that OJJDP is not a social agency"—in the words of Barbara A. Mandel, president of the National Council of Jewish Women—see Senate, Committee on the Judiciary, *Confirmation Hearings on Federal Appointments*, 188; Senate, Committee on the Judiciary, *Oversight: Office of Juvenile Justice and Delinquency Prevention*, 10; Regnery, "Getting Away with Murder," 67.

25. US Congress, House of Representatives, Committee on Education and Labor, *Juvenile Justice, Runaway Youth, and Missing Children's Act Amendments of 1984: Hearing before the Subcommittee on Human Resources*, March 7, 1984, 69–70.

26. Regnery, "Getting Away with Murder," 65; Ira M. Schwartz, *(In)Justice for Juveniles: Rethinking the Best Interests of the Child* (Lexington, MA: Lexington Books, 1989), 26; Stephen J. Brodt and J. Steven Smith, "Dialogue, Part 1: Public Policy and the Serious Juvenile Offender," *Criminal Justice Policy Review* 1, no. 1 (April 1988): 71.

27. Joe Soss, Richard C. Fording, and Sanford F. Schram, *Disciplining the Poor: Neoliberal Paternalism and the Persistent Power of Race* (Chicago: University of Chicago Press, 2011). Contrary to popular belief, "liberal law and order" policies in the early Cold War era laid the groundwork for the contemporary carceral state. Naomi Murakawa, *The First Civil Right: How Liberals Built Prison America* (New York: Oxford University Press, 2014); Brodt and Smith, "Public Policy and the Serious Juvenile Offender," 75–76. Brodt and Smith mistakenly used the term "Chicano" here. "Chicano/a," "Chicanx," and other terms refer specifically to the Mexican American community, oftentimes in the context of Mexican Americans' political mobilizations in the twentieth century's latter half. In all likelihood, Brodt and Smith were trying to discuss the potentially deleterious effects of "tough on crime" policies on Latinx Americans, not just Chicanx people. Special thanks to Anita Casavantes Bradford for her insight on this point.

28. Alfred S. Regnery, "Dialogue, Part II: Response to Critique of Brodt and Smith," *Criminal Justice Policy Review* 1, no. 1 (April 1988): 81, 82 (emphasis in original). For liberalism and "political whiteness," see Daniel Martinez HoSang, *Racial Propositions: Ballot Initiatives and the Making of Postwar California* (Berkeley: University of California Press, 2010).

29. Senate, Committee on the Judiciary, *Missing Children's Assistance Act*, 166; Justice Assistance Act of 1984, PL 98-473, 98 STAT. 2082; Sickmund and Puzzanchera, eds., *Juvenile Offenders and Victims*, 163, 86; Rebecca Dingo, "Securing the Nation: Neoliberalism's US Family Values in a Transnational Gendered Economy," *Journal of Women's History* 16, no. 3 (Fall 2004): 173–86; Melinda Cooper, *Family Values: Between Neoliberalism and the New Social Conservatism* (Cambridge: Massachusetts Institute of Technology Press, 2017).

30. Advisory Board on Missing Children, *Their Safety and Their Future*.

31. Christopher Lasch, *Haven in a Heartless World: The Family Besieged* (New York: Basic Books, 1977); US Congress, House of Representatives, Committee on Education and Labor, *Oversight Hearing on the Missing Children's Assistance Act: Hearing before the Subcommittee on Human Resources*, Ninety-ninth Congress, first session, May 21, 1985, 58; US Congress, House of Representatives, *Title IV: Missing Children's Assistance Act—Hearing before the Subcommittee on Human Resources*, Ninety-eighth Congress, second session, April 9, 1984, 51; Ronald Reagan, "Radio Address to the Nation on the American Family," December 3, 1983, Ronald W. Reagan Presidential Library, Simi Valley, CA, https://www.reaganlibrary.gov/research/speeches/120383a; Natasha Zaretsky, *No Direction Home: The American Family and the Fear of National Decline, 1968–1980* (Chapel Hill: University of North Carolina Press, 2007).

32. CBS, *Evening News*, October 19, 1984, record no. 293913, Television News Archive, Vanderbilt University, Nashville (hereafter VTNA); Senate, Committee on the Judiciary, *Oversight: Office of Juvenile Justice and Delinquency Prevention*, 31. See also House of Representatives, Committee on Education and Labor, *Oversight Hearing on the Juvenile Justice and Delinquency Prevention Act*, 111–12.

33. US Congress, House of Representatives, Committee on Education and Labor, *Oversight Hearing on the Missing Children's Assistance Act: Hearing before the Subcommittee on Human Resources*, Ninety-ninth Congress, second session, August 4, 1986, 146; House of Representatives, Committee on Education and Labor, *Oversight Hearing on the Missing Children's Assistance Act*, 61–62. According to the NCMEC's own website, the Center has "assisted law enforcement in the

recovery of more than 222,000 missing children." See National Center for Missing and Exploited Children, "Key Facts," www.missingkids.com/keyfacts.

34. House of Representatives, Committee on Education and Labor, *Oversight Hearing on the Missing Children's Assistance Act*, August 4, 1986, 144, 146; NBC, *Nightly News*, December 6, 1985, record no. 541637, VTNA; CBS, *Evening News*, March 27, 1985, record no. 302658, VTNA.

35. Advisory Board on Missing Children, *Their Safety and Their Future*, 20, 15, 1, 2, 3; House of Representatives, Committee on Education and Labor, *Juvenile Justice, Runaway Youth, and Missing Children's Act Amendments of 1984*, 67.

36. Advisory Board on Missing Children, *Their Safety and Their Future*, 1, 2–3; ABC, *World News Tonight*, June 4, 1981, record no. 72458, VTNA.

37. Advisory Board on Missing Children, *Their Safety and Their Future*, 7, 15.

38. Alfred S. Regnery to William Bradford Reynolds, May 15, 1986, Juvenile Justice: Report on Missing and Exploited Children, box 379, Jennifer Boeke files, subject files of the special assistants to the assistant attorney general (compiled 1974–2000), record group (RG) 60: General Records of the US Department of Justice, National Archives and Records Administration, College Park, MD (hereafter NARA II).

39. The ABMC report did allude to "in-home physical, sexual, or psychological abuse," though it is unclear whether this was a reference to rape and molestation by parents or relatives. Advisory Board on Missing Children, *America's Missing & Exploited Children*, 6, 12, 5. See also Zaretsky, *No Direction Home* .

40. Advisory Board on Missing Children, *Their Safety and Their Future*, preface, 1, 2, 5, 14, 15.

41. Gillian Frank, "Save Our Children: The Sexual Politics of Child Protection, 1965–1990" (PhD diss., Brown University, 2009), 243, quoted in Whitney Strub, *Perversion for Profit: The Politics of Pornography and the Rise of the New Right* (New York: Columbia University Press, 2010), 205; Advisory Board on Missing Children, *Their Safety and Their Future*, 26, 31.

42. Strub, *Perversion for Profit*, 198, 202.

43. "Federal Study of Sex Magazines Assailed," *Los Angeles Times*, May 8, 1985, B8; Philip Shenon, "Projects of a Provoking Sort," *New York Times*, May 23, 1985, B12; "Al Regnery's Secret Life"; Senate, Committee on the Judiciary, *Missing Children's Assistance Act*, 225; US Congress, Senate, Committee on the Judiciary, *Oversight of the Office of Juvenile Justice and Delinquency Prevention: Hearing before the Subcommittee on Juvenile Justice*, Ninety-ninth Congress, first session, May 7, 1985, 64, 160, 161. The 1986 ABMC report called for such research. "There has been a proliferation of material," the publication read, "in records, videos, motion pictures, and magazines that would have been considered obscene or dangerous even for adults a generation ago. The apparent glorification of drugs, suicide, murder, rape, incest, torture, bondage, and blood rituals and rites raises serious questions about the images and values held out to children as counterculture attractions." The publication went on to encourage "intelligent study and consideration" of such matters. Advisory Board on Missing Children, *Their Safety and Their Future*, 30.

44. Julilly Kohler-Hausmann, "Guns and Butter: The Welfare State, the Carceral State, and the Politics of Exclusion in the Postwar United States," *Journal of American History* 102, no. 1 (June 2015): 89 (emphasis in original); Brent Cebul, Lily Geismer, and Mason B. Williams, "Introduction—Beyond Red and Blue: Crisis and Continuity in Twentieth-Century US Political History," in *Shaped by the*

State: Toward a New Political History of the Twentieth Century, ed. Cebul, Geismer, and Williams (Chicago: University of Chicago Press, 2019), 3–23.

45. Advisory Board on Missing Children, *Their Safety and Their Future*, 22. For more on "victims' rights," see Carrie A. Rentschler, *Second Wounds: Victims' Rights and the Media in the US* (Durham, NC: Duke University Press, 2011).

46. Protection of Children Against Sexual Exploitation Act, PL 95–225, 92 STAT. 7, February 6, 1978; Child Protection Act, PL 98–292, 98 STAT. 204, May 21, 1984.

47. Child Sexual Abuse and Pornography Act, PL 99–628, 100 STAT. 3510, November 7, 1986; Child Protection and Obscenity Enforcement Act, PL 100–690, 102 STAT. 4486, November 18, 1988; Child Protection Restoration and Penalties Enhancement Act, PL 101–647, 104 STAT. 4816, November 29, 1990; United States Sentencing Commission, *The History of the Child Pornography Guidelines*, October 2009, https://www.ussc.gov/sites/default/files/pdf/research-and-publications/research-projects-and-surveys/sex-offenses/20091030_History_Child_Pornography_Guidelines.pdf; James R. Kincaid, *Erotic Innocence: The Culture of Child Molesting* (Durham, NC: Duke University Press, 1998), 95.

48. Even after Regnery resigned, the Reagan administration tried (to no avail) to "terminat[e]" the OJJDP. See Ronald W. Reagan, "Message to the Congress Reporting on Federal Juvenile Delinquency Programs," February 25, 1987, American Presidency Project, University of California, Santa Barbara, https://www.presidency.ucsb.edu/documents/message-the-congress-reporting-federal-juvenile-delinquency-programs.

49. CBS, *Evening News*, December 14, 1985, record no. 301299, VTNA; "Talking Points: Juvenile Office Intact Despite His Efforts, Regnery is Quitting," *Washington Post*, May 30, 1986, A13; Lasch, *Haven in a Heartless World*.

CHAPTER 6

1. Suzanne Gamboa, "4,000 Runaways Go Home Via Free Trailways Trips," *Schenectady Gazette* (NY), June 7, 1985, 3; Ronald Reagan, "Remarks at a Ceremony Marking the Beginning of the President's Citation Program for Private Sector Initiatives," December 10, 1984, Ronald W. Reagan Presidential Library (hereafter RR), Simi Valley, CA, https://www.reaganlibrary.gov/sspeeches/121084a.

2. Carrie Rentschler, *Second Wounds: Victims' Rights and the Media in the US* (Durham, NC: Duke University Press, 2011).

3. That Code Adam and other instruments successfully recruit the public into projects of policing and surveillance evince the Foucauldian concept of governmentality. See Graham Burchell, Colin Gordon, and Peter Miller, eds., *The Foucault Effect: Studies in Governmentality* (Chicago: University of Chicago Press, 1991).

4. David Harvey, *A Brief History of Neoliberalism* (New York: Oxford University Press, 2005), 42; Benjamin C. Waterhouse, *Lobbying America: The Politics of Business from Nixon to NAFTA* (Princeton, NJ: Princeton University Press, 2013); Diane Negra and Yvonne Tasker, eds., *Interrogating Postfeminism: Gender and the Politics of Popular Culture* (Durham, NC: Duke University Press, 2007); Nancy Fraser, "Feminism, Capitalism, and the Cunning of History," *New Left Review* 56 (March–April 2009): 97–117; Walter Benn Michaels, "Against Diversity," *New Left Review* 52 (July–August 2008): 33–36.

5. Karen Staller, "Social Problem Construction and Its Impact on Program and Policy Responses," in *From Child Welfare to Child Well-Being: An International Perspective on Knowledge in the Service of Policy Making*, ed. Sheila Kamerman, Shelley Phipps, and Asher Ben-Arieh (New York: Springer, 2009), 165; Jeffrey S. Turner, *American*

    Families in Crisis: A Reference Handbook (Santa Barbara, CA: ABC-CLIO, 2009), 217; Abraham B. Bergman, "The Business of Missing Children," *Pediatrics* 77, no. 1 (January 1986): 120; Rentschler, *Second Wounds*. For the neoliberal construction of "the market" and "the state" as "separate and antagonistic spheres," see Waterhouse, *Lobbying America*, 67.

6. CBS, *Evening News*, December 1, 1981, record no. 274755, Television News Archive, Vanderbilt University, Nashville (hereafter VTNA); CBS, *Evening News*, June 13, 1984, record no. 297468, VTNA; ABC, *World News Tonight*, June 4, 1981, record no. 72458, VTNA.

7. US Congress, Senate, Committee on Labor and Human Resources, *Missing Children: Hearing before the Subcommittee on Investigations and General Oversight*, Ninety-seventh Congress, first session, October 6, 1981, 27, 28, 29; CBS, *Evening News*, December 1, 1981, VTNA.

8. US Congress, Senate, Committee on the Judiciary, *Exploitation of Children: Hearing before the Subcommittee on Juvenile Justice*, Ninety-seventh Congress, first session, November 5, 1981, 74; US Congress, House, Committee on the Judiciary, *Missing Children's Act: Hearings before the Subcommittee on Civil and Constitutional Rights*, Ninety-seventh Congress, first session, November 18 and 30, 1981, 112, 117.

9. Ronald Reagan, "Remarks at a White House Ceremony Marking the Opening of the National Center for Missing and Exploited Children," June 13, 1984, RR, https://www.reaganlibrary.gov/research/speeches/61384a.

10. Ronald Reagan, "Radio Address to the Nation on the American Family," June 16, 1984, American Presidency Project, University of California, Santa Barbara (hereafter APP), https://www.presidency.ucsb.edu/documents/radio-address-the-nation-the-american-family-0. See also Robert O. Self, *All in the Family: The Realignment of American Democracy since the 1960s* (New York: Hill and Wang, 2012); Melinda Cooper, *Family Values: Between Neoliberalism and the New Social Conservatism* (Cambridge: Zone Books / Massachusetts Institute of Technology Press, 2017).

11. Paul C. Light, "The Volunteering Decision: What Prompts It? What Sustains It?" Brookings Institution online, Fall 2002, https://www.brookings.edu/research/articles/2002/09/fall-civilsociety-light; Executive Order 12427: President's Advisory Council on Private Sector Initiatives, June 27, 1983, APP, https://www.presidency.ucsb.edu/documents/executive-order-12427-presidents-advisory-council-private-sector-initiatives; Reagan, "Remarks at a Ceremony Marking the Beginning of the President's Citation Program for Private Sector Initiatives," December 10, 1984, RR.

    For the intertwined fears of national and familial decline, see Natasha Zaretsky, *No Direction Home: The American Family and the Fear of National Decline, 1968–1980* (Chapel Hill: University of North Carolina Press, 2007). See also J. Brooks Flippen, *Jimmy Carter, the Politics of Family, and the Rise of the Religious Right* (Athens: University of Georgia Press, 2011); Whitney Strub, *Perversion for Profit: The Politics of Pornography and the Rise of the New Right* (New York: Columbia University Press, 2010); Self, *All in the Family*.

12. Executive Order 12511: President's Child Safety Partnership, April 29, 1985, APP, https://www.presidency.ucsb.edu/documents/executive-order-12511-presidents-child-safety-partnership; John L. Marion Jr. to Edwin Meese, through T. Kenneth Cribb Jr. and Stephen Galebach, April 11, 1985, box 248, Stephen Galebach files, subject files of assistants to the Attorney General (1974–94), record group (RG) 60: General Records of the Department of Justice (1790–2002), National Archives

and Record Administration, College Park, MD (hereafter NARA II); Lois Haight Herrington to Edwin Meese III, April 23, 1985, box 18, John L. Howard files, personnel hiring and appointment files of the Associate Deputy Attorney General (1981–93), RG 60, NARA II; President's Child Safety Partnership and the Office for Victims of Crime, *A Report to the President*, 15, 16, enclosed in Richard B. Abell to Edwin Meese III, September 25, 1987, box 269, Edwin Meese files, subject files of the Attorney General (1975–93), RG 60, NARA II.

13. Ronald Reagan, "Remarks on Signing the Proclamation and Executive Order on Child Safety," April 29, 1985, APP, https://www.presidency.ucsb.edu/documents/remarks-signing-the-proclamation-and-executive-order-child-safety; President's Child Safety Partnership, *A Report to the President*, 18, 16, NARA II.

14. For the Gramscian construction of "commonsense," see especially Harvey, *A Brief History of Neoliberalism*; Laura Briggs, *Somebody's Children: The Politics of Transracial and Transnational Adoption* (Durham, NC: Duke University Press, 2012).

15. US Congress, Senate, Committee on the Judiciary, *Private Sector Initiatives regarding Missing Children: Hearing before the Subcommittee on Juvenile Justice*, Ninety-ninth Congress, first session, May 22, 1985, 19, 21; US Attorney General's Advisory Board on Missing Children, *Missing & Exploited Children: The Challenge Continues* (Washington, DC: US Department of Justice, 1988), 17.

16. Ronald Reagan, "Remarks at a White House Meeting with Members of the National Newspaper Association," March 7, 1985, RR, https://www.reaganlibrary.gov/research/speeches/30785a.

17. ABC, *World News Tonight*, April 3, 1985, record no. 95787, VTNA; "Congressman Mickey Edwards Leads Effort to Use Televised House Proceedings to Help Find Missing Children," press release, Office of Congressman Mickey Edwards, June 13, 1984, box 71, folder 15, Mickey Edwards Collection, Carl Albert Center Congressional Archives, University of Oklahoma, Norman (hereafter MEC).

Edwards orchestrated similar efforts throughout 1984 and 1985. See "Oklahoma Congressman Mickey Edwards Will Deliver Floor Speech to Help Find Kidnapped Children," press release, Office of Congressman Mickey Edwards, June 27, 1984, box 106, folder 14, MEC; "Ten Members of Congress Will Deliver Floor Speeches Wednesday to Help Find Kidnapped Children," press release, Office of Congressman Mickey Edwards, July 24, 1984, box 71, folder 15, MEC; "Congressman Mickey Edwards Asks Television Stations to Help Find Kidnapped Children," press release, Office of Congressman Mickey Edwards, August 8, 1984, box 71, folder 15, MEC; "Edwards Will Use Televised House Proceedings to Help Find Kidnapped Ponca City Child," press release, Office of Congressman Mickey Edwards, March 21, 1985, box 106, folder 14, MEC; "News Advisory," press release, Office of Congressman Mickey Edwards, May 21, 1985, box 106, folder 14, MEC; AP, "House Members Help Focus Attention on Missing Children," *Ponca City News* (OK), April 3, 1985, 1, box 59, folder 13, MEC.

C-SPAN was established in 1979. By 1985, approximately 43 percent of households with televisions had "wired cable," while 26 percent had "wired pay cable." See David Sedman, "The Legacy of Broadcast Stereo Sound: The Short Life of MTS, 1984–2009," *Journal of Sonic Studies* 3 (October 2012): https://www.researchcatalogue.net/view/252502/252503.

18. H.J. RES. 291, House of Representatives, Ninety-ninth Congress, first session, May 21, 1985, box 106, folder 14, MEC. Edwards's proposed resolution was referred to the House Subcommittee on Telecommunications, Consumer Protection, and Finance, but no further action was taken. Penny Pagano, "FBI Enlists Bill Cosby in

Search for Missing Kids," *Los Angeles Times*, June 12, 1985, 1; Patrick Goldstein, "TV's Power Found in Missing," *Los Angeles Times*, April 29, 1985, 9; Associated Press, "CBS Public-Service Ads to Seek Missing Children," *New York Times*, July 18, 1985, C22—all enclosed in letter and accompanying materials, Terri Rabel to Mickey Edwards, n.d., 1985, box 106, folder 41, MEC.

19. Advisory Board on Missing Children, *The Challenge Continues*, 15; Senate, Committee on the Judiciary, *Hearing on Private Sector Responses*, 18, 20; President's Child Safety Partnership, *A Report to the President*, 44, NARA II.

20. PL 99–87, 99 STAT. 290, Ninety-ninth Congress, first session, August 9, 1985; Marilyn Ivy, "Have You Seen Me? Recovering the Inner Child in Late Twentieth-Century America," *Social Text*, no. 37 (Winter 1993): 229. See also Eric Freedman, *Transient Images: Personal Media in Public Frameworks* (Philadelphia: Temple University Press, 2011), 25–53.

21. "Fingerprinting of Children Spreading," *New York Times*, February 22, 1983, A12; Stanley Patz, letter to the editor, *New York Times*, December 7, 1980, E22; Senate, Committee on the Judiciary, *Private Sector Initiatives regarding Missing Children*, 38; United Press International, "Fingerprinting Law for Pupils Signed," *New York Times*, September 29, 1983, B9.

22. "Fingerprinting of Children Spreading"; "Does fingerprinting children make sense?" *Changing Times* (August 1983): 24; Laurie Johnston and Susan Heller Anderson, "A Foe of Fingerprinting for Children Speaks Out," *New York Times*, May 19, 1983, B3.

23. Sandy Banks, "LA Schools Put Fingerprinting Program on Hold," *Los Angeles Times*, March 27, 1983, V1; "Does fingerprinting children make sense?"; Ralph Blumenthal, "Groups Offering to Seek Missing Children are Springing Up Across the Nation," *New York Times*, May 25, 1984, A14; Hanke Gratteau and Ray Gibson, "In missing-child business, fear sells," *Chicago Tribune*, September 1, 1985, 1. For more on Child Find's "Child Finder Kit," see "Does fingerprinting children make sense?"; US Congress, Senate, Committee on Labor and Human Resources, *An Overview on Missing Children: Hearing before the Subcommittee on Children, Family, Drugs, and Alcoholism*, Ninety-ninth Congress, first session, May 23, 1985, 23. For more on the investigation into Child Find's internal affairs, see Senate, Committee on the Judiciary, *Private Sector Initiatives regarding Missing Children*, 46; Associated Press, "Internal strife, state probe beset Child Find," *Des Moines Register*, April 29, 1984, 12A; Ralph Blumenthal, "Registry of Missing Children Faces State Inquiry," *New York Times*, May 21, 1984, B2.

24. It is unclear whether Reagan consented to the Moral Majority's use of his image and rhetoric. Lamarr Mooneyham, "Missing child outrage prompts MM to form Child Protection Task Force," *Moral Majority Report* (April 1985): 1; Child Protection Task Force advertisement, *Moral Majority Report* (April 1985): 3; Proclamation 5194, Missing Children Day, May 15, 1984, RR, https://www.reaganlibrary.gov/research/speeches/51584c; Gratteau and Gibson, "In missing-child business, fear sells."

25. William E. Geist, "About New York, Videotaping Youngsters to Foil Kidnappers," *New York Times*, November 16, 1985, 30; Laurie Krauth, "Missing Children: A Manipulated Issue?" *Toledo Blade* (OH), October 5, 1985, B1; Neal Karlen with Nikki Finke Greenberg, David L. Gonzalez, and Elisa Williams, "How Many Missing Kids," *Newsweek* (October 7, 1985); Nitika Vij, Gulsheen Kaur Kochhar, Sanjay Chachra, and Taranjot Kaur, "Dentistry to the rescue of missing

children: A review," *Journal of Forensic Dental Sciences* 8, no. 1 (January–April 2016): 7–12; Kate Moore, "Lasting impression," *News-Herald* (Willoughby, OH), August 10, 2003, https://www.news-herald.com/news/lasting-impression/article_82309c94-8675-517c-9086-d57fb3e751dc.html; Colleen Sheridan, "Local Dentist Aids Child Safety Program with Charts and Microdots," *The Hour* (Norwalk, CT), November 25, 1985, 35; "Dental Microdots Protect Children," *Observer-Reporter* (Washington, PA), August 5, 1985, B-3; Alan Bavley, "With New Dental Microdots, People's Teeth Can Tell a Tale," *Sun-Sentinel* (Fort Lauderdale and Broward County, FL), May 24, 1985, https://www.sun-sentinel.com/news/fl-xpm-1985-05-24-8501210393-story.html.

26. Carol Tavris, "Child Abuse: Real Dangers and False Alarms," *New York Times*, November 10, 1985, BR48; CBS, *Evening News*, July 2, 1985, record no. 304808, VTNA; Gratteau and Gibson, "In missing-child business, fear sells"; John Hood, *The Heroic Enterprise: Business and the Common Good* (Hopkins, MN: Beard Books, 2005), 125–26; Mommy's Helper company website, "Kid Keeper," mommyshelperinc.com/kidkeeper.htm.

27. Gratteau and Gibson, "In missing-child business, fear sells." For the news media backlash to the stranger danger panic, see especially Diana Griego and Louis Kilzer, "Truth about Missing Kids: Exaggerated Statistics Stir National Paranoia," *Denver Post*, May 12, 1985, 1A; Albert Scardino, "Experts Question Data about Missing Children," *New York Times*, August 18, 1985, 22.

28. Krauth, "Missing Children: A Manipulated Issue?"; US Congress, House of Representatives, Committee on Education and Labor, *Oversight Hearing on the Missing Children's Assistance Act: Hearing before the Subcommittee on Human Resources*, Ninety-ninth Congress, first session, May 21, 1985, 57, 58.

29. Krauth, "Missing Children: A Manipulated Issue?"

30. Bergman, "The Business of Missing Children," 119, 120.

31. Advisory Board on Missing Children, *The Challenge Continues*, 1.

CHAPTER 7

1. William Plummer and Margaret Nelson, "A Town Prays for a Missing Son," *People* 32, no. 21 (November 20, 1989); Sharon Cohen, "Life without Jacob: 'I'm Just a Mom Who Wants Her Kid,'" Associated Press, February 10, 1990; Dirk Johnson, "Kidnapping Sows Suspicion in Trusting Town," *New York Times*, April 29, 1990, https://www.nytimes.com/1990/04/29/us/kidnapping-sows-suspicion-in-trusting-town.html; David Unze, "20 Years After Wetterling Abduction, Cases Have Changed Society," *St. Cloud Times* (MN), October 22, 2009; Madeleine Baran, "In the Dark," *American Public Media Reports*, December 30, 2016, https://www.apmreports.org/story/2016/12/30/27-years-wetterling-child-abduction; "Timeline of the Jacob Wetterling Case," *Star Tribune* (Minneapolis–St. Paul, MN), September 6, 2016, www.startribune.com/timeline-of-jacob-wetterling-case/392244731; "The Hunt: Jacob Wetterling's Abductor," CNN, July 9, 2015, https://www.cnn.com/2015/07/03/us/jacob-wetterling-abductor-the-hunt-johwn-walsh [sic].

2. Mary Divine, "In chilling confession, Jacob Wetterling's fate is finally revealed," *Pioneer Press* (Minneapolis–St. Paul, MN), September 6, 2016, https://www.twincities.com/2016/09/06/jacob-wetterling-suspect-danny-heinrich-court-today/; Baran, "In the Dark"; Plummer and Nelson, "A Town Prays for a Missing Son."

3. Other similar legal instruments created in the nineties included the National Child Protection Act (NCPA) of 1993 and the Jimmy Ryce Law Enforcement Training Center. The former, for which Oprah Winfrey petitioned, offered a federal response to the 1980s child sexual abuse panic. In the wake of the high-profile sexual abuse scare at the McMartin preschool in California, the 1993 NCPA formalized a national system through which childcare providers would undergo criminal background checks. Established in 1996 by the federal government, the Ryce Center took its name from nine-year-old Jimmy Ryce, who was kidnapped, sexually assaulted, and slain in Florida the previous year. Administered through the Office of Juvenile Justice and Delinquency Prevention, the Ryce Center continues to furnish "training and technical assistance," including the provision of bloodhounds, to law enforcement in the search for missing children. See National Child Protection Act, PL 103–209, 107 STAT. 2490, December 20, 1993; Michael Medaris, "Jimmy Ryce Law Enforcement Training Center Program," Office of Juvenile Justice and Delinquency Prevention, Office of Justice Programs, US Department of Justice, fact sheet no. 62 (March 1997), https://www.ncjrs.gov/pdffiles/fs9762.pdf.
4. Gallup, "In Depth: Topics A to Z—Crime," https://news.gallup.com/poll/1603/crime.aspx. See also Naomi Murakawa, *The First Civil Right: How Liberals Built Prison America* (New York: Oxford University Press, 2014), especially chapter 4; Peter Applebome, "Arkansas Execution Raises Questions on Governor's Politics," *New York Times*, January 25, 1992, https://www.nytimes.com/1992/01/25/us/1992-campaign-death-penalty-arkansas-execution-raises-questions-governors.html; Michelle Alexander, "Why Hillary Clinton Doesn't Deserve the Black Vote," *The Nation*, February 29, 2016, https://www.thenation.com/article/hillary-clinton-does-not-deserve-black-peoples-votes; Nathan J. Robinson, "The Death of Ricky Ray Rector," *Jacobin*, November 5, 2016, https://jacobinmag.com/2016/11/bill-clinton-rickey-rector-death-penalty-execution-crime-racism [sic].
5. Alexander, "Why Hillary Clinton Doesn't Deserve the Black Vote"; Joe Soss, Richard C. Fording, and Sanford F. Schram, *Disciplining the Poor: Neoliberal Paternalism and the Persistent Power of Race* (Chicago: University of Chicago Press, 2011).
6. Julilly Kohler-Hausmann, *Getting Tough: Welfare and Imprisonment in the 1970s* (Princeton, NJ: Princeton University Press, 2017), 293; Kaaryn S. Gustafson, *Cheating Welfare: Public Assistance and the Criminalization of Poverty* (New York: New York University Press, 2011), 51.
7. Violent Crime Control and Law Enforcement Act, PL 103–322, 108 STAT. 2038, 2042, September 13, 1994; Rick Hampson, "'Apostrophe laws' named for kid victims on the wane," *USA Today*, June 12, 2013, 1; Benjamin Gray, "Deviance and Discourse: Child Molesters in the United States" (MA thesis, University of Kansas, 2011), 27; Arizona Code, § 43–6117 (1939, supp. 1952); California Penal Code § 290 (1947). In 1990, Washington State instituted its Community Protection Act, which prefigured the adoption by other states of registration and notification statutes as mandated by the Wetterling Act and Megan's Law. See Revised Code of Washington, chap. 71.09 (supp. 1990–91).
   As historian Scott De Orio shows, California's SOR, implemented in the early Cold War period, focused primarily on gay cruising and other counternormative sexual offenses which fell under the state's "lewd conduct" statute. After decades of organizing against the statute, gay rights activists and civil libertarians eventually succeeded, in 1983, in removing "lewd conduct" from the list of offenses

for which one could be forced to register as a sex offender in California. By the mid-1990s, of course, sex offender registration had emerged as "a ubiquitous legal response to rape and child sexual abuse." Accordingly, De Orio writes, "the cast of characters to which sex offender registration applies has changed," but "the policy's narrow-minded reliance on stigmatizing individuals as a way of controlling sexual violence persists." Or, as Joseph Fischel puts it, "sex offenders are the new queers." Scott De Orio, "The Creation of the Modern Sex Offender," in *The War on Sex*, ed. David M. Halperin and Trevor Hoppe (Durham, NC: Duke University Press, 2017), 261; Joseph J. Fischel, *Sex and Harm in the Age of Consent* (Minneapolis: University of Minnesota Press, 2016), 20.

8. Violent Crime Control and Law Enforcement Act, HR 3371, One Hundred and Second Congress, first session, introduced September 23, 1991; Jacob Wetterling Crimes against Children Registration Act, HR 324, One Hundred and Third Congress, first session, introduced January 5, 1993; Violent Crime Control and Law Enforcement Act, PL 103–322, 108 STAT. 2039; "The President's Directive to the Attorney General to Develop a National Sexual Offender Registration System," June 19, 1996, "Mayors [4]" folder, J. Terry Edmonds files, Office of Speechwriting, Office of Communications, White House Staff and Office Collections, William Jefferson Clinton Presidential Records, Clinton Digital Library, William Jefferson Clinton Presidential Center, Little Rock, AR (hereafter CDL), https://clinton.presidentiallibraries.us/items/show/33648.

9. "Revised Justice Proposed Report re: HR 3355, Violent Crime Control and Law Enforcement Act of 1994," May 31, 1994, "Crime–Views Letter" folder, Bruce Reed files (crime series), Domestic Policy Council, White House Staff and Office Collections, CDL, https://clinton.presidentiallibraries.us/items/show/22638; "Accomplishments" folder, n.d. [likely early 2001], Edmonds files, CDL, https://clinton.presidentiallibraries.us/items/show/34097.

10. Kevin Fagan, "20 years after Polly Klaas killing, attitudes change," *San Francisco Gate* (CA), October 2, 2013, https://www.sfgate.com/crime/article/20-years-after-Polly-Klaas-killing-attitudes-4861976.php; California, AB 971, Chapter 12, 1994; "A Primer: Three Strikes—The Impact After More than a Decade," California Legislative Analyst's Office, October 2005, https://lao.ca.gov/2005/3_strikes/3_strikes_102005.htm; Mike Males and Dan Macallair, "Striking Out: The Failure of California's 'Three Strikes and You're Out' Law," *Stanford Law and Policy Review* 11, no. 1 (Winter 1999): 65–72.

11. Marc Klaas, "Polly's legacy: to make the state safer for kids," *San Diego Union-Tribune* (CA), October 27, 1994, enclosed with Marc Klaas to Bill Clinton, December 14, 1994, "Klaas [2]" folder, Reed files (crime series), CDL, https://clinton.presidentiallibraries.us/items/show/22584; Marc Klaas to Bill Clinton, December 23, 1993, "Klaas [2]" folder, Reed files (crime series), CDL.

12. Marc Klaas to Bill Clinton, February 1, 1994, "Klaas [2]" folder, Reed files (crime series), CDL.

13. Orrin G. Hatch, "The administration's silent assault on truth-in-sentencing law," *Washington Times*, January 25, 1994, press clips: January 25, 1994, David Kusnet files, Office of Speechwriting, Office of Communications, White House Staff and Office Collections, CDL, https://clinton.presidentiallibraries.us/items/show/47343.

14. Don Feder, "Bench press test for crime candor," *Washington Times*, February 2, 1994, press clips: February 2, 1994, Kusnet files, CDL, https://clinton.presidentiallibraries.us/items/show/47350.

15. Draft, speech to Ohio Peace Officers Training Council and Academy, London, Ohio, February 15, 1994, "POTUS Speeches—London, Ohio (2/15/94)" folder, Reed files (crime series), CDL, https://clinton.presidentiallibraries.us/items/show/ 22602; Julia Moffett to Don Baer, July 4, 1996, "Updated Anecdotes" folder, Don Baer files, Office of Communications, White House Staff and Office Collections, CDL, https://clinton.presidentiallibraries.us/items/show/34789; Bruce Reed to unknown administration official, "Meeting with Marc Klaas," February 28, 1994, "Klaas [2]" folder, Reed files (crime series), CDL.

16. Klaas to Clinton, February 1, 1994, CDL. Marc Klaas remained in contact with administration officials into Clinton's second term, and he delivered an address at the 1996 Democratic National Convention in New York City. See Marc Klaas to Bruce Reed, September 9, 1996, "Klaas [1]" folder, Reed files (crime series), CDL.

17. For discussions of California as a bellwether state in the criminal justice realm, see Ruth Wilson Gilmore, *Golden Gulag: Prisons, Surplus, Crisis, and Opposition in Globalizing California* (Berkeley: University of California Press, 2007); Kelly Lytle Hernández, *City of Inmates: Conquest, Rebellion, and the Rise of Human Caging in Los Angeles, 1771–1965* (Chapel Hill: University of North Carolina Press, 2017).

18. Jo Ann Harris to all US Attorneys, March 13, 1995, Criminal Resource Manual: Sentencing Enhancement—"Three Strikes" Law, Office of the United States Attorneys, US Department of Justice, https://www.justice.gov/usam/ criminal-resource-manual-1032-sentencing-enhancement-three-strikes-law; "The Three Strikes and You're Out Law," California Legislative Analyst's Office, February 22, 1995, lao.ca.gov/analysis_1995/3strikes.html; "A Primer: Three Strikes—The Impact after More than a Decade"; Alex Hannaford, "No Exit," *Texas Observer*, October 3, 2016, texasobserver.org/three-strikes-law-no-exit; David Schultz, "No Joy in Mudville Tonight: The Impact of Three Strikes Laws on State and Federal Corrections Policy, Resources, and Crime Control," *Cornell Journal of Law and Public Policy* 9, no. 2 (Winter 2000): 572–73.

19. Schultz, "No Joy in Mudville Tonight," 573; Leon Neyfakh, interview with John Pfaff, "The Clintons Aren't to Blame for Mass Incarceration," *Slate*, February 11, 2016, https://slate.com/articles/news_and_politics/crime/2016/02/michelle_ alexander_blames_hillary_clinton_for_mass_incarceration_she_shouldn.html. See also John F. Pfaff, *Locked In: The True Causes of Mass Incarceration and How to Achieve Real Reform* (New York: Basic Books, 2017).

20. Neyfakh, interview with Pfaff; Sentencing Project, "Trends in US Corrections," March 2017, https://sentencingproject.org/wp-content/uploads/2016/01/Trends-in-US-Corrections.pdf; Nathan James, "The Federal Prison Population Buildup: Options for Congress," Congressional Research Service, May 20, 2016, https://fas.org/sgp/crs/ misc/R42937.pdf; "Fact Sheet: Violent Crime Control and Law Enforcement Act of 1994," US Department of Justice, October 24, 1994, https://www.ncjrs.gov/txtfiles/ billfs.txt.

21. CNN, *Larry King Live*, interview with Marc Klaas, transcript, December 14, 1993, enclosed with Liz Bernstein to Mark Gearan, "POTUS meeting with Mark [*sic*] Klaas," December 17, 1993, "647420–events" folder, Reed files (crime series), CDL; "Mission, Philosophy, Goals and History," Klaas Foundation for Children, enclosed with Marc Klaas to Bruce Reed, November 3, 1996, "Klaas [2]" folder, Reed files (crime series), CDL; Megan's Law, PL 104–145, May 17, 1996, 110 STAT. 1345.

22. "Sex Offender Registration and Community Notification," February 11, 1996, "Domestic Violence" folder, Reed files (crime series), CDL, https://clinton.

presidentiallibraries.us/items/show/22560; John J. Goldman, "Details Convey Horror of Megan's Death," *Los Angeles Times*, May 6, 1997, https://www.latimes. com/archives/la-xpm-1997-05-06-mn-55980-story.html; Rich Schapiro, "Parents of little girl who inspired Megan's Law recall brutal rape, murder of their daughter 20 years later," *New York Daily News*, July 27, 2014, https://www.nydailynews. com/news/crime/parents-girl-inspired-megan-law-recall-tragedy-article-1.1881551; Associated Press, "Man Charged in 7-Year-Old Neighbor's Killing," *New York Times*, August 1, 1994, B5.

23. Associated Press, "Man Charged in 7-Year-Old Neighbor's Killing"; "Sex Offender Registration and Community Notification," Reed files (crime series), CDL; Goldman, "Details Convey Horror of Megan's Death"; Schapiro, "Parents of little girl who inspired Megan's Law recall brutal rape, murder of their daughter 20 years later"; William Glaberson, "Man at Heart of Megan's Law Convicted of Her Grisly Murder," *New York Times*, May 31, 1997, nytimes. com/1997/05/31/nyregion/man-at-heart-of-megan-s-law-convicted-of-her-grisly-murder.html.

24. James Barron, "Vigil for Slain Girl, 7, Backs a Law on Offenders," *New York Times*, August 3, 1994, B4; Jan Hoffman, "New Law is Urged on Freed Sex Offenders," *New York Times*, August 4, 1994, B1; Associated Press, "Whitman Latest to Urge Laws on Notices of Sex Offenders," *New York Times*, August 6, 1994, 24; Kimberly J. McLarin, "Trenton Races to Pass Bills on Sex Abuse," *New York Times*, August 30, 1994, B1; Jerry Gray, "Sex Offender Legislation Passes in the Senate," *New York Times*, October 4, 1994, B6; Joseph F. Sullivan, "A Crackdown on Sex Offenders in New Jersey," *New York Times*, October 21, 1994, B6; Joseph F. Sullivan, "Whitman Approves Stringent Restrictions on Sex Criminals," *New York Times*, November 1, 1994, B1.

25. Violent Crime Control and Law Enforcement Act, PL 103–322, 108 STAT. 2041; "Sorting It Out: Megan's Law and More," *New York Times*, November 1, 1994, B6; Sullivan, "Whitman Approves Stringent Restrictions on Sex Criminals."

26. "Remembering Megan," *New York Times*, November 5, 1994, 22; US Congress, House of Representatives, Conference Report to Accompany HR 3355, Violent Crime Control and Law Enforcement Act of 1994, report no. 103–694, One Hundred and Third Congress, second session, August 10, 1994, 283; "Revised Justice Proposed Report re: HR 3355," Reed files (crime series), CDL; Violent Crime Control and Law Enforcement Act, PL 103–322, 108 STAT. 2042.

While deliberations about New Jersey's Megan's Law and the federal VCCLEA did overlap—both chronologically and thematically—it would be inaccurate to assert that "the New Jersey bills" somehow "inspired" the Wetterling Act or the broader crime bill in which it resided. Indeed, Clinton administration officials discussed the need for community notification protections as early as May 1994, almost two full months before Megan Kanka was murdered. Moreover, a House version of the VCCLEA—the subject of a conference report published August 10, 1994, less than two weeks after Megan's slaying and well before the New Jersey General Assembly produced its version of Megan's Law—empowered law enforcement agencies to release offender information, if they chose to do so. In addition, only with the passage of Megan's Law on the federal level in 1996 would community notification become federally mandated.

27. "Megan's Law," *Washington Times*, January 6, 1995, "White House News Reports—January 6, 1995" folder, Ira Magaziner files, Health Care Task Force, CDL, https:// clinton.presidentiallibraries.us/items/show/39374.

28. Robert Hanley, "Judge Curbs Law on Sex Offenders," *New York Times*, January 4, 1995, A1; Robert Hanley, "'Megan's Law' Suffers Setback in Court Ruling," *New York Times*, March 1, 1995, A1.

29. Suzanne Fields, "The rights and wrongs of Megan's Law," *Washington Times*, March 6, 1995, "White House News Reports—March 6, 1995" folder, Magaziner files, CDL, https://clinton.presidentiallibraries.us/items/show/39415; Maureen and Rich Kanka, letter to the editor, *USA Today*, March 3, 1995, "White House News Reports—March 3, 1995" folder, Magaziner files, CDL, https://clinton.presidentiallibraries.us/items/show/39414.

30. "Nationline," *USA Today*, January 6, 1995, "White House News Reports—January 6, 1995" folder, Magaziner files, CDL; Jon Nordheimer, "'Vigilante' Attack in New Jersey is Linked to Sex-Offenders Law," *New York Times*, January 11, 1995, A1. For more on the Guardian Angels, see Reiko Hillyer, "The Guardian Angels: Law and Order and Citizen Policing in New York City," *Journal of Urban History* 43, no. 6 (November 2017): 886–914.

31. Jerry Seper, "Justice Dept. backs NJ on sex-offender notification," *Washington Times*, February 10, 1995, "White House News Reports—February 10, 1995" folder, Magaziner files, CDL, https://clinton.presidentiallibraries.us/items/show/39399.

32. Robert Hanley, "New Jersey Supreme Court Hears Bitter Legal Argument over 'Megan's Law,'" *New York Times*, May 3, 1995, B5; "Megan's Law, Rewritten," *New York Times*, July 29, 1995, 18; Robert Hanley, "Federal Appeals Court Rejects a Challenge to 'Megan's Law,'" *New York Times*, April 13, 1996, 23.

33. Hanley, "New Jersey Supreme Court Hears Bitter Legal Argument over 'Megan's Law'"; "Megan's Law, Rewritten"; Robert Hanley, "'Megan's Law Reactivated, with Offenders' Protections," *New York Times*, September 15, 1995, B5; "Sex Offender Registration and Community Notification," Reed (crime series), CDL; Lord Windlesham, *Politics, Punishment, and Populism* (New York: Oxford University Press, 1998), 181; Robert Hanley, "Mounting Legal Assault against 'Megan's Law,'" *New York Times*, March 16, 1996, nytimes.com/1996/03/16/nyregion/mounting-legal-assault-against-megan-s-law.html; Hanley, "Federal Appeals Court Rejects a Challenge to 'Megan's Law'"; Robert Hanley, "Judge Upholds Law Requiring Notice about Sex Offenders," *New York Times*, July 2, 1996, B1; Robert Hanley, "State's Notification Law Faces New Challenge, This Time from Public Defender," *New York Times*, April 9, 1997, B6; "US Court Bars Hearing in a 'Megan' Challenge," *New York Times*, April 15, 1997, B4.

34. "Sex Offender Registration and Community Notification," Reed files (crime series), CDL; Jerry Gray, "House Approves Bill to Require Notification on Sex Offenders," *New York Times*, May 8, 1996, A1; Jerry Gray, "Senate Approves Measure Requiring States to Warn Communities about Sex Offenders," *New York Times*, May 10, 1996, A28; Megan's Law, PL 104-145, 110 STAT. 1345.

35. US Congress, House, Committee on the Judiciary, *Minor and Miscellaneous Bills (Part 2): Hearing before the Subcommittee on Crime*, One Hundred and Fourth Congress, second session, March 7, 1996, 98; William J. Clinton, "Remarks by the President in Bill Signing Ceremony for Megan's Law," White House Office of the Press Secretary, May 17, 1996, https://clintonwhitehouse6.archives.gov/1996/05/1996-05-17-president-remarks-at-signing-of-megans-law.html.

   For "everychild," see Anita Casavantes Bradford, *The Revolution is for the Children: The Politics of Childhood in Havana and Miami, 1959–1962* (Chapel Hill: University of North Carolina Press, 2014).

36. Max B. Baker and Stephen G. Michaud, "Tracking Sexual Offenders," *Fort Worth Star-Telegram* (TX), n.d., enclosed in Grace Mastalli to Dennis [?], Bruce Reed, and Rahm Emanuel, March 4, 1996, "Sex Offenders" folder, Reed files (crime series), CDL, https://clinton.presidentiallibraries.us/items/show/22617.

37. "The President's Directive to the Attorney General to Develop a National Sexual Offender Registration System," Edmonds files, CDL; "President Clinton's weekly radio address," CNN, June 22, 1996, http://edition.cnn.com/US/9606/22/clinton.radio/transcript.html; "President William J. Clinton Radio Address to the Nation," June 22, 1996 (taped June 21, 1996), "6/22/96 Radio Address" folder, Edmonds files, CDL, https://clinton.presidentiallibraries.us/items/show/33800; Richard Tewksbury, Wesley G. Jennings, and Kristen Zgoba, "Sex Offenders: Recidivism and Collateral Consequences," report funded by the US Department of Justice, grant no. 2009-IJ-CZ-0203, September 30, 2011, https://www.ncjrs.gov/pdffiles1/nij/grants/238060.pdf.

38. Pam Lychner Sexual Offender Tracking and Identification Act, PL 104–236, October 3, 1996, 110 STAT. 3093–94.

39. Steven Yoder, "Why Sex Offender Registries Keep Growing Even as Sexual Violence Rates Fall," *The Appeal*, July 3, 2018, https://theappeal.org/why-sex-offender-registries-keep-growing-even-as-sexual-violence-rates-fall.

40. "Innocent Images National Initiative," Federal Bureau of Investigation, www2.fbi.gov/publications/innocent.htm; "OJJDP [Office of Juvenile Justice and Delinquency Prevention] Activities to Combat Child Abduction," n.d. [likely 2002], box 45, folder 16, Jay Lefkowitz subject files, Domestic Policy Council, White House Staff Member Office Files, George W. Bush Presidential Library and Museum, Southern Methodist University, Dallas, Texas.

41. Laura Rogers, "Sex Offender Registry Laws: From Jacob Wetterling to Adam Walsh," Sex Offender Sentencing, Monitoring, Apprehension, Registration, and Tracking Office, Office of Justice Programs, US Department of Justice, July 2007, https://ojp.gov/smart/pdfs/so_registry_laws.pdf; Paul Mokrzycki Renfro, "Keeping Children Safe is Good Business: The Enterprise of Child Safety in the Age of Reagan," *Enterprise & Society* 17, no. 1 (March 2016): 181. For "flesh-and-blood children," see Casavantes Bradford, *The Revolution is for the Children*.

42. Jonathan Simon, *Governing through Crime: How the War on Crime Transformed American Democracy and Created a Culture of Fear* (New York: Oxford University Press, 2007).

CHAPTER 8

1. Adam Walsh Child Protection and Safety Act of 2006, PL 103–322, 120 STAT. 617, July 27, 2006.

2. George W. Bush, "Remarks on Signing the Adam Walsh Child Protection and Safety Act of 2006," July 27, 2006, American Presidency Project, University of California, Santa Barbara (hereafter APP), https://www.presidency.ucsb.edu/documents/remarks-signing-the-adam-walsh-child-protection-and-safety-act-2006; "Child Protection and Safety Act Signing," July 27, 2006, C-SPAN, video, https://www.c-span.org/video/?193619-1/child-protection-safety-act-signing; President's Child Safety Partnership and the Office for Victims of Crime, *A Report to the President: President's Child Safety Partnership* (Washington, DC: President's Child Safety Partnership, 1987), enclosed in Richard B. Abell to Edwin Meese III, September 25, 1987, Edwin Meese: Children—Partnerships in Child Safety, 1987, box 269, entry 1092, subject files of the Attorney General, compiled 1975–93,

Office of the Attorney General, general records of the Department of Justice (1790–2002), Record Group 60, National Archives and Records Administration, College Park, MD.

3. George W. Bush, "Remarks Announcing the White House Conference on Missing, Exploited, and Runaway Children," August 6, 2002, APP, https://www.presidency. ucsb.edu/documents/remarks-announcing-the-white-house-conference-missing-exploited-and-runaway-children; Agenda: White House Conference on Missing, Exploited, and Runaway Children, October 2, 2002, box 46, folder 2, Jay Lefkowitz subject files, Domestic Policy Council, White House Staff Member Office Files, George W. Bush Presidential Library and Museum, Southern Methodist University, Dallas, Texas; Iris Marion Young, "The Logic of Masculinist Protection: Reflections on the Current Security State," *Signs: A Journal of Women in Culture and Society* 29, no. 1 (Autumn 2003): 8; George W. Bush, "Remarks on Children's Online Safety," October 23, 2002, APP, https://www.presidency.ucsb.edu/documents/remarks-childrens-online-safety. This "wave of horrible violence" likely included the abduction and murder of seven-year-old Danielle van Dam in February 2002; the kidnapping of fourteen-year-old Elizabeth Smart in June 2002; the July 2002 kidnapping and murder of five-year-old Samantha Runnion; and the abduction of seven-year-old Erica Pratt, also in July 2002. These cases were not interrelated.

4. Rebecca Wanzo, "The Era of Lost (White) Girls: On Body and Event," *differences: A Journal of Feminist Cultural Studies* 19, no. 2 (Summer 2008): 100; Eugene Robinson, "(White) Women We Love," *Washington Post*, June 10, 2005, www. washingtonpost.com/wp-dyn/content/article/2005/06/09/AR2005060901729. html.

5. Unborn Victims of Violence Act of 2004, PL 108–212, 118 STAT. 568, April 1, 2004; "President Bush Signs Unborn Victims of Violence Act of 2004," Office of the Press Secretary, White House, April 1, 2004, https://georgewbush-whitehouse. archives.gov/news/releases/2004/04/20040401-3.html.

6. Bush, "Remarks on Signing the Adam Walsh Child Protection and Safety Act of 2006," APP; Itir Yakar, "Ad campaign combats global child sex tourism," *Salt Lake Tribune* (UT), October 16, 2004, https://archive.sltrib.com/story.php?ref=/faith/ ci_2427428; Eric Lichtblau and James Dao, "US is Now Pursuing Americans who Commit Sex Crimes Overseas," *New York Times*, June 8, 2004, A1; CNN, *Anderson Cooper 360*, November 12, 2010, record no. 979710, Television News Archive, Vanderbilt University, Nashville; Valeri Hudson, Bonnie Ballif-Spanvill, Mary Caprioli, and Chad F. Emmett, *Sex & World Peace* (New York: Columbia University Press, 2012), 144.

7. *Sin City*, dir. Robert Rodriguez and Frank Miller (2005); *Hard Candy*, dir. David Slade (2005); Melissa Wangenheim, "'To Catch a Predator,' Are We Casting Our Nets Too Far?: Constitutional Concerns Regarding the Civil Commitment of Sex Offenders," *Rutgers Law Review* 62, no. 2 (Winter 2010): 559; Amy Rokuson, "'To Catch a Predator' Gets Caught: Are NBC's Television Journalists Sacrificing Media Ethics and Legal Procedures for a Chance in the Spotlight?" *Seton Hall Journal of Sports and Entertainment Law* 19, no. 2 (2009): 511. For an analysis of filmic representations of sex offenders, see Samuel M. Jay, "Transforming the Predator: Representations of the Child Sexual Abuser in 21st Century American Visual Media" (MA thesis, University of North Texas, 2009).

8. Clemens Wergin, "The Case for Free-Range Parenting," *New York Times*, March 20, 2015, https://www.nytimes.com/2015/03/20/opinion/the-case-for-free-range-parenting.html?_r=0; Jeffrey S. Dill, "The Irony of the Overprotected Child,"

Institute for Family Studies blog, University of Virginia, April 8, 2014, https://ifstudies.org/blog/the-irony-of-the-overprotected-child; Jeffrey S. Dill, *Culture of American Families: Interview Report*, Institute for Advanced Studies in Culture, University of Virginia, Charlottesville (2012), s3.amazonaws.com/iasc-prod/uploads/pdf/19e53db9c6c6b180e7b0.pdf.

9. Lenore Skenazy, "Why I Let My 9-Year-Old Ride the Subway Alone," *New York Sun*, April 1, 2008, https://www.nysun.com/opinion/why-i-let-my-9-year-old-ride-subway-alone/73976. Elizabeth Smart is probably the "Mormon girl in Utah" Skenazy mentioned, and "the little girl in Spain" is likely Madeleine McCann, who actually disappeared from Praia da Luz, Portugal, not Spain, in 2007.

10. Lenore Skenazy, *Free-Range Kids: How to Raise Safe, Self-Reliant Children (Without Going Nuts with Worry)* (New York: John Wiley & Sons, 2009); Lizzie Widdicombe, "Mother May I?" *New Yorker*, February 23, 2015, https://www.newyorker.com/magazine/2015/02/23/mother-may; "Unsere hysterische Kultur," *Der Spiegel*, May 16, 2015, https://www.spiegel.de/spiegel/print/d-134995283.html.

11. Joseph E. Stiglitz and Linda J. Blimes, "The true cost of the Iraq war: $3 trillion and beyond," *Washington Post*, September 5, 2010, www.washingtonpost.com/wp-dyn/content/article/2010/09/03/AR2010090302200.html; "Child Poverty in America, 2010," Children's Defense Fund, September 2011, https://www.childrensdefense.org/wp-content/uploads/2018/08/child-poverty-in-america-2010.pdf; Ronald Brownstein, "Closing the Book on the Bush Legacy," *Atlantic Monthly* (September 11, 2009), https://www.theatlantic.com/politics/archive/2009/09/closing-the-book-on-the-bush-legacy/26402/.

12. Lenore Skenazy, "A Great Depression for Kids?" Free-Range Kids blog, September 19, 2008, www.freerangekids.com/a-great-depression-for-kids. To its credit, the Free-Range Kids blog does occasionally address the unspeakable tolls of mass incarceration and SORs. After police in Baton Rouge, Louisiana, killed thirty-seven-year-old Alton Sterling, a registered sex offender, Skenazy astutely observed, "Only in death, it seems, can a sex offender on the registry be considered a human worthy of love and sympathy." Lenore Skenazy, "Alton Sterling: A Sex Offender Rendered Human Again by His Shocking Death," Free-Range Kids blog, July 10, 2016, www.freerangekids.com/alton-sterling-a-sex-offender-rendered-human-again-by-his-shocking-death.

13. Robert Joseph Taylor, Linda M. Chatters, Amanda Toler Woodward, and Edna Brown, "Racial and Ethnic Differences in Extended Family, Friendship, Fictive Kin, and Congregational Informal Support Networks," *Family Relations* 62, no. 4 (October 2013): 609–24, https://www.ncbi.nlm.nih.gov/PMC/articles/pmc4116141; Skenazy, "Why I Let My 9-Year-Old Ride the Subway Alone."

14. Mark Hugo Lopez and Gabriel Velasco, "Child Poverty Among Hispanics Sets Record, Leads Nation: The Toll of the Great Recession," Pew Research Hispanic, September 28, 2011, https://www.pewhispanic.org/2011/09/28/childhood-poverty-among-hispanics-sets-record-leads-nation; Hanna Rosin, "The Overprotected Kid," *Atlantic Monthly* (April 2014), https://www.theatlantic.com/magazine/archive/2014/04/hey-parents-leave-those-kids-alone/358631/.

15. Josh Gerstein, "Obama talks DNA on 'America's Most Wanted': transcript," *Politico*, March 9, 2010, https://www.politico.com/blogs/under-the-radar/2010/03/obama-talks-dna-on-americas-most-wanted-transcript-025589; "President Obama on 'America's Most Wanted,'" White House blog, March 6, 2010, https://obamawhitehouse.archives.gov/blog/2010/03/05/president-obama-americas-most-wanted.

16. International Megan's Law to Prevent Child Exploitation and Other Sexual Crimes through Advanced Notification of Traveling Sex Offenders, PL 114-119, 130 STAT. 15, February 8, 2016; Leon Neyfakh, "Obama Just Signed a Really Bad Criminal Justice Law," *Slate*, February 9, 2016, https://slate.com/articles/news_and_politics/crime/2016/02/the_international_megan_s_law_obama_just_signed_is_bad_law.html; Louis Nelson, "Trump: 'I am the law and order candidate,'" *Politico*, July 11, 2016, https://www.politico.com/story/2016/07/trump-law-order-candidate-225372.

17. "Statement of Principles," Right on Crime website, originally published November 2010, rightoncrime.com/wp-content/uploads/2010/11/roc-Statement-of-Principles11.pdf; John J. DiIulio Jr., "Stop Crime Where It Starts," *New York Times*, July 31, 1996, A15. See also Marie Gottschalk, "Conservatives against Incarceration?" *Jacobin*, December 23, 2016, https://jacobinmag.com/2016/12/carceral-state-mass-incarceration- conservatives- koch-trump.

18. Judith Levine and Erica R. Meiners, "Are Sex Offenders Human?" *The Baffler*, November 15, 2016, https://thebaffler.com/latest/sex-offenders-human-levine-meiners; Tom Perrotta, *Little Children* (New York: St. Martin's Press, 2004); *Little Children*, dir. Todd Field (2006); Sufjan Stevens, "John Wayne Gacy Jr.," *Sufjan Stevens Invites You to: Come On Feel the Illinoise* (2005); *Pervert Park*, dirs. Frida Barkfors and Lasse Barkfors (2014).

19. Richard Tewksbury, Wesley G. Jennings, and Kristen Zgoba, "Sex Offenders: Recidivism and Collateral Consequences," report funded by the US Department of Justice, grant no. 2009-IJ-CX-0203, September 30, 2011, ncjrs.gov/pdffiles1/nij/grants/238060.pdf; Center for Sex Offender Management, "Exploring Public Awareness and Attitudes about Sex Offender Management: Findings from a National Public Opinion Poll," Office of Justice Programs, US Department of Justice, August 2010, https://csom.org/pubs/csom-Exploring%20Public%20Awareness.pdf; Lydia Saad, "Sex Offender Registries are Underutilized by the Public," Gallup, June 9, 2005, https://news.gallup.com/poll/16705/sex-offender-registries-underutilized-public.aspx.

ARCHIVES CONSULTED

Carl Albert Congressional Research and Studies Center, University of
    Oklahoma, Norman
Archives of Iowa Broadcasting, Wartburg College, Waverly, Iowa
Archives Research Center, Robert W. Woodruff Library, Atlanta University Center,
    Atlanta
George W. Bush Presidential Library, Southern Methodist University, Dallas
William Jefferson Clinton Presidential Center, Little Rock
KCCI–TV, Des Moines, Iowa
National Archives I, Washington, DC
National Archives II, College Park, Maryland
New York Public Library, New York City
William S. Paley Center for Media, New York City
Ronald W. Reagan Presidential Library, Simi Valley, California
Roper Center for Public Opinion Research, Cornell University, Ithaca
Stuart A. Rose Manuscript, Archives, and Rare Book Library, Robert W. Woodruff
    Library, Emory University, Atlanta
State Historical Society of Iowa, Des Moines
Television News Archive, Vanderbilt University, Nashville
Benjamin N. Woodson Research Center, Walter W. Fondren Library, Rice University,
    Houston

INDEX

For the benefit of digital users, indexed terms that span two pages (e.g., 52–53) may, on occasion, appear on only one of those pages.